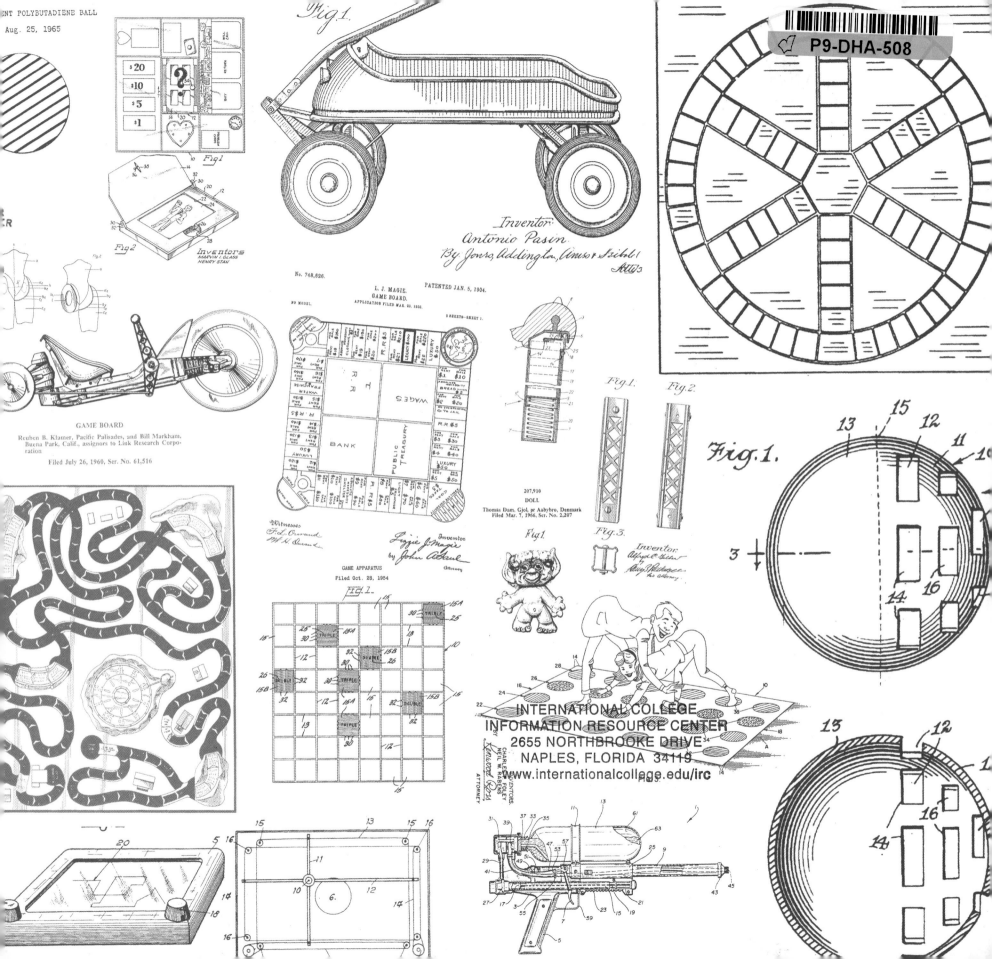

THE

Playmakers

MAGIC *Etch A Sketch* SCREEN

THE
Playmakers

AMAZING ORIGINS *of* TIMELESS TOYS

TIM WALSH

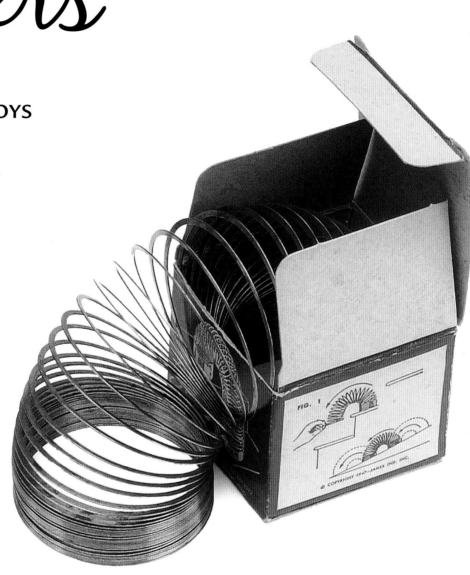

Keys
Publishing

SARASOTA, FLORIDA

Keys Publishing
PMB 180
5370 Clark Road Suite A
Sarasota, FL 34233-3227

Web site: www.theplaymakers.com

ISBN: 0-9646973-4-3
Library of Congress Control Number: 2003096499

Library of Congress Cataloging-in-Publication Data

Walsh, Tim.
    The playmakers : amazing origins of timeless toys /
Tim Walsh.

    p. cm.
    Includes bibliographical references and index.
    LCCN 2003096499
    ISBN 0-9646973-4-3

    1. Toys—United States—History. 2. Inventions—
    History.   I. Title.

GV1218.5.W35 2004   688.7'2'09
                                 QBI03-700682

Written by Tim Walsh
Design by Giles Hoover, *osprey*design
Printed by Regent Publishing Services, China

05 04   10 9 8 7 6 5 4 3 2 1

FOR
SARAH, EMMA, AND KATE

Contents

Author's Note

In the business of toys, ideas abound. This book is about entrepreneurs who dreamed of creating fun *and did it!* They are *The Playmakers*.

Like any creative industry, the business of toy making has its share of egotists. Press releases often credit a toy to a single person, when in fact many people played a role in refining it. This book is meant to be a giant thank-you to the individuals responsible for the biggest, brightest and best playthings ever created. That's a good thing, but a bit dicey to attempt in the black and white of a book. An effort to spread credit around runs the risk of offending someone by omission. Rather than throw up my hands, I decided

to chance it. I hope the people who receive some well-earned credit within these pages far outnumber the people who feel snubbed by a lack of recognition.

At the beginning of each chapter, a block of pertinent information answers the "What, When and Who" of each plaything. I use the term toy to mean any plaything, including a game, doll, action figure, plush animal, building set, and so forth.

Debut: The year in which a toy was released to a mass audience in its first successful incarnation. Toys are placed within sections chronologically, based on their U.S. debut.

Predecessor: The toy that led directly to the development of the toy covered.

Inventive idea: The person responsible for the core concept for a toy, but not necessarily the toy's inventor.

Inventor: The person most responsible for the creation of the toy.

Developer: The person responsible for the improvement and/or popularization of the toy.

Insider: A person crucial to the successful development of the toy. Typically an insider is employed within the toy company (licensee) that brings the toy to the market.

Companies: The businesses that put the toy on the market by offering it for sale, usually through a licensing arrangement with the inventor or developer (licensor). Sometimes, the inventor forms his or her own company to market the toy, in which case the inventor's company is included also. Companies are arranged chronologically from first to most recent. Companies listed are not necessarily the owners of the toy. For complete trademark and copyright information, please see the credits page.

RULES OF THE GAME
(OR HOW I CHOSE THE TOYS I CHOSE)

1 **The toy had to have sold at least ten million copies.** That's a big number in any industry.
2 **The toy had to have been on the market for at least ten years.** The toy industry is a fashion business riddled with one-hit wonders. The longevity of the products selected sets them apart.
3 **The toy had to have been invented outside of the major toy companies.** This being a celebration of entrepreneurs, great toys like Easy-Bake Oven (Kenner, now Hasbro) and Hot Wheels (Mattel) were excluded for being "inside" jobs.
4 **The toy had to have been invented by an identifiable person or persons.** Ancient playthings like tops, marbles, chess and checkers were excluded for being too generic.
5 **The toy had to have significance to me or my friends.** If your favorite toy was excluded, I encourage you to write your own book. It's a very liberating experience.

I conducted over 150 interviews for *The Playmakers,* making every effort to contact as many of the inventors and developers of these toys as possible. Some declined my request for an interview. In the case of inventors and developers who have died, I include the year of their birth and death, if known. This is a book for adults, in that the stories of the creation of the toys are presented as truthfully as possible, warts and all. I included personal information regarding inventors or developers only as it pertained to the story at hand.

Author's Note

Author's Note

I refer to "Toy Fair" throughout *The Playmakers*. This important trade event is officially called the American International Toy Fair and first took place in 1903. Since 1934, the show has been held annually in New York (except for 1945 when World War II caused its cancellation). Managed by the Toy Industry Association, Inc. (TIA), formerly known as Toy Manufacturers of America, Toy Fair welcomes thousands of hopeful toy inventors every year. All of the toys covered in *The Playmakers* have logged their share of time at this show, which has grown from a handful of salesmen gathering in a Manhattan hotel, to the largest toy trade show in the Western Hemisphere.

A few words about the timelines that introduce each section: Here you'll find pictures of the classics covered in these pages, in their original packages when possible. Obviously, the packages are not to scale (imagine a Super Ball the size of a Hula Hoop!), but they do help to recreate that sense of anticipation we felt before we tore into the box to get at the treasure. The timelines include major industry events and the debut of other significant toys. All the toys listed in the timelines, but not covered in this book, were also invented by individual designers and not large toy companies (*The Playmakers 2*, perhaps?). Note that the timelines are specific to the section they introduce. For instance, the timeline introducing the Marvin Glass section details only the toys that came from his design firm and the timeline before the WHAM-O section details only WHAM-O toys.

I didn't want to write a book that contained information anyone could readily find by searching the Internet in an afternoon. That meant much digging and a lot of help from people willing to share. I was privileged to have spoken to many toy "legends" and to all of them, I say thank you. There are rare interviews in this book and pictures of some even rarer toys. The photograph of The Landlord's Game on pages 46–7, the Streater vehicle on page 67, The Syco-Seer on page 94, the Bild Lilli doll on page 131, and the Operation prototype on page 162, typify toys or prototypes seldom seen in print anywhere.

While I am happy to be able to include these rare toys in *The Playmakers,* I am equally proud to share the universal toys, the ones *we all played with.* So pull up a comfortable chair and settle in for some fun.

Tim Walsh
Sarasota, Florida
October 14, 2003

The Toy Center at 200 Fifth Avenue has been the main exhibition site for the American International Toy Fair since 1934.

Introduction

TOYS ARE MAGICAL

So much so, that it's easy for kids to believe that elves make them. But even after we turn from the North Pole and begin looking to Toys R Us for our playthings, there's still this sense that our favorite toys have always just existed. Naturally God created GI Joe in his image, and that primordial soup that supposedly oozed so many millennia ago? Surely it contained coenzymes, water and the first developing wad of Silly Putty.

I was seven years old when I etched away a window on my Etch A Sketch to reveal a silvery display of rods, pulleys and strings. "How did they get in there?" Then it dawned on me. *Someone made this thing. I wonder who?*

The makers are not Santa's elves, but they've spun magic nonetheless. Some were full-time professionals, but most were moonlighters, holding down serious *jobs* as professor (Rubik's Cube), barber (Uno), waiter (Pictionary), and piano tuner (View-Master). Some had professional design studios, but more likely they created fun on a kitchen table in Connecticut (Wiffle Ball), in a basement in California (Frisbee) or in a cramped apartment in Montreal (Trivial Pursuit). Inspiration struck them while

Introduction

Part of the fun is that we are in control, using toys and our imaginations as a means toward adventure or, maybe, escape. A trip in a Radio Flyer wagon can take us much farther than the mere distance we move in it. Later, games like Pictionary and Jenga bond us to our family and friends.

Over time, our childhood toys are given away, sold off at garage sales, lost but not forgotten. Then, with kids of our own, a pleasant revelation. . . .

Toys Are Timeless

As parents or grandparents, we give our little ones a piece of ourselves in a toy we once treasured. It's *more* than a brand new box of Crayola crayons; it's that shared experience, the smell, the waxy coat of color— you did the same thing when you were four years old. Raggedy Ann looks different today than she did when you first had tea with her, but somehow she's still the same. Toys connect us.

Here, then, is a trip to toyland.

Once onboard (yes, it's a Lionel), you'll meet the people behind some of your favorite playthings, past and present. Along the way, you'll grow your own pet, adopt your own "kid" and build your own skyscraper once again. You'll find out how that Etch A Sketch works and what that mysterious liquid is inside the Magic 8 Ball.

Welcome to a trip for the senses, where, through your imagination (and wonderful photos), you'll see the rainbow of colors in a favorite Matchbox collection, hear the familiar sound of a Slinky again, feel the fur of a cherished teddy bear and breathe deep the aroma only Play-Doh can deliver. Unfortunately the only taste you'll experience is that of Pez, but take heart. If you're so hungry for fun that *beans* make you think of stuffed animals and the term *doughnut* makes you reach, not for a Krispy Kreme, but the hand brake on your boyhood Big Wheel, then you picked up the right book.

walking in downtown Manhattan (Lite-Brite) or deep within the rural mountains of Georgia (Cabbage Patch Kids).

Meet *The Playmakers,* imaginative designers, developers, *doers.* The playthings they created merit our admiration.

Toys Are Important

From the moment we grasp our first rattle, toys help us to discover our world. We learn fine motor skills with Lego blocks and Lincoln Logs, counting and colors in Candy Land. Later, toys allow us to role-play our futures, envisioned behind the wheel of a Tonka truck or through the eyes of a Barbie doll.

THE PLAYMAKERS
Toy Timeline

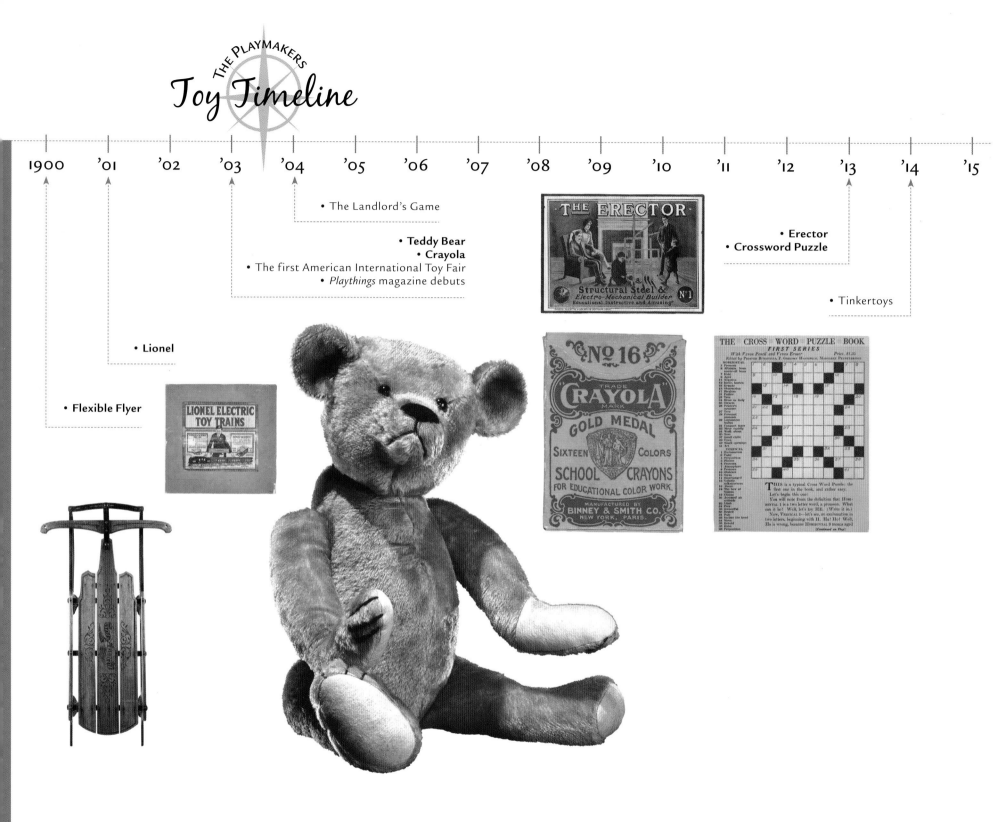

1900   '01   '02   '03   '04   '05   '06   '07   '08   '09   '10   '11   '12   '13   '14   '15

• The Landlord's Game

• **Teddy Bear**
• **Crayola**
• The first American International Toy Fair
• *Playthings* magazine debuts

• **Erector**
• **Crossword Puzzle**

• Tinkertoys

• **Lionel**

• **Flexible Flyer**

1900s–1920s

'15 ’16 ’17 ’18 ’19 ’20 ’21 ’22 ’23 ’24 ’25 ’26 ’27 ’28 ’29 1930

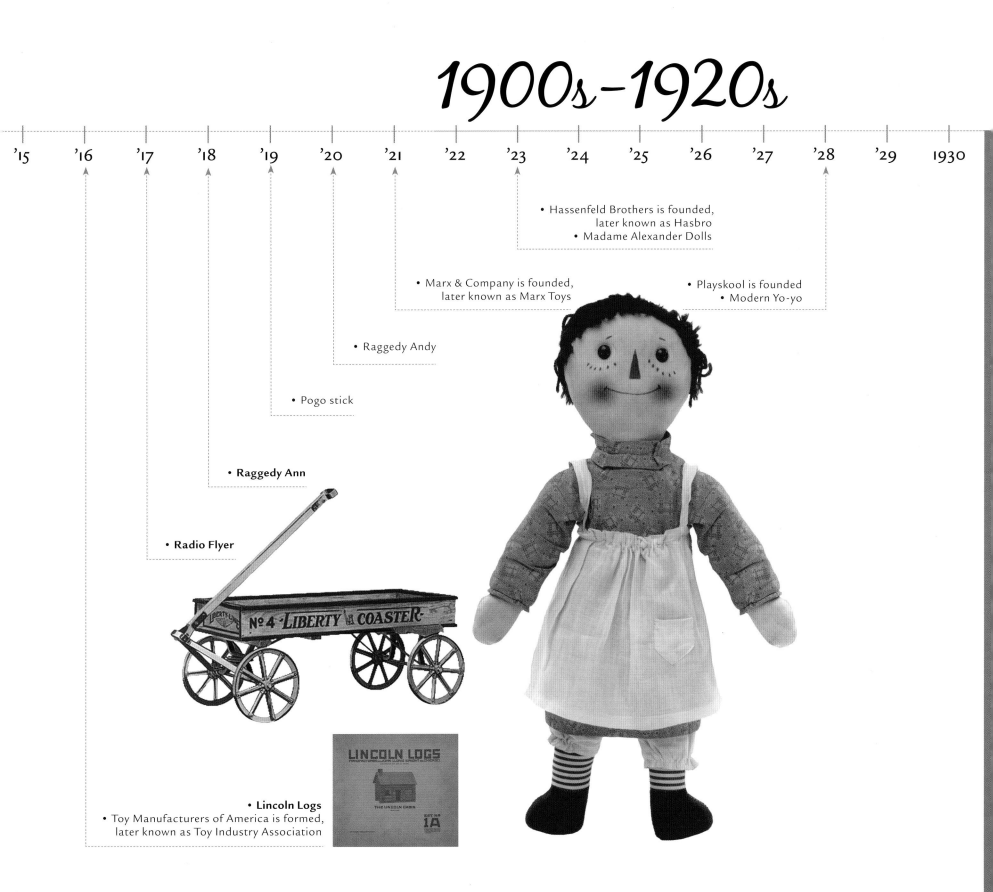

• Hassenfeld Brothers is founded,
later known as Hasbro
• Madame Alexander Dolls

• Marx & Company is founded,
later known as Marx Toys

• Playskool is founded
• Modern Yo-yo

• Raggedy Andy

• Pogo stick

• **Raggedy Ann**

• **Radio Flyer**

N° 4 ·LIBERTY COASTER·

LINCOLN LOGS
MANUFACTURED BY JOHN LLOYD WRIGHT INCORPORATED

THE LINCOLN CABIN

SET N°
1A

• **Lincoln Logs**
• Toy Manufacturers of America is formed,
later known as Toy Industry Association

Debut: 1900
Predecessor: The Fire Fly (1890)
Inventor: Samuel Allen (1841-1918)
Companies: S.L. Allen Company, Leisure Group, Blazon-Flexible Flyer, Roadmaster Industries, Brunswick Corporation, Pacific Cycle

Flexible Flyer

Sam Allen's first successful steerable sled was the Fire Fly (produced from 1890–1900, then reissued in 1935). It was named after the company's Planet Jr. seeder.

A Family Love Affair

It's the winter of '72 in South Jersey, not far from the birthplace of Flexible Flyer sleds. My sister and I sit and listen intently. The number we are trying to *will* from the radio is our school code, a number that only matters in the winter, on the morning after a snow storm. It's a magical thing, a winter passage of youth. "It's a snow day!"

Samuel Allen didn't invent the snow day, but he came close to perfecting it when he invented Flexible Flyer, his "sled that steers." Prior to his gift, steering a stiff sled was done by leaning and dragging one foot. It was an awkward maneuver at best, one that compromised a big reason we loved to sled in the first place: speed. His revolutionary design allowed us speed *and* the possibility of controlling our course. Although Sam Allen steered us into the modern era of sledding, he wasn't trying to leave his mark. He was trying to keep good workers from leaving his business.

Allen was an inventive and hardworking man from a prominent Quaker family whose ancestors helped William Penn and others establish the city of Philadelphia. In 1866, at the age of 25, he founded a farm equipment company with his father. The S.L. Allen Company's first products were farming machines of Allen's design. One, a seed spreader that resembled the planet Saturn in shape, was dubbed "Planet Jr." The production of Planet Jr. farm equipment was the sole operation of the company for 23 years. Despite its success, the S.L. Allen Co. was a seasonal business and

would lose many of its workers in the summer months when production of farm equipment dropped. To slow the migration, Allen set out to develop a winter product. According to Joan Palicia's wonderful book, *Flexible Flyer Sleds and Other Great Sleds for Collectors,* Allen got his idea while paging through the dictionary, his eyes falling on the word *sled.*

Allen was uniquely qualified to improve upon this plaything of his past. As a boy, he had attended a Quaker academy called Westtown School, where "coasting" was the winter pastime of choice. His daughter, Elizabeth, and nearly every generation of the Allen family since have attended the school, maintaining the extracurricular tradition of taking to the nearby slopes. "It's a hilly campus," said Westtown archivist Mary Brooks. "Back when Sam Allen was here the students would build a sled track every year. They'd stomp it down and then run toboggans and bobsleds down the hill, through the woods and then out into the open meadow."

By 1884, sled prototypes were being sent off to Westtown for testing by Elizabeth and her friends on the very same Pennsylvania hills where Allen had discovered his own fondness of flying. He developed "The Phantom," "The Fleetwing," "Ariel" and "Fairy Coaster"—all failed attempts at producing a sled with the affordability and steerability he wanted. When

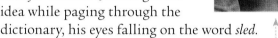

Samuel Allen

Flexible Flyer
postcard, 1907

he finally envisioned a sled with grooved, T-shaped runners (where a cross section of the steel runner would look like an inverted T), his dream began to materialize.

On February 14, 1889 Sam applied for a patent on his "improved sled." His design featured runners that were weakened at a crucial point, allowing them to flex when a steeringbar was manipulated. This, together with the sled's improved speed, inspired Allen to name it Flexible Flyer. He received patent approval in August of that same year and went to production on his first steerable model, the Fire Fly.

The sporting goods industry was a far cry from the farm and garden trade to which he was accustomed. Department store buyers thought that Allen's Fire Fly sleds would not sell and refused to stock them. Salesmen from within his own company, angry that their summer vacations would be cut short in order to sell sleds, encouraged Sam to sell the patent and stick to farm and garden equipment. He refused to give up despite the pessimism and languishing sales. He tried advertising his line of sleds, which initially resulted in a net loss when the sales dollars didn't cover his advertising expenses.

By the turn of the century, however, when skating and tobogganing began to rise in popularity along with other outdoor sports like golf and tennis, Allen recognized the trend and increased his efforts. "The Fire Fly was his first sled that sold well," author Joan Palicia told me. "But no one called it a Flexible Flyer." Up until that time, the Flexible Flyer name had only been used to describe his entire line of sleds, and was never put on the sleds themselves. Other S.L. Allen models from that time featured

decks decorated with roses, triangles and other patterns, but it wasn't until 1900 that they wore their famous name and logo.

FROM "THE SLED THAT STEERS" TO "THE SLED OF THE NATION"

Early advertisements for Flexible Flyer sleds touted steering, speed, safety, and oddly enough, shoe preservation. One read: "Don't kick steer—Get a real self-steering sled, the famous Flexible Flyer and save your shoes. . . ." Another ad sang this tune to the Allen invention: "The Flexible Flyer is a sled up-to-date, In all other makes it hasn't a mate, It takes from the father all signs of the blues, For the self-steering sled is a saver of shoes."

As Flexible Flyer soared, other sled manufacturers weren't about to drag their feet in coming out with their own steering models. There was The Speedplane, The Storm King and The Lightning Glider, to name a few. Sears and Roebuck

Inspired by the two legendary department stores that first decided to stock his reintroduced line — Wanamaker's in Philadelphia and R.H. Macy Co. in New York — Allen designed an emblem. According to author Joan Palicia, "He took the Wanamaker eagle and the red ribbon from Macy's to create his logo for Flexible Flyer."

released their own models like The Snow Bird and The Flying Arrow, but none could catch the original. Steerable sleds became the standard because of Flexible Flyer, and as the rest of the sledding industry tried to keep up, the front-runner was pushed into national prominence. Flexible Flyer became "The Sled of the Nation." In a few years, Allen's salesmen were taking orders for over 120,000 sleds per year. Baseball may have been the national pastime, but that was only in the summer.

When sled sales began to outperform the farm equipment side of his company, Sam Allen surely shared that fact with his former naysayers. Allen's continued success allowed his company to expand in the 1920s, when they offered wooden skis for older kids whose interest in sledding had melted away. For many, no matter what their age, the joy of sledding returned every winter when thoughts turned to flying on an icy cloud of white.

THE SNOW DAY

In the quiet stillness that follows a heavy snowstorm, my sister and I pulled our sleds to a nearby golf course where we met scores of other kids. Over a foot of snow had fallen, so as the days went by, the trails packed down more and the sledding got better. When it drizzled lightly one day and then froze overnight, the Flexible Flyers really lived up to their name.

In our neighborhood, you were king of the hill if you could make it all the way to the bottom while standing on your sled, the frayed rope attached to your steering bar like the reins of a runaway horse. If you were a specialist, you could run with your Flexible Flyer in hand, dive headfirst and land with your sled sandwiched perfectly between you and the icy slope. Get it wrong and you bounced off the sled painfully, but time it right and you'd *fly* — six inches off the ground with a glistening runway blurry beneath.

DOWNHILL

Over time, an aging Flexible Flyer faced new and stiffer competition. The battle came in the form of molded plastic and eventually erupted into a price war that Sam Allen's classic invention simply could not win. Starting in the 1960s, inexpensive plastic toboggans, snow disks and even rolled-up vinyl mats ate away at the runner sled's market share. Later, inflatable snow tubes and the soaring popularity of snowboards marked the grounding of Flexible Flyer.

By 1939, most straight-runner sleds were replaced by models with "safety-runners." This change prevented the sharp runners on a capsized sled from impaling a sledder who trailed a friend down the hill. Older "coasters" might recall "staking their claim" by plunging their sled into the snow by its pronged runners, like Admiral Byrd at the top of the world.

In 1968, the S.L. Allen Company was sold to the Leisure Group. The Flexible Flyer name switched hands again in 1973, 1993, and in 1996 when the Brunswick Corporation became its owner. In 1999, Brunswick stopped making Flexible Flyer runner sleds and sold the trademark to Pacific Cycle the following year. The sled with classic runners of red, hardwood decking and the unique steering bar has all but faded from sight. "The sledding industry has been going downhill for sometime now," Joan Palicia said. "Paris Sleds in Maine were the first manufacturers of wooden sleds in America, starting in 1861. Now they're also the last."

It's comforting to remember our Flexible Flyer sleds, cherished and named, deck art worn away and underside branded with our initials. Toys connect us. My Dad did things with his Flexible Flyer sled that I duplicated 45 years later. Sam Allen would be pleased to know that one wintry day, this family ritual will be passed on to my daughters.

Likewise, within the family known as Westtown School, customs die hard. "We have a lot of old restored Flexible Flyers hanging up in the old gymnasium," Mary Brooks said. "They are taken down at least once each winter and brought outside for the kids to ride. It's an annual tradition."

Only time will tell if production will one day resume and a new generation of eagles will take flight. Until then, we are left with the fond memory of hills conquered and the bittersweet realization that even the greatest run must eventually come to an end.

Family Tradition

In 1952, my mother and father were married and when a blizzard hit their honeymoon, the sleds came out. "We went up to a resort in the Pocono Mountains and met four or five other couples," my Dad said. "We all went sledding on this steep hill that I bet was a half mile long. We had great time—just flying down that mountain."

"The resort had Flexible Flyers hanging in this old barn. Oh, I'll never forget this," he laughed as he recalled the story. "Some of the sleds had been put away wet the previous winter and their runners were pretty rusty. You had to use steel wool to clean them off or the sled wouldn't slide worth a lick. Well, this farm boy wearing a big pair of baggy overalls came up carrying this rusty old sled. He's going to show off for his new wife, so he sets it down at the top of this hill and walks back 40 feet or so. He takes off running and then does a big belly flop on that sled and it doesn't move an inch! He went cartwheeling down that mountain—we couldn't stand up we were laughing so hard. He came lumbering back up with those overalls stuffed with snow. He looked like a walrus. Oh, it was fun. We sledded the whole week and met friends that we've kept for life."

In the '20s, Allen introduced Flexy Racers, a line of sled-like vehicles with wheels for use after the ice and snow melted.

Lionel

Debut: 1901
Inventor: Joshua Lionel
Cowen (1877-1965)
Companies: Lionel Manufac-
turing Company, Lionel
Corporation, Lionel
Trains Incorporated,
Lionel LLC

ROLLER-COASTER RAILROAD

At 1:00 p.m. on September 5, 2000, a group of weary but excited travelers gathered in lower Manhattan on Murray Street. Unfortunately, taking the train, which would have been perfectly appropriate, was not an option. Transporting a four-foot by four-foot mahogany table that held a circular train layout powered by a car battery was impossible by subway car. So, Joe Mania along with his eight-year-old daughter, Danielle, and his father, Leo, drove to a small anniversary celebration for which he'd built a reproduction of an early gondola train.

With a handful of train lovers and three generations of the Mania family present, the 100-year-old articles of incorporation for The Lionel Manufacturing Company were read aloud. As the growing crowd gathered closer to hear, the gondola circled the track.

Imagine looking down from the third floor loft of the building that stands at 24 Murray Street, at the mingling crowd as they watch the toy

train completing circle after circle. Now imagine the street changing. Graffiti fades away. Taxi horns soften and then disappear, replaced by the soft clip-clop of hooves. Cars become horse-drawn buggies. We've departed the station in the year 2000 and have arrived 100 years before—in the same place, but at a very different time.

On September 5, 1900, Joshua Lionel Cowen formed The Lionel Manufacturing Company, a firm that planned to make and sell "electric novelties." Several years earlier, Cowen had put his genius to work to create a "flash lamp," a method by which an electrical current could be used to light a fuse. A consummate tinkerer, Cowen had also created what he later claimed to have been the first portable electric fan. While these two inventions provided the basis on which his

Joshua Lionel
Cowen took his
middle name and
made it synony-
mous with model
railroading.

Lionel's 260E Steam Locomotive from the early 1930s.

company was founded, the reality was that the flash lamp had limited uses and the electric fan never really worked well. So there Cowen found himself at the turn of the century, 23 years old and the owner of a company with no viable product.

THE FUTURE IN A STOREFRONT

In the days before radio and television, products and services were sold largely by printed advertisements in newspapers, magazines or on billboards. Even the foremost marketing tool of the times, the Sears & Roebuck catalog, relied on black and white pictures or artists' renderings to sell their goods. Stores built elaborate window displays to attract customers, but they too were static, lacking action or excitement. It was within these circumstances that, as legend has it, Joshua Cowen approached a local shop owner named Robert Ingersoll with an idea.

In the book *All Aboard! The Story of Joshua Lionel Cowen & His Lionel Train Company,* author Ron Hollander writes that Cowen offered to give Ingersoll's storefront window *movement* through the use of an electric carriage that would carry any goods the shop owner wished to feature. Cowen would build his rail-riding carriage from the motor he had designed for his electric fan, powered by a dry cell battery. Ingersoll bought the idea, and soon his shop window was alive with motion. In today's high-tech world of advertising, where "motion pictures" play on billboards the size of the *building* at 24 Murray Street, it is hard to imagine just how revolutionary Cowen's gadget was. Powered by that still mysterious energy called electricity, the carriage (or Electric Express, as Cowen called it), *moved by itself* and passersby froze in their tracks at the sight of it.

Whatever product this primitive retail display might have carried is lost to time and the telling of a good toy story, because as the legend goes, Ingersoll's customers wanted to buy the display more than the goods. The shop owner obliged. Cowen replaced it and another Electric Express was sold the very next day. Hollander reports that Ingersoll placed an order for six more and the same thing happened. When other shop owners got on board too, the third-floor loft at 24 Murray Street buzzed with activity.

The Electric Express gondola is often romanticized as the rail car that launched Lionel trains, but due to its origins as a display it lacked any connection to the real world of trains. Recognizing this, Cowen took a step in 1901 that would characterize his company's products for the next century, adding realism to his line with the introduction of an electric trolley. A replica of the trolley cars that existed at the time, Lionel's new rail car was immediately familiar and gave his customers a plaything to which they could relate. The next year, the Lionel Manufacturing Company released their Electric Express with a significant addition: a coupler that allowed the gondola and the trolley to attach to each other. It was Lionel's first train set.

A replica of the motorized window display that marked the beginning of contemporary model railroading. Lionel's Electric Express, introduced 1901.

GAUGING SUCCESS

Perhaps because the fan motor Cowen had invented needed to fit between the wheels of his Electric Express, he made the "gauge" or width of his earliest tracks $2\,^7/_8$ inches between the rails. In 1906, however, Cowen introduced a three-rail sectional track system. The change from the previous setup (where short-outs were common) was a major improvement. Additionally, Cowen reduced the gauge of his new three-rail track to $2\,^1/_8$ inches and dubbed it "standard."

"All other track was, by inference, rendered nonstandard," authors Gerry and Janet Souter state in their book, *Classic Lionel Trains.* "This marketing coup forced 2- and $1\,^3/_4$ inch track . . . to eventually disappear. Standard Gauge became the standard . . . ." This introduction of the standard gauge track marked the beginning of Lionel's dominance in the toy train industry.

Also in 1906 came Cowen's first transformer, which took the 110-volt current within homes (that were fortunate enough to have electricity) and dampened it down to a safer and manageable 30-volt maximum. A lever on the transformer thus became a throttle, enabling the user to increase or decrease the voltage and thereby increase or decrease the speed of the train. These clunky black boxes transformed electricity—*and us*—from passive observers to active conductors.

In 1915, Lionel introduced a smaller line of O gauge trains that ran on track measuring $1\,^1/_4$ inches between the rails. These smaller, more affordable trains would soon become the dominant gauge in model railroading, a segment of the toy industry that Cowen was determined to lead. At a time when war in

Prior to the transformer, the only option for a toy train operator was "on" or "off." The transformer became a throttle to regulate speed and would later be used to change a train's direction, make its whistle blow and more. Of course, no electrical current passed into the body of the "Conductor," but try telling that to anyone transformed by the magic of a model railroad.

Europe had ended German dominance of the toy industry, Lionel in New York, Ives in Connecticut and American Flyer in Illinois all raced to fill the gap. The war also brought additional opportunities for Lionel as Cowen landed military contracts for navigational equipment. The company grew, and in 1918 changed its name to The Lionel Corporation. The war ended in the same year, marking a new beginning for Lionel trains and the nation.

The roaring twenties were marked by extravagance and fun for both the nation and Lionel. According to Hollander, train layouts came alive as "crossing gates dipped, block signals changed colors, traffic warning bells sounded, highway flashers twinkled—all automatically as the train passed." Beautifully illustrated company catalogs were produced and distributed to hardware stores, toy and hobby shops, and directly to households. Gorgeous, full-page advertisements appeared in comic books and boys' magazines. Lionel was barreling down the track and like many American companies in the late '20s was unaware that the light at the end of the long tunnel of prosperity belonged to another train.

1900s–1920s

LIONEL

THE WRECK

In the same year as the economic crash of 1929, Lionel produced some of their most expensive trains. Ignoring the economic climate, the company continued to introduce ever more expensive trains *during* the Depression, based solely on Joshua Cowen's optimism. In 1931, Lionel introduced what many train enthusiasts consider his crowning glory in locomotives: The 400 E, a toy steamer trimmed with copper piping and red-spoked wheels. At nearly 12 pounds, the standard gauge 400E was a monster, but even this formidable beast would be derailed by the crumbling economy.

To address the economic times, Cowen shifted his company's focus from the big, standard gauge trains (with their big price tags to match) to their O gauge line. Additionally, he introduced lower priced trains under the Winner brand, a name that was later changed to Lionel Jr. Despite these efforts the company went into receivership and according to Hollander, endured losses in 1931, 1932 and 1933. In order to survive, Cowen would need to streamline both his business practices and his trains. He copied the railroad industry's new lightweight streamliner passenger trains, which had become symbols of recovery for a nation eager to move forward.

Cowen spiced up his traditional trains through the use of endorsements. Although celebrities like Tommy Dorsey and Frank Sinatra enjoyed Lionel trains in the 1930s, Cowen chose to use real-life train engineers to help drive Lionel out of receivership. Just as NASCAR drivers do today, these men "drove" for teams like the New York Central Railroad and the Santa Fe Railroad. Conductors like Bob Butterfield and W. P. McAfee told kids that "Lionel trains are real—like mine!" Lionel boasted that their little locomotives were "The Trains that Railroad Men Buy for Their Boys!" These tactics pulled Lionel out of financial peril. It was a mouse, however, that got them back in the black.

In the fall of 1934, Lionel introduced a windup handcar that featured Walt Disney's Mickey and

Minnie Mouse. Hollander reports that Lionel sold 253,000 of them that fall; another 100,000 orders had to go unfilled because the company could not make the trains fast enough. Lionel released a handcar that also included Donald Duck and Pluto, and later a toy circus train featuring the entire Disney menagerie of characters.

The animal magnetism of Mickey and his friends brought Lionel plenty of media attention in the mid-'30s.

In 1937, before the economy had recovered, Cowen invested an unbelievably risky sum of money in dies and tooling to create the 700E Hudson, a replica of the New York Central steam locomotive. As always, Cowen's attitude was *full steam ahead*. In fact the only thing that could stop Lionel was World War II. The company suspended all train manufacturing in mid-1942 until 1945 to focus on producing wartime materials, and although no trains chugged out of the Lionel factories those years (except for some paper punch-out trains that kids assembled themselves), the company profited financially from its many government contracts. The result was a cash flow when the war ended that made the following decade one of their most prolific.

The Santa Fe twin diesel engine was introduced in 1948 and would become Lionel's best-selling train.

RIDIN' HIGH

According to Gerry and Janet Souter, "Lionel achieved peak earning of $32.9 million [in 1953]. Two-thirds of the toy trains sold in America were Lionels . . . ." However, Lionel's financial stability was more akin to a ride on roller coaster than a railroad, and despite just completing their best year ever, a dark cloud loomed.

As more travelers chose to drive or travel by air, the sinking popularity of our nation's railroads foretold the future of Lionel. Television was booming, ushering in "passive entertainment." Seemingly overnight, the hands-on building of elaborate train layouts had become tedious and toy trains old-fashioned.

Lionel's sales dropped dramatically from 1953 to 1955. In reaction, Lionel produced a line of smaller HO ("Half O") scale trains in 1957, which Lionel's competition had been producing with great success for decades. HO's promise of affordability in the face of a looming recession made the move a good business decision.

Unfortunately, other HO manufacturers were not willing to let go of their market share easily and sales of Lionel's HO line fell flat. The same year, Lionel's desperate attempt to garner sales in any way possible led to the ill-fated "New Exclusive Pastel Train Set for Girls." This infamous train with its Easter-colored cars laid an egg. Lionel executives failed to realize that when it came to toy trains, girls wanted exactly what boys did: realism. Today the train is sought as a collector's item because so few were ever sold.

Cowen's time had passed. As his company began to fade, he retired in 1958. Cowen's son had been working alongside his father within Lionel officially since 1937, and unofficially much longer than that, posing for pictures in Lionel catalogs when he was still a boy. As expected, Lawrence took over the controls of the company. What came next was anything but expected.

A year after he retired, the elder Cowen sold his stock and interest in Lionel to his nephew Roy Cohn, much to the surprise and dismay of his son. While no one may ever know the reasons behind this decision (Hollander reports that Joshua Cowen sold his stock while Lawrence was out of the country), it was incongruent with the legacy of Lionel trains. After creating a toy that had bonded fathers and sons like no other, Cowen's decision remains a sad and ironic footnote in the annals of model railroading.

The '60s were turbulent times for Lionel and the

Lionel's famous milk car was introduced in 1947. After loading the magnetic-based milkcans into the roof hatch of the car, a push of a button on the remote control caused a little milkman to deliver "authentically styled milkcans, one by one, out onto the platform."

Lionel introduced trains that smoked in 1946. Ammonium nitrate pellets were dropped down the engine's stack and came to rest on a specially made light bulb (which also doubled as the engine's headlight). Once the pellet heated up, it liquefied and began to smoke. After ammonium nitrate was found to be unstable (it's basically a minature fertilizer bomb!), pellets were changed to the safer SP Pellets shown here. Later, pellets were heated by a wire element. Today, a liquid is used.

company diversified into numerous directions, all of which burdened the company further. In 1965, Joshua Lionel Cowen died and four years later the company that bore his name stopped producing electric trains. It licensed the name Lionel to Fundimensions, a subsidiary of General Mills, who took over the brand under the familiar dark blue and orange banner. Despite its rocky ride, the name Lionel still carried clout.

With slogans like "Not Just a Toy, A Tradition," Fundimensions called upon the spirit of Joshua Cowen (not to mention the dies and tools from Lionel's glory days of the early '50s) and resurrected many of the company's most popular models. Fundimensions drove Lionel through the turbulent '70s and into one of their best years in 1981, followed immediately by the filing of Chapter IX bankruptcy protection in 1982. The next year manufacturing was moved to Mexico. Finally in 1985 Lionel trains returned to glory at the

hands of man who, in a symbolic turn of foreshadowing, salvaged his first train from a garbage can at the age of seven.

Richard Kughn was walking home from school when he spotted the trashed train. He redeemed the railroad, cleaned it up and got it running again. Years later, he shared how he had bonded with his father over that train and many others like it throughout his childhood. By the time he made his first million in commercial real estate Kughn had left childhood behind, but not his love of trains; he was an avid collector and member of the TCA (Train Collectors Association) when he bought Lionel's licensing contract from General Mills in 1986.

Under his conductor's cap, the company was renamed Lionel Trains Incorporated and its original reputation for quality was reestablished. Kughn introduced trains in virtually all known sizes in an effort to appeal to every collector and every budget. But his most significant contributions were in technological advancements like a fully digital collection of railroad sounds that included, quite literally, all the bells and whistles of a real railroad.

In 1992, Kughn formed LionTech (short for Lionel Technology) in an effort to develop a wireless remote control system for running a model railroad. Kughn's unlikely partner in the venture was singer-songwriter Neil Young. Young was an avid Lionel fan and the father of two boys with cerebral palsy. In an effort to develop a remote control system that was easier for his sons to use, Young's path crossed Kughn's and a partnership was formed. Young also helped LionTech develop advanced sound systems for trains. Hollander writes, "From this partnership came the electronic mainstays of current Lionel Trains, TrainMaster Command Control and advanced RailSounds." With this new setup, engineers could control their trains via radio signals and with the push of a button, create smoke, hear engine sounds and even listen to miniature railroad workers talk to each other.

Kughn had bought out his licensing contract from General Mills early in 1994 and was now the outright owner of the greatest name in model railroad history. But while the name had value, the business behind it continued to run out of steam. After Lionel filed for Chapter IX protection again in late 1994, Kughn decided to sell the business to an investment firm made up of Neil Young and several partners. In 1995, Lionel Trains Incorporated and LionTech were consolidated under the new name Lionel Limited Liability Corporation, or Lionel LLC. No matter what it's called, for many "Lionel" remains not just a name, but a family tradition.

"My father's the one that got me involved in trains," Joe Mania told me. Joe was eight years old at the time, the same age his daughter was when she accompanied her father and her grandfather to Lionel's 100th birthday celebra-tion. Joe remembered, "I was home from school sick and I called him at work and asked to play with the trains which were in a wooden crate in the back of our basement. He said yes, but added, 'They've got to be put away when you're done.' Well, they just never went back in the crate. It's been 30 years now."

Whether rediscovered in a dusty basement or revealed in a shiny new box at a local hobby shop, this is Lionel's legacy—a passion that ties the past to present with an alluring call of "All aboard!"

✳ The first electric toy trains in America were made by Cincinnati's Carlisle & Finch Company, founded in 1893.

✳ The Train Collectors Association, located in Strasburg, Pennsylvania, has over 31,000 members.

Teddy Bear

Debut: 1903
Namesake: Theodore "Teddy" Roosevelt (1858-1919)
Inventive Idea: Cartoonist Clifford Berryman
Inventors: Morris & Rose Mitchtom
Companies: Ideal Toy and Novelty Company, Margarete Steiff GmbH and many others

A FEROCIOUS FRIEND

Of all the stuffed animals in the world, our love of the stuffed bear puts us on a first-name basis; there's Winnie, Paddington, Rupert and Corduroy. In the animal world, their real names (like Grizzly and Kodiak) are much more threatening. Bears are not the most gentle of creatures to be providing us one of our most cherished creature comforts. Yet psychologists suggest that it is precisely the bear's formidable size and strength, hidden within the teddy bear, which permits that unexplainable feeling of comfort and security. Plaything *and* protector. Before he became our favorite kind of bear, even before he became Christopher Robin's bear, he was simply Teddy's bear.

Theodore Roosevelt was born in 1858. Although sick with asthma through most of his childhood, "Teddy" increased his strength through rigorous exercise, advocated "the strenuous life," as he called it, and built himself into a rough and tumble outdoorsman. Both his personal and political lives bore scars of sorrow that he masked with a gruff manliness. In 1884, he endured the death of his first wife soon after she gave birth to their only child. His mother died on the same day. Later, during the Spanish-American war in 1898, Roosevelt led the First Volunteer Cavalry Regiment, known as the Rough Riders, in a daring charge at the battle of San Juan Hill. He returned home a national hero and two years later, ran for vice president alongside presidential candidate and friend, William McKinley. The McKinley-Roosevelt ticket won, but tragedy struck again when McKinley was assassinated on September 6, 1901, elevating Roosevelt to president. It's fitting that a man so hardened by life's blows inspired a toy companion that comforted and softened the hearts of so many.

The event that inspired the creation of "Teddy's bear," as the toy was first called, happened just a little over a year after Roosevelt took office. While working to resolve a border dispute between the states of Mississippi and Louisiana, Roosevelt took time off for a hunting trip for black bear in Smedes, Mississippi. Apparently, the hunting was not good and for

Early Ideal teddy bear, circa 1907.

days the press reported the president's inability to bag a black bear. Finally his aides trapped a bear near a watering hole and tied it to a tree. Offering the bear to the president for an easy kill, the aides were surprised when Roosevelt declined to shoot the animal in such an unsportsmanlike manner. Such an act of compassion from this rugged new president was unexpected and news of the incident soon spread. Before the days of press photographers, newspapers utilized the services of talented cartoonists to tell a visual story. News of the bear incident inspired Clifford Berryman, cartoonist for the *Washington Post,* to draw a panel that cleverly spoke to both the president's political agenda for the trip and his refusal to kill a trapped animal. Berryman titled it, "Drawing the Line in Mississippi."

Berryman was flooded with requests for more drawings of the cute bear cub from his cartoon. As the artist obliged, the frightened beast changed from its original adult appearance to a cute and tattered little cub, which embellished the story even further. The subsequent drawings were irresistible—the disheveled cub sported cute Mickey Mouse ears before Mickey Mouse even existed! The public's immediate affection

Theodore "Teddy" Roosevelt was the 26th president of the United States.

for the little bear, combined with Roosevelt's noble self-restraint, proved to be a political windfall for the president. His popularity soared. When the cartoon reached New York it caught the attention of a shop owner in Brooklyn.

Morris Michtom and his wife Rose were Russian-born immigrants who owned a small store that sold candy and other penny items. Sometimes to make ends meet, the Michtoms would sell dolls that Rose had sewn at night. After seeing Berryman's drawing, Morris asked Rose if she could make a few toy replicas of the bear in the cartoon. Rose did just that, the legend goes, using plush velvet and shoe buttons for eyes. Calling the little fellows "Teddy's bears," the Michtoms displayed them in their store window for $1.50. When they sold quickly, Morris and Rose reportedly sent a sample of the bear to Roosevelt along with a letter asking permission to use his name. The president is said to have responded favorably and the Michtoms found themselves in the business of making stuffed bears.

The demand for Teddy's bears grew so quickly that the Michtoms could not possibly keep up with the orders, so with the help of a wholesale company named

Clifford Berryman's caricature of the president, with his back turned to the frightened bear and his hand up in disdain, first ran in the *Washington Post* on November 16, 1902.

Butler Brothers, they founded The Ideal Toy & Novelty Company in early 1903—the first teddy bear manufacturing company in the United States. Unknown to the Michtoms, at the same time in Germany, a remarkable woman who survived childhood polio was about to change the little bear's destiny.

Margarete Steiff's company created the first stuffed bear with movable limbs. These early Steiff bears had a humped back and a long snout like an actual bear. That's because Margarete's nephew, Richard Steiff, designed the toy from drawings he made of bear cubs at Germany's Stuttgart Zoo. The finished toy featured a round, hard body and arms that allowed it to sit or stand on all fours. It was not called a teddy bear, for that name was not yet known to the Steiffs. According to Leyla Maniera's book *Christie's: A Century of Teddy Bears,* they called it "Bär 55 PB" in their catalogs, then named it Petsy, after the German term *Meister Petz,* meaning bear or bruin. For these reasons, neither Margarete Steiff nor her nephew Richard can truly be called the inventors of the "teddy bear," any more than the first rag doll maker can be credited as the inventor of Raggedy Ann. However, the Steiff family's contribution to the popularity of the toy is undisputed, for after displaying these bears at the Leipzig Trade Fair in 1903 they reportedly sold 3,000 of them to a New York wholesaler. Later, with feedback from the fair and possibly in response to the emerging Teddy's bear mania in the United States, the Steiff Company created a thinner, softer stuffed bear, and began shipping them in larger quantities to America.

When the Michtoms altered their bear to look more like the Steiff bears, the war of the baby bruins was on. To this day the debate rages as to who "invented" the teddy bear, with the Michtom supporters noting that the early Steiff bears had multiple names, none of which included "Teddy's" or "teddy bear," while the Steiff defenders point out that neither the letter to Roosevelt from the Michtoms nor his letter supposedly mailed back to them has ever surfaced. Silent in this debate is Clifford Berryman, who created Teddy's bear

and profited little from his creation monetarily, while Ideal, Steiff and others manufactured Teddy's bears by the bushel.

In 1906, Teddy Roosevelt ran again, this time adopting Berryman's little bear as his political mascot, and won in a landslide. The subsequent four years witnessed continual use of the bear icon in all the Berryman cartoons featuring the second-term president. That same year the term teddy bear (without the possessive "s" attached) first appeared in the October 1906 issue of *Playthings* magazine and the term officially entered the toy business vernacular.

THE YEAR OF THE BEAR

In 1907 teddy bears overran the toy world. Steiff company records show that they sold 974,000 teddy bears that year, most shipped to the bear's birthplace, the United States. While scores of other German manufacturers followed suit, Ideal acquired larger facilities to keep up with the competition from foreign importers and the growing number of domestic makers trying to capitalize on the fad-turned-fashion piece.

The practice of photographing a child with his or her favorite teddy bear was common by 1907. Songwriters published tunes like "The Teddy Bear's Picnic" and "Teddy Bear's Lullaby" that same year, demonstrating the rising trend of adults buying and wanting more of the bears. It's long been known that in order for a toy to reach fad proportions it must appeal to adults, but once scores of adults want the toy more than the kids, the fad turns into a craze. In the book, *Kids' Stuff* by Gary Cross, the author quotes ads of the time to reveal how this seemingly innocuous stuffed creature had bear-hugged adults and would not let go.

Specialized bear "fashions" were sold separately in 1907. Even magazines like the *Ladies' Home Journal* offered patterns for teddy bear clothes.

These included pajamas, Rough Rider, fireman, sailor, and clown suits. . . . Teddy bears were all the "rage in the cities." . . . They had become a fashion accessory.

FEROCIOUS, FANCIFUL, FASHIONABLE

Hindsight helps in defining a toy craze. In this case, we can claim we identify with bears because of the human qualities they possess, like the ability to stand and walk on their hind legs or, in the case of the Panda bear, the ability to use its forepaws like hands. Likewise, Berryman's rendition of the hapless bear cub featured human eyes open wide in fear and a human mouth agape at Roosevelt's refusal to shoot. Readers empathized with this little guy, and later when teddy bear artists rendered their versions of the cub, even more human attributes showed up in all the mohair and stitching. The adorably sad eyes, cocked head, long "give me a hug" arms and pathetically big feet all contributed to the bear's popularity.

Teddy bears were pricey because of the hand labor and expensive materials needed to make them, yet they sold well for reasons beyond craftsmanship. They appealed to boys because bears had a reputation for being rugged, ferocious animals. In light of the aforementioned clothes in which these early teddies were outfitted (Rough Riders, firemen, sailors) it is fair to call teddy bears the first action figures! To little girls, their appeal involved something more fanciful. Teddies were poseable and unlike the dolls of that period that consisted mostly of wood, composition or porcelain, teddy bears were also huggable.

By 1905, so many manufacturers were copying the superior Steiff design that the company trademarked the "button in ear" model of their bears, which to this day differentiates a Steiff bear from all others.

By 1908, the teddy bear fad faded with Teddy Roosevelt's refusal to run for a third term. William Taft, the man whom Roosevelt decided should be his successor, campaigned on a platform based on the old Roosevelt ideals and a brand new mascot. The Taft team created post cards and buttons featuring *Billy Possum,* a reference to Taft's love of "possum and 'taters." Although he won the election, Taft's marsupial never caught on as a stuffed animal (perhaps because Taft's relationship to the furry fellas consisted of his desire to ingest them). The teddy bear's status as the most popular toy ever named after a president remained intact, surrendering that claim only briefly in the 1950s when Lincoln Logs surged in popularity.

The appeal of the teddy bear remained steady through both World Wars and the Depression . In those troubled times, the most famous of all stuffed animals provided comfort and a needed reprieve from the worries of an uncertain future.

Winnie the Pooh

In the mid-1920s, English author A. A. Milne created the most famous teddy bear of all time. Winnie the Pooh began his life with the name Edward Bear, named by Milne's son, Christopher Robin Milne. The story is told that Christopher Robin became enamored with a black bear cub at the London Zoo named Winnie. The bear had belonged to a British soldier who had rescued her, named her after his hometown of Winnipeg, Canada, and later donated her to the zoo. Christopher Robin renamed Edward Bear "Winnie." The name Pooh came later, courtesy of Christopher's famous father. The book *Winnie-the-Pooh,* first published in 1926, secured the popularity of the stuffed toy for generations.

Millions of teddy bears are still sold each year, many finding themselves in the arms of adults who cherish them no less than the child who sees their teddy as play pal, confidant and guardian angel. Today more than ever, a teddy bear's hug remains one of life's simple pleasures, and his multifaceted reputation as security blanket, plaything and comforter remains intact.

This ad from 1907 claims that, "Teddy is all the rage in the cities. The children carry him to school and even the grown-up ladies carry him with them when they go out for a walk or ride, or to the theater."

While Ideal and Steiff both took credit for having originated the teddy bear, the two men who had the most to do with its creation gave each other the credit. Teddy Roosevelt never referred to the toy as a Teddy's Bear, but called it a Berryman Bear. Clifford Berryman referred to his creative work as a Roosevelt Bear.

Debut: 1903
Inventor: Edwin Binney and
    C. Harold Smith
Company: Binney & Smith

Crayola

COLORING THE SENSES

See the brilliant colors, smell that distinct aroma. Listen for the tiny smack of the point separating from the colored page and feel the waxy blanket you've just laid down. No other plaything appeals to the senses like Crayola crayons. That's why, according to the company, a typical child between the ages of two and eight spends twenty-eight minutes a day coloring, wearing to the nub 730 crayons by the time he or she turns ten. And that's why there's a factory near Easton, Pennsylvania that makes an average of 12 million Crayola crayons *per day*.

The factory is actually more of an industrial campus. Seven acres of Crayola paradise. Joseph Binney cast the die for that factory back in the 1800s when he founded the Peekskill Chemical Company. Its specialty was making pigments, the kind that turned barns of that era their distinctive red color. In 1885, Joseph Binney retired, handing over control of the company to his son, Edwin Binney, and his nephew Harold Smith. They changed the name to Binney & Smith, a company that communicated to the world in terms of color.

Edwin
Binney

Although the company would soon have a bright future, a deep black pigment colored the new generation's start. Binney & Smith was the first company to discover the secret of using carbon in making a really dark black. Soon it was used in the production of goods like shoe polish, printing inks and car tires. Binney & Smith's carbon black earned them a gold medal at the 1900 Paris Exposition and marked the beginning of the company's long use of the term "gold medal" on their product packaging.

As the company expanded, it began to specialize in providing safe, educational art products for children. Slate pencils and other pigment-based writing tools were merely a fraction of their growing product line. This meant that

C. Harold
Smith

In 1903, the very first Crayola school crayons were shipped to schools at the affordable price of five cents a pack.

thousands of boxes containing the company's various products needed to be marked and inventoried using ink labeling markers, which were common at the time, but messy. Not necessarily looking to invent a new product, but more interested in solving an untidy problem, Binney and Smith developed a mess-free marking crayon by mixing their carbon black with paraffin wax. To make the marker clean and easy to use they wrapped it in a paper sleeve. Little did they know what they had just created.

By the early 1900s, Binney & Smith sold pencils and dustless chalk to schools throughout America. Some company representatives who visited the schools noticed that the children often used expensive artist's crayons from France or simply went without. After learning of the need for an inexpensive alternative, Edwin Binney & Harold Smith decided to adapt their carbon/paraffin marking crayon for use in schools. They altered the formula, added some talc, and created the future of their company in the form of a 3-inch stick of color. Alice Binney, Edwin's wife and a former schoolteacher, named these humble crayons. By combining the French word for chalk, "craie," with the term "oleaginous," which means oily and referred to the paraffin wax, she christened the school crayons "Crayola."

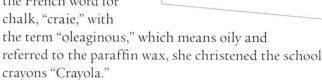

Crayola, Grant Wood and the American Farm Family

In 1930, artist Grant Wood produced his most famous painting, American Gothic. Wood was inspired to become an artist after winning third prize in a Crayola drawing contest when he was 14. In the background of Grant's famous painting sits a barn in a famous hue of red — more than likely courtesy of Binney & Smith.

Farmers had a long association with Binney & Smith. Local farm families worked hand wrapping Crayola crayons during the Depression (automatic wrapping machines were not used until the late '40s). Binney & Smith's support of the local community continued even after the economy recovered, as farm families found valuable off-season winter jobs at the Crayola plant.

The famous box of 64 Crayolas was released in 1958. While Bing Crosby was dreaming of a *White Christmas* that year, American kids longed for one filled with 64 colors and a built-in sharpener.

The eight original colors included black, brown, purple, blue, red, orange, yellow and green. The package described them aptly, as "Clean, Compact, Convenient" and touted their use "for educational color work." Their use and value far exceeded the company's expectations. Crayola crayons became an indelible part of our American culture.

From the success of Crayola crayons, Edwin and Harold grew their company into a giant in the art supply industry. Modeling clay and paints were some of their new product lines, but it was the varied Crayola crayon assortments that propelled the company forward. Crayola offered a box of 16 crayons shortly after the original eight of 1903. In 1949, the company introduced the Crayola box of 48 and marked the beginning of a whole new palette of colors from which budding artists could choose. Colors like Carnation Pink and Periwinkle began to grace the artwork on refrigerator doors across America. The famous box of 64 Crayolas came out in 1958, and in 1972, fluorescents were added to the color mix with explosive names like Atomic Tangerine and Laser Lemon.

Currently over 120 colors are available from the more than 600 shades of Crayola crayons that have been produced over the years. Over 100 billion Crayola crayons have been sold in eighty-plus countries. Their exact chemical composition remains one of the most guarded secrets in the toy industry. It's that secret formula that gives Crayola crayons their feel, quality of line and distinctive aroma—the very same scent that a Yale University study cited as number 18 on a list of the 20 most recognizable scents to adults.

But why stop there? Go ahead. Let your other senses play a part. Is there anything more luscious than a brand-new box of Crayola crayons? Rows of colored sticks standing perfectly at attention, awaiting your artistic whims? Slide one out of the box and feel its weight. Hold it by the perfect paper wrapper and transfer some color onto a page. Press hard if you want, even the soft click of a Crayola crayon breaking is somehow oddly satisfying.

Of course the Crayola creations are the most rewarding part. It's the sharing of feelings through color, both the dark ones and the light ones. Those are the gifts from my kids that I cherish the most. After the hugs and kisses, I'll take their ideas, fears, thoughts and dreams all expressed on paper. Long before they can articulate themselves adequately with words, kids can speak in shades of Pacific Blue and Wild Watermelon. Mr. Binney and Mr. Smith would be pleased.

Erector

Debut: 1913
Inventor: A. C. Gilbet (1884–1961)
Companies: Mysto Manufacturing, The A. C. Gilbert Company, The Jack Wrather Corporation, Gabriel, Ideal, Meccano

MAGIC MAN

While it's true Alfred Carlton Gilbert became a Yale-trained physician, a world-class athlete and a gifted entrepreneur, when he was a boy all he wanted to be was a magician. By many accounts he was an accomplished performer of magic tricks, and by adulthood his skills were so proficient that he earned money for his medical school tuition by making magic in shops around New Haven, Connecticut. In 1907, at the age of 25, he formed a company called Mysto Manufacturing to sell magic kits to kids.

Apparently this magic man could also levitate, for in 1908 he willed himself over a 12-foot bar and earned a gold medal in the pole vault at the Olympics in London. In 1909 he graduated with his medical degree but decided to focus on entertaining and educating children through toys and magic.

The legend is that while on a train traveling from New Haven to New York City, Gilbert witnessed some workmen riveting steel beams in the construction of an electrical power-line tower and decided then and there to create a construction set made of steel with real metal beams, nuts, bolts, gears, wheels and even engines. Although it's a nice story, surely Gilbert was also influenced by the tin and brass construction sets patented by Britain's Frank Hornby in 1901. Hornby's Meccano sets had been marketed successfully in England and sold in America as early as 1910. While Gilbert may not have been first to make these metal marvels, his were the sets that captivated America.

In *The Man Who Changed How Boys and Toys Were Made*, author Bruce Watson explains how Gilbert made a prototype of his idea by cutting cardboard into tiny girders, braces and trusses. Once he perfected the size and shape of the various parts, he hired a local machinist to build a prototype of his creation from steel. Progressing from cardboard model to steel prototype proved easy enough, but taking the leap of faith into production of such an elaborate toy was another matter. Gilbert's business involved making simple, inexpensive magic kits, not toys.

1915 Erector set

He showed the idea to his father, a pragmatic man who could not understand why his son would waste a Yale education making magic tricks. Perhaps the father saw the value of this construction toy idea, but more likely, Watson contends, Frank Gilbert just believed in his son. In 1913, with a $5,000 loan from his father, A. C. Gilbert produced his Mysto Erector Structural Steel Builder.

When these simple sets of metal were introduced, America had recently witnessed all the wonders that man could build. In 1902, New York's first skyscraper, the uniquely triangular Flatiron building, captivated the world. In 1903 the Wright brothers built the world's first flying machine, and in 1908, just five years before the launch of Erector, Henry Ford began mass-producing the Model T. The era just after the industrial age continued to produce never-before-seen marvels and American kids eagerly joined in the revolution on a miniature scale. Gilbert marketed Erector sets directly to boys, although little girls certainly constructed too. He sold the more elaborate sets in heavy wooden cases that made them feel more like tools than toys—but then, that's exactly what Gilbert wanted to provide; tools to make just about anything a creative mind could dream up.

He introduced his toy with a range of sets numbered one through eight; the low numbered sets came in cardboard boxes and were affordable to nearly everyone. They contained enough parts to make a few models, but more importantly, they were the "hook" that pulled kids into the corps of Erector engineers. With a taste of Erector glory, a kid would soon long for the bigger and more expensive sets. For instance, set No. 3 allowed a builder to construct fifty-five

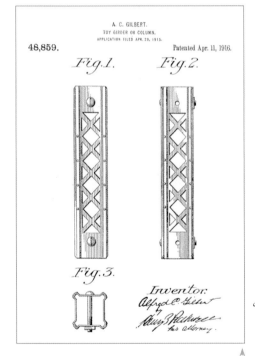

A. C. Gilbert improved on the British Meccano sets by designing his Erector sets with "interlocking grooved girders" that gave considerably more structural support to the buildings, bridges and vehicles that kids could create.

different models at a cost of only $3. The Cadillac of construction sets, the revered No. 8, came with 740 parts, a screw driver and a motor. "Put them all together, and a boy could build one hundred different models, not to mention whatever implements of destruction he could design himself," Watson writes. The No. 8 was encased in a gorgeous walnut box with sliding drawers, complete with lock and key to keep your little brother from messing with your girders. It cost $25 in 1915, which would equate to nearly $450 today. Just how well these elaborate and expensive construction sets sold testifies to Gilbert's belief in the imagination of children and his own irrepressible will. A. C. Gilbert proved to be as gifted at marketing as he was at pole vaulting (or seemingly anything else he endeavored to do).

The Erector brand catapulted to national fame as Gilbert engineered one of the most shrewd promotions of a toy ever launched in America. According to Watson, Gilbert offered huge prizes in Erector design competitions. Kids from across the country entered to win sporting goods, motorcycles and even an actual automobile in 1915. With thousands of fans writing him every week, the entrepreneur created his Gilbert Institute of Erector Engineering, which offered the title of "Engineer" to anyone who submitted a new design for an Erector model. Earning the title of "Expert Engineer" or "Master Engineer" required more effort. A kid had to submit a self-designed model but also sell a certain number of subscriptions to Gilbert's *Erector Tips* magazine.

These clever cross-promotions proved wildly successful, making The A. C. Gilbert Company the

His ads didn't speak down to children, but directly to them—as if Gilbert himself were down on the floor with his sleeves rolled up and ready to play. This ad ran in 1914.

The roaring twenties were the heyday for Erector sets and in 1924 they were totally revamped. The company reduced the size of some parts and added many new ones, exponentially expanding the creative possibilities. Sets that built a single elaborate model balanced the other end of the design spectrum. Coveted by collectors today, these sets created a Ferris Wheel, Zeppelin or Locomotive.

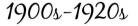

Gilbert's company persevered through the Depression and prospered in the period leading up to World War II. Around this time the company introduced the classic, metal boxes, sets galvanized in the minds of big kids everywhere. When World War II ended and our heroes returned home, they settled down and raised the vast group of consumers known as baby boomers. Through the late '40s and early '50s, this horde of tinkerers made Erector sets a must-have toy.

biggest toy company in America. Using his own likeness and reputation in advertisements that ran across the United States, A. C. Gilbert became not just a spokesman but a personal friend to legions of kids. He spoke from his heart because he actually believed in the constructive value of his toys, and when he spoke, A. C. Gilbert could be very persuasive.

Gilbert secured his place in history by a legendary incident that rivals his gold medal performance and his invention of one of our nation's most beloved toys. In 1918, as World War I raged in Europe, the U.S. Council of National Defense debated whether to restrict or even ban the sales of toys for the 1918 holiday season in order to conserve materials needed for the war effort. Gilbert had been named president of the newly formed Toy Manufacturers of America just two years prior, and even though his tenure as president expired by 1918, he arranged for an audience with the Council in Washington. His moving plea, pointing out the educational value and immeasurable importance of toys in the nurturing and development of children, caused the Council to declare toys "essential" and therefore exempt from the proposed ban. The *Boston Post* reported the incident, dubbing Gilbert "The Man Who Saved Christmas."

Cherry-red Erector sets like this one from the '50s turned many baby boomers into lovers of heavy metal.

ROCK AND BLOCKS

When rock 'n' roll hit the scene, teenagers turned their envious gaze from Charles Lindbergh to Elvis Presley. Erector sets began losing the older market share to adolescent rebellion. The classic toy wasn't "cool" anymore and, to make matters worse, younger builders were about to discover the new kid in blocks.

Erector sets had weathered the competition from Tinkertoys, which were also released in 1913, and even Lincoln Logs, introduced three years later. For nearly 45 years these classic construction sets of wood and metal were the only ones kids wanted. That is until 1958, when the new and improved Lego plastic building brick hit the market. Lego sets were cheaper, lighter and more colorful, offering vast design possibilities. Lego really excelled, however, in its ease of use, a challenge that Erector, with all the nuts, bolts, screwdrivers and wrenches, could not answer. Little engineers who had once played with Erector Brik-tor sets "for young builders" left Erector to construct their dreams in Lego bricks.

A. C. Gilbert's company survived two World Wars and the Depression, but it would not survive losing the interest of children. Gilbert died at the age of 77 in 1961, and six years later the company he founded fell as well. The Erector trademark has been passed around from toy company to toy company since 1967, but none could raise the toy to its previous glory. Some point to the fact that building with an Erector set takes patience and planning, attributes more suited to children of another era. For baby boomers,

A. C. Gilbert poses with a giant Erector Ferris Wheel.

who toiled with girders and screws for hours on end, building with an Erector set was a labor of love.

BUILDING ON A LEGEND

Erector's current owner is a French company with the familiar name Meccano. In the United States, Brio Corporation distributes the latest Erector sets with innovations that have given the 90-year-old toy a real boost. For 2003, Brio introduced Erector models with "molecular metal," a revolutionary building material with memory. Featured within the Erector "Design" line, this advancement features parts that bend and then spring back to their original shape, ready for the next wave of inspiration.

If A. C. Gilbert were alive to see these new models with "molecular metal," the toy maker in him would certainly have many questions, but the child in him would have but one: "Hello Boys!" he'd say, "What shall we build first?"

The new face of Erector

Crossword Puzzle

1900s–1920s

Debut: 1913
Inventor: Arthur Wynne (1862-1945)
Developer: Margaret Petherbridge (1895-1984)
Companies: *New York World* newspaper, Simon & Schuster, anyone with a printing press

THE CROSSWORD CONNECTION

Nine letter word, starts with C, ends with D, "immensely popular game." Easy right? C-A-N-D-Y-L-A-N-D. Oops. I knew I should have done this one in pencil.

The most popular game in the world calls itself a puzzle, and depending on who you talk to, it's a hobby that can become a habit—or an addiction that can become an obsession.

It all started on December 21, 1913, when an unassuming, diamond-shaped collection of numbered boxes appeared in the Sunday issue of the *New York World* newspaper. It occupied the "Fun" section of that day's edition, with simple instructions that read, "Fill in small squares with words which agree with the following definitions." The man who wrote those instructions is the man credited as inventor of the crossword puzzle, "Fun" editor, Arthur Wynne.

The English-born Wynne was trying to think of a new item for a section that regularly featured anagrams, rebuses, and other games that turned words into playthings. According to Charles Panati's *Extraordinary Origins of Everyday Things,* Wynne based this "Word-Cross," as the innovation was first called, on a Victorian word puzzle that his grandfather had taught him called Magic Square. After the third week of the puzzle's run, the compositor at the *New York World* wrote the title "Can you fill in the Cross words?" above the puzzle. By the fourth week, the title had changed to Cross Words.

Although simple compared to today's mega-grids, the puzzles quickly became a reader favorite. Amazingly, no one from the newspaper ever tried to copyright the proprietary play of the puzzles or trademark the name Cross Word. Despite the angry letters that Wynne received whenever the section ran without a Cross Word, his bosses dismissed the puzzle as a fad and remained deaf to his suggestion that they protect their rights.

Almost a decade later, the *New York World* was still the Cross Word's sole distributor, but the monopoly didn't last. As the puzzle's appeal continued to grow, other newspapers created their own versions. By the early 1920s, according to Panati, every major U.S. paper featured its own crossword puzzle. As its fame spread, the cleverly addictive clues and boxes caught the eye of a man named Richard Simon.

Arthur Wynne, creator of the crossword puzzle.

The first published crossword puzzle ran on December 21, 1913, in the *New York World.*

The World.

"Circulation Books Open to All."

"Circulation Books Open to All."

NEW YORK, SUNDAY, DECEMBER 21, 1913.

FUN'S Word-Cross Puzzle.

FILL in the small squares with words which agree with the following definitions:

2–3. What bargain hunters enjoy:

4–5. A written acknowledgment.

6–7. Such and nothing more.

10–11. A bird.

14-15. Opposed to less.

18–19. What this puzzle is.

22–23. An animal of prey.

26–27. The close of a day.

28–29. To elude.

30–31. The plural of is.

8–9. To cultivate.

12–13. A bar of wood or iron.

16–17 What artists learn to do.

20–21. Fastened.

24–25. Found on the seashore.

10–18. The fibre of the gomuti palm.

6–22. What we all should be.

4–26. A day dream.

2–11. A talon.

19–28. A pigeon.

F–7. Part of your head.

23–30. A river in Russia.

1–32. To govern.

33–34. An aromatic plant.

N–8. A fist.

24–31. To agree with.

3–12. Part of a ship.

20–29. One.

5–27. Exchanging.

9–25. To sink in mud.

13–21. A boy.

Simon was a hopeful book publisher, and together with his friend and partner Max Schuster, decided that the promising popularity of Cross Words just might be the perfect launching pad for their fledgling firm. In 1924, Plaza Publishing printed 3,600 copies of *The Cross Word Puzzle Book,* a collection of Cross Words edited by Wynne's successor at the *New York World,* Margaret Petherbridge, and others. With a lot on the line, the two entrepreneurs packaged the book with a free pencil and eraser and gave copies away in the hope of luring orders from bookstores. The books sold quickly. Plaza Publishing rushed back to print and sold out of the new run as well. The phenomenon had begun.

In 1924, the *New York Times* reported that the puzzles were causing "temporary madness," and that "all ages, both sexes, highbrows and lowbrows, at all times and in all places, even in restaurants and in subways, pore over the diagrams. . . ." From 1924 to 1930, the crossword craze had millions of steadfast solvers in its grip. While the New York Public Library began to limit the use of their dictionaries to five minutes per patron, the B & O Railroad stocked dictionaries in their cars for travelers smitten with all those squares.

When Wynne retired sometime in the 1920s (he was 53 when he invented the puzzle), Margaret Petherbridge became the editor in charge of the *New York World's* "Fun" section and overseer of the crossword puzzle. No person outside of Arthur Wynne himself had such a huge impact on the development of the genre of crosswords. In the book *The Crossword Obsession,* author Coral Amende tells more about the remarkable woman who made influential changes to "the world's most popular pastime."

Beyond co-editing the book that launched crosswords to prominence, Petherbridge established what Amende describes as "the crossword layout rule . . . of diagonally symmetrical grids with no isolated sections, or 'islands,' of answer words." Her work at the *World* eventually gained the attention of publisher Arthur Hays Sulzberger, who brought her on board to edit an ongoing crossword puzzle for the *New York Times*. The first crossword to appear in the *Times* was edited by Petherbridge-Farrar (who'd since married) and ran on February 15, 1942. She remained at the *Times* as their crossword editor for another 27 years, creating a legacy that has continued ever since. Will Shortz, the current *New York Times* crossword editor, recognizes her influence on puzzle history. "Margaret always said that she took the best ideas from contributors and encouraged the ones that made sense," Shortz said. "Over the years she began introducing themes for puzzles, wordplay and trickery as she adopted those ideas."

Within the puzzle clues, Petherbridge-Farrar coupled her love of puns and a British knack for wordplay. Combined with her self-established American style grid, she'd created the modern crossword puzzle. She established the *Times*-tested tradition of making their daily puzzles easier in the beginning of the week and then progressively harder, culminating with the most vexing of all puzzles on Saturday, a day of penciling for millions. "She made the Saturday puzzle extra hard, reasoning that most people didn't have a job to go to that day," said Shortz.

Petherbridge-Farrar was forced to retire from the *New York Times* in 1969, but not from crossword puzzles. "The *Times* had a mandatory retirement age at the time and it was really a ridiculous thing, because she was still so good and so beloved, but they had to enforce this rule," Shortz told me. "So she went to General Features Syndicate, which was owned by the *LA Times*." She edited the

Los Angeles Times crossword until her death in 1984 at the age of 89.

I asked Will Shortz if he planned to edit the *Times* crossword until he was 89. "Hopefully as long as I live!" he laughed. "It's a prestigious job and a great job."

And a job that touches the lives of many—celebrities included, as evidenced by the mail he receives: a birthday note from former president Bill Clinton. A poem from actor Paul Sorvino. He gets all kinds of compliments and critiques. "Artie Johnson wrote me once after I had used the clue 'Jovial Johnson' for the clue 'A-R-T.' He sent me a card and the entire message was 'Jovial?' And if you know his kind of humor, there's nothing jovial about it. I wrote him back and said 'You're right—that's not a good clue, but I went with it for the alliteration.'"

Before the end of 1924, over 150,000 copies of *The Cross Word Puzzle Book* had sold all across the country, launching not only the popularity of the puzzles, but a printing dynasty as well; Plaza Publishing soon became Simon & Schuster.

Crosswords have even become the barometer by which fame is measured. Make it as a clue or answer within the *New York Times* crossword puzzle and you've really made it. "Rita Braver, the CBS newswoman, wrote me a thank you note after her name appeared,"

At the height of the craze in 1925, crosswords turned into a lifestyle. Everything from jewelry, furniture, clothing (including bathing suits) featured the puzzle's indicative black and white box pattern. Photograph circa 1925.

Shortz said. "She said she had no idea how many of her friends solve the *Times* crossword by 7:00 a.m., because that's when her phone started ringing." So, you may ask—have many lobbied him for inclusion? "Yes, and I won't tell you who." Shotrz laughed. "I never pay attention to lobbyists, because if you have to lobby, then there's a problem."

While some long for the day when fame (or Will Shortz) puts them on a pedestal, others are content to enjoy the fun of trying to solve these addictive puzzles. Shortz said that Steven Sondheim and Bill Gates solve them, as does Steven King, Lee Iacocca and Yo-Yo Ma. It is estimated that 27% of Americans work crosswords at least occasionally, putting the number of fans at 50 million. With nearly every newspaper running its own, this ubiquitous puzzle has indeed become the most popular game in the world.

So lovers of language unite! In an often chaotic world, crossword puzzles offer us order and perhaps even a metaphor for life better lived. They challenge us, and when we endure, they give us a tangible sense of satisfaction. Their intelligent design and simplicity remind us to reach across (or down) to others, and that no matter how difficult or infuriating life becomes, we are not alone. In the end, we're all connected . . . like the letters in a puzzle.

Wynne's puzzles evolved in name from Word-Cross to Cross Word to Cross-word to crossword. The addendum to 1928's Merriam-Webster's *New International Dictionary* became the first dictionary to include the term "crossword."

Starting in 1960, the *New York Times* crossword puzzle was syndicated to other newspapers around the world.

In 2003, the 26th annual World Puzzle Championship took place in Stamford, Connecticut. Founded by Will Shortz, this Super Bowl of crosswords draws over 400 contestants from the United States, Canada, and Europe.

Lincoln Logs

1900s–1920s

Debut: 1916
Inventor: John Lloyd Wright
Companies: John Lloyd
Wright Company, Play-
skool, Hasbro licensed to
K'Nex

CABIN FEVER

The log cabin of the western frontier ranks along-side the red barn of our farmlands as the most American of all buildings. It has come to represent America—formed rugged and sturdy through great effort. Products from maple syrup to vacation resorts use the image of the log cabin in hopes that consumers will associate its qualities with the commodity on which its likeness appears. No product has raised the log cabin to icon status more than Lincoln Logs. Since 1916, this simple construction toy has helped entertain and educate generations of children in patriotic fashion. John Lloyd Wright, the son of architect Frank Lloyd Wright gave us the logs, wooden slats and chimneys needed to design our own rustic homes and frontier villages. For all their rich history associated with the American West, however, Lincoln Logs were in fact inspired by a trip to the Far East.

John Lloyd Wright was also an architect and in 1916, he accompanied his famous father on a visit to Tokyo. They traveled there to observe the construction of the famed architect's Imperial Hotel. Designed to withstand an earthquake (which it did during the Great Kanto earthquake of 1923), the building utilized an interlocking beam design known as "floating cantilever construction." This design feature intrigued John and as he watched, mesmerized by the sight of the huge timbers being stacked into place, he conceived the idea that eventually became Lincoln Logs.

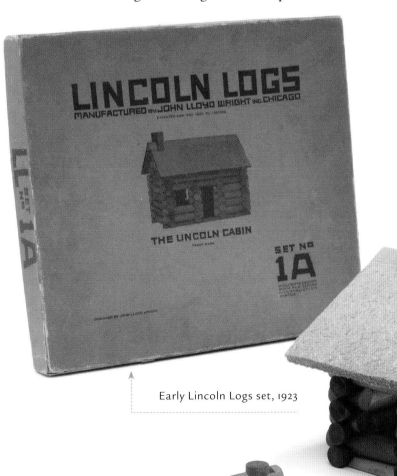

Early Lincoln Logs set, 1923

Undoubtedly influenced by already successful Tinkertoys and Erector sets, Wright formed John Lloyd Wright, Inc. to introduce Lincoln Logs in 1916. America was fighting in World War I when this new construction system was conceived, and the association with our beloved 16th president certainly helped establish the toy with families feeling patriotic, and harkened back to the days of good old-fashioned wooden blocks.

BLOCK PARTY

Wooden blocks have been around forever—or at least since kindergarten. When a man named Friedrich Froebel founded the first kindergarten in 1837, the building block of his curriculum was . . . well, building blocks. They improved motor skills and taught the basics of math. With their open-ended play, blocks could be anything a child's imagination could dream up or knock down. In Froebel's Blocks, as they were called, future architects like Frank Lloyd Wright found their calling at their fingertips. " . . . Now came the geometric by-play of these charming checkered colour combinations!" Frank Lloyd Wright wrote in his Autobiography. " . . . The smooth shapely maple blocks with which to build, the sense of which never afterwards leaves the fingers. . . ."

While building blocks influenced the father to become an architect, it was the architect in the son that led him to create Lincoln Logs. They were made from redwood cut to various lengths. Small notches in the ends or middle of each piece allowed beams to lock into place, but remain flexible enough to withstand the occasional (cow) poke or (cattle) prod. The snaky way a Lincoln Log building would slide and flex was cool.

Like any construction toy, the process of constructing and destroying was a big part of the fun. You had the supreme power to build a ridiculously tall log cabin that resembled the Leaning Tower at Pisa more than the Ponderosa; then that same power allowed you to go Godzilla, scattering Lincoln Logs to the far corners of the Western Frontier or maybe just under the living room sofa.

Through the '30s and '40s, Lincoln Logs grew in popularity, and in 1947, Playskool purchased them from Wright. The acquisition paid off handsomely as the 1950s mania of all things western branded Lincoln Logs with baby boomers and beyond. In 1954, Walt Disney launched *Davey Crockett, Indian Fighter* starring Fess Parker. An instant hit, it spurred the creation and sales of coonskin caps, toy guns, cowboy play sets and wagon loads of other western-related toys. By this time Lincoln Logs had been an established brand for over 30 years, and the subsequent rush of families buying sets was akin to a stampede. The boom lasted well into the 1960s, fueled in 1964 by Fess Parker (again), this time starring in *Daniel Boone* for NBC.

A new enlarged Design Book containing many novel and original ideas in log construction suggests endless building possibilities with **LINCOLN LOGS** — "America's National Toy."

BE BUILDERS
The glory is, if you build what you can,
That all the while you are building a man.

J. LL. WRIGHT, Designer.

Although this early ad shows a young girl joining in the fun, Lincoln Logs were marketed directly at boys, as this poem found in the back of an early design book reflects.

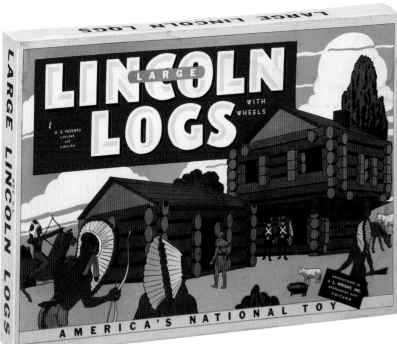

As the popularity of Lincoln Logs grew, competition surfaced in the form of Halsam's American Logs and others, but the original outlasted all imitators. Even after the cowboy phenomenon died and most western-themed toys faded into the sunset, Lincoln Logs remained a staple. Over 100 million sets have been sold since 1916, making them one of the most enduring and best-loved toys. The logs just keep on rolling, as cabin fever strikes a new generation of American kids.

By the 1940s, Lincoln Logs were "America's National Toy."

Today, a company called K'Nex makes Lincoln Logs under special arrangement with Hasbro.

Liberty Coaster Debut: 1917
Little Red Wagon Debut:
    1933
Inventor: Antonio Pasin
    (1897–1990)
Companies: Liberty Coaster
    Wagon Company,
    Liberty Coaster
    Manufacturing
    Company, Radio Steel &
    Manufacturing
    Company, Radio Flyer,
    Inc.

Radio Flyer

LEARNING TO FLY

Today it's one of our most identifiable pieces of Americana, but the Radio Flyer wagon actually started its long journey toward icon status 4,000 miles from the United States in a small town near Venice, Italy. From there, a 16-year-old boy named Antonio Pasin boarded a boat with no more to his name than his talents as a wood craftsman and a dream of owning his own business.

On April 19, 1914, Pasin landed at Ellis Island in New York Harbor within the majestic shadow of the Statue of Liberty. With a cousin in Chicago, his aim was to eventually find work in that city's cabinetmaking trade. For three years the immigrant boy took whatever odd job turned up in a tight labor market. He served water to a crew of sewer diggers, washed vegetables, finished pianos and even posted watch at a cemetery.

Finally, by 1917 he had saved enough money to buy some used woodworking tools and started constructing handcrafted wooden wagons at night in a rented one-room workshop. During the day, Pasin lugged a ragged old suitcase containing an unassembled wagon from store to store, and when a prospective buyer would allow, he'd assemble the parts to illustrate just how well his wagons were made. By 1923, he was successful enough to hire several employees and founded the Liberty Coaster Wagon Company, named after the statue that had welcomed him to the land of opportunity.

The company succeeded and changed its name to The Liberty Coaster Manufacturing Company, reflecting its expansion into other childhood vehicles. By 1925, the Liberty line included wooden scooters and tricycles. As word spread of his well-built playthings, Pasin realized that he would never be able to continue crafting them in wood and still meet the growing demand. Incorporating the mass manufacturing techniques of the auto industry, Pasin began

Radio Flyer wagon, circa 1935

Antonio Pasin was a skilled cabinetmaker, like his father and grandfather before him, but it wasn't until his parents sold their family mule that they had enough money to send Antonio gliding off toward his future in America.

and hard work had transformed him from a penniless, immigrant teen to the world's largest producer of coaster wagons.

In 1987, the company was renamed Radio Flyer, Inc. after its best-selling wagon. Today, Robert and Paul Pasin, grandsons of the company's founder, run the 86-year-old family business. The company keeps up with the changing times by adding new models that reflect contemporary popular culture.

In 1927, it was radio and Lindbergh. In 2003, it's Land Rovers and Hummers. Radio Flyer, Inc. now makes an "ATW," or All-Terrain Wagon, with wide, air-filled tires for both a quiet ride on pavement and smooth transport over loose ground, such as a trip

making metal wagons out of stamped steel in 1927. He was inspired by the proliferation of the relatively new invention of radio and by Charles Lindbergh's solo, non-stop flight across the Atlantic that same year. Combining those two marvels, Pasin christened his new metal wagons Radio Flyer.

Using the assembly line methods pioneered by Henry Ford, Pasin's company grew exponentially and in 1930 he renamed his business the Radio Steel & Manufacturing Company. The shift from wood to steel allowed him to retain his old-world standards of quality (his steel-bodied wagons were virtually indestructible), while increasing production and lowering the price. Pasin's vision allowed him to make an affordable wagon, as his slogan read, "For every boy. For every girl." He was given the nickname "Little Ford" by the steel companies who sold him the raw materials necessary to transform 25 pounds of metal into a toy that transported many of us through childhood. Just 16 years after setting foot in America, Pasin's vision

Big and Small: During the Depression, Antonio Pasin went against the advice of many within his company and built a 45-foot-tall "Coaster Boy" outside his display at the 1933 Chicago World's Fair. Inside, he sold miniature versions of his wagon like the one pictured here for 25 cents. The gamble paid off as Radio Flyer became the talk of this global event.

to the beach. For kids looking for more cargo space, there's the extra big "SUW," or Sport Utility Wagon, with room for twice the Girl Scout cookies and three times the rock collection they've ever carried. Although the Pasin family continues to add to their legacy, they remain true to their origins with a toy that's both the center of child's world and an invisible prop in a much bigger play.

Our little red wagon possessed the selfless ability to blend into the background. We remember it, but even more than that, we remember what was carried in it, who was pulling us along, where we were going and what it became through our imaginations. We recollect the pumpkins it collected and that litter of kittens it held. We remember our older siblings or our parents as they pulled us along and it's those images that bring the memories flooding back. We loved our Radio Flyer because its familiar shape transformed into a lemonade stand, a getaway car or, filled with water, a swimming pool on a hot summer day. Your mom may remind you that you once pulled your Radio Flyer full of dolls, but you remember it as a school bus full of kids. Because of the Radio Flyer's rare ability to become less, in our minds and hearts it has become so much more.

The Radio Flyer story is a tale of transportation both real and imagined. It's mules and boats and the auto industry, but it's also spaceships and flying carpets. According to Webster's dictionary the word *transport* means "to carry from one place to another," but it also means "to move to strong emotion." This is our little red wagon, the transporter of dreams.

"For every boy. For every girl."

A Radio Flyer wagon is one of those rare toys that grows with us. At first we are pulled as passive participants, simply along for the ride. Then we take the handle and an active role in our wagoneering, pulling along anyone or anything light enough to lift, and small enough to fit inside. As we grow older and bolder, we turn the handle around and transform our wagon into a scooter, sitting on one knee within the wagon and using the other leg to propel ourselves down the driveway or down the street.

Even the Depression couldn't halt the demand for Antonio Pasin's wagons. He often boasted that through those terrible economic times, his company made 1,500 wagons a day. What *did* stop production was World War II. From 1942-1945, Pasin's company produced "Blitz Cans" for the war effort. They were five-gallon, steel containers designed to transport fuel and water to troops stationed overseas.

As a piece of Americana, Radio Flyer received the star treatment in 1992, when it served as the centerpiece of the Richard Donner film, *Radio Flyer*. Starring Elijah Woods (and featuring an uncredited Tom Hanks), the movie chronicles the story of two brothers and their fantasy travels as they use their little red wagon to escape a troubled family life.

In 1997, Colin Powell founded America's Promise, a non-profit organization dedicated to improving the lives of our at-risk youth. The symbol the organization chose to represent their efforts was a Radio Flyer wagon. (Visit America's Promise at: WWW.AMERICASPROMISE.ORG)

Antonio Pasin passed away in 1990. In 2003 he was inducted into the Toy Industry Hall of Fame.

Antonio Pasin named his futuristic Streak-O-Lite wagon of 1934 after the Chicago Burlington & Quincy Railroad's new Pioneer Zephyr train, which debuted the same year. The wagon had control dials, a horn and headlights!

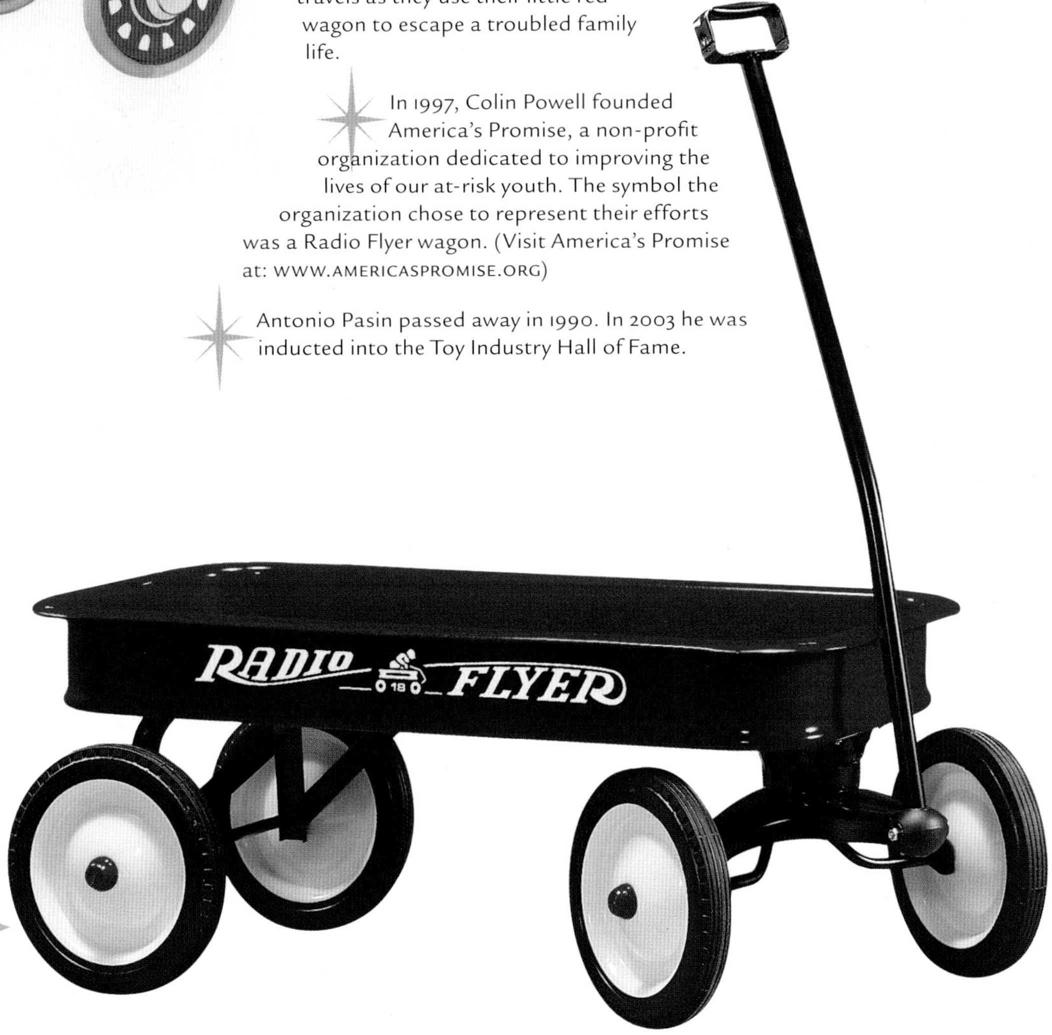

The distinctive shape of Radio Flyer Inc.'s #18 is trademarked. The model has been in continuous production for over 70 years.

Debut: 1918
Raggedy Andy Debut: 1920
Inventor: Johnny Gruelle
Companies: P. F. Volland,
Exposition Doll & Toy
Manufacturing,
Georgene Novelties,
Knickerbocker Toy,
Applause

Raggedy Ann

FLOPPY LOVE, FRAGILE LOVE

What is it about floppy characters that makes us want to hug them? Is it their vulnerability in an unkind world, or perhaps our own frailty that draws us to them? Beanie Babies, Sock Monkeys, teddy bears—all floppy. The Scarecrow from *The Wizard of Oz?* Dorothy comes right out and says it; she likes him the best. In the world of toys, the floppiest and most enduring character is a little rag doll named Raggedy Ann, and if her story doesn't pull on your heartstrings then you just might need a hug yourself. We met her in 1918, making Raggedy Ann the oldest continuously licensed character in the toy industry. The reason for her survival

when other seemingly more commercial characters have come and gone is a topic of conjecture. Conceivably, she endures because of her folk status as a handmade rag doll, which evokes feelings of nostalgia. Or perhaps because of her fanciful stories retold over the years to generations of children. More likely it's a less tangible reason and the purest of notions . . . she was born out of a father's love for his daughter.

Cartoonist Johnny Gruelle met and married Myrtle Swan in 1901 and the couple's only daughter, Marcella Delight Gruelle, was born in 1902. She was a creative child like her father and her imaginative, make-believe worlds left their mark on her father's famous work.

THE LEGEND

The story goes that Marcella, while exploring her grandmother's attic, happened upon an old, tattered rag doll. The doll was faded and had lost one of her shoe button eyes. Still, it was love at first sight as Marcella rushed off to her father's studio with the floppy old doll and an uncontainable smile. Johnny, with brush and ink in hand, took a long enough break to paint a new face on the old doll.

Johnny Gruelle, a fan of James Whitcomb Riley, borrowed two of his classic poems, "The Raggedy Man" and "Little Orphan Annie," to christen his little doll, "Raggedy Ann."

Raggedy Ann's creator, Johnny Gruelle, was also a political cartoonist, a gifted illustrator, an imaginative writer and a successful businessman.

Whether or not Raggedy Ann came to be in just this fashion is anybody's guess. One thing is known for sure—Marcella had a rag doll that she cherished and Johnny Gruelle, the consummate observer, watched his little girl play and gathered wonderful ideas for his stories. Soon a droopy rag doll called "Rags" began appearing within the panels of Gruelle's *Mr. Twee Deedle* comic strip. Rags continued to have a limited role in Gruelle's stories until she came to life one day in 1915. On September 7th of that year, Gruelle received confirmation of a design patent he had filed on everybody's favorite rag doll, but it would be another three years before children got to meet Raggedy Ann. Johnny's heart and mind were elsewhere.

Marcella was sick. According to Patricia Hall, Gruelle's biographer and author of *Johnny Gruelle: Creator of Raggedy Ann and Andy,* Myrtle Gruelle had given her daughter's school permission to give Marcella a vaccination, the medical community's new (and controversial) treatment to pre-empt epidemic illnesses. For reasons unknown, Marcella was given a second vaccination shot a few days later without her mother or father's consent. A short time after the second shot, Marcella fell ill. As she battled a terrible fever, Johnny read her stories he had written about Mr. Twee Deedle and other characters she loved. He tried to comfort her by making up stories about her favorite toys. After months of struggle, Marcella Gruelle died on November 8, 1915. She had just turned 13.

Many things could have occurred after such a devastating blow: a bitter lawsuit with the school, a sad divorce over regrets and unfulfilled dreams, or an addiction to numb the pain. None of these happened. In her book, Patricia Hall shares her insight into a strong man at a sorrowful crossroads:

> According to friends who visited Gruelle [in the days following Marcella's death], Johnny was keeping in his studio a single, tangible reminder of his daughter, one of the few that he could bear to have near. This memento, made so many years before by Alice Gruelle, had been adopted

and loved by Marcella as her own. According to the accounts, when all else would fail, it was this plaything—a floppy, tattered little rag doll, with a crooked smile and scraggy hair—that seemed to give Johnny Gruelle consolation and inspiration, as he worked to lift himself out of a pool of incredible sorrow.

Eventually Johnny Gruelle was ready for Raggedy Ann to be loved by a wider audience of children, just as she had been so adored by Marcella. In his *Raggedy Ann Stories,* Gruelle wrote a poignant dedication that revealed his own ascendancy out of the darkness: "As I write this, I have before me on my desk, propped up against the telephone, an old rag doll . . . what joy and happiness you have brought into this world! And no matter what treatment you have

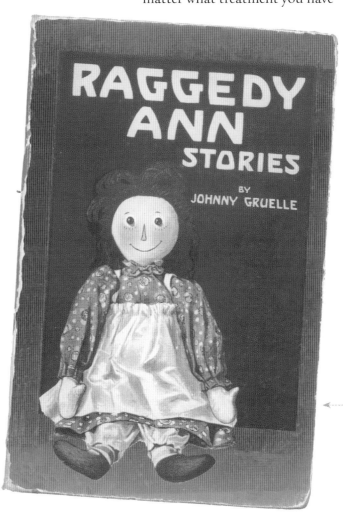

Gruelle's book was released in time for the 1918 Christmas shopping season and was a colossal success for the book's printer, P. F. Volland.

received, how patient you have been! What lessons of kindness and fortitude you might teach could you but talk. . . . So, to the millions of children and grown-ups who have loved a Rag Doll, I dedicate these stories of Raggedy Ann."

In 1918, P. F. Volland brought out their first Raggedy Ann doll. She wore a helpless yet happy expression, disheveled clothes, twisted yarn hair and overall ragamuffin appearance. Her arms seemed to be perpetually turned outward, waiting for a child's hug.

The very first Raggedy Anns were produced by hand with facial features changing from doll to doll. This "homemade" appearance—intentional or not—contributed to Raggedy Ann's warm public acceptance. According to Hall, the basis for her appropriate "raggedy" appearance derived from the fact that Volland had referred to handmade prototypes made by the Gruelle family in preparation for the final product. Between the time Johnny first developed the doll in 1915 and when they went into production in 1918, the Gruelle family made and sold Raggedy Ann dolls as a cottage industry. These first Gruelle family-made dolls are extremely rare because of their limited quantity and historical value.

A REAL SWEET HEART

In the stories of Raggedy Ann, Johnny explained that it is Raggedy Ann's candy heart that makes her so sweet. Today it is a point of legend among Raggedy Ann fans and a question that still remains: *Were there ever real candy hearts sewn into Raggedy Ann dolls?* Johnny's son, Worth Gruelle, has stated that he remembers his family sewing candy hearts into the early dolls. No Gruelle-made Raggedys have ever surfaced with a candy heart, but some still believe.

Raggedy Ann's brother Andy arrived in 1920. By 1922, Johnny Gruelle was producing newspaper serials chronicling the adventures of Raggedy Ann and her now famous brother. Although he drew other characters, Raggedy Ann & Andy remain Gruelle's most enduring creations, and through the early part of the Depression the Gruelle family and the P. F. Volland Company survived, due largely to the Raggedys. But in 1934, Gruelle lost his publisher when Volland decided to leave the book publishing business. In 1935, Johnny signed an agreement with the Exposition Doll & Toy

Early Raggedy Ann dolls had a thick cardboard heart sewn inside. Later the love was spelled out in stencil form.

Manufacturing Company. Business improved until a company by the name of Molly-'Es Doll Outfitters began a brazen campaign to wrestle exclusive rights to Raggedy Ann and Raggedy Andy away from their creator.

A lapse in the usage of the Raggedy Ann and Raggedy Andy trademarks had occurred between the time Volland reassigned all rights to the Raggedys and Gruelle contracted with Exposition, resulting in a brief period of legal limbo. Mollye Goldman, the owner of Molly-'Es Outfitters, saw an opportunity in the post-Depression toy business where few existed. In 1935, she began to make and sell her own Raggedy Ann dolls in the hopes of cashing in on a sure bet.

Gruelle vs. Goldman dragged out over three years, costing Johnny his contract with Exposition, thousands of dollars in legal fees and more in lost revenue. During the battle, Mollye Goldman's company continued to sell unauthorized versions of Raggedy Ann and Raggedy Andy. Eventually Johnny prevailed, winning the battle, but losing the war. The stress of the prolonged fight proved to be too much, and on January 9, 1938, at the age of 58, Johnny Gruelle died of heart failure.

Soon after his untimely death, the Gruelle family set to work preserving his legacy. In 1938, Georgene Novelties became the producer of officially licensed Raggedy Ann and Raggedy Andy dolls. In 1939, the newly formed Johnny Gruelle Company self-published four Raggedy Ann books. In 1940 Raggedy Ann & Andy starred in their first animated cartoon.

For twenty more years Myrtle Gruelle oversaw the future of Raggedy Ann & Andy while preserving their treasured past. In 1960, at the age of 71, she no longer felt up to the task of running the Raggedy Empire with only the family's help. Myrtle chose the Bobbs-Merrill Company to carry the Raggedys into the future, transferring all rights to the Raggedy trademarks and likenesses on June 20, 1960. In 1965, the company chose the Knickerbocker Toy Company to take Raggedy Ann and Andy dolls into their 50th year.

For many doll lovers, they don't get any bigger than Raggedy Ann. Here she sits exhausted after a long day of shopping at FAO Schwarz in Orlando.

Still very much a family affair, Johnny's son Worth Gruelle continued to provide illustrations for Raggedy Ann and Andy books, and when deadlines got tight, Worth called on his daughter, Joni. She was named after her grandfather and her talent confirms that a whimsical and deft hand definitely runs in the Gruelle family.

For 86 years Raggedy Ann and her equally raggedy brother have endured. Although they are internationally recognized (their popularity in Japan rivals their status here) they will forever be slices of pure Americana. Who could have imagined in 1918 that a simple rag doll could captivate so many people? Thirty million books and 15 million dolls later, Raggedy Ann & Andy have gone beyond what their creator could ever have imagined . . . or have they? Johnny Gruelle could imagine quite a lot.

Raggedy Ann was inducted into the National Toy Hall of Fame on March 27, 2002.

The Johnny Gruelle Raggedy Ann & Andy Museum, located in Arcola, Illinois, opened to the public in May of 1999.

THE PLAYMAKERS
Toy Timeline

1930	'31	'32	'33	'34	'35	'36	'37	'38	'39	'40

• Monopoly
• Magic Slate

• Go to the Head of the Class
• Criss-Cross Words, predecessor to Scrabble

• The first FAO Schwarz store opens in New York City
• The Connecticut Leather Company is founded, later known as Coleco
• Ole Kirk Christiansen's woodworking company is founded, later known as LEGO.

• View-Master

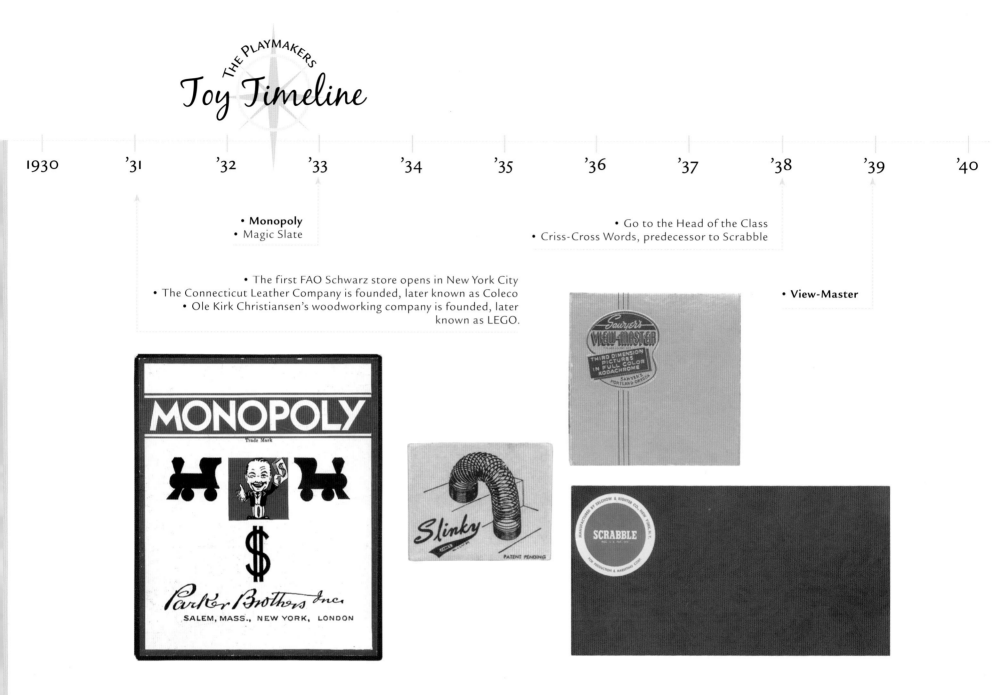

1930s-1940s

'40　　　　'41　　　　'42　　　　'43　　　　'44　　　　'45　　　　'46　　　　'47　　　　'48　　　　'49　　　　1950

- **Slinky**
- Ruth and Elliot Handler form Mattel with Harold Matson

- *New York Times* runs its first crossword puzzle

- Mound Metalcraft is formed, later known as Tonka Toys
- The Syco-Seer, predecessor to Magic 8 Ball

- Playskool buys the rights to Lincoln Logs
- Bouncing Putty, predecessor to Silly Putty

- **Tonka**
- Kenner is founded

- **Scrabble**
- Cluedo debuts in England
- Flyin' Saucer, predecessor to Frisbee

- **Cootie**
- **Candy Land**
- **Clue**
- Automatic Binding Bricks, predecessor to Lego bricks
- Yakity Yak Talking Teeth

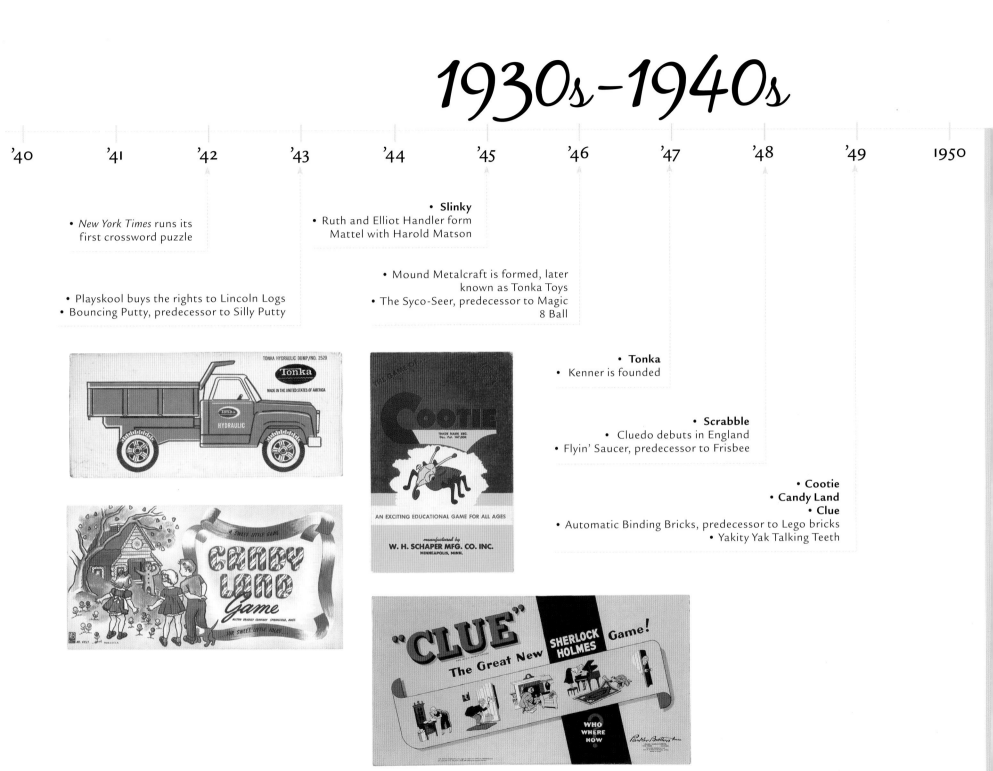

Debut: 1933
Developers: Charles
  Darrow (1889-1967),
  Ruth Hoskins (1904-
  1986), Cyril Harvey
  (1901-1981), Ruth Harvey
  (1899-1962), Jesse
  Raiford (1900-1960)
Companies: Parker
  Brothers, Hasbro
Predecessor: The
  Landlord's Game (1903)
Inventor: Elizabeth Magie
  (1866-1948)
Companies: Economic
  Game Company (1904),
  Adgame Co. (1932),
  Parker Brothers (1939)

Monopoly

AMERICA'S FAVORITE PLAYGROUND

Contrary to popular belief, there's no FREE PARKING in the real Atlantic City, but it's cheap. I come to rest on a space that sits at the corner of Boardwalk and Park Place. Someone has erected a hotel and I'm cringing at the thought of what landing here might cost me. Turns out the hotel on this historic site is Bally's Atlantic City Hotel and Casino, and I can stay here all day for $2. The parking is discounted to entice me to come inside and play, but I walk through the gleaming interior, right past the action and out onto the Boardwalk. At this historic corner stands a sign:

In 1930 an unemployed Philadelphian named Charles Darrow dubbed a board game MONOPOLY. He labeled its streets after avenues along the Boardwalk. It became the most popular game of all time, and gave new meaning to the word "gaming" in Atlantic City. . . .

It's a nice tip of the hat, complete with a picture of the smiling entrepreneur. This rags-to-riches tale, however, is not entirely true. Charles Darrow did not name the game and he most certainly did not label its streets. He copied both from an already existing game. Then how can this tribute even *exist?* The answer occurred to me after I strolled south along the Boardwalk a few blocks and looked up. If you ask anyone, "Who built Trump Plaza?" the response you'll always get is "Donald Trump." The real answer, of course, is the scores of contractors and thousands of workers who contributed various parts to the whole. *They* built the hotel, but the quick and simple

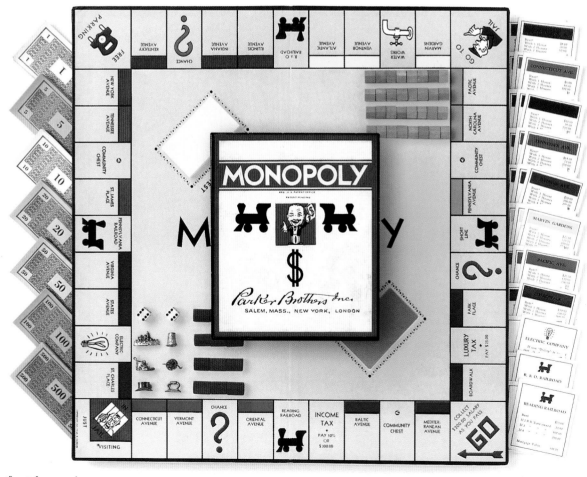

answer is more marketable, pointing to one dynamic individual whose money backed it all. No, Charles Darrow didn't invent Monopoly, but he developed it just like real estate, and in doing so made it more valuable. So much so, it made him a multimillionaire.

Monopoly is the best-selling proprietary game of all time. More than 200 million sets have been sold in over 80 countries, according to its maker, Parker Brothers. No amount of marketing spin will accomplish that unless the game is good, and Monopoly is one of the best ever. It balances skill and luck, provides shifts in power and moments of great suspense. The fantasy of holding all that cash, building houses and even hotels—pretend as they all may be—still lures us to play. Such a celebrated game deserves that the whole truth be told. While *many* refined the game along its historic path to greatness, a single inventor started it all. If Darrow was the developer of Monopoly, then a woman named Elizabeth was its architect.

THE LADY AND HER LANDLORD'S GAME

Elizabeth Magie was born near Canton, Illinois, in 1866. Raised during the infancy of the women's suffrage movement, Magie was ahead of her time. She was a writer and public stenographer, and in 1893 patented a "type-writing machine" that allowed a typist to fill a page of paper more efficiently. The pages of Magie's life were most certainly full. "Lizzie," as she was known, was a gifted actress who gave dramatic readings and performed in "trouser roles," impersonating boy characters to the delight and amazement of many in her hometown. Her most historic role, however, was that of a game inventor.

In 1903, Magie applied for a patent on a diversion she called The Landlord's Game. The patent, granted

Elizabeth Magie invented at least seven published games over her 33-year career.

a year later, stated that "the object of the game is to obtain as much wealth or money as possible. . . ." Beyond the same ultimate goal as Monopoly, Lizzie's game contained many other familiar elements. Both games feature a square board with 40 spaces and 22 properties, both have four railroads and both contain JAIL and GO TO JAIL spaces. In both games, a player can get out of jail by rolling doubles or by paying $50. Each game has a luxury tax and two utilities (one water, one electric). The Landlord's Game had a Public Park space, while the same space shows up in the exact same spot on the Monopoly board as "FREE PARKING."

Magie created The Landlord's Game as a practical example of the immorality of rent gouging, land monopolies and other corporate monopolies. Her choice of using railroads to illustrate her latter point was significant, because the first case of federal regulation on businesses occurred in the late 1870s and concerned the railroad industry. She played her game with friends in the town of Brentwood, Maryland, and in doing so planted the seed of the game on the East Coast. In 1906, Magie moved to Chicago, bringing the game with her to the Midwest. In 1910 she married Albert Phillips, a Chicago businessman, and around this time decided to produce a version of The Landlord's Game that was slightly different than the game described in her 1904 patent. Thus began the 30-year transformation that turned The Landlord's Game into Monopoly.

Her first printed version of The Landlord's Game contained most of the rules described in her 1904 patent, but with several new additions including properties with street names and a telling rule she

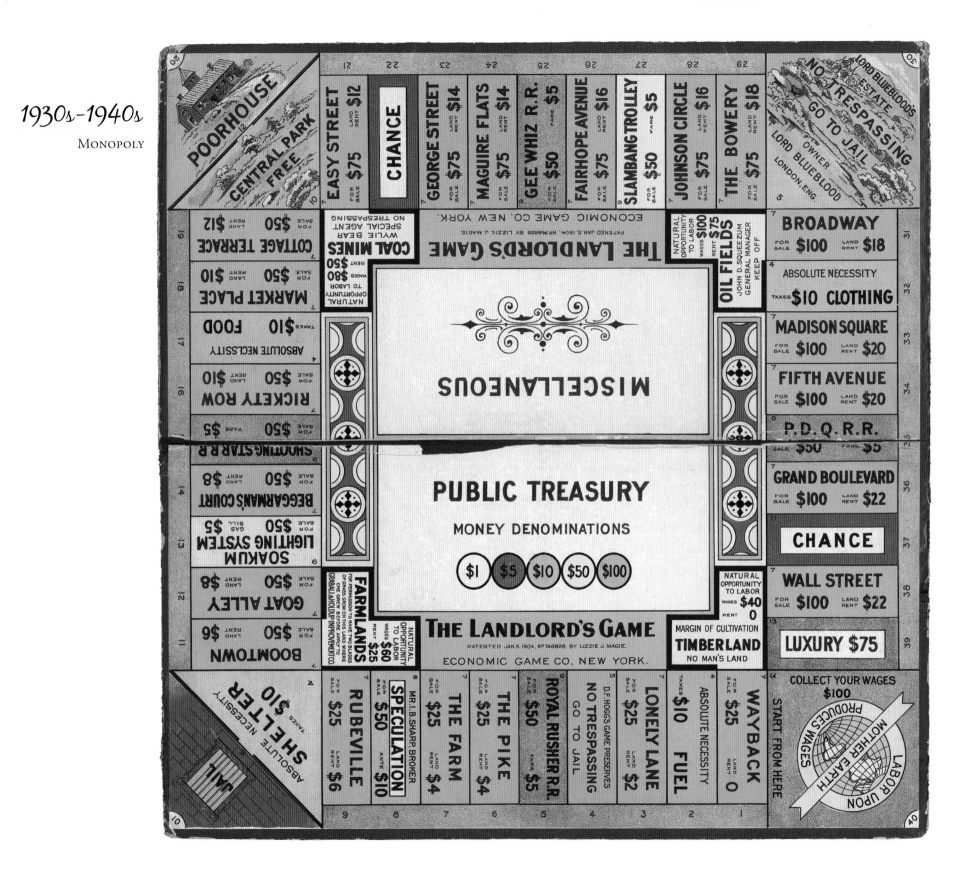

There is no longer any doubt that Monopoly descended from The Landlord's Game. Pictured here and opposite is an extremely rare copy of what is believed to be Elizabeth Magie's first printed version of the game, produced around 1910 by a New York firm called Economic Game Company. Photograph © 2003 Thomas E. Forsyth.

called "Monopoly—If one player owns 2 railroads, he charges $10 fare; if 3, he charges $20; 4, $50." Lizzie included an auction rule which allowed players to buy a property, "provided no other player bids more for it," and a set of instructions to play the game in a new way.

ECONOMICS OR ENTERTAINMENT?

In 1879, Henry George wrote his revolutionary book *Progress and Poverty,* which argued that unearned increases in land value (inflation of real estate prices) benefited the few (wealthy landlords) while it crushed the masses (tenants) who were charged rent reflective of ever escalating land values. His solution was "The Single Tax," a proposed economic reform asserting that all government could be funded by a single tax

on land alone. Lizzie Magie Phillips had become a devoted "Single Taxer" and instituted rules in her game to promote the theories of Henry George. Unfortunately for her, the original play pattern she established in her 1904 patent ("obtain as much wealth or money as possible") overtook her altruistic intentions of benefiting society. Back on the East Coast, The Landlord's Game had found a following and taken on a life of its own.

According to Ralph Anspach's groundbreaking book, *The Billion Dollar Monopoly Swindle,* as early as 1910 Magie's game had become a folkgame played on homemade boards at colleges such as Princeton (NJ), Haverford and Swarthmore (PA) and Williams (MA). Scott Nearing, an economics professor at the Wharton School of Finance at the University of Pennsylvania, used the game in his classroom to illustrate the harm monopolies caused, exposing the game to possibly thousands of students.

In 1923 Lizzie Magie Phillips was back living near Washington D.C. when she applied for the second patent on her creation. While her 1904 patent was fairly silent on the lessons her game tried to teach, her new patent left no doubt: "The object of the game is not only to afford amusement to the players, but to illustrate to them how . . . the landlord has an advantage over other enterprises and also how the single tax would discourage land speculation." Lizzie brought her new version to Parker Brothers, which turned it down, probably because it was so politically charged. Although she continued her quest to bring about serious economic change, her sense of humor remained. In her new patent she states: "Caught robbing a hen-roost—go to jail; . . . caught robbing the public . . . the players will now call you Senator."

Lizzie would not have been so comedic had she realized the changes inflicted by those who made their own versions of her game. Anspach discovered that some early players stayed true to her beliefs, like brothers Fred and Louis Thun, who produced an anti land-ownership version of Magie's game after learning a form of it from Wharton students. Others who adapted the game did not share the same fervor for reform, but instead focused on the game's fun.

Atlantic City was founded in 1854 as "America's City." Many of its streets were named after American states, while others were named after oceans and seas like "Pacific Avenue" and "Baltic Avenue." In this picture taken around 1915, strollers "take a walk on the boardwalk" near Steel Pier.

In 1932, just after an adaptation called The Fascinating Game of Finance appeared, Lizzie released her second printed version of The Landlord's Game, but added her single tax game under the name Prosperity in the same box. She called this double game The Landlord's Game and Prosperity. But as Lizzie continued to play reformist, her game found favor with people who just wanted to play. The transformation of The Landlord's Game was long in coming, attracting an eclectic following in the process. The acolytes of Henry George were first, and then collegiate liberals fell under its spell. But it was a very unlikely group of people who would make the most significant changes in Lizzie's game, providing some of the last pieces to a 30-year puzzle.

THE FRIENDS

Ruth Hoskins was a Quaker (The Religious Society of Friends) living in Indianapolis when she was introduced to The Fascinating Game of Finance in 1929. When Ruth left the Midwest in 1930 for a job as principal of a Friends School in New Jersey, she brought along her version of the game to share with her fellow teachers. As Anspach details in his book, this group of "Friends" played the game most every night, and again the game was altered. First, Ruth and her friends discarded the auction rule and introduced fixed property prices. This simplified the game and allowed children to play along with adults, making Monopoly the family game it is today. Then they renamed the properties to match the streets found in their beachfront town. The Landlord's Game was about to advance to Boardwalk.

Ruth Hoskins and her friends named the streets in their version of Monopoly after the real Atlantic City streets on which they lived and worked. The Atlantic City Friends School was located at the corner of Pacific and North Carolina. Other game players lived south of Atlantic City, just past the city of Ventnor, within an enclave of town houses in Margate City called Marven

The only known surviving example of Charles Darrow's handmade, circular Monopoly board. In 1992, it was bought at auction for $64,350 and now resides at The Forbes Magazine Collection in New York City along with other early examples of Monopoly.

Gardens (named by combining MARgate and VENtnor).

The game of Monopoly as we know it today had nearly reached perfection in Atlantic City at the hands of Ruth Hoskins and her Quaker acquaintances. Among them were Cyril Harvey and Eugene Raiford. Raiford's brother, Jesse, who sold real estate in Atlantic City has been credited with devising the property values in Monopoly. Another player introduced to the game in Atlantic City was Charles Todd, a hotel manager from Germantown, Pennsylvania, who brought the game back to this northwest suburb of Philadelphia in 1932. There he showed it to his friend Esther Darrow and her husband, Charles.

Charles Darrow was born in Maryland in 1889, grew up in Pittsburgh and moved to Germantown after marrying Esther in 1927. He lost his job at a steam boiler company to the Depression in 1930. Darrow had been a plumber, an engineer, and a radiator repairman. "His interest was in steam equipment," his son Bill Darrow told me. "He referred to himself as a practical engineer, which denoted in his mind that he'd never been to college." With no job, a four-year-old son and Esther expecting their second child, Darrow's resume was forced to expand even further by 1932. He repaired electric irons, patched concrete, walked dogs and peddled just about anything. When he ran out of odd jobs and still couldn't find work in the steam trade, he turned to toys.

Darrow devised an improved bridge score pad, but when it didn't sell well, he tried working in wood. He hand cut plywood to make jigsaw puzzles and a game called Bug (which was reminiscent of Cootie). When neither of those caught on, Darrow might have thought about selling his jigsaw to help feed his family, but it's a good thing he didn't. Soon he was cutting out little wooden houses and hotels as fast as he possibly could.

When Charles Todd introduced the Atlantic City version of Monopoly to him, Darrow had been unemployed nearly three years. Monopoly fell into the lap of a desperate man with a penchant for games and the mechanical skills to produce them. According to Anspach, Darrow received 12 copies of the Monopoly rules from Charles Todd and then began making his own version of the game, just as many had done since 1910. Taking oilcloth (a cheap fabric with a washable surface used for tablecloths), Darrow first tried making a circular game board.

Darrow added more color to the property spaces and, more importantly, illustrations that brought the game to life. The famous black RAILROAD silhouettes, the red car on FREE PARKING, the red arrow and boxy letters on the GO space, the WATER WORKS faucet, the CHANCE question marks and the pointing hand for the space marked GO TO JAIL did not appear on any pre-existing Monopoly games. Bill Darrow contends that all of these legendary icons were the direct work of his father. "He didn't have any money to hire an artist yet. He used stencils for the railroads and the rest were all hand-painted." Phil Orbanes, former senior vice president of research and development at Parker Brothers, says, "Darrow gave Monopoly its first visual signature. His artist stylized the corners of the board . . . and created the first copyrightable look, the look that all of America has come to know, the look that represents the game of Monopoly."

In 1933, Darrow copyrighted his version of the game and began selling homemade copies of it to friends and associates. "It took him all day to turn out a single game," Bill Darrow said. "A local lumber yard gave him some old pine moldings that he cut to make the houses and hotels." Darrow produced the game for about $1.00 and sold it for $2.00, not a bad profit in

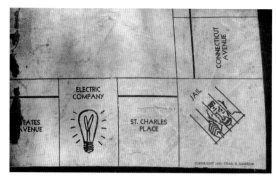

the dark days of the Depression, yet he knew he could sell more if he could make them faster. "As you can well imagine it was pretty damn labor intensive," Bill said. "He just got snowed in and it was just a matter of time before he went running down to Patterson."

"Patterson" was Lytton Patterson, Jr., a friend of Charles Darrow and owner of Patterson and White Printing in Philadelphia. To automate whatever part of the manufacturing process he could at an afford-

Only six known copies of Darrow's "blank" oilcloth board exist. This is how it appeared before Darrow hand-painted the individual spaces. Printed by Patterson and White for Charles Darrow in 1933.

Who was Charles Darrow?

He has been both immortalized in bronze in Atlantic City and demonized by researchers looking into the truth about Monopoly. What can't be ignored is the fact that Charles Darrow improved Monopoly by risking his own money, producing the game himself and selling it for nearly two years—all in an impossible economic climate. Yet, equally apparent is the fact that Darrow acted dishonestly when he claimed to be the sole creator of the game in the process of patenting it.

Beyond the numerous similarities between the game he "invented" and the game Magie patented 30 years prior, there's an error Darrow unknowingly perpetuated that many historians point to as a smoking gun of evidence proving that at least a part of the game was copied. Researcher Ralph Anspach discovered that when Charles Todd copied his version of the Monopoly board from Ruth Hoskins, he miscopied the property Marven Gardens as Marvin Gardens, with an "i." Not knowing Atlantic City intimately, Todd never noticed his error. Darrow copied Todd's misspelling in his game and then Parker Brothers copied Darrow, perpetuating the misspelling to this day.

All this evidence precludes Darrow as the "inventor" of Monopoly, but it does not diminish his role as the game's developer. He retired at the age of 46, helped his wife Esther import exotic orchids and then spent his remaining years traveling to ancient cities in the study of archaeology. He died in 1967.

Today, a sign made to look like the Monopoly property it inspired stands at the entrance of the real Marven Gardens, albeit with the name spelled correctly.

In 1934, Darrow printed 500 copies of his first version of Monopoly, later known as the "white box" edition.

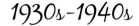
for the game's box top. The first printed version of Monopoly was born.

Darrow sold his new version of the game to John Wanamaker's Department Store in Philadelphia. At the same time he tried to drum up interest from the larger game companies, but both Milton Bradley and then Parker Brothers turned it down. Monopoly seemed to break all the rules. Parker Brothers cited "52 fundamental errors" in the game, most notably the time in which it took to win, and they also believed that the masses would never play such a complicated game. In the book, *90 Years of Fun,* produced by Parker Brothers in 1973, Edward P. Parker recalled, "After Darrow left, the executives played the game several times, and although we personally enjoyed it, everyone felt it could never be a popular success. . . . The decision to turn it down was unanimous." Darrow was on his own.

With money from the sales of his first print run and his life savings on the line, Darrow went back to press,

able cost, Darrow hired Patterson and White to print only the black outlines on a limited number of oilcloth boards, which he would then hand color.

With Patterson's help, Darrow doubled his output to two games a day, but demand still outpaced his ability to hand color the board, hand cut the hotels and houses, and type up the rules and game cards. When Patterson and White took over the bulk of the production, leaving Darrow to paint the boards and assemble the sets by hand with the help of his wife and young son, the entrepreneur was able to make six games a day. It still wasn't enough.

THE DIE ROLL

Darrow realized that printing a finished version of the game would allow him time to concentrate solely on selling. His increasing volume of customers convinced Darrow to upgrade the game's graphics and go to print. He hired an artist who improved on his rudimentary scribblings and created the first "Monopoly Man" icons

Arguably the most infamous rejection letters in toy history.

taking a tremendous risk in making 7,500 new games. "Wanamaker's in particular complained that Darrow's first version of the game took up too much shelf space and was too expensive," said Phil Orbanes. What resulted was his "black box" edition that featured a much smaller package containing all the playing pieces, with the board separate. Darrow's new version of Monopoly was made to meet the mass-market and he soon landed other accounts in Philadelphia like Gimbel's and Lit Brothers. Parker Brothers took notice, and then, they took over.

Manufactured by
CHARLES B. DARROW
40 Westview Street
Germantown, Philadelphia

The legendary game maker struck a deal with Darrow and began production of Monopoly in March of 1935. According to Orbanes, the contract between Darrow and Parker Brothers stipulated that the firm buy out Darrow's remaining inventory. Still concerned that the game took too long to play, they released it with rules added for a version of "Short Monopoly." By cannibalizing most of Darrow's 7,500 black box games for components and printing new game boxes on their own, Parker Brothers produced a run of 10,000 new games in 1935. It became known to collectors as "the trademark" edition.

The Depression had nearly devastated Parker Brothers, and by many accounts, Monopoly saved the 52-year-old game firm from financial ruin. "Monopoly got off to a phenomenal start in a set of circumstances that has not existed before or since," Orbanes said. "No one had any money and along comes this chance for people to vicariously wheel and deal for a few hours and get their minds off their own personal limitations." For Charles Darrow, the agreement with Parker Brothers would eventually net him millions. Parker Brothers sold 250,000 copies of Monopoly in 1935 and soon all of America was surprised by this new and exciting board game, but no one was more taken aback than Lizzie Magie Phillips.

On February 3, 1936, *Time* ran a story on Monopoly. "Erroneous is the popular legend that Monopoly was originally devised by Henry George to demonstrate the validity of his single tax theories," the article read. "The basic patent on Monopoly was obtained by Mrs. Elizabeth M. Phillips . . ." The editorial went on to credit Darrow as the patent holder of Monopoly "in its current form."

Both true statements. Here's

After FAO Schwarz sold 200 copies of Darrow's "black box" edition (pictured here), Parker Brothers decided those "52 fundamental errors" could be overlooked after all. "[My father] used to get a lot of mail," Bill Darrow said. "One letter I recall was from someone who wanted to know how you ended the damn game. They'd been playing for 4 ½ days!"

what happened, according to Ralph Anspach.

Parker Brothers helped Darrow file for his patent on Monopoly in August of 1935, granted by the United States Patent and Trademark Office four months later. To protect their investment, Parker Brothers contacted Lizzie Magie Phillips and struck a deal in which she agreed to assign her 1924 patent to them (her 1904 patent had expired in 1921) in exchange for $500 and the promise of printing three of her other games, with full credit given to her on the cover of each. Around that same time, Parker Brothers also bought the rights to The Fascinating Game of Finance.

Lizzie's credit as the original patent holder on the game that became Monopoly faded over time, while

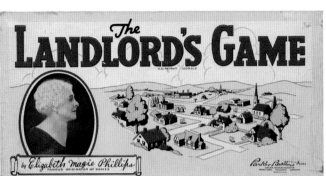

Elizabeth Magie Phillips licensed King's Men (1937), Bargain Day (1937) and The Landlord's Game (her third version—1939), to Parker Brothers in exchange for the rights to her patent on The Landlord's Game. Unfortunately, all sold poorly and were soon off the market.

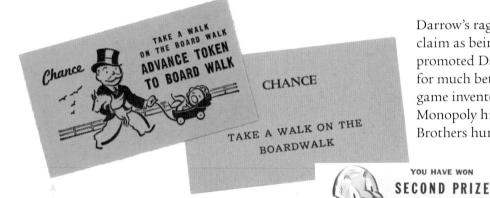

By 1936, Parker Brothers was advertising Monopoly with a mustached tycoon. He first graced the community chest and chance cards in 1936, after Parker Brothers decided to spruce up Darrow's pictureless cards (above right). He didn't get an official name until 1946, when his likeness was used on a Parker Brothers game called Rich Uncle and he was dubbed Rich Uncle Pennybags. In 1999, Parker Brothers changed his name to Mr. Monopoly.

Darrow's rags-to-riches story endured despite his false claim as being its sole "inventor." Parker Brothers promoted Darrow partly because his story made for much better PR than a story about a tax reform game invented by a little old lady (Lizzie was 70 when Monopoly hit it big in '36). More than anything, Parker Brothers hung their hat on Darrow because *his name was on the patent that the company now owned and which superceded all others.* How the patent office missed *both* of Magie's patents in granting Darrow his, is a mystery that will perhaps never be solved.

In 1936, just a year after its release, Parker Brothers sold an amazing 1.8 million copies of Monopoly, at one point making 20,000 games *a week* to keep up with demand. They were leery at the end of 1936, fearing a sharp decline in sales, but the demand for Monopoly let up only slightly. When the Depression

Charmed, I'm sure...

So what is it about Monopoly that has made it the most successful proprietary game in history? "It's the play," Monopoly historian Phil Orbanes contends. "It's the interaction between the players, the deal making and the decision making . . . It's not the game pieces, the money or the board."

I took my own informal survey and was surprised at what I heard over and over again. Sorry, Phil, the players have spoken. It's the game pieces. Whether you're a race car buff, a sucker for that cute little dog or have a shoe fetish, it seems that everyone has a favorite Monopoly token. And as you'd expect from a game with such a rich history, the tokens have a story of their own.

"In the early games he took about a ¾-inch dowel, cut off thin wafers and painted them different colors for tokens," Bill Darrow said of his father's early handmade games. "But that got cumbersome real quick so he said, 'Just let the players use their own.'" In his game rules Darrow wrote "see that each player is provided with some TOKEN (Key, Ring, etc.) to represent him in his travels around the board . . ." It has been surmised that the thimble was the one household object, small and made of metal, which inspired the creation of the famous Monopoly tokens. However, another story rings so much sweeter.

In 1932, Mary Utterback and Mary Jean Boston were 10 years old and best friends. Since they both had younger brothers who were chums, the four kids would often meet at Mary Jean's house in West Philadelphia. "After school we would go to her house because her Uncle Charles had this game he had showed us how to play," Mary told me. "He had made colored wooden pieces and at times we'd take a break from the game and leave it set up, but when we'd come back the next day, we'd forget whose color was whose." Mary and Mary Jean found a fun solution dangling from their wrists.

"Mary Jean lived near several five & dime stores that carried these tiny metal toys you could buy for a nickel," Mary recalled fondly. "Woolworth's had displays where you could buy a link bracelet to hang the toys as charms. They were so cheap—you could only wear the bracelet for so long before it turned your wrist green!" She laughed. "We took our favorite charms from our bracelets and our brothers took their toy vehicles and we used them as our tokens."

It seems plausible that Darrow passed the "charms as tokens" idea on to Parker Brothers. The most telling evidence that supports the theory is the appearance of holes in several of the tokens found in the earliest Monopoly games. In most cases these holes were subtly placed, as in the pull tab on the shoe or in the smokestacks of the battleship. In other tokens, the holes were obvious.

"History is replete with examples of games that were never commercial until someone came along and added just a little bit of pixie dust at the right time and then off they went," says Orbanes. While it's true that this is a fairly common phenomenon in the toy business, there's an unexplainable magic to Monopoly that perhaps only pixie dust and lucky charms can ever hope to explain.

In the brim of the earliest top hats there's a mysterious hole. Could Parker Brothers have sourced these early tokens from the makers of bracelet charms before creating their own molds?

The first Parker Brothers Monopoly games contain these six classic tokens.

In the '30s and '40s these three rare tokens were introduced in certain editions . . .

. . . followed by these four classics.

In the late '30s a deluxe version with composite or bakelite tokens was released in limited quantities.

Wooden tokens first showed up in 1936 when demand for Monopoly grew so fast that Parker Brothers couldn't keep up with the production of the metal tokens, and again during WWII, after a ban on the use of nonessential metals was imposed.

In 1999, a new token was added, the ever-so-appropriate "Sack of Money."

Esther and Charles Darrow pose for a publicity picture for Waddington's Games in England. The version of Monopoly shown dates from the 1960s.

Millions still play Monopoly with a dream to "Own it All." If you're one of them and you find yourself among a gathering ready to wage real estate war, thank Ruth Hoskins and her friends as you set up the game. Next, thank Charles Darrow as you dole out the money. Then, with your favorite tokens resting on GO, raise a glass to Elizabeth Magie Phillips, for 2004 marks the 100th anniversary of her original patent on The Landlord's Game.

In 1913, a version of The Landlord's Game emerged in Annan, Scotland. That same year in Dumfries, Scotland, a game bearing the unmistakable imprint of The Landlord's Game was released under the title Brer Fox an' Brer Rabbit.

An early monopoly folkgame player named Dan Layman adapted the game into "The Fascinating Game of Finance," which was the first commercially printed example of the "monopoly" game. It was printed in 1932 by Knapp Electric Inc.

During World War II, Monopoly games were sent into German POW camps by Allied intelligence agents. The games were made by Waddington's, the company that manufactured and sold Monopoly for Parker Brothers in England and who had developed a way to print on silk. Allied prisoners who received the games were surprised to discover escape maps hidden within the game boards, miniature compasses, and real money stashed within the packets of Monopoly money.

Game historians owe a debt of gratitude to Ralph Anspach, who unearthed much of Monopoly's early history in the process of defending himself against a trademark infringement lawsuit brought by General Mills, then owner of Parker Brothers. The suit was over his 1974 Anti-Monopoly game and lasted until 1984, when he won his case.

lifted and better economic times followed, people still wanted to fantasize about untold fortunes in paper money.

Monopoly's global success was inescapable to Elizabeth Magie Phillips. If she had any regret, it probably wasn't about the deal she made or her lack of public recognition, but over the loss of her original intent. The game she created to mock the monopolists was changed by others into a celebration of the monopolists, eventually banned in Russia, China, North Korea and Cuba for its "representation of the evils of a capitalistic society." The world, it seemed, had missed her point. She died in 1948, in Arlington, Virginia. She was 82 years old.

View-Master

Debut: 1939
Inventor: William Gruber
Developers: William Gruber and Harold Graves
Companies: Sawyer's Inc., GAF, View-Master International, View-Master Ideal, Tyco Toys, Fisher-Price, a subsidary of Mattel

WINDOW TO THE WORLD

View-Master emerged from its debut at the 1939 New York World's Fair to give us a look at who and what we were as a nation. The country stood at a crossroads then, not wanting to look back at the aftermath of the Depression, while gazing outward toward a hopeful tomorrow. Through the lenses of a View-Master the future was bright in all its three-dimensional glory. We've been looking ever since.

William Gruber, a fan of stereography, invented View-Master as a home entertainment gadget for adults.

In 1938, a German immigrant named William Gruber was recovering from minor surgery in an Oregon hospital, when he was struck with a brilliant idea. He conceived of a way to use movie film to make stereo pictures and group them for viewing in a very efficient and inexpensive manner. A piano tuner by trade and photography buff by passion, for years he had taken his own 3-D pictures, an avocation too expensive for the average consumer. His new idea would make his hobby accessible to people of all walks of life.

The potential excited him, but reality soon set in. He had recently married and the idea of starting a risky new venture without the necessary capital seemed too daunting. His idea may have died in that Oregon hospital had it not been for a chance meeting.

On a piano tuning trip that July, Gruber visited the Oregon Caves National Monument with his stereo camera in tow. There, a man also carrying a camera bumped into him. The accidental

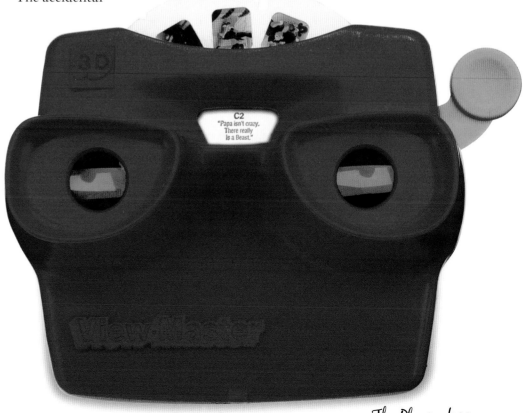

tourist happened to be Harold Graves, president of Sawyer's Photographic Services, a company specializing in picture postcards. A more serendipitous meeting would be hard to find! Harold noticed William's unusual camera setup (dual cameras mounted side by side) and the two men chatted about their mutual love of stereography. The two clicked and Gruber decided to share his unpatented ideas with Graves.

Gruber's innovation was a reel that held seven pairs of pictures on 16-millimeter movie film using Kodachrome, Kodak's relatively new color transparency film. Each pair of pictures would be mounted on a circular disk 2 $\frac{1}{2}$ inches across from each other—approximately the same distance between the human eyes. Add an inexpensive, plastic viewer that could magnify the images when the user peered inside and you had a 3-D goldmine of a concept. Graves was hooked.

Less than a year after their meeting, Sawyer's Photographic Services invested $50,000 to build machinery that William Gruber helped design. Soon Gruber and Graves produced their new device, called View-Master, or as the Associated Press called it, "a wondrous three-dimensional world viewed through a plastic machine." Before long, Gruber and Graves's invention incited the masses, but this was not stereography's first ascension to popularity. View-Master owes

Harold Graves, president of Sawyer's Photographic Services.

The very first View-Master viewer. It may look much different than the ones seen today, yet any reel from any given year will fit any View-Master viewer. Want to view your *Finding Nemo* reel in my '39 viewer? Not a problem—and a testament to the Gruber design.

its royal standing as one of the most popular toys ever, to a pair of knights and a rather famous poet.

STEREOGRAPHY'S START

In 1838, precisely 100 years prior to the chance meeting of Gruber and Graves, Sir Charles Wheatstone published a paper on "binocular vision" and presented it to the British Royal Society. His work demonstrated the "depth of vision principle" based on the fact that our eyes see slightly different images when directed at a given object. Wheatstone explained that the two images we see are combined by our brains to produce the sensation of perspective or depth. He called the device he built to demonstrate his idea a "stereoscope" from the Greek words *stereo* (solid) and *scope* (view), and although it now has the distinction of being the Granddaddy of the View-Master, in 1838 it was a large and cumbersome laboratory machine meant only for experimentation.

The next advance in the evolution of stereo photography struck in 1850 when Sir David Brewster (knighted by William IV for his many inventions, including the kaleidoscope) introduced his tabletop stereoscope at the International Exhibition in London. His design allowed the observer to look through twin magnifying lenses at images mounted side by side. The London exhibition exposed the device to many people and by 1852, over a half million Brewster viewers were reportedly sold throughout England and France. Among its many fans, Brewster's stereoscope found its way onto the desk of Dr. Oliver Wendell Holmes.

Holmes was a Harvard educated physician, essayist and poet, but it was his love of stereography that would turn him into an inventor. Envisioning a stereoscope that was less expensive and smaller than the Brewster version, Holmes teamed with a man named Joseph Bates to create just that. The Holmes-Bates stereoscope held stereo views mounted on a stiff card and brought these wondrous views off the tabletop and into the hands and homes of people everywhere.

Stereography was to the 1850s what television was to the 1950s—a new, never-before-seen view of the world *from the comfort of your living room.* As the twentieth century dawned, stereo views recorded the events of the age, like McKinley's inaugural parade and the aftermath of the San Francisco Earthquake of 1906. For a century, the Holmes-Bates stereoscope engaged the imagination of millions by capturing the images that helped record our culture, our country and our world.

President Rutherford Hayes was one of the first well-known collectors of stereo views. Many more would follow, including a certain piano tuner named William Gruber. While the Holmes-Bates stereoscope offered broader accessibility than the Brewster tabletop model, it was still largely a device for the middle to upper class. William Gruber took stereography to the masses. Where stereoscopes once held only one black and white 3-D view, View-Master held seven images in brilliant color.

VIEW-MASTER HITS THE SCENE

In the book entitled *View-Master Memories* by Mary Ann & Wolfgang Sell, William Gruber is quoted:

. . . the old-time stereoscopes . . . they gave you the illusion of reality and yet you were only looking at a black & white picture stereo card, right? Now, imagine the

In 1859, the Holmes-Bates stereoscope made stereography portable for the first time. The pictured view is marked "President and Mrs. Taft in Home Life."

thrill of looking not at, but through a translucent stereo picture in full Kodachrome color, with light coming through the film from behind to give you the illusion that you're standing in the middle of a real scene!

View-Master was released in Portland, Oregon, in 1939 and immediately marketed to adult nature lovers; the first reels were views of national parks and scenic attractions like Colorado's Pikes Peak. The inaugural View-Master stereoscope, Model A, included 15 scenic reels. In 1943, the Model B viewers came out, followed by the most popular square version, or Model C, in 1946. Soon, over 1,000 dealers around the country were selling the View-Master system. Reels were sold individually at the start, but later came in themed packets of three. William Gruber himself photographed many of the earliest images, as the success of his invention allowed him to pursue his passion for photography full time. Soon hundreds of additional photographers were needed to fill the growing demand for 3-D pictures.

It wasn't until 1951 that the View-Master name became synonymous with kids. Sawyer's purchased the Tru-Vue Company of Illinois, effectively eliminating their biggest competitor. Tru-Vue had made quite a market for itself in stereo filmstrips. But most important was the fact that Tru-Vue owned the licensing rights to Disney characters. By acquiring

them, Sawyer's was preparing to take View-Master into the children's market, riding securely on the coattails of Mickey Mouse and his powerful friends.

The 1950s brought with it everything that Disney and the rest of Hollywood had to offer. Sawyer's produced View-Master reels like the Mouseketeers and Captain Kangaroo alongside educational reels such as Monticello, Home of Thomas Jefferson. From this period on, View-Master followed the trends and hot licenses of the day. When westerns rode into popularity, so did View-Master reels featuring Roy Rogers, Dale Evans and Hopalong Cassidy. The '60s saw groovy reels of *Flipper, The Monkees,* and *Lost in Space.* One of Sawyer's most popular reels from the late '60s was The Moon Landing, evidence that Sawyer's still kept their educational origin in sight.

William Gruber died suddenly in 1965 at the age of 62. His assessment of Harold Graves had been accurate, for Sawyer's continually paid Gruber a royalty based on sales of View-Master products that, over the years, made him a wealthy man. A year after his death, the General Aniline and Film Corporation (or GAF) bought Sawyer's, Inc. With the advantage of a bigger advertising budget, View-Master flourished, and with more licenses being added every year, there seemed no end to the toy's growing popularity.

Then the circuits came to town.

View-Master ad, circa 1955

VIEW-MASTER FANS
GROW UP

Sales of View-Master products slowed in the mid-'70s as the toy business ushered in an age of electronic playthings. Challenges from competing toys were to be expected, but more troubling for View-Master was the fact that their target market was shrinking. View-Master once sold to a preteen market, but as kids grew more socially mature the View-Master brand saw its market share dwindle. This was dubbed "age compression" and it continues in the toy industry today. Simply put, kids outgrow toys faster than they used to and smart toy companies often need to revamp their products in an attempt to reverse the alarming trend.

It's tough keeping up with today's sophisticated five-year-old. This might explain the new space age, goggle-like View-Master viewers now in the marketplace. Despite the update, View-Master has evolved into a strictly juvenile toy—ironic considering the content of the first reels. Today, Mattel sells View-Master under the Fisher-Price brand name.

It's been sold and resold to various companies and repackaged numerous times. Except for a brief time when talking and lighted View-Masters were available, it has not changed in the way it functions for 65 years. Over a billion View-Master reels have been sold since Graves bumped into Gruber back in 1938. Oliver Wendell Holmes and other pioneers of stereography would be amazed.

Perhaps View-Master's appeal is in its simplicity. No batteries, no electricity needed, just a lamp or window at which to point. It's a visual toy, but *its sounds* are so distinctive; the windshield wiperish swoosh of the reel advancing, the echoey clack of plastic when your finger slips off the lever, the hollow reverberations of the hidden spring. The sounds I like best though are the "Oohs" and "Aahs" that come from my seven-year-old when she slides a new reel in and looks out her window to the world.

In 1981, View-Master was sold for $24 million to a group of investors and renamed View-Master International. Eight years later, Tyco Toys became its owner. Finally in 1997, View-Master became a Mattel brand.

Baby boomers would barely recognize the viewers of today if not for the telltale reels.

Debut: 1945
Inventor: Richard James
(1918-1974)
Developer: Betty James
Companies: James Industries, Poof Products

Slinky

WIRE WALKER

Slinky is the most unlikely toy, encircled with the most unlikely tale of steps and missteps. In 1943, while working on a ship, mechanical engineer Richard James saw a coiled pile of metal move in the most interesting way. Hired by the Navy to create a system by which sensitive equipment could function on rough seas, James thought that torsion springs (springs with no tension on them) were the answer. During a trial run on a boat from Philadelphia's Cramp Shipyard, he experimented and rejected many sizes of springs. One such rejection sat on a desk motionless until he accidentally knocked it off its perch. Instead of landing in a heap, the spring became a marvelous thing. James watched it bounce, and then for one brief moment actually appear to *walk*. A few trial pushes off a stack of books later and James knew that the incident was no fluke. The discovery intrigued him, so he took the spring home to show his wife, Betty.

The Slinky story may not start with Betty James, but it certainly ends with her. I had the privilege to interview Mrs. James and found her as fun and endearing as the toy she made famous. Her stories often end with a chuckle and her positive spirit is at once apparent, although she recalled her immediate reaction to Richard's idea was anything but upbeat.

"When Richard came home with this spring, I thought 'Oh, Boy. Here we go again.' You know, he had a lot of ideas." She told me of the time he created a compressor that pumped soda from their basement and into their kitchen refrigerator. "You could push a button and get an ice-cold Coca-Cola anytime. That was one of his good ones." But this time, when

The first Slinky, 1945

Together, Richard and Betty James stepped into the toy business in 1945 with their toy that walked.

Richard the dreamer predicted, "I think with the right properties in the steel and the right tension in the wire, I can make this spring walk," Betty the realist, was unconvinced. After working on it off and on for about a year, James showed his wife. "It walked alright," Betty said. "But I was still doubtful it could be a toy until we showed it to some neighborhood children and they absolutely loved it. That's what convinced me."

When it came time to name it, Betty combed through a dictionary looking for the perfect word to describe this "stealthy, sleek and sinuous" plaything. The word she found was Slinky.

With $500 in borrowed money, they formed James Industries and had 400 springs made by a local machine shop. The 80 feet of twisted wire was then hand-wrapped by Betty. "Richard would bring the Slinkys home at night from the shop and I would roll them up in this yellow paper that had instruc-

tions printed on one side," she recalled. "That was our packaging! Oh, it was dreadful." When I asked her if any of those rare original Slinkys still exist, she said no. "We were trying so hard to just get enough money to keep going—we never thought to keep any. We sold everything we had." But not right away.

For all the lasting charm that it possesses today, in 1945 it was just a fat spring—a circular pile of coiled wire that sold for $1.00. Richard and Betty had little luck convincing toy stores to buy their new creation. Slinky was a hands-on toy. It walked only when pushed and it made a "slinkity sound" only when handled. It was a product that begged for in-store demon-

stration. After some begging of his own, Richard convinced Philadelphia-based Gimbel's department store to place an order.

Alongside a sloped board he had fashioned, Richard piled those first 400 Slinkys, wrapped in their bright yellow paper packaging. Before long he sent a few loose ones on their way, down the board and into the hands of astonished Gimbel's customers. Ever the pragmatist, Betty planned to surprise her husband by visiting the store with a friend, both of whom would buy a Slinky, assuring Richard of at least some success. But when Gimbel's elevator doors opened, Betty and her friend witnessed a crowd of customers waving their own dollar bills and clamoring for the few Slinkys that remained. In less than 90 minutes Richard sold all 400!

After Slinky's amazing introduction, Richard and Betty opened shop on Portico Street in Philadelphia. Slinky left its paper packaging behind for a modest tan box with red lettering that looked conspicuously hand-drawn. Betty took the orders while Richard

Shortly after Slinky's launch, Richard James replaced his rudimentary sloped board with store displays like this one, which showed off what his wire walker could do.

The Slinky Jingle

Betty James credits Tom Cureton, James Industries' head of advertising, for hiring Homer Fesperman and Charles Weagley to write this classic toy tune in 1962. It became the longest running jingle in advertising history.

What walks down stairs alone or in pairs and makes a
slinkity sound?
A spring, a spring, a marvelous thing,
ev'ryone knows it's SLINKY!
It's SLINKY, it's SLINKY, for fun, it's a wonderful toy.
It's SLINKY, it's SLINKY, it's fun for a girl and a boy.
It's fun for a girl and a boy.

1930s–1940s

SLINKY

perfected the engineering behind a machine that could transform 80 feet of wire into a 2 ¼-inch column of 98 coils in about 10 seconds. By 1950, James Industries was so successful that they had to build five more coiling machines to keep up with demand. Slinky appeared in newspapers across the country and Richard James became something of a celebrity, appearing on TV shows and telling the world about his toy. Just 10 years from its humble introduction, over 100 million Slinkys had been sold. But despite skyrocketing sales, all was not well inside James Industries. At the height of its success, Slinky was pushed to the edge of peril by the very same man that invented it.

In 1960, like Slinky, Richard James simply . . . walked. Leaving his wife, six kids and the company he founded, he went to Bolivia and joined what Betty James described as a religious cult. In the months leading up to his departure, Richard forwarded a considerable amount of "charitable contributions," leaving Betty both in shock and thousands of dollars in debt. "It doesn't bother me now," she told me. "I think in the early days of Slinky, he was given a lot of press and really felt important. So when he wasn't getting the same applause, I think that outfit made him feel important again because he was giving them so much money." Why Richard James didn't feel that being a husband and father was important enough, we'll never know. "He said he was going and asked if I wanted to sell the business or run it," Betty recalled. "Without any hesitation I said I'd run it."

Betty James was 42 years old when the reins of James Industries were forced into her hands. "I was scared, I'll admit that," she recalled. "I wasn't sure if

For a brief time in the late 1940s, colored Slinkys were available in red, blue or green. Beyond a choice of colors, this vintage ad promised that "Even grownups are goggle-eyed at its lifelike capers."

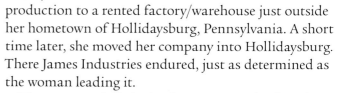

At Last...'A Different Toy!
Lots of Action

Nothing to Wind Up
Nothing to Wear Out

COMMENDED BY THE CONSUMER SERVICE BUREAU OF PARENTS' MAGAZINE

SEND FOR

SLINKY

only $1.00 postpaid

TODAY!

Let your child be the first in your neighborhood to own and enjoy this amazing coiled spring toy. It slithers, squirms, wiggles. It flip-flops down stairs and slopes. Even grownups are goggle-eyed at its lifelike capers. Three bright colors. Send only $1.00. We pay postage. 10-day money-back guarantee.

JAMES INDUSTRIES, INC.
359 E. Madison Ave., Clifton Heights, Penna.
Please rush . . . SLINKYS at $1.00 ea. Red ☐
Green ☐ Blue ☐. Enclosed find $.........
You pay the postage.

Name...
Address...
City.........................State.............

James Industries built a new factory in Hollidaysburg, Pennsylvania in 1964, providing over 120 needed jobs to the town. Over 30 years later, the town honored Betty James and James Industries on Slinky's 50th year.

I could do it or not, but you know when you have six kids, you do what you have to do and you don't think too much about it." She called all the creditors Richard had left behind and negotiated for more time. She sold the Philadelphia factory and moved production to a rented factory/warehouse just outside her hometown of Hollidaysburg, Pennsylvania. A short time later, she moved her company into Hollidaysburg. There James Industries endured, just as determined as the woman leading it.

The success of Slinky in the 1960s was due largely to Betty's fortitude. Her grit came as no surprise to those who knew her. Once, when a steel strike threatened to bankrupt the company, she took characteristic action. "I didn't know what to do, so I just called the president of Pittsburgh Steel and I told him that I felt he had to know what it was like to struggle, and that he wouldn't be where he was if he didn't have some feeling for people. I explained our case and asked him to please ship me the steel. I don't know if he felt sorry for me or what, but he shipped the steel."

Over the years Betty's company introduced junior Slinky and a plastic Slinky, the latter a response to the cheap imitation ones that flooded the market from overseas. Next came the Slinky Dog in 1952, followed by Slinky glasses. Through it all, the biggest seller remained the plain wire original. Except for the replacement of foreign steel by a domestic metal and the crimping of the sharp ends for modern safety standards, the Slinky has not changed much in over half a century.

Although Slinky remained consistent, James Industries was forced to change. Through it all Betty remained its anchor and guardian. Richard James tried to convince his wife to join him on his crusade, but she refused. "He wrote me and wanted me to come to Bolivia and leave the children here. I never answered his letters." Richard James died of a heart attack in 1974 while still in Bolivia, somewhere far south of home.

Betty's oldest son, Tom, later joined his mother in the business and James Industries remained a family affair until 1998. In that year, after talking it over with her kids, 80-year-old Betty James sold her company to Michigan-based, Poof Products, Inc. "I had been courted by a number of bigger companies over the years, but I always refused to sell because my employees have been so wonderful. This area needed the work and the bigger toy companies would have moved it," Betty said. "Poof promised me they'd leave it here. So far it's still here." And so is Betty James, the Mrs. Claus of a town called Hollidaysburg, a living icon of the toy industry, and the grand matriarch of a toy named Slinky.

In 2000, Betty James was inducted into the Toy Industry Association's Hall of Fame, a fitting tribute to the woman who named Slinky in 1943, saved it in 1960 and marketed it for 55 years.

Over 300 million Slinkys have been sold since the original walked on the scene over five decades ago. That equates to 50 tons and 3 million miles of wire—enough to circle Earth 126 times.

The Slinky Dog

"We got a prototype in the mail from a lady named Helen Malsed," Betty said of the classic Slinky Dog. "I thought it was really great and told her if she got a patent on it, we'd sell it and pay her a royalty—and that's what we did." Betty James was thrilled to see her Slinky Dog featured in 1995's *Toy Story* and its sequel. "I have 16 grandchildren," she beamed. "We went en masse and we were so excited—you just have no idea." The Slinky Dog debuted in 1952.

THE PLAYMAKERS
Now and Then

Debut: 1947
Developers: Russ
Wenkstern (1912-2000),
Charlie Groschen
Predecessor: Streater Steam
Shovel (1946)
**Founders of Mound
Metalcraft:** Lynn Baker
(1899-1964), Avery
Crounse and Alvin Tesch
Companies: Mound
Metalcraft, Tonka Toys,
Hasbro

Tonka

THE TOUGH TOY

A sunny day. A mound of dirt. A toy truck. What more could a 5-year-old kid want? Tonka Toys were first introduced in 1947, but to get the real history of this American legend you have to go back 30 years *more,* to a different day, in a different kind of mound.

In 1917, in the town of Mound, Minnesota, a man named L.E. Streater founded the Streater Lumber Company after buying several lumberyards around Minneapolis. In 1928, his son Edward joined the company to develop

Lynn Baker, co-founder of Mound Metalcraft, Inc.

a new manufacturing arm and soon a subsidiary called Streater Industries began producing kitchen cabinets, store fixtures and wooden toys in an old brick building that was once Mound grade school. In the early 1940s, Edward Streater hired a sheet metal worker, Charlie Groschen, and a former school teacher, Russ Wenkstern, to help spearhead the company's production of sheet metal store fixtures and wartime materials, which included steel shell boxes.

During the same time, Streater Industries created the Streater Excavating Contractor, a toy steam shovel with a wooden cab and metal base, boom and bucket. Possibly because their business was moving more towards metal products or perhaps influenced by the success of Structo Manufacturing's line of sturdy metal vehicles, Streater Indus-

Wrecker Truck, 1955

The toy that led to Tonka, the 1946 Streater Steam Shovel featured one winding wheel that raised and lowered the boom and another that directed the bucket. The label above appears on the rear of the vehicle.

tries revamped their hybrid wood and metal toy into the Streater Steam Shovel, a toy made almost entirely from pressed steel. They took it to Toy Fair in 1946 but experienced little interest from buyers. With their store fixture production increasing, Streater decided to sell their toy division.

While lunching with a friend named Lynn Baker, Ed Streater mentioned that his company's Mound plant was for sale. Baker was a car salesman who, along with accountant Avery Crounse and machinist Alvin Tesch, had founded a metal stamping company called Mound Metalcraft in 1946. The trio planned to make metal-stamped garden tools in Mound and saw the Streater plant as the perfect launching pad for their venture. In early 1947, Mound Metalcraft bought the plant and all of Streater's dies and tools, including those that made the Streater Steam Shovel.

SHOVELS OR SHOVELS?

Experience told Baker and his partners that their mostly spring/summer business of selling shovels, rakes, hoes and other gardening implements needed to be balanced by a product line that sold well in the fall and winter. Looking at the miniature Streater Steam Shovel, Baker thought toys might fill that need. After simplifying the mechanism that raised and lowered the boom of the Streater vehicle, Baker and his team made an almost identical steam shovel toy. They changed Streater's red, blue and black color scheme to orange and black. Then, with the same die, they created a crane in the soon-to-be-famous yellow and black.

They named their two-toy line Tonka Toys after nearby Lake Minnetonka. The word *tonka* also means "great" in the language of the Native American Sioux.

1930s–1940s

Tonka

In 1947, the company's first full year in the toy business, they produced 37,000 units of their Steam Shovel and Crane. It was a modest beginning, with six employees making toys in an old schoolhouse. In 1948 they added a lift truck and trailer and changed the hard rubber wheels on some of their toys to the more realistic rubber tracks. By 1949 the Tonka line had grown to thirteen vehicles including the company's first dump truck. Just a sideline at first, Tonka Toys were now outperforming Mound Metalcraft's garden implements. With such explosive growth, Baker turned his attention exclusively to toys and then to an experienced hand for help.

These two products, the #150 Crane (or Clam) and the #100 Steam Shovel marked the beginning of Mound Metalcraft's toy division.

MR. TONKA

Russell Wenkstern joined Mound Metalcraft in 1952. In most accounts of Tonka history, Avery Crounse and Alvin Tesch are mentioned, and rightly so, since they

Russell Wenkstern was CEO of Tonka from 1961 until 1977, when he retired.

co-founded Mound Metalcraft along with Lynn Baker. Yet, what is widely unreported is the fact that Crounse and Tesch had sold their interest in the company and left it by 1953. "There was talk about relocating around that time," Lloyd L. Laumann, Tonka's former VP of manufacturing, told me. "There was a disagreement as to the direction of the company, so Baker, Wenkstern, and others bought them out. No question about it, if there ever was a Mr. Tonka, Russ was it."

In the later part of 1955, Mound Metalcraft officially changed its name to Tonka Toys, Inc. In *100 Greatest Baby Boomer Toys,* author Mark Rich writes, "Tonka remained a relatively low-profile player in the toy world during its early years, dwarfed by the pressed-steel powerhouses of Marx, Structo, Wyandotte, and Buddy L. . . . By the 1960s, however, most major toy catalogs reflected the fact that Tonka was the company to watch."

TONKA GOES HI-TECH

Speaking of other toy trucks, Baker noted in a 1953 *Minneapolis Times* article, "They didn't resemble real trucks and they could be demolished by any active boy in no time." Baker rightly surmised that parents wanted durability and affordability, while boys wanted realism. Pleasing the perceptive 5-year-old proved very difficult. Making toys detailed enough to match the real vehicles on the road required a labor-intensive series of steps that added tremendous cost. Only a progressive manufacturing process could solve the problem.

Lloyd L. Laumann described the tedious process of making a cab for a dump truck. "Blank steel would come in and go through eight separate punch presses or dies. The windows were punched out, the holes for the wheel wells and so forth. The parts were manually transferred from one die to another for each operation. Around 1956–'57, Tonka developed six- and eight-stage progressive tooling [where all eight stages would occur within a single, elaborate die]. A piece of steel went in raw and came out as a finished part—ready to be assembled. It was such an advancement, [technology company] Honeywell came out and looked at what Tonka was doing." Tonka was one of the first companies in the Midwest to incorporate the technique of progressive tooling, and soon their competitors were forced to follow.

The progressive tooling advancement gave Tonka the ability to make their toy vehicles truer to their real-world counterparts. Working in an 18-to-1 scale, Tonka's line accurately reflected the same vehicles that hauled the dirt, mixed the cement and put out the fires in towns across America. This accuracy prompted prestigious companies like Allied Van Lines, Green Giant Foods, Ace Hardware and Star-Kist Tuna to commission Tonka to make promotional replicas of their company trucks. Today, these utility trucks, box vans and semis are sought-after prizes for Tonka collectors.

POSITIVE PAINTING

Another innovation that helped secure Tonka Toys' reputation for quality and durability was electrostatic painting. In order to achieve total coverage with a protective coating, Tonka utilized a relatively new process of painting where the paint was electri-

The waves on the first Tonka Toys logo represent Lake Minnetonka. "Lynn Baker had the logo made for $25 dollars," Russ Wenkstern once said. "We came to New York, but who wants to buy toys from company called Mound Metalcraft? So it [the company] became Tonka Toys."

cally charged. "Paint having a positive charge was spun off a disk. As the toys went through a spray booth on a conveyor, the paint would be drawn to them," Laumann said. "It gave the toy a nice smooth finish and made it more durable."

Once again the Tonka team perfected an elaborate process. There were three stages to Tonka's painting, where wet paint was applied to wet paint—another industry first. "Dupont was very instrumental in helping us develop that process," Laumann noted. But painting the parts was just the beginning. Next, drying ovens baked the enamel coating into a semi-permanent finish. "Via conveyor, a part would go into a bake oven at 325 degrees, and by the time it came out and was taken by conveyor to the assembly line, the paint was dry," explained Laumann. After traveling some 300 feet on Tonka's elaborate conveyor system, the parts were then cool enough to be picked up by hand and transferred to the assembly line.

By 1961, the Tonka assembly line was at full throttle. The company produced a line of 41 models that year and made their 15 millionth Tonka toy—all under Wenkstern's watchful eye. "Russ ran the

1961 Green Giant
Stake Truck

1930s–1940s

TONKA

An early model of The Mighty Tonka Dump Truck from the '60s. After its release, Tonka ran a TV ad showing an elephant stepping on the toy with no ill effects. Before the six-ton pachyderm could trumpet at the end of the ad, Tonka's legendary toughness was secured.

company long before he became CEO in 1961," Laumann said. "Lynn Baker had health problems and spent a lot of time in Florida. He operated the company over the phone through Russ. Russ was really the guy that called the shots." During Wenkstern's tenure, Tonka went from being "dwarfed by pressed-steel powerhouses," to earning its Sioux name. Then, in 1964, Tonka advanced from being "great" to "mighty great."

"Wow! Just like real!"

TOY EXPERTS APPRAISE DESIGN OF TONKA TOYS

The Cement Mixer (No. 120) is typical of the "Tonka touch" in designing realistic toys. It is an exact scale model, right down to dual headlights, wrap-around, tinted windshield, wheel discs, all-rubber tires, and real truck paint. Truck is fully operational. Fills through hopper on top. Mixer assembly, made of extra-tough Implex Material, geared to turn as truck moves. Mixer can be tilted for emptying down adjustable chute in back. 15½" long, 8" high, 6¾" wide. Packed 4 to a shipper, weight 21 lbs. Retails at $6.98.

PART OF A CHILD'S WORLD   TonkaToys inc.

YELLOW FEVER

The Mighty Tonka Dump Truck, in all its yellow glory, was released in '64 and its oversized wheels and huge payload capacity made it big enough for little kids to ride. With one or both knees tucked into the spacious bed, kids could roll down the driveway if they wanted. More likely they used their Tonka to haul dirt, mud or rocks, all in indestructible fashion.

Today, the Tonka watchwords of durability, affordability and realism remain firmly in place, with "interactivity" recently added for the preschool set. In 2000, Tonka released Chuck My Talkin' Truck and Tucker My Talkin' Truckbot. When Tucker says any of his 47 different phrases (like, "We mean business, right buddy?"), his eyes light up and his head turns. For nearly 50 years, Tonka Toys have been lighting up the eyes and turning the heads of youngsters all over the world.

Realism rules in this ad from 1961.

Mound Metalcraft grew from just two toys to an entire line of "Tonka Tough" vehicles produced and marketed across the globe. Over 250 million Tonka trucks have been sold since the Mound schoolhouse was turned into a toy factory. Now that's one tough act to follow.

According to Hasbro, who purchased Tonka Toys in 1991, more than 119,000 pounds of yellow paint and 5.1 million pounds of sheet metal are used each year to make Tonka toys.

Upon Russell Wenkstern's induction into the Toy Industry Hall of Fame in 1998, the Toy Industry Association wrote: "He turned Tonka into the largest volume manufacturer of vehicles of any type in the world, and insisted that Tonka trucks be the safest and most durable toys of their time, a tradition that continues today." Russ Wenkstern died in 2000.

Charlie Groschen designed this 1956 Suburban Pumper with a threaded hydrant that reduced the water pressure from a garden hose and allowed kids to play fire chief.

CHARLIE GROSCHEN

*M*y early career was in air-conditioning and heating. I was a sheet metal man," Charlie Groschen said. "After Streater was sold, I had a little sheet metal shop in my basement." From that shop, Groschen freelanced for Mound Metalcraft, designing their first road grader vehicle in 1953. Later that year, he came to work for the company full-time as assistant plant manager.

During his two-decade career with Mound Metalcraft (renamed Tonka Toys in 1955) Groschen advanced to VP of production and eventually president of the toy division. Russ Wenkstern created the Tonka culture and Charlie Groschen created the toys. In 1956, Groschen designed a Suburban Pumper, a fire truck that kids could hook up to a

THE PLAYMAKERS
Insider Profile

garden hose. It was an immediate hit, leading to many more fire trucks introduced over the years. "I was a fireman too, so that helped," Groschen told me. "We had our own pumper [at the fire department] that I referenced, but we also went to other towns and looked at theirs. We tried to take the best from all makes. It wasn't a Ford or a Chevrolet. It was a Tonka. That was the idea."

Groschen created a bulldozer, dump truck, delivery truck and more, all with the help of designers Lee Pheilsticker and Ted Zbikowski. Later, Pheilsticker worked with Groschen on The Mighty Tonka Dump Truck. "I liked the looks of one particular heavy-duty mining truck we found and so I sat down with Lee and we built the prototype based on that. They [Tonka executives] liked what they saw, so we went ahead with it. Boy, that one was a real winner."

Debut: 1948

Predecessors: Lexiko (1931-1938), It, Criss-Cross Words (1938-1947)

Inventor: Alfred Butts (1899-1993)

Developers: James Brunot (1902-1984), Helen Brunot

Companies: Production & Marketing Company, Selchow & Righter, Milton Bradley (North America), Mattel (outside of North America)

Scrabble

A NUMBERS GAME WITH LETTERS

B-A-L-A-N-C-E. I earn 14 points for the word and a 50-point bonus for using all seven tiles in my rack. A good start and a fitting word for the game I'm playing.

Every game of Scrabble starts with balance. It has an ingenious equilibrium that draws comparisons to the greatest games in history. It may be the most famous word game in the world, but Scrabble owes its longevity—even its very origin—to numbers as much as it does to letters. An easy assumption is that Scrabble sprang from the mind of a linguist with a vast vocabulary or some loquacious wordsmith with an English degree. Not true. Its balance was meticulously developed over a seven-year period by a shy statistician with a degree in architecture, a mathematical mind and an aversion for spelling. Go figure.

Early Scrabble produced by Selchow & Righter for James Brunot's Production & Marketing Company.

BUTTS

After losing his job as an architect to the Depression in 1931, Alfred Butts tried his hand at painting before finding part-time work as a statistician. Somehow he hit upon the idea of creating and selling a game as a means of income and decided to figure out, quite analytically, what kind of game to create.

He segmented games into three categories: strategy games (like Chess or Backgammon), numbers games (Bingo and Dice) and word games (Cross-word puzzles and

anagrams). Noting that most games fell into one or the other of the first two categories, Butts decided to focus on developing a word game for the masses. Next, all he needed was an idea for one.

According to the book *Word Freak* by Stephan Fatsis, Butts's "eureka moment" came while reading Edgar Allen Poe's short story "The Gold Bug," wherein a character deciphers a secret message by comparing its symbols to letters in the alphabet. In the story, Poe wrote: "Now, in English, the letter which most frequently occurs is e. Afterwards, the succession runs thus: a o i d h n r s t u y c f g l m w b k p q x z." The statistician in Butts had to find out if the rate of occurrence for each letter was accurate. As it was, Poe ran way off the track, but he set Butts on the right track to inventing a word game whose central scoring mechanism revolved around *the frequency with which letters appear in words.*

"The popular story is that Butts figured out the breakdown of the letters in Scrabble by counting the letters from the front page of the *New York Times,*" Fatsis writes. "Actually, he used several sources, including the *Times,* the *New York Herald Tribune* and *The Saturday Evening Post.*" From just one such study, Fatsis reports that Butts sampled "a total of 12,082 letters and 2,412 words," providing adequate (and exhaustive) proof that Scrabble began as a statistician's obsession.

Butts called his game Lexiko. The object was to score the most points by building a nine- or ten-letter word while drawing and discarding from your "hand" of nine letter tiles. There was no board. Even in its early incarnation, Butts's game found a wonderful balance between the conclusions drawn (skill) and the tiles drawn (luck). From 1934 through 1938, Butts made sets of Lexiko by hand and sold them to friends and acquaintances. More significantly, he tried to license his

creation to Milton Bradley and Parker Brothers, among other publishers, but was rejected each time. Thinking the game needed something more, he began to experiment.

He changed Lexiko so that words could be built crossword style on a board. At a loss for what to call his new creation, it was labeled It for a time, and then Criss-Cross Words.

Butts assigned each letter a specific value based on its occurrence in everyday language; the more common a letter, the less it was worth, yet the more of them there were in the game. For instance, Butts placed twelve Es in the game but made them worth only a point a piece. By contrast, there was only one

Alfred Butts poses with an early version of Criss-Cross Words, which he hand made with blueprinting paper pasted on folding checkerboards.

Q and one Z, but they were both worth 10 points. By using this criteria, there should have been more Ss in the game than the four that Butts introduced, but he correctly surmised that the game would be too unbalanced if easy points were often scored by pluralizing. He shrewdly added two blank tiles, which could become any letter a player wanted, and lastly he reduced the number of tiles on a player's rack from nine to seven.

The final board layout added more intricacies to the game. Scoring was based on the points marked on each letter tile, with premium spaces added that doubled or tripled the value of a letter or word. Play a "Triple Letter Score" and you'll gain more points, but you may open up a "Double Word Score" for an opponent. Butts placed the coveted "Triple Word Score" spaces out on the fringes of the board, giving players the opportunity to catch up late in the game.

Butts sold Criss-Cross Words from his Queens, New York, home for $2 a set. Those early games "were hand drawn with his architectural drafting equipment . . ." Hasbro's website reports. "The tiles were similarly hand-lettered, then glued to quarter-inch balsa and cut to match the squares on the board." Although he enjoyed some modest

James Brunot posed for this publicity photo in 1953, when his company was still helping Selchow & Righter fill demand by making 150,000 Scrabble tiles a day.

success, seven years of this tedium finally took its toll and Butts stopped producing the game sometime in the early 1940s.

BRUNOT

Butts had planted the seed, however, and with the end of World War II came a period of prosperity that gave Americans more leisure time than they had ever before enjoyed. In 1947, Butts was contacted by James Brunot, a former welfare worker looking to start a home-based business. Another version of the story (as reported in *Life)* claims Brunot was an "old friend" and had been playing the game with Butts as early as 1933. In either case, Butts must have been delighted to license the rights to a 16-year-old game in which he still had hope. A deal was struck that paid Butts a small royalty and his game went into production once again.

One of several names that Brunot considered superior to Criss-Cross Words was "scrabble," which meant "to scrape or grope about frenetically with the hands." Of course it still means that when it's a verb, but to most people the word has taken on a secondary meaning as one of the most recognizable trademarks in the world. The success of Scrabble was far from immediate, however.

In the summer of '48, Brunot's Production & Marketing Company produced the first Scrabble sets. According to Fatsis, "Brunot bought a supply of birch plywood that had been advertised as scrap lumber in the *New York Times*. He hired a few local woodworkers who sawed into tiles the long strips of wood onto which letters and point values had been silk-screened." The game boards were a bit more complicated, so Brunot ordered them from Selchow & Righter, a New York game-manufacturing firm.

The 80-year-old game company was best known for Parcheesi, but they were also a "jobber" in the industry, printing game components for other companies. As such, they had a front row seat to the labored growth of Scrabble under Brunot's fledgling enterprise. James Brunot and his wife Helen showed as much drive as Butts had in the early days of Lexiko and Criss-Cross Words. *Life* reported that, "During 1949, their first full year of operation, they assembled and sold 2,251 games and lost $450." They limped along for three more years assembling Scrabble games in the living room of their Newtown, Connecticut, home. On average, they sold a few hundred games a week. Then, in the summer of 1952, they returned from a weeklong vacation and were shocked to find orders totaling over 2,000 games. In the weeks that followed, the orders only grew.

WORD OF MOUTH MEETS MACY'S

It's been widely reported that a Macy's department store executive "discovered" Scrabble at a resort that summer and was dismayed to find Macy's shelves Scrabbleless upon his return. He instructed his buyer to place an order and when other retailers followed suit, Scrabble found its following.

A *Time* magazine article the following year stated that "the emergence of Scrabble has been volcanic and unexplained." The Brunots moved production from their living room to an abandoned schoolhouse, and then to a converted woodworking shop. There in the Connecticut woods, the Brunots made Scrabble games just as fast as they could. They hired workers to help assemble the game, but the orders swelled beyond their maximum output of 6,000 games per week. By the fall of 1952, they sold 37,000 sets. Selchow & Righter had certainly noticed the ever-growing number of game boards the Brunots had been ordering, and although the game company had rejected the prospect of licensing Scrabble earlier in the year, they were

now "groping about frenetically," anxious to sign a deal.

Selchow & Righter produced a "standard set" that sold for $3, but Brunot shrewdly retained the rights to produce a deluxe version of Scrabble that he continued to make in his woodshop-turned-production facility. It sold for $10 and featured a red leatherette carrying case with white plastic tiles and plastic racks (in a time when wood was common and newfangled plastic was considered "deluxe"). For the lower-end market, Brunot licensed the rights for a cheaper $2 version to a game company called Cadaco-Ellis. It was dubbed Skip-A-Cross and featured cardboard tiles with a game board that was nothing more than a tray that rested within the box.

Although Selchow & Righter was brought in to do the heavy lifting, they couldn't keep up with orders either. It was estimated that Selchow & Righter sold

Poor Man's Scrabble. After Scrabble took off and a "$3 standard set" was hard to find, many gamers settled for a $2 Skip-A-Cross.

800,000 Scrabble games in 1953. That year *Life* reported "Christmas shoppers in search of the standard $3 Scrabble set can get it in only two ways: they can place their names on the bottom of waiting lists, or they can lurk for hours beside a counter until a shipment arrives, at which time they take their chances like football players going after a fumble. No game in the history of the trade has ever sold so rapidly and few have shown such promise of consistent, long-term popularity." How right *Life* was. Nearly four million Scrabble sets were sold in 1954, and although that was the game's peak sales year, its following grew over time.

50 YEARS AND 10 BILLION TILES LATER . . .

The shy statistician who changed the landscape of games retired on his modest Scrabble royalties. (Brunot made the bulk of the money, 12 cents per game compared to Butts's 2.5 cents, Fatsis reports.) Ever the numbers man, Butts was fond of noting that "one-third went to taxes. I gave one-third away, and the other third enabled me to have an enjoyable life." He made wooden jigsaw puzzles for friends and remained relatively unknown after the original Scrabble craze of the 1950s died down. However, in 1981, 50 years after he first conceived of Lexiko, Selchow & Righter sent the 82-year-old Butts on a media tour and he enjoyed some newfound recognition in the twilight of his life. He died in 1993 at the age of 94.

BY THE NUMBERS

An expert player can regularly score more than 400 points per game. Hasbro sells between 1.5 and 2 million games per year. There are over 120,000 possible words that can be spelled with just seven letters or less, according to the National Scrabble Association, which oversees the activities of over 200 official Scrabble Clubs in North America, sanctions 170 tournaments each year (including the National and World Scrabble Championships) and maintains a rating system for over 10,000 tournament players. Over 100 million sets have been sold around the world, making it the #1 proprietary word game ever created.

Scrabble is so perfect, what could anyone possibly add to improve it? A tribute would be proper. The official tournament rules state that for a word to be judged acceptable *"it must appear as a main entry . . . in Merriam-Webster's Collegiate Dictionary, 10th Edition."* Two fitting exceptions to that rule would be the names:

and

James Brunot gave Scrabble its name and brightened the game board by coloring the premium spaces their famous shadings of blue and red. He also conceived the 50-point bonus for using all seven tiles, a move known as a "Bingo."

Brunot and Butts sold all their rights in Scrabble to Selchow & Righter in 1971.

The National Scrabble Association was founded in 1978.

Selchow & Righter was purchased by Coleco in 1986. Hasbro bought Coleco three years later, making Scrabble a part of their Milton Bradley division.

Debut: 1949
Developer: Herb Schaper
Companies: W.H. Schaper Manufacturing Company, Inc., Tyco Toys, Milton Bradley

Cootie

"COOTIES!"

Have you ever watched a little boy douse himself with an imaginary bug spray after being touched by a girl? "Aarghh . . . Cooties!" he yells. Most times the girl just rolls her eyes, which erases any doubt that girls mature faster than boys. Minnesotan Herb Schaper was an adult when he developed The Game of Cootie, but he had a little boy's love for fishing and bugs. While whittling a wooden fishing lure one day, it occurred to him that his creation had a sort of funny appeal. After showing it around, he was convinced that what he had carved would lure the attention of children more than fish.

The year was 1948, and one story about the origin of the Cootie toy (the lore as opposed to the lure) is that Schaper whittled 40,000 Cootie bugs by hand that year. That equates to hand-carving over 14 an hour, 8 hours a day, 7 days a week for an entire year—a true fisherman's tale if there ever was one. A more believable version has him hand-carving about two hundred while sitting on his mother's front porch.

Today's Cootie and the original 1949 version. While Schaper's Cooties could give you the creeps or the giggles, depending on your disposition, Milton Bradley's updated bugs are just plain silly.

Cooties, Cooties Everywhere!

Herb Schaper's version was not the first "Cootie" game produced in America. The name originally came from World War I soldiers who (when faced with duty in lice-infested trenches), gave the squirmy pests their infamous name. It's believed that the first Cootie game was made around 1915 by the Irvin-Smith Company and consisted of weighted caplets within a box that contained a wire trap at one end. The object was to tilt the box and try to maneuver the "cooties" into the trap.

The second generation of the game was made around 1927 by both the J.H. Warder Company and the Charles Bowlby Company. These games came much closer to Schaper's version, in that players tried to "build a bug." Both were paper and pencil games, however, where the bug parts were simply checked off or drawn as their corresponding numbers were rolled on a die. Warder's version was named Tu-Tee, while Bowlby called theirs Cootie. In

1937, a company called Rork's produced The New Game of Cootie, which was almost identical to Warder's version.

Then in 1939, Transogram took the first step toward a 3-dimensional bug building game. In this adaptation, players placed cardboard eyes, a body and a head along with wooden legs, antennae and a tail, into a board that was die-cut in the shape of the bug.

Did Herb Schaper know of these games when he created his version of Cootie? Being a toy man, he probably was aware of at least the Transogram game. Just like Marvin Glass & Associates would do in the '60s with hits like Hands Down and Toss Across, Schaper took a popular paper game and updated it into the post-World War II world of plastics. His version of Cootie was the first fully three-dimensional one, and so it replaced all previous editions, becoming a permanent part of pop culture.

Early Cootie games. Clockwise from left: Transogram, 1939; Rork's, 1937; and Irvin-Smith Company, 1915.

What *is* known for a fact is that Herb Schaper owned a store in which he sold hand-carved Cootie bugs and other wooden toys. Schaper developed Cootie into a game where the object was to put a bug together. In 1949, he created a mold from his original wooden carving and turned his creation into plastic, forming the W. H. Schaper Manufacturing Company, Inc. in the process.

Dayton's of Minnesota gave Schaper's bugs their big break. Having convinced the legendary department store to carry a dozen games on consignment, Herb was tickled that they sold over 5,000 copies of Cootie by the end of 1950. By 1952, his company made and sold over 1.2 million Cootie games, and a great game company was born. Herb's love of bugs (and certainly his success with Cootie) led him to release other bug-themed games over the years including Tickle Bee, Tumblebug and Ants in the Pants.

Cootie proved to be his biggest seller. Spin-offs included Deluxe 6 Cootie, which offered six bugs instead of the standard four, Giant Cootie and a Cootie House game. Each featured characteristically simple graphics. When Tyco Toys bought W.H. Schaper Manufacturing in 1973 the graphics improved, but play varied from the classic only slightly. In the game, kids still try to roll a "1" and then a "2" to get a body and

a head of their choice. From there, a "3" gets players an antenna, a "4" an eye, "5" a proboscis—the most titillating part—and a "6" earns one of the six legs necessary to complete a Cootie bug first and win the game.

In the mid '70s the Cootie bugs evolved into an entirely different species, which carries on today. Where many games have been cheapened over time with less expensive parts than their original inspirations, the modern Cootie game comes with more than before, thanks to Cootie's new owner, Milton Bradley. The newest version has a board with each part numbered as a visual reminder for young players. Additionally, each bug is bigger and has its own personality—or, better said, the *parts* have their own personalities. In legs, you can opt for ones clad with in-line skates, sneakers, human feet or alien hands. Today's discerning Cootie bug may have typical antennae, or sport a porkpie hat. And the classic "proboscis"? It's still there, along with a tongue, a pair of buckteeth and some chubby lips.

Herb Schaper's idle whittling and the power of plastics combined to create an American classic that has lasted for 55 years. Over 50 million Cootie games have been sold since 1949. That's over 200 million Cootie bugs and one gigantic infestation of fun.

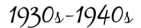

1930s–1940s

COOTIE

1950s

1966

1972

Debut: 1949
Inventor: Eleanor Abbott
   (1910-1988)
Company: Milton Bradley

Candy Land

RECIPE FOR FUN

There's no formula for a hit game. If there were, there'd be hit games introduced every year. As it is, they come along ever so rarely, which makes 1949 a vintage year.

Three classics were introduced in '49, with themes as contrary as they could be. Schaper Manufacturing had us overrun with fun in The Game of Cootie; Parker Brothers divulged Clue; and Milton Bradley introduced what became "a child's first game." While Cootie was clothed in bug parts and Clue was cloaked in murder, Candy Land was covered with chocolate.

The first children to play Candy Land were in the polio ward of a San Diego hospital in 1948. The game's creator was a retired schoolteacher by the name of Eleanor Abbott. In addition to being a former educator, Eleanor was also a patient in the same hospital, suffering from the same dreadful disease as the children. Thus, she was uniquely qualified to understand their circumstances and equally fit to provide a fantasy world into which they could escape. Eleanor's young friends loved the game, and soon she was encouraged to submit it to Milton Bradley. Milton Bradley executive Mel Taft began working for the

The original "sweet little game for sweet little folks."

The boy in the illustration on this early 1949 board at left has an odd line running up his leg. The board on the right represents a later version where the line is removed. Could this have been a hint of a leg brace, subtly added by the artist or inventor? If so, it would certainly go unnoticed to the casual player, but would speak volumes to the young polio victims for whom the game was initially created.

1930s-1940s

CANDY LAND

game giant in 1949, the same year that Candy Land debuted. "Eleanor brought us her game sketched out on butcher's paper," Taft said. After speaking to her on the phone, he decided to pay her a visit. "Eleanor was just as sweet as could be. She was a schoolteacher who lived in a very modest home in San Diego," he said. "She was a real sweetheart. I liked her immediately."

Although the executives at Milton Bradley liked Eleanor Abbott and her game, they had no idea how big it would become. Taft recalled that they decided to produce the game as a temporary fill-in, a small step away from the school supply business that had dominated their line since the end of World War II. In fact, prior to Candy Land, a game called Uncle Wiggly was Milton Bradley's biggest hit, with rival Parker Brothers far outperforming them in the game trade. That is until this sweet lady brought them Candy Land.

What a world Abbott created! The board has always been a map, laid at the feet of two happy travelers. These explorers have always been a little boy and girl, who with hands clasped, set out on a journey through a candy-covered countryside. The "Candy Hearts" reminded them that they were loved. They were called

to come inside the "Lollipop Woods," and if ever there was a tree to be climbed, the "Gingerbread Plum Tree" was it. The crude renderings of the "Crooked Old Peanut Brittle House" and the "Home" on the earliest boards looked more like log cabins than anything edible. Was Eleanor Abbott's artwork used in the very first Candy Land games produced? It's a romantic notion, but one mystery that may forever remain hidden.

Candy Land required no reading. Cards with one or two colored squares made it clear to kids as young as three where to go next on the rainbow path,

The 1962 version of Eleanor Abbott's creation.

The Playmakers 81

with the goal to reach "Home Sweet Home" first. Play pieces were pawns initially, but later became gingerbread men, who, if they were lucky, found shortcuts like the "Rainbow Trail" and "Mountain Pass." If unlucky, the dreaded "Cherry Pitfalls" or the sticky "Molasses Swamp" slowed down the gingerbread men, seemingly forever. It could have been some suppressed guilt over my own sweet excesses, but I always saw the black dots that represented the "Cherry Pitfalls" as cavities.

Dental worries aside, Candy Land was a quick hit, earning its creator her just desserts. "I remember when it really started to take off," Mel Taft told me. "Eleanor gave most of her royalties right back to the kids. She bought supplies and equipment for all the schools."

Today's Candy Land provides new characters for every area of the board, like Princess Lolly, who reigns over the "Lollipop Woods," and Queen Frostine, who floats on the "Ice Cream Sea." I suppose the characters add a semi-human element to which kids can relate, but for me the changes have made the game semi-sweet, with some of the original innocence lost, too. For instance, there's a plot in today's Candy Land, complete with an antagonist in the form of Lord Licorice. Mr. Mint

Today

1978

1962

1949

The earliest games had wooden pawns, but once Candy Land became a hit, Milton Bradley introduced gingerbread men pieces.

1950s   1960s   1970s   1980s

Through the decades, Milton Bradley frequently updated the art of Candy Land, with each generation having at least one version to call its own.

is depicted with a peppermint axe, hacking down peppermint trees, and a monster named Gloppy wades in the Molasses Swamp. Many adults remember Candy Land very differently, yet today's young Candy Land player won't miss what they never knew.

Be the first to find the Candy Castle

The best part of playing is playing together.

Ages 3 to 6

Today's Candy Land has new art, but remains as big as ever, selling well over a million units per year.

No, there's no formula for a hit game, but there are eternal truths. Kids will always love candy, and since its introduction, kids have loved Candy Land. In the time it takes you to say "Peppermint Stick Forest" or "Gumdrop Mountains," Candy Land's magic can send mature adults back to their childhood.

The little travelers at the start of the game have names now (they're called The Candy Land Kids), but at least they're still holding hands. Some things remain as they should . . . still sweet after 55 years.

> Surveys find that 94% of mothers are aware of Candy Land and over 60% of households with a five-year-old child own the game.

> Techie treats. There's a handheld electronic Candy Land and even a CD-ROM version for your home computer—just be sure to keep your mouse away from the goodies.

MEL TAFT

Insider Profile

Milton Bradley executive Mel Taft graduated from Harvard Business School in 1949 and went to work for the legendary game company that same year. One of the first game executives to embrace

television, Taft encouraged his company to advertise on TV like toy giants Hasbro and Mattel. The result propelled Milton Bradley past rival Parker Brothers as the biggest game company in the world. In 1958, Taft secured the license for a home version of the NBC hit game show Concentration. Password followed in 1962, but only after Taft convinced TV producers Mark Goodson and Bill Todman that a home version could be done by devising a red plastic window that ingeniously revealed the word. The result was Milton Bradley's first game to sell over 1 million copies in a single year. Taft spearheaded many other Milton Bradley hits including The Game of Life, Operation and Twister in the '60s, and Simon in 1978. Mel Taft retired as Milton Bradley's senior vice president of research & development in 1984, after 35 years in the game trade.

Debut: 1948
U.S. Debut: 1949
Inventor: Anthony Pratt
(1903-1994)
Developers: Anthony Pratt
and Elva Pratt
Companies: John
Waddington Games Ltd.,
Waddington's Games,
Parker Brothers

Clue

"The Envelope Please . . ."

Tuxedos and gowns shimmer and glitter on Hollywood's biggest night—the Oscars. The late-great Madeline Kahn approaches the podium; the equally witty Martin Mull escorts her. After Ms. Kahn reads a short list of nominees, the posh and powerful shift in their seats. The envelope is handed to her and as she opens it a hush falls over the crowd of renown. Seconds seem like minutes. At last she reveals: "Mr. Green did it in the Study with the Rope!"

So this didn't really happen, but it could have in 1985. That's the year *Clue* opened in theaters nationwide, starring Madeline Kahn as Mrs. White, Martin Mull as Colonel Mustard, and a great cast portraying the other Clue characters we have grown to love and suspect. Silly Putty and Slinky have both traveled into

It never won an Academy Award, but Clue was a pretty funny film with three alternate endings.

space—but a *movie based on a plaything?!* Somehow that seems even grander. Conquer Hollywood, it seems, and you conquer the world.

Long before Madeline Kahn was offered the role of Mrs. White, Clue was a game that gave new meaning to the expression "foul play." It was first released by John Waddington Games Ltd. (later Waddington's

The 1949 version of Clue.

Clue inventor Anthony Pratt surely was influenced by a murder mystery game called Mr. Ree, released by Selchow & Righter in 1937. The game board featured an overhead view of a dwelling (in this case Aunt Cora's red brick house) and contained four metal murder weapons.

Games), the Parker Brothers of England. Waddington named the game Cluedo as a play on the word "ludo," which means "I play" in Latin. Cluedo, or its American alias Clue, is well-known in over 73 countries. But how did this devilishly clever game come to be? Or, in the Clue parlance: Who? Where? How?

Mr. Pratt did it in the town of Leeds with a brainstorm.

In 1943, Anthony Pratt was a patent clerk serving as a fire warden during the war. On patrol throughout Leeds, England, one quiet night, he got to thinking about an old parlor game that he used to play with his friends called Murder. The idea of trying to simplify the entertainment into a board game of his own struck Pratt. He shared his plan with his wife Elva, and together they designed the first Clue game board. It took them several years of tinkering to figure out the mechanics of play, but eventually Pratt received a patent on the game and submitted it to Waddington's in 1947. After test-playing the game, the Waddington's executives knew they had a hit. The first Cluedo games debuted in London in 1948, and the game came to America as Clue one year later.

The marketed game did not change much from Pratt's ingenious prototype. It was called Murder, with Mr. Green originally named Reverend Green. Pratt's first choice of weapons included an axe, a bomb, a hypodermic needle and poison. Those weapons were eventually replaced by the now infamous lead pipe, candlestick, rope, revolver, knife, and wrench—(even Inspector Clouseau would know if a bomb was used, right?). Working out which unique

The first Clue games from 1949 were subtitled The Great New Sherlock Holmes Game. The earliest rare sets, like the one pictured here, contained real rope that was replaced by plastic-molded rope shortly after production began.

combination of "Who?" "Where?" and "How?" is what makes the game so addictive for budding detectives.

At the start of the game, one suspect card, one weapon card and one room card are placed inside the envelope. These three cards represent the murderer, the weapon he or she used, and the room in which the dastardly deed was committed. All the other cards are then dealt out to the players. As they move into rooms the players make *suggestions;* "I suggest that Mrs. White did it in the billiard room with the rope," for example. The player to the left of the suggester then looks at his or her cards to try and prove the suggestion false. From here it is a race, through a process of elimination, to deduce what three cards are within the envelope. Along the way, Pratt's design allows for an element of any great murder mystery: deception. By suggesting a card from his or her own hand, a crafty player may trick others into thinking that particular card is in the envelope.

The climax of any Clue game came when you thought you'd solved the crime. There was always a bit of suspense when the envelope was checked. Wrong, and you sat out the rest of the game; but if you were right you were Sherlock Holmes, at least until the next game. Whether we fancied ourselves Sherlock, Nancy Drew, Perry Mason or Agatha Christie, Clue provided fun *and* justice. The case was always solved and nobody got hurt. Mr. Boddy has been murdered over a billion times since Clue's introduction, and just like us he keeps coming back for more.

While we dreamed of becoming detectives, Anthony Pratt aspired to be a concert pianist. In the mid-'50s he sold the worldwide rights to Clue for a relatively small upfront fee and a limited-term royalty. This initial windfall allowed him to pursue his lifelong dream, tickling the ivories across Europe. In a few years, however, Pratt ran out of money and was rumored to have gone back to his original career as a patent clerk.

1956

1972

1963

1986

Meanwhile, Waddington's made a mint licensing the game around the world.

According to a *New York Times* article by Robert McG. Thomas, Jr., Waddington's executives found themselves tangled in their own Clue mystery in 1996. Planning to celebrate the sale of their 150 millionth Clue game worldwide, they could not locate Anthony Pratt. They set up a hotline and called upon the English populous to help solve the mystery. Finally, the case was cracked when Waddington's received a call from a cemetery superintendent who reported that Anthony Pratt had been buried there in 1994. His headstone read

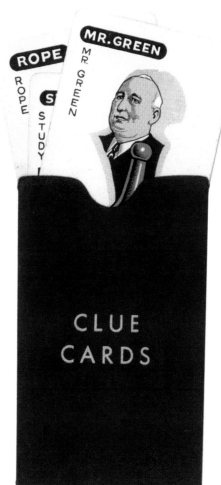

With six suspects, six weapons and nine rooms, there are 324 possible combinations to the crime in every game of Clue.

"Inventor of Cluedo." Unlike his youthful and oft murdered creation Mr. Boddy, Anthony Ernest Pratt died peacefully at the age of 90.

We love Clue for its simplicity, but also for its moments of fun. There's that occasion when you suggest one of your own cards, bluffing your opponents. The flash of brilliance when you think you've cracked the case. And finally, the instant when you cross the threshold of that dubious room, solving the murder with a boastful—"Elementary my dear Watson, the envelope please . . . ".

1992

1998

2002

In 1999, a bottle of poison was added to celebrate Clue's 50th Anniversary, just like the one Pratt originally intended back in 1943.

Three million Clue games are sold around the world each year. It has spawned several computer editions, an Alfred Hitchcock edition, as well as versions featuring *The Simpsons* and *Scooby Doo*. Cluedo has inspired a game show and even a soap opera in its native Britain.

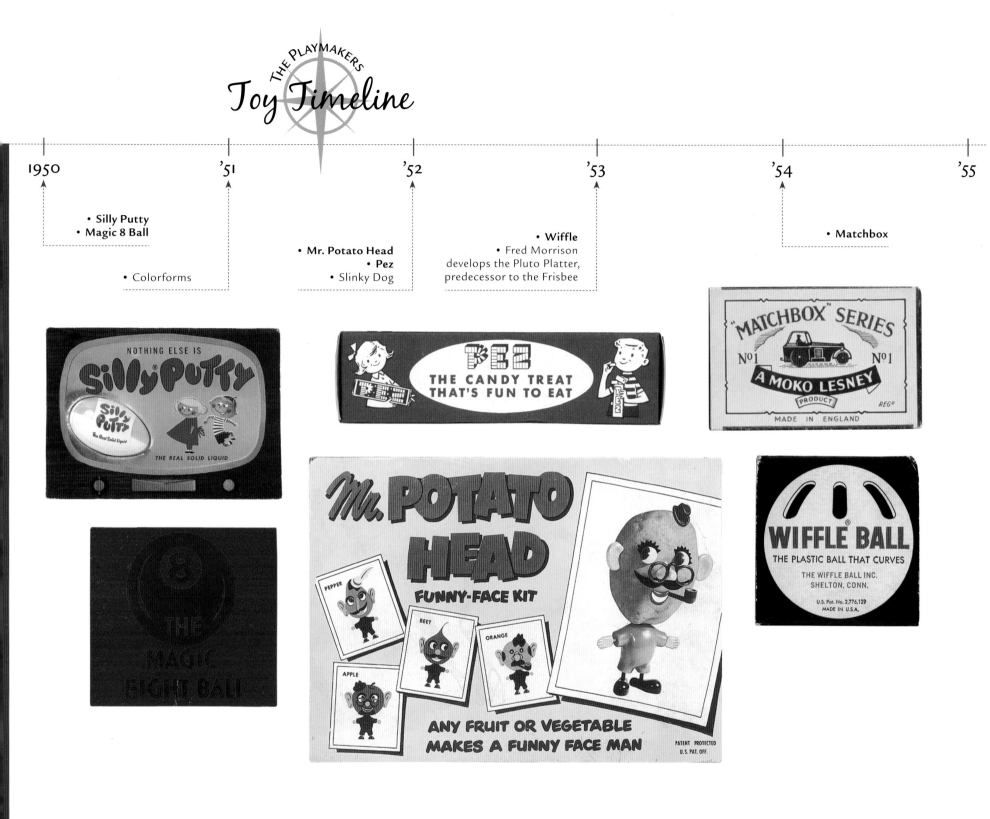

THE PLAYMAKERS
Toy Timeline

| 1950 | '51 | '52 | '53 | '54 | '55 |

• Silly Putty
• Magic 8 Ball

• Colorforms

• Mr. Potato Head
• Pez
• Slinky Dog

• Wiffle
• Fred Morrison develops the Pluto Platter, predecessor to the Frisbee

• Matchbox

NOTHING ELSE IS
Silly Putty
Silly Putty
The Real Solid Liquid
THE REAL SOLID LIQUID

PEZ
THE CANDY TREAT
THAT'S FUN TO EAT

"MATCHBOX" SERIES
No 1   No 1
A MOKO LESNEY
PRODUCT   REGᵈ
MADE IN ENGLAND

THE
MAGIC
EIGHT BALL

Mr. POTATO HEAD
FUNNY-FACE KIT
PEPPER
BEET
ORANGE
APPLE
ANY FRUIT OR VEGETABLE
MAKES A FUNNY FACE MAN
PATENT PROTECTED
U.S. PAT. OFF.

WIFFLE BALL
THE PLASTIC BALL THAT CURVES
THE WIFFLE BALL INC.
SHELTON, CONN.
U.S. Pat. No. 2,776,139
MADE IN U.S.A.

1950s

'55 '56 '57 '58 '59 1960

• Yahtzee
• Ant Farm

• Skateboard

• Barbie
• Risk
• Instant Life, predecessor to Sea-Monkeys

• Play-Doh
• Lilli doll, predecessor to the Barbie doll, first appears in Germany

• Charles Lazarus creates the toy supermarket, later known as Toys R Us

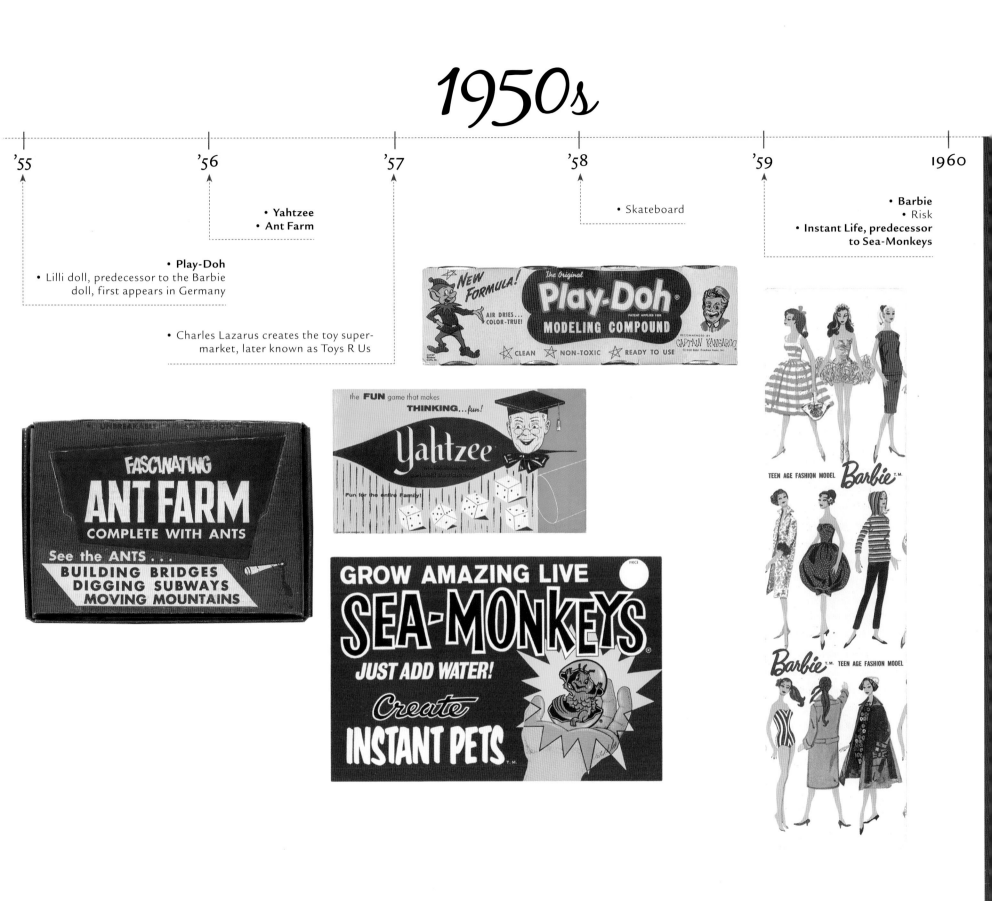

Debut: 1950
Predecessor: Bouncing Putty (1949)
Inventor: James Wright
Developer: Peter Hodgson
Companies: Silly Putty Marketing, Binney & Smith

Silly Putty

BOUNCING BABY

They met during World War II. It was a chance encounter, but one that changed them forever. It was a secret at first, but soon the chemistry between them became evident to everyone. They were inseparable.

Yes, the union of boric acid and silicone oil produced a bouncing baby ball that changed the toy industry forever. And to think, if rubber trees were indigenous to the United States, these two may have never come together on that fateful day in 1943.

As World War II dragged on, the ability to get rubber for essentials like boots, gas masks and tires was hindered to the point that our government's War Production Board asked for assistance. Calling on the ingenuity of American industry, Uncle Sam sought the development of a synthetic rubber. James Wright, a chemical engineer working in General Electric Company's New Haven, Connecticut, laboratory took up the challenge. Wright tried numerous chemical combinations. When he mixed boric acid and silicone oil in a test tube, he was surprised to discover that the two "polymerized." He removed the gummy substance, and in his desire to test any rubberlike properties it might possess, threw it on the floor. Wright named his glob, Bouncing Putty.

Wright soon discovered that despite its rebounding quality, Bouncing Putty was not a suitable synthetic rubber. It broke under pressure and was way too soft, flattening into a thick puddle if left for just a few minutes. Still, G.E. thought it might have *some* application. So while Wright applied for a patent in 1944, G.E. sent it out to their engineers all over the world. Many brilliant minds pondered the putty, and after five years the verdict came down—no practical use.

Peter Hodgson is the man credited with finding the many *impractical* uses for Bouncing Putty. A Canadian-born copywriter, Hodgson was 37 when his path crossed with bounding fame. Binney & Smith, today's maker of Silly Putty, reports that Hodgson met a toy shop owner named Ruth Fallgatter at a party hosted by a G.E. executive and that together they were introduced to the silly compound. Between 1944 and 1949 the educated upper class around New England made this

Silly Putty first came in a box with copy that told of all it could do then added, "Let it alone, it settles slowly and majestically into a tired little puddle. SEE?"

James Wright created his "Bouncing Putty" in a G.E. laboratory.

This '50s ad touted Silly Putty's many exploits.

silicone/boric acid mixture an adult party fad. Labeled Gupp in some circles and Nutty Putty in others, it was just a matter of time before someone tried to market the stuff.

In 1949, Fallgatter and Hodgson began selling Bouncing Putty from Ruth's store, the Block Shop in New Haven, Connecticut. Using Hodgson's marketing experience and copywriting skills, they produced a toy catalog offering Bouncing Putty in a small, clear case for $2.00. Despite some moderate success, Fallgatter decided to discontinue the stuff, but Hodgson did not give up so easily. He was reportedly $12,000 in debt when he threw caution to the wind and dove headfirst into this "solid-liquid." He signed a deal with G.E. and with borrowed money purchased $147 worth of the gooey stuff for which no one seemed to have a use. But Peter Hodgson hatched a plan.

WHICH CAME FIRST, THE SILLY PUTTY OR THE EGG?

For no other reason than the fact that Easter was right around the corner, Hodgson hit upon the idea of selling the putty in an egg-shaped container in the spring of 1949. After the season was over he decided to keep the unique package, reasoning that it set his product apart.

The second key change Hodgson made was to the name. In his experimenting with the stuff he found that it did a lot more than just bounce. When he pulled it apart slowly it stretched further than his arms could spread, but when he gave it a quick yank, it snapped in half. It was susceptible to air pockets, which snapped and popped delightfully when it was squeezed. Yes, Hodgson decided that naming it Bouncing Putty would be an injustice to its many silly antics, and that's how Silly Putty found its name.

From a converted barn in North Branford, Connecticut, Peter Hodgson started shipping his newly named product to retailers in a package that was logical and ludicrous at the same time. The world was introduced to Silly Putty by the dozen, inside pasteboard egg crates. With such a package, it's no wonder that toy industry professionals were not as enamored with Silly Putty as the man who named it. At its public debut during the 1950 International Toy Fair in New York, Hodgson was urged repeatedly to give it up. After six more bleak months, Hodgson discovered Silly Putty's most amazing trick yet: He found that if you gave Silly Putty a little press, it would explode!

The "press" in question was *The New Yorker* magazine. In the summer of 1950, a writer for the prestigious publication stumbled upon Silly Putty at a Doubleday store in Manhattan. He was so taken by the squishy, pinkish stuff that he decided to feature it in the column, "Talk of the Town." After the August 26th issue of *The New Yorker* hit the stands, Hodgson was immediately deluged with phone calls. Reportedly, in just three days, orders for over 250,000 eggs of Silly Putty were placed. Hodgson secured loans, ordered

Silly Putty hasn't changed since the days of pulling comics off the page, but printing has. Inks have greatly improved since the '50s and '60s. As a result, today's comics won't allow Silly Putty to perform one of its most memorable tricks. Here Marvel Comic's Iron Man gets a facelift.

plastic eggs, and geared up production. After shipping nearly seven tons of the stuff and being stretched to the brink of its capacity, Peter Hodgson's company almost snapped.

Just after Silly Putty took off, Hodgson was almost forced into bankruptcy in an ironic twist that harkened back to the creation of the substance. In 1950, the U.S. government set restrictions on the use of silicone to aid, this time, in the Korean War effort. Production drastically dropped and Hodgson limped along through the rest of the year trying to keep his company afloat. Luckily the demand for Silly Putty never slowed, so when the ban was lifted in 1951, Silly Putty hit the ground bouncing.

As the sales of Silly Putty climbed, it found a new audience. Its initial market was adults, but almost immediately after its release children discovered it in full force. Picking comics off a page and stretching faces into silly contortions was a kid-favorite beginning in the mid-'50s. Hodgson recognized the shift and began advertising Silly Putty on TV's *Captain Kangaroo* and *The Howdy Doody Show*.

The '60s were good to Silly Putty. Hodgson's son, Peter Hodgson Jr., often lent his dad a hand in the family business and was instrumental in the introduction of Silly Putty to the USSR and Western Europe. In 1963, he introduced it to England and stayed involved with the company until his father's death in 1967. One year later, Peter Hodgson, Jr. sold the rights to Silly Putty to Crayola crayon maker, Binney & Smith.

While this strange silicone polymer continues to suffer from a solid/liquid identity crisis, we've never failed in identifying with its most crucial chemical component . . . fun. Three hundred million eggs have rolled off the production line since the first blob oozed out of the test tube and Binney & Smith still makes 12,000 eggs of the stuff per day. It has evolved from a peculiar fad to an indelible part of our pop culture. In the 50 years that it has existed, we have learned one timeless toy truth: *Nothing else is Silly Putty.*

- After a batch of Silly Putty is made (still from silicone oil, boric acid and other secret ingredients), it is formed into large bricks. Silly Putty maker Binney & Smith uses marshmallow cutting machines to separate the bricks into small square chucks, which are then packed into the classic, egg-shaped container.

- Originally produced only in its natural shade of basic beige, Silly Putty is now available in 14 colors. There's a heat-sensitive line that changes colors and even a glow-in-the-dark variety. Metallic gold Silly Putty first appeared in 2000, in honor of the classic toy's 50th anniversary.

- All Peter Hodgson's eggs were in one basket. His company never made any product other than Silly Putty, yet when the entrepreneur died, he reportedly left an estate worth close to $150 million.

- The Apollo 8 astronauts took Silly Putty to space in 1968 where it was used as a stress reliever and to help fasten down tools in the weightlessness of space.

POLYMERS IN THE PUTTY

Silly Putty is known as a "dilatant" or a compound that resists flow as a result of force. Technically, it is a liquid containing long molecules called polymers that can slip and slide over one another and flow like a liquid. These polymers are linked however, and if rapid force is applied to them they will become tangled, catch on each other and resist force like an elastic solid. Extremely rapid force will cause the polymers to snag even more and break apart. This is why a ball of Silly Putty will settle into a blob if left alone, spring back if bounced and shatter if struck with a hammer.

Silly Putty was one of the first TV-advertised toy items after Mr. Potato Head, and Hodgson was shrewd in his package execution. To reinforce Silly Putty's TV connection, he switched from a box to a package that looked like a TV screen, complete with knobs.

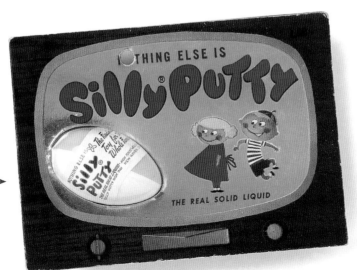

Magic 8 Ball

1950s

Debut: 1950
Predecessors: The Syco-Seer (1946), Syco-Slate (1948)
Inventors: Albert Carter and Abe Bookman
Developer: Max Levinson
Companies: Alabe Crafts, Ideal, Tyco, Mattel

The Magic 8 Ball levitates here in its original packaging from 1950.

BEHIND THE 8 BALL

"*Will I ever finish this book on time?*"
Magic 8 Ball: DON'T COUNT ON IT

So went my reintroduction to this classic toy. Like most of us, I had one when I was a kid and wondered if it really could tell me the answers to my biggest questions.

"*Will Carole Piccoli marry me?*"

AS I SEE IT YES

"*Alriiight, I'll tell her at recess. Will the Phillies win the World Series?*"

MY REPLY IS NO

Even when it proved to be wrong (she didn't, they did) I was always drawn back to its circular window and that wonderful moment of suspense as my "future" floated to the surface.

It's really a 20-sided polygon, floating inside a liquid-filled tube, fitted within a 3-inch-diameter hollow plastic ball. The answers or predictions appear on each triangular face of the polygon, also known as the "Spirit Slate." It feels heavy in your hands. Gaze at the "8" (so that the window is facing down) and ask your "yes or no" question. When you turn the window up, the polygon rises to the surface and comes to rest against the window, revealing

Al Carter's patent drawing for a "liquid filled dice agitator."

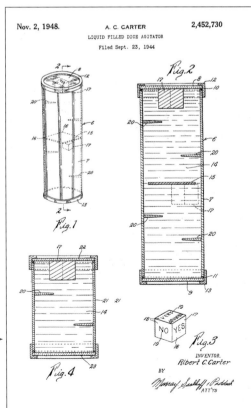

your answer. Like the best toy ideas, it's simple and yet very clever. It's hard to walk past a Magic 8 Ball sitting on a desk or table and *not* pick it up looking for fun and good fortune.

Fortune-telling and the movement known as Spiritualism (the belief that the dead communicate with the living) enthralled America in the years just before the Civil War. Séance parties and psychic mediums were all the rage, while in Europe the first Ouija boards, or "talking boards" as they were called, appeared in 1850. Then, as the Civil War erupted, the uncertainty of the times fueled a desperate desire to know what the future held. It's no surprise that during World War II the idea for what became the Magic 8 Ball originated—or so I would eventually learn after weeks of trying to make contact with a dead man.

I didn't need a séance. I knew a great truth: If the deceased person you are trying to find happens to be an inventor, your single best source of divination is the U.S. Patent and Trademark Office. Printed on the early Magic 8 Ball packages is "Pat. No. 2452730," which names Albert C.

Carter as the inventor of the same type of contraption that sits inside every Magic 8 Ball. The problem was, Albert C. Carter wasn't the man I was trying to find.

The man I was looking for was named Abe Bookman, because everything I read stated that "Abe Bookman invented the Magic 8 Ball in 1946." *That* was the answer that had continually floated to the surface—on the Internet, in books and in newspaper articles. Appropriately, the origin of the Magic 8 Ball is masked in mystery.

The document I found at the USPTO stated that Albert C. Carter had assigned his patent rights to a man named Abe Buchmann. *"Could this be the Abe Bookman often credited as its inventor?"*

SIGNS POINT TO YES.

Despite all its psychic ability, the Magic 8 Ball can only answer a "yes or no" question. That leaves quite a few others to ponder. Who *really* invented it? Why is it a billiard 8 ball? What is that murky blue/black liquid in there? Why are air bubbles preventing me from seeing my destiny? After weeks of searching, the answers were finally revealed—not through a psychic but a reference librarian.

The Magic 8 Ball was first produced by a company called Alabe Crafts in Cincinnati. After trying unsuccessfully to find information on the company at two local library databases and the Internet, I decided to go to the toy's hometown. A call to The Public Library of Cincinnati turned up nothing. OUTLOOK NOT SO GOOD. I decided to CONCENTRATE AND ASK AGAIN; a call to the Cincinnati Historical Society Library led to the reference librarian, who uncovered the truth in an article from the *Cincinnati Post*.

According to this 30-year-old newspaper story which quotes both Abe Bookman and then-president of Alabe Crafts, Sid Korey, the idea for the Magic 8 Ball began with Alfred Carter's mother.

Wait a minute—*Alfred?* The patent was filed by an Albert Carter. First it was Buchmann/Bookman, now it's Albert/Alfred? I was convinced that mischievous

spirits were trying to misdirect anyone looking into the origin of the toy.

REPLY HAZY, TRY AGAIN.

Regardless of the spelling, this article went on to state that Carter's mother, Mary, was a well-known Cincinnati clairvoyant and medium in the '40s. She revealed the future for Sherlock Holmes creator and supernatural enthusiast Sir Arthur Conan Doyle, among other celebrities. Mary Carter created a mysterious device called a Psycho-Slate, which was a blackboard with a lid that closed over its writing surface. After asking a question and closing the lid, the sounds of squeaking chalk, or "spirit writing" as it was called, were heard. Mary would then open the board to reveal the answer, to the bewilderment of her patrons. No one knew how she did it.

Certainly inspired by his mother, Al (let's just leave it at that) Carter created a tubelike, fortune-telling device. Inside was a pair of floating dice (with responses printed on each side) separated by a panel in the center. The tube was completely filled with a dark, viscous fluid

The Syco-Seer came with instructions and a guarantee that "answers obtained are equally as reliable as those received through the greatest living psychic mediums."

(some say it was molasses); when placed on one of its clear windowlike ends, one die would float to the top, revealing an answer. Once it was flipped over and set back down, the other die would work its way to the top.

Carter took his unique idea to a local Cincinnati store owner named Max Levinson, who was so intrigued by Carter's device that he not only wanted to stock it in his store, but wanted to produce it for sale to other stores. Levinson turned to his brother-in-law, who was a graduate of Ohio Mechanics Institute, for ideas on the best way to produce the device. Enter Abe Bookman, a meticulous genius and the perfect man for the job. Levinson formed a novelty company with Bookman at the helm and Carter as his silent (and very inventive) partner. In 1946, the company was founded and named Alabe Crafts, Inc. by combining Al and Abe's first names. Together, the men produced The Syco-Seer, a 7-inch-tall tube touted as a "Miracle Home Fortune-Teller."

Al Carter filed for his patent on Sept. 23, 1944, and assigned it to Bookman, Levinson and some other partners in Alabe Crafts. Before the patent was granted in 1948, Carter died. It's not clear whether he lived to see his invention "attract hordes of curious shoppers in department stores from Chicago to New York," as the *Cincinnati Post* says it did by 1947. He lived a gypsy lifestyle and died unknown. "When he was sober, he was a genius," the article quotes Abe Bookman as saying. "He stayed in flophouses . . . he was always broke, but I bought every idea he ever had, and that gave him enough to keep going."

While Alabe carried on without Carter, The Syco-Seer went through some improvements as Abe Bookman sought to make it better and less expensive to manufacture. First it was reduced in size to include only a single window on one end and given the new name, Syco-Slate: The Pocket Fortune Teller.

A gypsy woman graced the package of Alabe's new product and as a promotion, Bookman hired models to stand in stores dressed as gypsies. When the ladies quickly grew bored with the long demonstrations, Abe Bookman decided to adapt the Syco-Slate into a self-demonstrating device.

In 1948, they encased Al Carter's tube within an iridescent crystal ball, a step toward the spherical fortune-teller we know and love. It was not successful, but attracted the attention of Brunswick Billiards in Chicago, who commissioned Alabe Crafts to create a promotional fortune-teller in the likeness of a classic, black, number 8 billiard ball. The year was 1950, and a legend was born.

After the promotion ran its course, Abe Bookman decided to offer this "Magic 8 Ball" to the public. The fortune-telling craze continued through the '50s. Fortune cookies were at their peak in popularity and many diners featured napkin holders that sold fortunes for a penny; the timing was perfect for the Magic 8 Ball Fortune Teller. It was released as a paperweight and conversation piece. Later packaging touted it as the Magic Answering 8 Ball Fortune Teller, but the directions remained identical:

(1) Hold "8" BALL with black window down.

(2) Ask a "YES" or "NO" question about the future.

(3) Wait 10 seconds.

(4) Turn "8" BALL over, with black window up in level position.

Around 1948, Syco-Slate debuted in department stores, including Gold-blatt's in Chicago and Shillito's in Cincinnati.

(5) Written answer will appear on Spirit Slate in window.

Many fortune seekers had their own rituals. "I always kissed mine before asking a question," one lady told me. Others had their own rules that they rigorously enforced. "Don't shake it!" I was warned by one enthusiast. "People complain about air bubbles and yet they still shake it! Where does it say to shake it? Nowhere. Just turn it over!"

"Is this man taking the Magic 8 Ball too seriously?"

AS I SEE IT YES

Trapped air bubbles have been reduced greatly, but it's good to know that if you need help, there are websites devoted to the Magic 8 Ball that show you how to dispel them by tapping the toy in a process called "burping."

About a million Magic 8 Balls are sold each year and they seem to occupy a permanent space on children's dressers, corporate desks and toy store shelves everywhere. There have been several

The Magic 8 Ball has racked up more than its share of imitators over the years. There's Madame Zelda's Crystal Ball, The Orb, and even the Q Ball, which talks. The Sarcastic Ball answers, "Yeah, and I'm the Pope"; and the Sunshine Smiley Face responds with compliments like "Your breath is so minty!"

Have a Ball

Fans are surprised to learn that the Magic 8 Ball has been around for so long. Children of the '50s, '60s, '70s, and '80s all tend to claim it was first produced during their childhood.

THE PLAYMAKERS
Now and Then

Clockwise from left: early-'50s, mid-'50s, '60s, '80s, '90s, Today

BURSTING BUBBLES

The Syco-Seer was filled with a gooey liquid that prevented air bubbles and resisted freezing. Unfortunately, it also kept users waiting for the die as it would creep s-l-o-w-l-y to the surface. Alabe Crafts switched to an "anti-freeze" type fluid that consisted of alcohol and blue dye. When Ideal Toys bought Alabe Crafts in 1971, they made several additional improvements to the toy's design. In 1975, they filed a patent for a "Bubble free die agitator," which splits the Magic 8 Ball's inner tube into two different-sized compartments separated by a funnel-like wall that helps trap the bubbles. Tyco Toys bought Ideal in 1987 and benefited from this patented improvement. Today, the Magic 8 Ball calls Mattel home, where the patent is still in use.

THE PLAYMAKERS
How It Works

Magic 8 Ball games, key chains and a talking telephone. There's the Magic Date Ball that comes in hot pink and has become a girls' sleepover essential. There are even licensed versions based on *The Simpsons* and *SpongeBob SquarePants*.

The concept has been used in fortune-tellers shaped like Yoda from *Star Wars*, Dogbert from *Dilbert* and even the Chihuahua from the Taco Bell ads. For all their efforts, none can compare to the classic original. It's a fun novelty, which means you shouldn't pick your spouse or stocks by it. As the box says: "Magic 8 Ball to be used for entertainment purposes only." Still, I had to ask one more question, even though I already knew the answer . . .

"You'll be around for another 50 years, won't you?"

YOU MAY RELY ON IT

According to the book *Inside the Magic 8 Ball* by Miriam Zellnik, Dr. Lucien Cohen, a psychology professor at the University of Cincinnati, was consulted to establish the 20 responses hidden within each Magic 8 Ball. The same ratio of ten affirmatives, five negatives and five neutral, or "teaser" responses are used to this day.

Debut: 1952
Inventor: George Lerner
(1910-1995)
Company: Hasbro

Mr. Potato Head

A HALF-BAKED IDEA

Since discovering them in 3,000 B.C. we've found that potatoes can be fried, mashed, whipped, boiled, steamed, baked, and of course, adorned with plastic human body parts.

Yes, when Mr. Potato Head debuted he really was a potato. He may not be an actual vegetable anymore, but he's not just a toy anymore either—he's a movie star. But before the *Toy Story* films, this potato's underground start took root in the fertile mind of a Brooklyn-born toy inventor, a man who for a brief time made it okay for us to play with our food.

In 1949, George Lerner came up with the idea for a toy that allowed kids to press sharp-pronged plastic face and body parts into vegetables and fruits in order to create "a funny face man." There had been a variety of popular "make a face" toys out before this time, but none that included three-dimensional props, and certainly none that encouraged the mutilation of produce. A few years before, Lerner had formed a toy development firm called The Lernell Company, with his friend Julius Ellman. The two had combined their talents (and their last names) to create a company that played for a living. "George was brilliant," Ellman told me. "I was there, but he was the true inventor of Mr. Potato Head."

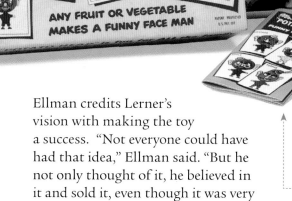

ANY FRUIT OR VEGETABLE
MAKES A FUNNY FACE MAN

The first Mr. Potato Head, 1952

Ellman credits Lerner's vision with making the toy a success. "Not everyone could have had that idea," Ellman said. "But he not only thought of it, he believed in it and sold it, even though it was very controversial."

Controversial? It's hard to imagine a more innocuous toy than Mr. Potato Head, but in 1949, with the Depression and World War II food rationing still fresh in consumers' memories, the idea of turning food into a toy was considered irresponsible and wasteful. All the toy companies rejected Lerner's idea for fear of a public backlash. "George had done some work for Buddy L Toys during the war and even they turned it down," Ellman recalled. Finally, after several years of

George Lerner, the patriarch of Mr. Potato Head.

trying, Lerner convinced a food company to use the idea as a giveaway prize in cereal boxes. They offered George $5,000 to buy the idea outright. "That was a lot of money in 1951," Ellman said. "Not bad for a little raw potato." George took it. If not for a fateful trip to a small play kit company, the toy that became Mr. Potato Head might have remained a breakfast trinket.

Brothers Henry and Hillel Hassenfeld formed Hassenfeld Brothers, Inc. in 1923 to sell scrap textiles. Once stuck with an excess inventory of book-binding cloth, they decided to make pencil boxes. Over the years, they turned their box-making enterprise into a school supply company by filling their boxes with pencils, erasers, compasses and rulers. A doctor's kit and nurse's kit followed, and the Hassenfeld Brothers' line of play kits was born. When Henry's son Merrill later joined the company, he expanded the idea to include a mailman's kit, a cosmetics kit and others. Then one day in 1951, George Lerner showed Henry and Merrill a box filled with plastic face parts.

Merrill loved it. More than any other kit they had produced, this one was *fun*. Compared to their Junior Air Raid kit (no, really), this one was downright silly. The war was over and despite the controversy over wasting food, the Hassenfelds decided that maybe it was time to let a kid be a kid again. They were sold on the idea; unfortunately, the idea had been sold to a cereal company. Regardless, the Hassenfelds didn't give up. According to Ellman, they contacted the owners and offered them $2,000 to stop production and an additional $5,000 reimbursement for the money they had paid George for the idea. Lucky for all of us, the cereal company agreed. Lerner then signed a new deal where the Hassenfelds paid him a $500 advance against a 5% royalty on every kit sold. Since potatoes were a staple and seemed to be the produce that worked best when pierced with the plastic parts, it was named Mr. Potato Head.

On April 30, 1952, Hassenfeld Brothers (later Hasbro) did something that no other toy company had ever done. They put a toy on television.

Just five years earlier, only 250,000 TV sets were in use in the United States. By the end of 1951, just before the launch of Hasbro's new toy, there were nearly 8 million, by 1955 the number mushroomed to 32 million. Television had reached the baby boomers, who watched awestruck as that magical box of flickering gray pictures introduced them to their new friend. "Meet Mr. Potato Head," the TV voice said. "The most wonderful friend a boy or girl could have." And with that came those immortal words parents have heard a million times since: "Ooo, I want *that!*" Hasbro changed forever the marketing of toys when they sold over one million Mr. Potato Head Funny-Face Kits in the first year.

When it was released, the Mr. Potato Head kit contained no potato, just a Styrofoam head to give kids a clear picture of what it was they were supposed to do with all the wonderful Potato Head paraphernalia in the package. In fact, the original set contained 30 accessories including a body, hands, feet, ears, two mouths, two pair of eyes, four noses, three hats, eye glasses, a tobacco pipe, and eight felt pieces cut out to resemble facial hair—all for just 98 cents! Soon after its release, Hasbro added an order form to each kit that read, "Hey Kids! Get Loads of Extra Mr. Potato Head Parts—50 Different Pieces for Only 50¢."

Mr. Potato Head's continued success and our nation's post-war affluence gave children of the '50s the unalienable right to accessorize their favorite spud. In kits that followed, Mr. and Mrs. Potato Head got a car, a boat trailer, a kitchen set, a stroller and even pets known as the Spud-ettes. In 1964 our favorite potato got something really special . . . his very own head.

Mr. and Mrs. POTATO HEAD
the joyful toy of 1001 faces!

1950s

MR. POTATO HEAD

Hasbro introduced Mrs. Potato Head in 1953. That same year the couple produced a son named Spud and a sweet potato of a daughter named Yam.

1950s

MR. POTATO HEAD

Mr. Potato Head unveiled his new plastic head in 1964, complete with ready-made holes for the insertion of the face parts, hats, a pipe, and glasses.

News Flash: Kids don't always put away their toys (*Gasp!*) and all organic matter eventually rots (*Yuck!*). This volatile combination meant that Mr. Potato Head, with his organic noggin, really grew on us over time, especially when abandoned under the sofa for a few days. This probably influenced Hasbro's introduction of a plastic potato head, but the real agent of change was the new safety regulations within the toy industry. The sharp-pronged accessories in the original Mr. Potato Head kit had to go.

When Hasbro saw that the change didn't slow sales, they introduced a line of plastic-headed friends for the Potato Head family, called the Tooty Frooty Friends. With only one fruit in the bunch, the name made about as much sense as another set from this era: Mr. Potato Head on the Moon. Courtesy of themed play sets, Mr. Potato Head became the tuber-turned-tourist and visited other hot spots in the late '60s including the Wild West, a Circus, a Masquerade Party, a Parade, a Farm and the Railroad.

Things only got stranger. In 1974 his head doubled in size and his legs and arms disappeared—he was now a head resting on two big feet. These kits had fewer accessories that were larger, changed this time to conform to safety standards concerning choking hazards. For some reason he also became much darker with the new makeover, looking more like a Mr. Slightly Over-Cooked Potato Head. Various size slots

replaced the round holes in his head, a change that allowed the pieces to be inserted in only one direction. "Where was the fun in that?" asked Dennis Martin, a Mr. Potato Head collector and creator of the website www.potatoheadcollector.com. "No more crooked mouths or twisted ears!"

Thankfully, the '80s marked a turnaround. Mr. Potato Head acquired the more realistic golden brown color and basic shape we recognize today. His arms returned along with round holes that replaced the awkward slots. "Once again you could stick a cockeyed nose in his ear hole or have the freedom to give him feet growing out of his head," Martin enthused. For him and others, this was a step back to the best kits—the ones for use with real potatoes.

The '80s version improved over sets of the past with the addition of Mr. Potato Head's patented drawbridge posterior. For the first time all those accessories had a place to be stored. Kids may still have trouble picking up after themselves, but at least the "I lost the box" excuse is history.

Through the late '80s and into the '90s his popularity and emerging personality helped launch his career as spokes-potato. In 1987, Mr. Potato Head surrendered his tobacco pipe to the U.S. Surgeon General in support of the American Cancer Society's Great American Smokeout. In 1992, he lent a hand by giving up his couch potato reputation and received an award from Arnold Schwarzenegger and the President's Council for Physical Fitness. Four years later Mrs. Potato Head and he joined the League of Women Voters in a campaign that encouraged Americans to vote. Mr. Potato Head had transcended his

In 1964, vegetables Katie Carrot, Pete the Pepper, and Cooky the Cucumber joined Oscar Orange as the oddly titled Tooty Frooty Friends.

Mr. Potato Head lost his arms and legs in 1974 and he was not happy about it.

standing as a plaything, and for the first time his *image* had become bigger than his brand name. And he wasn't finished yet.

In 1995 Mr. Potato Head appeared in the Disney/Pixar Pictures hit movie, *Toy Story*. Don Rickles supplied the voice in a persona that presented Mr. Potato Head as a cynic, but somehow lovable just the same. Even without legs, Mr. Potato Head was hip! With his appeal now broadened to include adults, Hasbro released sacks of Mr. Potato Head merchandise. In 1998, the first toy to ever be advertised on television got his own TV show, airing on The Fox Kids Network and featuring him as a Muppet-like character. Just one year after that, he returned to the big screen in 1999's *Toy Story 2*.

Today he's a celebrity icon, having conquered the toy world and tinsel town. Mr. Potato Head has appeared on merchandise as diverse as neckties, boxer shorts, vibrating massagers, inflatable chairs, salt & pepper shakers and beauty aids. He's adorned T-shirts, hats, pajamas, slippers and the pages of numerous children's books. He's been the focus of board games, handheld electronic games and computer games. His drawing power has made him a premium toy at Burger King, McDonald's, Wendy's and Hardee's. It's no surprise that he has harvested multigenerational appeal—he's been a top-selling toy for over *half a century,* and today remains one hot potato.

THE PLAYMAKERS
Now and Then

Mr. Potato Head has always been synonymous with fun. Today he is as lovable as he was 52 years ago.

Debut: 1927
U.S. Debut: 1952
Inventor: Edward Haas III
Company: Pez Candy, Inc.

Pez

THE TOY THAT KEEPS ON GIVING

In the 1982 movie *E.T. The Extra-Terrestrial*, a little boy named Elliot tries in vain to describe Pez to the little guy from space. You don't need to be from another galaxy to wonder what on earth were they thinking?

Try to explain this humanoid candy cylinder to the uninitiated and the world of Pez rears its peculiar head. First you take Snoopy or whatever lovable cartoon character that adorns the top of your dispenser and pull his head off his body. Next you take the 12 candy bricks (which look for all the world like a spinal column) and insert them into his stemlike body. Now, just bend Snoopy's head waaaaay back and viola! The candy is pushed out from his throat area. Welcome to earth, where over 3 billion of these little candies are sold each year.

With the momentum of 76 years on the market and a fan base that spans generations, Pez has triumphed over its weirdness as the first interactive candy. Yes, the long road to Spin-Pops and Pop Rocks was paved by all those Pez candy bricks. The cool dispenser stands as the first toy that *gave you candy,* and to a kid, what could possibly be better than that? Truth is, the phenomenal popularity of Pez has always been more about the toy dispenser. The candies as E.T. discovered, taste more like Rolaids than Reese's Pieces. Any big league pitcher or stand-up comedian will tell you; sometimes it's in the delivery.

Austrian Edward Haas III didn't intend for his mint to become a candy, much less a toy. In 1927, Haas was a successful food company executive in Vienna when he developed an inexpensive way to make compressed mints from peppermint oil and sugar. They were originally formed in their classic rectangular shape so that they could be wrapped quickly and easily by machine. Marketed as a strong breath mint for adults and used as an alternative to smoking, these little rectangular

It has been presumed that the first character Pez dispenser was this "full body" Santa Claus from the 1950s.

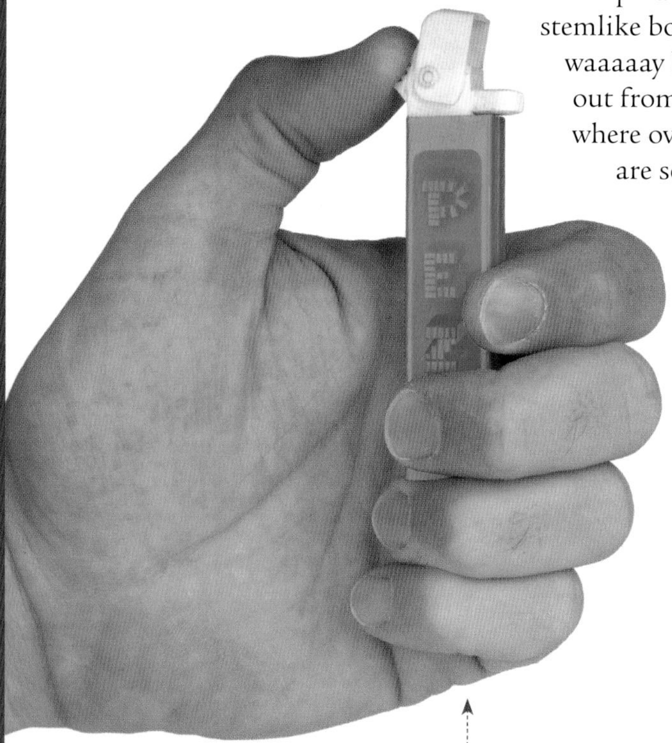

In 1948, to sell its benefit to smokers who were trying to quit (or mask their breath), Edward Haas hit on the idea of stacking his mints inside a dispenser that looked like a cigarette lighter.

Pez produced sexy ads like this one throughout the late '40s and early '50s. Influenced by the "Varga" girl paintings of Alberto Vargas, the "PEZ girls" clearly established Pez as an adult breath mint.

treats sold in pocket tins named Pez, after the abbreviated German word for peppermint—**P**feff**E**rmin**Z**.

In 1948, Haas engineered his first dispenser. It resembled a cigarette lighter and could be operated with one hand. Pez, Inc. touted its "easy, hygienic" properties. Today, these dispensers are known to the Pez collecting community as "regulars." What was next for Pez was anything but that.

In 1952 Pez came to the United States, but the American palate was not ready for such an intense peppermint breath mint (years later, the very successful Altoids proved that Pez was just ahead of its time). To crack the American market, the company did some consumer research, and the resulting changes meant a major makeover for the mint. After repositioning it as a candy, the company made Pez in fruit flavors.

To fit their new younger audience, the "cigarette lighter" had to go, and someone at Pez (no one knows exactly who) decided that topping them off with big plastic heads would do the trick. It's reported that Edward Haas didn't approve of this direction, but regardless of his concerns, these new character dispensers made his candy line an international success.

It is believed that the first Pez dispenser with a cartoon head was either Mickey Mouse or Popeye. Both dispensers pictured here date to the early '50s.

STAYING TOONED

Pez is the *Rolling Stone* cover of the cartoon world. Characters that have been immortalized in polystyrene over the years read like a virtual comic Hall of Fame: there's Daffy, Dopey, Droopy, Snoopy, Tweety, Speedy, Winnie, Wile E., Bozo, Pluto, Zorro, Dumbo, Leonardo, and Mario. From Spider-Man to Wolfman, Captain Hook to Captain America.

Approximately 35 dispensers are released each year, with a large number of dispensers being company creations and not famous cartoon characters. Holiday characters like Santa Claus (featuring just his head this time) and the Easter Bunny are popular, with Halloween having the greatest influence on new releases. In the past, characters like Mr. Ugly, Dr. Skull, and The Eerie Spectres series all spooked kids, but gave them candy nonetheless. A personal favorite was the One-Eye Monster that was released in the '60s, but returned a decade later having found his missing eye and the new name, Gorilla.

If yanking a candy brick out of a cartoon character's throat wasn't weird enough, the Pez company topped that

1950s

PEZ

It doesn't matter if you're Darth or Daffy, make it atop one of these plastic pedestals and you're a character that's truly arrived.

Pez Armory: The Pez Space Gun (top) was released in 1956 and remained on the market until the mid-'60s when it was replaced by the Pez Candy Shooter (modeled after a .32 caliber pistol). Finally in the early '80s, when Star Wars and its sequels fueled the space craze, Pez introduced its second version of a Space Gun.

by a long shot in 1956. That's when the first Pez gun came out and the collective parenting community cringed as kids put the barrel in their mouths and shot Pez candies in the back of their own throats. "Shoots delicious Pez candy bullets!" ads for the guns read.

Other non-character Pez dispensers included the Baseball Glove, Ball & Bat, whistles and even truck series (the only Pez dispensers designed to be viewed horizontally instead of on end). But more than anything, it was the characters that drove Pez sales.

Perhaps prompted by the royalties that Pez had to pay to the owners of these cartoon creations, in the '60s the company created its own line of characters called PezPals. They looked suspiciously like *Peanuts* characters with strange interchangeable hairpieces, hats and other prop parts. Speaking of props, the most sought-after Pez is the ultra-rare Make-a-Face Pez, which came with face parts, like a miniature Mr. Potato Head. It was introduced in the early '70s and then pulled off the market after only a few months due to safety concerns. This little collection of plastic pieces—which probably cost less then 25 cents to mold back then—can now fetch over $4,000 from fanatical collectors.

The '80s marked the beginning of Pez-mania, with collectors sending prices for discontinued or "retired" Pez dispensers sky-high. Plastic feet were added to the dispensers in 1987 to make them more displayable. Today there are no less than twenty-five websites and at least four books dedicated to Pez collecting. Five annual Pez conventions take place every year, including PEZ-A-MANIA in Cleveland, PEZ-A-THON in Los Angeles and the National Pez Convention in St. Louis.

Pez Candy, Inc. remains a privately held company with annual sales across 60 countries estimated at $27 million. All Edward Haas was trying to do, way back in 1927, was make a mint. He did it twice.

★ Because company records have never been released to the public, no one knows for sure how many Pez dispenser models have been made. Estimates range from 250 to nearly 300.

★ The only real people to be featured as Pez dispensers were Daniel Boone, Betsy Ross and Paul Revere. The company cites the fact that the human head is just too boring.

★ There never was an Elvis Pez dispenser made for consumers, but when a handmade prop appeared in the movie *The Client,* it sent the collector community into a frenzy. There have been Elvis sightings ever since.

★ New York was home to the Pez candy factory until 1973, when it moved to (appropriately) Orange, Connecticut. Dispensers are made in Austria.

Pez in Cyberspace

A quick search on eBay, the premier online auction website, can turn up from 3,500 to 4,000 auctions for Pez paraphernalia. Founded in 1995 by programmer Pierre Omidyar, eBay has nearly 45 million registered users and growing. How did it all start? As a home page Omidyar set up so that his girlfriend could sell some of her Pez collection. Add "The candy that launched a billion bids" to the Pez resume.

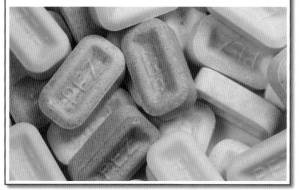

One of the most coveted non-character Pez dispensers is the Psychedelic Eye from the 1960s, also known as the Luv Pez.

Debut: 1953
Inventors: David N. Mullany and his son, David A. Mullany
Company: Wiffle Ball, Inc.

Wiffle Ball

WIFFLE'S BIG BREAK

Long before baseball became our National Pastime, it was a pastoral game played in wide open spaces. As its popularity grew, baseball spread into our suburbs and cities. In the 1830s a law was passed in Cooperstown, New York, restricting the play of baseball after shop owners complained about too many broken windows. They didn't know it at the time, but what the future home of the Baseball Hall of Fame needed wasn't another law, it was the Wiffle ball.

In 1952, 13-year-old David A. Mullany had an unquenchable need to play baseball but was faced with the friendly confines of his own backyard. Not content to give up on his game, David and his friends devised a way to play using a broomstick and perforated plastic golf ball. The ball worked well because no matter how hard he and friends connected with it, their ball was too light to travel very far and too soft to break any windows. Unfortunately, it was also next to impossible to make the ball curve and "break" like a big league pitcher. David tried harder and harder to snap off his curve, and inevitably complained to his dad that his arm "felt like jelly." His father, David N. Mullany, a former semi-pro pitcher, realized that throwing curveballs with a real baseball was hard enough on a young arm, let alone trying with such a small, light ball. Concerned, he set out to create a ball that would curve on its own.

The development of the ball that befuddles batters began with a rather unlikely source. The original Wiffle ball prototypes were hand cut from spherical moldings used to package Coty perfume bottles, procured through a friend who worked at a nearby cosmetics factory. The elder Mullany discovered these round plastic containers were just slightly smaller than a baseball. But, like many playthings chronicled in this book, the sweet smell of success was a long way off.

The former pitcher surmised that if he made the ball lighter on one side, it would curve. With a razor blade and some tape, David sat down at his kitchen table and cut the round plastic moldings in half. After taping a hemisphere in which he had cut holes to one that was complete, he gave the makeshift ball to his boy for testing. It didn't curve. After many trips back to the kitchen table, the father-son team learned that the shape and placement of the holes (and not necessarily the lopsided weight), held the keys to altering the ball's flight. Over the next few weeks father and son tested dozens of prototypes, all hand cut and taped together by the senior Mullany.

When the new ball's design was finally perfected—virtually anyone could throw

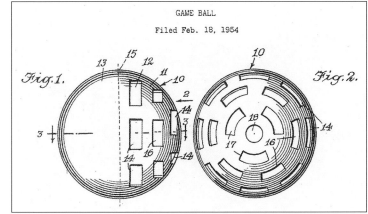

David Mullany filed a patent on his ball in early 1954. Eventually, however, a ball with eight oblong holes worked even better, and the definitive Wiffle ball design was discovered.

a pitch that would curve two feet or more—Mullany decided to venture into the toy business. David A., the boy who gave his dad the inspiration to develop the ball in the first place, also gave the ball its now famous name. This new ball was so hard to hit, it made batters "whiff," baseball slang for "strike out swinging."

When the elder David failed to get all the financing he needed, he borrowed money from friends and mortgaged his home to market the newly christened Wiffle ball. If fate meant for his new business to strike out, David N. Mullany decided that he was going to strike out swinging.

After buying an injection molding machine and leasing space in a nearby Woodbridge, Connecticut factory, the Mullany family business was off and running. Their first sale was to Three Judges Restaurant, a diner just down the street from the factory.

This unlikely outlet sold the Wiffle ball from its front window at the 1953 price of 49 cents. A humble start for sure, but one that led to orders from local sporting goods stores.

WIFFLE LANDS IN WOOLWORTH'S

Soon word of mouth propelled the ball beyond the backyards of Connecticut. Wiffle Ball, Inc. snagged its first major order from the dominant retailer at the time, Woolworth's. They were skeptical, but David closed the deal by throwing the Wiffle ball against the buyer's office window. Impressed, the buyer relented and the Wiffle ball was on its way.

The rules enclosed with the earliest balls suggested using a broom handle as a bat, but by 1954, just a year after the ball's debut, David had contracted with a wooden handle manufacturer to produce the very first Wiffle bat, called the Wiffle King. It was 31 inches long and had a barrel that was only $1\frac{1}{8}$ inches in diameter, not much thicker than the broomstick that inspired it. The classic yellow plastic bat did not show up for another seven years (see sidebar on page 108.)

Wiffle began in David's mind as just a ball that could curve, but with the help of his son, he shrewdly released it with instructions for an entirely new game. In 1953 (and today), kids faced three daunting obstacles if they wanted to play a game of baseball: Not enough players, not enough room, and not enough money for expensive

David A. Mullany (left) poses with his father, David N. Mullany, and their curving sensation. This publicity photo was taken in the mid-'80s for Wiffle Ball Inc.'s 30th Anniversary.

The first Wiffle ball, from 1955, was "designed to take the place of baseball in confined areas."

In the late '50s, the Mullanys made a two-piece, plastic bat by injection molding; however, little hands tended to be pinched where the two halves snapped together so that idea was abandoned. A process called blow molding (where air is forced into plastic "melts" encased within molds), made it feasible to make a plastic bat more efficiently, and the classic yellow Wiffle bat debuted in 1962.

equipment. The very first Wiffle balls came with a flyer that explained the solution:

. . . Wiffle Ball was designed to take the place of baseball and stick ball for boys and girls in back yards and city streets. It is made of a tough rubbery plastic—will not break glass or damage property—is light in weight and cannot be thrown or hit any great distance . . . ball chasing and base running have been eliminated . . . the minimum number of players required to play Wiffle Ball is two—the pitcher and batter—one player to a side.

The directions also suggested using an area 20 feet by approximately 60 feet, with scoring areas spaced away from the batter at 20-feet intervals. Hit a ball that lands uncaught up to 20 feet from home plate and you score a single. A distance of 21–40 feet is a double, 41–60 feet is a triple, and launch one more than 60 feet uncaught and you clear the bases without running a step. Of course, most of us had our own ground rules, which made a game of Wiffle Ball even more fun and uniquely our own.

The corner deck and clothesline posts marked the foul lines in my boyhood backyard. Anything off the tool shed was a ground rule double; into the oak tree branches scored a home run. Our strike zone was always a lawn chair set up against the side of our house. Years later we were still playing, having graduated to a new and bigger ball park—our high school parking lot. We were a little more official at that grander asphalt field, but the old lawn chair remained from our backyard days. The *clank* of the ball hitting the chair and the *clack* of the bat remain vivid memories of summers past.

By 1959, the success of their balls and bats allowed Wiffle Ball, Inc. to move into a modest two-story brick office/factory in Shelton, Connecticut. David A. Mullany, the 13-year-old who inspired his dad, started

Over 1,000 teams of 3 to 5 players compete in regional tournaments like the Suncoast Challenge in the hopes of making it all the way to the USPPBA Championship, which takes place each summer.

working for the company in the 1960s and became its president sometime in the early '70s. By the time Wiffle Ball entered its twentieth year in 1973, it was evident that kids weren't the only ones playing.

In the mid-'90s, the Internet began to connect older players with others of their kind; full-grown adults excited to find they were not alone in their passion for plastic. So in 2001, players from all over the country formed the United States Perforated Plastic Baseball Association. The USPPBA

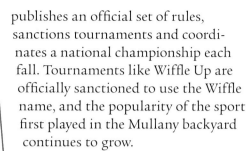

publishes an official set of rules, sanctions tournaments and coordinates a national championship each fall. Tournaments like Wiffle Up are officially sanctioned to use the Wiffle name, and the popularity of the sport first played in the Mullany backyard continues to grow.

Today, David A. Mullany's sons, David J. and Stephen Mullany, run the company their grandfather started a half century ago while resisting buyouts from the bigger toy and sporting goods conglomerates. "We're approached to

Pick Your Stick

The first Wiffle bat, the wooden Wiffle King, was produced for a limited time in 1954. The second generation of the wooden bat was the Official Wiffle Bat, made from 1955–1972. The classic, plastic yellow bat followed in 1962. In 1999, in response to the growing number of adult players, the Mullany family contracted with The Adeline Bat Company to make the first aluminum Wiffle bat.

sell all the time," says the third David to preside over Wiffle Ball, Inc. "We just really love what we're doing. We're making a product that people enjoy and have fun with." David's brother Stephen agrees. "Truthfully, we can't see ourselves doing anything else. It's a unique business." The summer of 2003 marked the 50th Anniversary of this unique business—a business of fun and family.

David N. Mullany died in 1990 at the age of 81. He saw his invention reach millions, passed the reins of his company to his son, and was alive to see it then passed on to his grandsons. "He was a really neat guy," says grandson David J. "I had a few years with him [at Wiffle Ball, Inc.] and I'm glad I had that opportunity."

The Mullany family does not divulge sales figures, saying only that they sell millions of balls per year. A hint of their success comes from one of their best accounts, The Connecticut Store, an outlet that has proudly shipped orders of Wiffle balls and bats to every state in the nation and 26 different countries. That's a long way for a ball to travel, especially from its rather modest beginning in the window of a small town diner.

To those who call themselves "Wifflers," the appeal of this classic plaything is deeply rooted in a place beyond the ball and beyond the game. It's better defined with words like *tradition, ritual* and even *rite of passage*. "It's incredible," says Hank Paine, president of The Connecticut Store. "We get young kids writing us. We get fathers saying 'I've been playing Wiffle Ball my whole life!' Then you get the grandfathers who were taught to play baseball with a Wiffle ball. I've seen it with my own grandkids, I keep getting slower and they keep getting faster, but Wiffle Ball stays the same."

In the face of corporate buyout attempts, it's comforting to know that Wiffle Ball Incorporated hasn't changed. It remains a family-owned company powered by just 12 full-time employees. They work to make a legendary product that continues to fly in the face of the $25 billion toy industry, which decrees that hit toys must be heavily advertised. Low overhead and no advertising budget mean you can still buy a

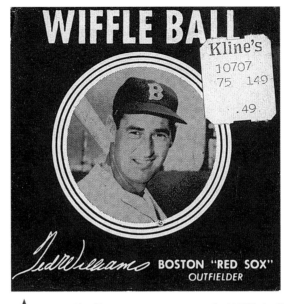

The first star to appear on the Wiffle ball box in the early '50s was Ted Williams. The last big leaguer to pitch for Wiffle ball was Rick Sutcliffe in the '80s.

Wiffle ball and bat set for under $3.50. In these days of greed, when for the love of money Major League Baseball players have insulted their fans in recent years with talk of "work stoppages," Wiffle Ball reminds us of a simpler time when playing was for the love of the game and the only "strike" you feared was your father's wicked Wiffle curve.

Wiffle balls are still made in the U.S.A. in Shelton, Connecticut.

In 1960, New York Yankee Pitcher Whitey Ford appeared in TV ads throwing a Wiffle ball against a plate glass window in order to show what the new ball would, and, thankfully, wouldn't do. Sales only increased enough to cover cost of the ads, and the Wiffle ball hasn't been advertised since.

If the Wiffle ball packaging seems frozen in time, it's by design. The artwork on the box is virtually identical today as it appeared in 1953. "The product doesn't change," David J. Mullany says. "That's one of the things we hear from people that they like. The balls are identical to the originals and the bats don't change from year to year. When we have new molds built, we use the original specs."

Debut: 1953
U.S. Debut: 1954
Founders of Lesney: Leslie
  Smith, Rodney Smith
Inventor: Jack Odell
Insiders: Moses and
  Richard Kohnstam, Fred
  Bronner
Companies: Lesney
  Products, Universal,
  Tyco, Mattel

Matchbox

INSIDE THE HOT BOX

Ever since I bought my first Matchbox car, I imagined building a flat-roofed, rectangular garage and painting it to look like a vintage Matchbox package. To further fuel this fantasy, I dreamed of pulling a real 1979 Corvette T-Top out of that cool, yellow and blue building. Or maybe easing a sleek 1962 Jaguar XKE inside, just before the door of the garage (flap of the box) closed behind the Jag's cherry-red trunk. It's a horrendously expensive fantasy, but one to which millions of collectors of Matchbox vehicles can relate. Thankfully, the hobby of collecting *die cast* cars has remained affordable, even after 90 years.

A shared boyhood in Enfield, England, made Leslie Smith and Rodney Smith friends, but it was a chance meeting some 20 years later that made them business partners. After their World War II service in the English Royal Navy, the two men went into business in 1947, combining their names to form Lesney Products. With £600 pooled from their military service pay, the partners bought a condemned tavern in war-torn London and some surplus die casting machinery. From this pub-turned-production facility, the two men helped rebuild

The first "Matchbox" vehicle was this No. 1 Diesel Road Roller, released in 1953.

While Dowst Manufacturing Company (later known as Tootsie Toy) mass-produced the first die cast car, a Ford Model T, another legendary name in die cast emerged across the Atlantic. Dinky vehicles started off in 1933 with the name Modelled Minatures because they were introduced as accessories to the successful toy train business of Liverpool's Meccano Company. Intended to bring realism to elaborate train layouts, Dinky vehicles were well detailed and soon rivaled the

Dowst Manufacturing's "Ford Tourer" was first made in 1914. It is believed to be the first mass-produced die cast car.

hugely successful toy train, eventually surpassing it in popularity. The path driven by Matchbox was blazed by Dowst, Dinky and other early die casters.

Die casting is the process of injecting a molten metal, like zinc, into a heated mold and then allowing it to solidify. When the piece (button, Monopoly token, toy car) has been sufficiently cooled, it's removed from the mold and trimmed of rough edges. The cleaned mold is then ready for the next "shot." The process takes only a few seconds and allows for the production of highly detailed items inexpensively and in mass quantites. No other die cast brand of toys would take fun to the masses like Matchbox.

their homeland by making die cast industrial parts and products.

Lesney Products may have remained an industrial manufacturer had destiny not stepped in. Less than a year after starting their company the Smiths rented space to an old acquaintance, a skilled die caster and mold designer named Jack Odell who envisioned starting his own casting company. After Odell landed a 10,000-piece order for a ceiling plate from General Electric (the very first mold he had designed for his new venture), Rodney and Leslie offered him a full partnership in Lesney Products.

Shortly thereafter, Odell developed a way to die cast that greatly eliminated the excess metal seepage from the area where the two halves of a mold met. Very little "finishing" was required, and this streamlined process reduced Lesney's unit price, giving them a distinct advantage over their competitors. Then Odell created dies for the first Lesney toys based on a line of toy vehicles by Dinky. In 1948, the company introduced the Diesel Road Roller, followed by other large scale toy vehicles that measured 3 $\frac{1}{4}$ inches to nearly 5 inches long. Because of Odell's new casting technique, these early models featured the same quality and detail as the Dinky models, but sold for a third of their price.

In 1949, Lesney introduced three additional vehicles and was just putting the final touches on the production dies for a 15 $\frac{3}{4}$-inch toy coach to commemorate the 25th wedding anniversary of King George VI and Queen Elizabeth, when a war halted production. Just five years removed from World War II, the trio of entrepreneurs was stopped in their tracks by another conflict, this time in Korea.

In 1950, restrictions on the use of zinc for nonessential products nearly crippled Lesney. Zinc was the primary metal used in die casting inexpensive toys and without it Lesney was in dire straits. The Wedding Coach was held out of production and the firm tried

to diversify into tin toys but they did not sell well. Rodney Smith became so discouraged that he left the company. Leslie Smith and Jack Odell weathered the storm, which eventually lifted in 1952, along with the ban on zinc.

Money was still tight—and it certainly didn't help that the expensive dies for the Wedding Anniversary Coach were gathering dust—when on February 6, 1952, King George died. As all of Britain prepared for the throne to pass to his daughter, Elizabeth II, inspiration struck. Lesney's Wedding Coach became a Coronation Coach, and the toy was released just before the official ascension of the new queen on June 2, 1953. The Coronation Coach was Lesney's first hit toy, reportedly selling 33,000 units. Smith and Odell next decided to make a smaller version of their Coronation Coach, and the miniature toy was a massive hit.

1950s

MATCHBOX

At left is one of Lesney's first toys, their 1948 Cement Mixer. At right is the scaled down version that became part of Lesney's Matchbox series in 1953.

Lesney's first vehicles were modeled after Dinky Toys like this "Dumper Truck." At first Lesney's toys were identical in size to Dinky, but in 1953, they were reduced to "Matchbox" size.

Lesney's 15¾-inch Coronation Coach was released in 1952 with great success, however when they reduced it to a 4½-inch size in 1953, it apparently became irresistible, selling over 1 million units and inspiring the launch of Matchbox.

Around the same time, as legend has it, Odell's oldest daughter had a "show and tell" event at school where the toys and trinkets the kids could present were limited in size—they had to fit in a matchbox. When even the small version of Lesney's Coronation Coach proved too big, Odell made a tinier version of his company's Road Roller for his little girl crafted out of brass. When all her friends wanted a tiny Roller too, Lesney Products obliged. Although they weren't the first company to offer toys in a matchbox-style package (that idea already existed in Germany before the war), Lesney was the first to use (and ultimately own) the legendary Matchbox trademark.

Flush with money from the phenomenal sales of the miniature Coronation Coach, Lesney financed the development of their new line. The vehicles in the Matchbox series were a Road Roller (No.1), Dumper truck (No. 2), Cement Mixer (No. 3), and Tractor (No. 4). These toys were die cast at an irresistibly small size never before seen, yet held an impressive amount of detail. Kids wanted all of those brightly colored boxes

with the toys tucked inside, and at the equivalent price of 40 cents each, parents let them have their way. The Matchbox series turned into a mini-gold mine for Lesney, and by the end of 1954, they phased out their line of larger vehicles.

In 1956, Jack Odell had the idea for a line of exquisitely detailed toys. Concentrating on vintage vehicles from the early half of the 1900s, he called his new line Models of Yesteryear, the beginning of a broader range for Matchbox featuring everything from buses, tramcars and luxury Bentleys, to locomotives, steam wagons and even a motorcycle with sidecar.

The years 1958 to 1968 proved to be the pinnacle of Matchbox success. Lesney went public in 1960, and in 1964 set their sights on America. Back in 1954, Lesney had contracted with American entrepreneur, Fred Bronner, to distribute their growing die cast series throughout the United States. Ten years later, Bronner was handpicked to lead Lesney Products (U.S.A.) and made Matchbox an American toy legend. According to Richard J. Scholl's book, *Matchbox Official 50th Anniver-*

The packaging for the SuperFast line was something special. Eye-popping paintings of cars in action (at extreme angles and perspectives) graced the famous yellow boxes. By 1971 most of the Matchbox line was converted to the SuperFast style.

sary Commemorative Edition, 100 million Matchbox vehicles were sold in 1966, and in three years that number had grown to 286 million—with 40% of sales coming from the United States. Matchbox had become a global name, and true to the first vehicle they made back in 1948, Lesney was rolling over their competitors.

That is, until Mattel released Hot Wheels.

THE NEED FOR SPEED

It's certainly true that the appeal of any toy vehicle is the promise of movement. But more than just a means of transportation, toy cars and trucks offer a fantasy and means of escape. Matchbox may have given us vehicles, but Hot Wheels gave us getaway cars.

By creating a die cast car with thin wire axles that allowed its wheels to turn with far less friction, Hot Wheels were by far the fastest toy cars on the market when they were released in 1968. Fueled by a high-octane, $10 million advertising campaign, Mattel promoted Hot Wheels full throttle. While the Matchbox series gave kids a world of travel, it lacked the sleek models and hot paint jobs present in the Hot Wheels line. Matchbox, for a short time anyway, got left in the dust.

According to Scholl, Matchbox sales plummeted from $28 million to $6 million after the release of Hot Wheels. Reacting quickly and efficiently, Lesney retooled in the latter part of 1969 and got back in the race with their own version of a low-friction car called SuperFast. The scorching new line featured hot rods

"What's a Moko?"

With the success of the Matchbox Series came the challenges of increased distribution, marketing, advertising, warehousing; all aspects of the toy business for which Lesney was not equipped. Needing immediate assistance in many areas of the toy trade, Smith and Odell turned to a renowned toy agent.

Moses Kohnstam (MoKo) came to England in the early 1900s to develop the country's growing toy industry. He hailed from Nuremberg, Germany

and was a knowledgeable agent who specialized in packaging, marketing and promotion of toys in exchange for a percentage of sales. In 1953, Moses Kohnstam's grandson, Richard Kohnstam, was in charge of the East London company and negotiated a deal with Leslie Smith and Jack Odell that made Moko the worldwide distributor of the Matchbox line.

and dragsters alongside Lesney's proven work vehicles. Bolder paint schemes and flat-out cooler cars made SuperFast an immediate hit.

The Matchbox 1-75 series meant that from year to year, Lesney's basic line always contained 75 vehicles. They retired old models and introduced new ones, but 75 was always the magic number—unless you count the variants and oddities that are sought-after collector's items. For example: A red, 1973 Formula 1 Racer with a white plastic driver, in its original box, is worth about $10. However, that same model in yellow will sell for well over $300. It's a different world when the kids are steering a toy's popularity, but when collectors are at the wheel, prices are often driven sky high.

During the '70s Lesney Products endured work stoppages, a major fire, a devastating flood and the 1973 retirement of Jack Odell. Business was so bad that by 1980 Odell came out of retirement to help Leslie Smith save the company, but Mattel had begun making their Hot Wheels line in China and the price of labor in England could not compete. In early 1982, a loss of over $15 million led to bankruptcy. A company called Universal Toys bought the rights to the legendary Matchbox trademark and moved production overseas, while Jack Odell personally bought

The success of models like this Massey Harris Tractor from 1954 (pictured in the background), inspired Lesney to produce a line made up of mostly work vehicles. But with the phenomenal success of Mattel's Hot Wheels, Lesney was forced to make faster, sportier models.

much of the Lesney dies and machinery to launch his own die cast company called Lledo (Odell spelled backwards).

From 1982 through 1992, Matchbox vehicles rolled alongside the many die cast companies with which they shared the retail road. In 1986, that competitive landscape shrunk when Matchbox bought the Dinky trademark. The first Dinky vehicles produced under the Matchbox label debuted in 1989, 40 years after Jack Odell was inspired by Dinky to create Lesney's immortal die cast line.

The Matchbox brand became the property of Tyco Toys when they bought the Universal Group in 1992. Then, in an ironic twist of fate, the company that nearly drove Matchbox out of business in 1969 became its new owner in 1997 when Mattel bought Tyco Toys. Today Matchbox continues to share a garage with Hot Wheels under Mattel's ownership, where they position Hot Wheels for a slightly older audience with the theme of "speed" throughout the line, while keeping the Matchbox vehicles true to their classic origins, complete with dual themes of "work" and "rescue."

Mattel continues to sell more Matchbox vehicles per year than Ford, GM and Chrysler *combined*. Collectors may keep them untouched within their sealed plastic shells, but the future of Matchbox vehicles rests in the palm of a million little hands. As long as the next generation of die cast devotees gets down on their hands and knees to discover the racin', crashin', flippin', skiddin' magic, then Matchbox will always roll on.

In 1999, in a move that angered Matchbox purists (but pleased collectors who just want as many models as they can get), Mattel increased the range of vehicles in the Matchbox line to 100. The change lasted two years before the traditional "Matchbox 75" returned.

Fifty years after their introduction, Matchbox vehicles are still about a buck, even though they no longer arrive in the box that made them famous.

Play-Doh

1950s

Debut: 1955
Inventors: N. W. McVicker,
    Joe McVicker (1929-1992)
Developers: Kay and Bob
    Zufall, Bill Rhodenbaugh,
    Dr. Tien Liu
Companies: Kutol Products,
    Rainbow Crafts, General
    Mills, Kenner, Tonka,
    Hasbro

GOOD, CLEAN FUN

Cans of it are in preschools, nursery schools and tucked away in kitchen cupboards and family playrooms around the world. Recipes on how to make it continuously pop up in magazines and on the Internet as its maker, Hasbro, fights to keep its name from becoming a generic label for all "modeling compounds." Its status as one of the most beloved toy products ever created makes its origin one of the weirdest of all toy stories. Play-Doh, that moldable stuff from childhood—sold in 75 countries in the staggering quantity of 95 million cans a year—was first invented as commercial wallpaper cleaner.

The legend of Santa Claus leaving lumps of coal in the stockings of bad little children has given the fossil fuel a bad reputation. Yet it was because of coal, or more accurately the messiness of heating with coal, that Play-Doh came into being. From 1885 until about 1950, coal was our nation's most widely used heating fuel. It produced four times the energy of wood at about half the cost, with the only downside being the sooty mess that coal furnaces produced. Non-washable surfaces like wallpaper presented a particularly troublesome problem. Spring-cleaning time found homemakers kneading a dough mixture of flour, water, salt and borax and rolling it up and down their papered walls to pull off the coal soot. Soon companies began offering premixed wallpaper cleaner. Play-Doh's off-the-wall journey from cleaning compound to modeling compound began in 1927, at a dying Cincinnati soap company called Kutol Products.

Cleo McVicker was just 21 years old and working for Kutol Product's parent company in Chicago when he was told to drive down to Cincinnati, sell Kutol's inventory and shut the place down. In peddling the remaining supply of powdered hand soap, McVicker had enough success to convince the parent company to allow him to stay in Cincinnati and try to turn the failing business around. He hired his brother, N. W. McVicker, as plant manager and maker of heir various cleaning compounds, and hit the road as a soap salesman. The turnaround came in 1933. "That's when Cleo went to Kroger grocery stores and asked to bid on their wallpaper cleaner," Bill Rhodenbaugh, former Kutol president and McVicker in-law said. "At the time Kroger bought private label wallpaper cleaner, so they asked him 'Do you know how to make this stuff?' and he said 'Oh yeah, we can make it.' Cleo was so gutsy."

According to Rhodenbaugh, Cleo signed a $5,000 performance bond against the order, which meant that if he didn't ship 15,000 cases of wallpaper cleaner on time, it would cost Kutol $5,000, enough to put the brothers out of business. "Cleo came back and told his brother about the order and N. W. asked, 'Well how do you make it?' and Cleo said, 'Hell if I know! That's your job!'" Bill laughed as he told the story. "N. W. figured out how to make the cleaner in time to get the order out."

Tragedy and the collapse of their core product line struck Kutol after World War II. Cleo McVicker died in a private plane crash in 1949. His widow, Irma, inherited the company and hired her son Joe McVicker and her son-in-law Bill Rhodenbaugh to help fill the void that Cleo's death had created and to try to reverse the company's plummeting sales. "After the war, conversion furnaces (powered by oil or gas) came out and the soot problem was gone. Then vinyl wallpaper was introduced, which could be washed with soap and water. All of a sudden there wasn't much market for wallpaper cleaner," Rhodenbaugh said. "The business was not in good shape." As Kutol faced a major financial crisis, Joe McVicker had a much bigger concern. He was 25 years old and had just found out he was dying.

McVicker was diagnosed with Hodgkin's disease, a rare form of cancer. His entire family rallied to help, including his sister-in-law Kay Zufall. "My husband Bob was a doctor in training in Bellevue, New York so we brought Joe up there," Kay recalled. They operated but it was unsuccessful. Bill Rhodenbaugh remembers it well. "They sent him back to Cincinnati to die, and damn if he didn't beat it."

Cleo and N. W. McVicker made this nontoxic, malleable cleaner for over 20 years, eventually bought Kutol and became the largest wallpaper cleaner manufacturer in the world.

After rounds of experimental radiation treatment, McVicker was struggling to recover while the business slid further toward collapse. Christmastime had always been when wallpaper cleaner production peaked, so that by the end of winter shipments could reach stores in time for spring-cleaning. The holiday season of 1954 found the Kutol plant eerily quiet. It turned out to be the calm before the storm.

THE FUTURE TAKES SHAPE

In New Jersey, Joe's sister-in-law, Kay, spotted a magazine article on decorating for the holidays. "I ran a community nursery school at the time and I was looking for inexpensive ways to decorate when I read that you could make Christmas tree ornaments by using wallpaper cleaner," Kay shared. "I immediately drove out to the local hardware store and asked if they had Kutol wallpaper cleaner. They had a hard time finding me a can, but they did. I remember being very excited, I mean, here my brother-in-law was dying of cancer, his business was failing and I just might have something here they could make." Kay brought the doughlike material into her nursery and the kids loved it. "We rolled this stuff out, and then took cookie cutters and cut out the shapes. We put little holes at the tops and then I dried them out in the oven at home. Afterwards, we called Joe. I told him 'You can make that stuff into a toy!' So he flew out, looked at those ornaments hanging on our tree and said. 'My God, we'll do it.'"

"Joe came back and told us what Kay had suggested," Bill Rhodenbaugh recalled. "It was so simple. Here it was right in front of us!" Kutol wallpaper cleaner was nontoxic, and unlike clay, it didn't stain. So after N. W. removed the detergents, added colorant and replaced the solventlike smell with a subtler almond scent, Kutol began introducing a brand-new product that they had already been making for 22 years. "We used 2 ½ barrel, industrial bread mixers," Rhodenbaugh said, "which of course, we already had. We had the flour conveyers. We had everything we needed and ran it on the exact same lines as we did the wallpaper cleaner." In no time, Kutol's Rainbow Modeling Compound was ready to meet the world.

RAINBOW MODELING COMPOUND!?

"'You can't call it that!' Kay said she told her brother-in-law. "Bob and I talked about it. Neither of us can remember who thought of it, but we came up with the name Play-Doh." Bill concurred. "Joe told me that Kay thought of the name. I've read places it was called Magic Clay, but that's not true. It was Play-Doh from the beginning." Kay and Bob Zufall downplay their significance in toy history. "People ask us, 'You gave the name away?!' Well, who knew it would sell anything?" Kay laughs now. "Joe did the hard work. We had a part in it for sure, but if it hadn't been sold, it wouldn't have been anything."

Kay Zufall suggested the idea for the world's most popular modeling compound and then she and her husband Bob named it Play-Doh.

The new company Joe formed with Bill Rhodenbaugh and his uncle N. W. was set up as a subsidiary of Kutol Products. Their new product came in single-gallon cans with colored lids that indicated the color of the Play-Doh inside, which from the beginning

was red, blue or yellow. By mixing those primary colors, kids could make "any color in the rainbow," and so they named their new company Rainbow Crafts. The reason Play-Doh came in such big cans at first was that none of the partners believed they would be able to sell it direct to retailers, so they focused instead on schools. "I called on the Cincinnati Board of Education because I had been trying to sell them soap, so I knew some people over there," Rhodenbaugh said. Soon Play-Doh was in every elementary school in the city.

Joe McVicker then took it to an educational convention for companies that sold school supplies. There, Washington DC's Woodward & Lathrop department store became Rainbow Craft's first major retail account. By 1956, Rainbow Crafts added a three-pack of smaller, seven-ounce cans to their product line. With successful in-store demonstrations, the colorful stuff soon reached Macy's in New York and Marshall Field's in Chicago, but the real breakthrough came in 1957 when Play-Doh was featured on TV sets across America. How Rainbow Crafts, a start-up company with few financial resources ended up with a national TV campaign is a testament to Joe McVicker's gift of persuasion and the intuition of a man named

It has been said that Play-Doh only came in an off-white color when it was originally made. "Not true," says Bill Rhodenbaugh. "It came in three colors in 1955, red, blue and yellow. In fact, we didn't add white to the mix until 1958, when we came out with a four-pack."

Play-Doh's inventors first thought they'd only sell their creation in schools, but it was soon in stores all over the country.

Bob Keeshan, better known as Captain Kangaroo.

By everyone's account Joe McVicker was a charismatic salesman, and when he talked his way in to see Keeshan, he ended up closing the deal that made Play-Doh famous. "Keeshan liked Play-Doh and wanted it on his show," recounted Rhoden-baugh. "But Joe told him that we didn't have any money for adver-tising. So Joe offered him 2% of our sales if he would feature it on the show once a week. Well, the Captain liked it so much that he started putting it on three times a week! I don't think there was ever a contract, but I remember signing checks and sending them to his production company. After that we got on *Ding Dong School* (with Miss Francis) and *Romper Room*. We had the country saturated with television."

Once it hardened, Play-Doh could be "sanded, filed or cut," the packaging claimed. Next kids could "paint their perma-nent sculptures." Note the ashtray on this 1959 package.

PLAY-DOH GOES GONZO

Once Play-Doh hit, it took Rainbow Crafts over 16 months just to fill all the back orders. According to Rhodenbaugh, trying to keep up with the demand was fun and extremely profitable. "We would sell wallpaper cleaner for 34 cents a can, but Play-Doh—same stuff, same can—we could sell for $1.50. We were just a couple young kids in our mid-20s," he laughed. "It was one hell of a run." Kutol went from sales of under $100,000 in 1954 to owning and operating Rainbow Crafts with sales of nearly $3 million just four years later.

In the mid-'50s, Rainbow Crafts encouraged kids to allow Play-Doh to harden, because it dried out so quickly. By 1957, Joe McVicker had hired chemist

Dr. Tien Liu to help his uncle N. W. improve on the Play-Doh recipe. "Dr. Liu made endless batches, tinkering with the formula," Rhodenbaugh said. "In the beginning, after it dried, it turned white. Dr. Liu took a lot of the salt out of the formula and that kept it from drying out so fast and losing its color."

Joe McVicker and his uncle N. W. filed for their patent on Play-Doh on May 17, 1960 and then split Rainbow Crafts from Kutol, leaving Bill Rhodenbaugh to run the less profitable hand soap company. "Joe had 51% of the two companies and I had 49%," Rhodenbaugh recalled. "He came to me and said 'I want to own this [Rainbow Crafts] entirely myself and I'm gonna give you Kutol Products as your share.' Play-Doh exists because of at least a half a dozen key people, but Joe had an ego, so he took all the credit." Despite the split, Joe McVicker and Bill Rhodenbaugh remained business partners. "I bought the building right next door and we still worked together. Kutol did all the packaging for Rainbow Crafts for years."

Rainbow Crafts was shipping well over a million cans of Play-Doh a year when they began exporting to England, France and Italy in 1964. Its success within the merger-laden toy industry meant it was only a matter of time before a bigger fish was attracted to all that colorful dough. When General Mills offered Joe $3 million for Rainbow Crafts, a price comparable to over $18 million today, he took it. Bill Rhodenbaugh wouldn't have sold. "The Rainbow Crafts employees wanted to buy the company and that would have been great, but it was Joe's decision," Bill said. "After he sold Play-Doh, it became a staple in the industry." By 1972, a year after General Mills had placed Play-Doh under its Kenner brand, and just eight years from the time Joe had sold out, the 500 millionth can of Play-Doh reached the market.

A decade later in 1983, four new colors were added to the Play-Doh mix. Hasbro became its owner in 1991, and although some new scents have been introduced over the years, the original smell of Play-Doh remains one of Toyland's most wonderful things.

THE SWEET SMELL OF SUCCESS

I pop the lid on a new can of Play-Doh and after emptying its bright blue contents, place the can to my face like it's an airplane oxygen mask. I inhale deeply and then, as if actually *on* some magical aircraft, I travel to a different place. At once I am at my parents' dining room table. I can see the pattern of the tablecloth, I can hear my mother in the kitchen behind me and I can taste the cherry Kool-Aid—the drink I used as a chaser after I ate a super-salty morsel of Play-Doh. It's a wonderfully vivid visit, 30 years in the past.

Scientists call my trip a "Proustian Memory," named after novelist Marcel Proust, who, in a 1913 novel, described how the smell of a certain cake dipped into lime-blossom tea had caused a flood of powerful memories. We now know there's a biological reason for what Proust described and what Play-Doh delivers. The sensation of smell, the retrieval of memories and our emotions, are all processed on the right side of the brain and are, therefore, closely linked. According to aromatherapy experts, that link has the ability to reduce stress, increase energy, and restore the lost balance of the mind, body and soul. Of course, they're referring to scents like nutmeg and lime-blossom tea, certainly not Play-Doh. Yet, give any surly adult a sniff of this magical modeling compound and you'll witness a transformation as remarkable as any from the most fragrant frankincense. The pleasant aroma of Play-Doh can move us and yes, restore our lost balance to mind, body and soul. It smells a little like almonds, a

little like grammar school, and a whole lot like childhood.

Unlike Play-Doh, Joe McVicker's story did not have a happy ending. According to Rhodenbaugh, Joe squandered the money he earned from the sale of Rainbow Crafts and years later struggled with other personal problems. He died in 1992. "Joe's story after Play-Doh is just a sad one all round," Rhodenbaugh says. When he thinks of his former partner, Bill prefers to think of the early days of Play-Doh. "It was exciting with Joe back then, seeing something grow like that—those were good times."

Kay Zufall believes in Joe's contribution to childhood. "Play-Doh is a beautiful tribute to a young man who tried very hard and succeeded in saving a failing business. He made a profit, not only for himself, but

Play-Doh Pete

The earliest cans of Play-Doh featured some children on the label, but by the mid-'50s the Play-Doh Pixie (who looked like a cross between Elmer Fudd and Peter Pan) was introduced to the packaging. In 1960, this pointy-eared pitchman became a boy mascot garbed in artist's smock and beret. Play-Doh Pete was his name, and his look has changed over the years. Most recently he gave up his beret for a baseball cap.

Clockwise from upper right: 1959, 1962, 1972, 2002.

for the millions of children who have enjoyed Play-Doh. That's the beautiful part of the story."

More than *2 billion* cans of Play-Doh have been sold since 1955, enough to roll out a Play-Doh "snake" that would wrap around the earth nearly 300 times. On this sometimes frightening planet, it's comforting to know that kids can still take a lump of Play-Doh and hold the future in their hands. That's the legacy of Joe McVicker and his Play-Doh compatriots—a world that kids can mold themselves.

✦ Dr. Tien Liu helped perfect the formula of Play-Doh for Rainbow Crafts and went on to work for Kenner and then Hasbro for many years, as the world's only Play-Doh expert.

✦ Both Play-Doh and Captain Kangaroo debuted in 1955.

EPILOGUE: LIFE AFTER PLAY-DOH

✦ Kutol Products went on to become one of the largest and most respected manufacturers of industrial and institutional hand soap in the United States. Bill Rhodenbaugh is retired now and his two sons, Joe and Tom, run the Cincinnati-based company, whose historic past is steeped in Play-Doh.

✦ Kay and Bob Zufall manage a successful clinic for the underprivileged in Dover, New Jersey. The thriving and esteemed Dover Community Clinic is staffed by 20 volunteer doctors who receive over 12,000 patient visits a year.

Inside the Fun Factory

Debut: 1960
Inventors: Bob Bogill and Bill Dale
Companies: Kutol Products, Rainbow Crafts, General Mills, Kenner, Tonka, Hasbro

Bob Bogill and Bill Dale were engineers for General Electric when they came to Rainbow Crafts with an idea for a three-stage rocket toy. "Needless to say, it didn't fit into our preschool line," Play-Doh co-developer Bill Rhodenbaugh recalled. "Instead I asked them to

scratch their heads and see if they could figure out something that would help us sell Play-Doh. They came back a little while later and took a plant tour."

The sight of Play-Doh being born brought out the little boy inside each of these engineers. The colorful, doughy stuff was mixed and then came down the line and was dropped into a big hopper, which then fed into a huge 200-horsepower extruder. The extruder forced the Play-Doh out through a 2½-inch outlet where it was cut off at the appropriate length and dropped into cans. "Bob and Bill saw our line and went back that very night and put the idea together for the Play-Doh Fun Factory. And that's exactly what it was, too—the kids put the Play-Doh into the top of it and used the pump to force it down and extrude it out the different holes," Rodenbaugh said. "I've heard it estimated, at one point, that over a third of the children in the United States had played with our Play-Doh Fun Factory."

1950s

Debut: 1956
Inventors: A Mysterious
  Canadian Couple
Developer: Edwin Lowe
Companies: E. S. Lowe,
  Milton Bradley

Yahtzee

A WINNING COMBINATION

Everyone writing about the history of Yahtzee seems to be reading from the same press release. The story goes something like this: A wealthy Canadian couple invents a dice game and plays it with friends aboard their boat. They call it their "Yacht Game." Soon their friends want copies too. The couple contacts Edwin Lowe, who back in the 1920s formed the E. S. Lowe Company and made a mint selling the game of Bingo. Lowe likes the idea of the Yacht Game so much that he offers to buy the rights. Being a wealthy Canadian couple, they're more interested in getting copies of their game, so instead they negotiate to have Lowe manufacture 1,000 copies (presumably for all their friends) in exchange for the complete rights to the game. Lowe obliges, and then relaunches the game as Yahtzee in 1956, eventually selling a bazillion of them.

But who were these inventors? I checked with the Association of Game and Puzzle Collectors, the Toy Industry Association, Milton Bradley (who bought E. S. Lowe in 1973), the Canadian Toy Collectors'

Society and everywhere else I could think to find this mysterious "wealthy Canadian couple." After having no luck, I turned to the game itself.

Five dice, twenty chips, a cup, score pad and pencils. The simplest of ideas often make for the best games. Fear of Yahtzee being labeled a gambling game prompted Lowe to declare on the game's first packaging: "The fun game

Yahtzee's original 1956 packaging featured heavy-handed referrals to the game's educational value.

long as possible. Finally, the grand pooh-bah was five of a kind, or the coveted Yahtzee.

Of course, it's all much simpler than it sounds, once you play it. At its debut E. S. Lowe had trouble explaining Yahtzee and early efforts to advertise it flopped. He ran an expensive campaign with Mays Department Stores in Los Angeles only to yield the sale of two games. According to Marvin Kaye's book *A Toy Is Born,* Lowe spent nearly a million dollars in the first three years of Yahtzee to no avail. Convinced against reason that he still had a winner, Lowe felt that to play Yahtzee was to love Yahtzee. Reading about it in an ad would not entice people to buy. So Edwin decided to throw some parties where people threw some dice.

Lowe sent his employees out to host Yahtzee parties and they in turn convinced others to do the same. Riding on his reputation and his historic Bingo sales, Lowe even contacted buyers from his various accounts and convinced them to host Yahtzee parties. The deal was simple. He would provide the games and refreshments while

that makes thinking . . . fun!" A professor with bowtie, bushy gray eyebrows and a smiling face looks on approvingly, peering over the top of his scholarly spectacles at a roll that looks like it's going to be . . . yes it is! A full house! The contrived cherry-on-top is his graduation cap (tassel to the left— he's earned his degree), as if long nights of rolling 'dem bones got him to graduation.

If it's true, he was a math major. Yahtzee was not a simple game to just pick up and play. The original came with a five-page booklet describing the rules of scoring. The score pad had an upper and lower section to fill out and the object was to roll five dice for specific scoring combinations and get the highest total score. Players achieved the combinations by rolling the five dice, up to three times per turn. With 13 categories to fill in, the strategy came from deciding which category to fill with each turn. Categories ranged from ones through sixes, to a group of poker-influenced combinations called three and four of a kind, small and large straights, and a full house. Chance was the easiest category to fill, but one that you'd hope to leave open as

This early ad called Yahtzee, "A party game that even party poopers can't resist."

Milton Bradley repackaged Yahtzee after buying E. S. Lowe in 1973.

forget the loud clacking of the dice within the cup? The original cardboard cup muffled the sound, but most of us played with the molded plastic variety that magnified the familiar rattle. The noise rose on the roll, five clattery cubes hitting against one another and then tumbling against the table before coming to rest. But the crescendo was what every roller hoped for, that moment when Lady Luck herself smiled in your direction and you yelled "YAHTZEEE!" Because they happened at a perfect rate of recurrence (they were difficult to roll, but not impossible), the suspense and subsequent satisfaction of rolling a Yahtzee was tangible. For some odd reason, rolling one with all sixes face up was even better.

In an interview conducted shortly before he died, Edwin Lowe claimed that he had forgotten the names of the inventors of Yahtzee. Perhaps they shunned any notoriety that Yahtzee's success would surely bring because of their purported wealth. Yet, we are the ones better off—heirs to a game that offers something priceless: Time spent with friends and family in play. No, you don't need a yacht to enjoy Yahtzee. All you really need is some dice, paper, a pencil and some friends who like to have fun. Call it a winning combination.

the hosts provided their homes. The winner would take home a free Yahtzee game while Lowe took some orders. Slowly but surely, party goers began to look for Yahtzee in stores and told their friends about it. The buzz that started with Lowe's parties got Yahtzee off and rolling.

Yahtzee's popularity grew through the '60s. By the early '70s, the P.R. man in Edwin Lowe had him bragging that Yahtzee was the biggest selling game in the world. Parker Brothers could have argued that claim, having nearly sold 100 million Monopoly games by that time. Milton Bradley could have also argued that their Candy Land game was bigger than Yahtzee, but if they took exception to Lowe's claims, they showed it in true toy industry fashion. They bought his company in 1973.

Today, over 50 million Yahtzee games have been sold all over the world. Its appeal is a combination of suspense, luck and loudness. Who can

Plan a Family Game Night

The classic shake and score dice game!

Ages 8 to Adult
1 or More Players

After nearly 50 years, Yahtzee is still rolling.

Ant Farm
Debut: 1956
Inventor: Milton Levine
Companies: E. Joseph
   Cossman & Company,
   Cossman & Levine, Inc.,
   Uncle Milton Industries

Sea-Monkeys
Debut: 1962
Predecessor: Instant Life
   (1959)
Inventor: Harold von
   Braunhut
Developer: Dr. Anthony
   D'Agostino
Companies: Honey Toy
   Industries, Transcience
   Corporation, Larami,
   Basic Fun, ExploraToy, a
   division of Educational
   Insights

Ant Farm & Sea-Monkeys

BY LAND, BY SEA . . . BY MAIL

If you were a kid in the '50s and wanted a toy with a biological bent, you had no shortage of choices. There were Magic Rocks (sodium silicate and magnesium sulfate) and the popular Mexican Jumping Beans (hatching moth eggs within the seed pods of the *Sebastiana pavoniana* shrub). During the '60s, pet seekers could turn to the back of any comic and find offers for critters like Japanese Fighting Fish and even Squirrel Monkeys. But you can well imagine the frenzied scene when Mom, opening that box she thought contained a lampshade from JC Penney encountered instead a small, freedom-seeking primate. For a Mom-approved pet, you were much better off with the captivating fun of Ant Farms or Sea-Monkeys. Underground or underwater, they could turn any kid into a basement biologist.

Pogonomyrmex

Artemia salina

DIGGING FOR GOLD

After World War II, Milton Levine and his brother-in-law, Joseph Cossman, returned from duty in Europe and started a novelty mail-order business. Their first successful product was "100 toy soldiers for a buck," as advertised in the pages of comic books. Being the nature of the novelty business, even their best ideas—like the Spud Gun, Balloon Animals and Shrunken Heads—lasted only a few years. "Two seasons, usually," Levine told me.

But that all changed on July 4, 1956, during an Independence Day picnic at Milton's sister's house in Southern California. The kids

The same classic farm scene has been the design of the upper part of the Ant Farm horizon for 48 years. The lower part of the horizon features a design always left up to the ants.

and when I questioned how he knew there were that many in there, he dumped the whole thing on my desk and said, 'You count them!' and stormed out." Through trial and error Levine and Cossman discovered that the best ants hailed from the West (there are more than 6,000 known species). The Harvester Ant, or "Pogis" as they are known, are one of only a few species that dig in daylight—a big plus if you want to watch your ants do something other than sleep.

The idea for the theme came from the farm in Jamestown, PA, where Milton first scooped up all those ants as a kid and the name Ant Farm was born.

were playing and everyone was relaxing . . . except for the ants. Beside the pool, the little workers were diligently going about their antly business, unnoticed by everybody except Milton. As he watched, he recalled his boyhood in Pennsylvania, where he would scoop up a mound of ants in a Mason jar and watch them dig tunnels. "It just came to me," he said. "Why not build an ant observation toy?" He was sketching out ideas long before the fireworks started.

"I made a prototype out of a clear, plastic gift box for handkerchiefs and put a wooden base on it," he recalled. From there the real work started, because, as Milton explained, "I knew nothing about ants at the time." The two brothers-in-law ran an ad in the newspaper saying "Ants Wanted!" and offered to pay "a penny per." People showed up with jugs of the bugs. "One guy came in with this big jar," Milton laughed. "He wanted 50 bucks for them,

KICKING THE TIRES (BEFORE BUYING THE FARMS)

The Ant Farm seemed a natural for Levine and Cossman's mail-order business. Before the entrepreneurs paid for the $18,000 tooling needed to manufacture Milton's brainchild, however, they ran a $200 ad in the *Los Angeles Times* just to be sure. A week after the ad appeared, they were deluged with orders and the Ant Farm was launched.

It was two panels of clear plastic held together by a green plastic frame. The distinctive green base read simply "Ant Farm" and held this six-by-nine-inch window of nature upright. Included was an "Ant Watcher's Manual," an 11-page booklet that touted the Ant Farm as " . . . a busy, bustling world that shows you that ants are a lot like the nicest people you know!"

For nearly five decades, Uncle Milton's Ant Farm has taught kids about hard work, community, teamwork, organization and even the cycle of life. "It's a good lesson for kids," Ant Farm inventor Milton Levine says. "Nothing lasts forever."

THE PLAYMAKERS
Now and Then

Today's Ant Farm and how it looked in 1956.

They may sport straw hats and baseball caps today, but in the '70s, the ants pitching the Ant Farm wore top hats.

About six months after launching their product, Levine and Cossman started to get interest from stores. This created a new conundrum, because ants don't stay alive for very long after leaving their colonies. Selling them inside a package—which could conceivably sit in a warehouse for months at a time—was out of the question. The simple solution was a slogan still used today, "You Take the Farm, We Mail the Ants." This new retail version of the Ant Farm included a stock certificate that could be redeemed for 25–30 ants via mail.

The Ant Farm, with its broader distribution, really took off after Cossman, the loud showman of the pair, scored big with a whopping 30-minute Ant Farms feature on *The Johnny Carson Show*. As its inventor, Milton Levine also pitched Ant Farms anywhere and everywhere. Even his young son Steven got into the act, appearing on children's shows in the 1960s touting his Dad's creation. At the Ant Farm's height of popularity, Levine and Cossman contracted with 35 ant harvesters who collected over one million ants per week to meet the demand.

YES VIRGINIA, THERE IS AN UNCLE MILTON

I asked the affable Levine how he came to be named Uncle Milton. "Someone asked me once, 'You have all these ants, where are the uncles?'" Milton recalled. So when Levine bought out his brother-in-law in 1965, he dubbed himself "Uncle Milton," thereby lending a sort of intimate legitimacy to his creation—if your "Uncle" recommended the Ant Farm, it had to be good, right? His live ant habitat then became Uncle Milton's Ant Farm and his company, Uncle Milton Industries.

Milton's son, Steve Levine, graduated from college (and from children's TV show appearances) and began working for his dad full-time in 1978. He's been the CEO of Uncle Milton Industries since 1989. The company continues to offer a diverse product line of science and nature toys, with the perennial Ant Farm brand continuing to be their biggest seller. Besides the original, there's Giant Ant Farm (15-by-10 inches), which has been in the line since 1958, and the new Xtreme Ant Farm, a multi-chambered affair in which ants "play" in a miniature extreme sports park, complete with BMX track and other ESPN2-inspired attractions.

Milton Levine, aka "Uncle Milton" poses with his famous creation and a few little friends.

Since that July 4th day back in 1956, over 20 million Ant Farms have been sold, much to the amazement of the company's patriarch. "I thought it would be good for maybe two years," Milton confessed. "Never in my wildest dreams did I think it would sell for over 45 years." Our favorite "Uncle" is retired now at the age of 89, but still very active and very passionate about his ants. Scientists may tout their ability to lift over fifty times their own body weight, an impressive exploit to be sure, but Milton Levine has discovered their most amazing feat yet.

"I love ants," he said to me. "They put my kids through college."

✳ Today, Western Harvester Ants, as well as California Harvester Ants are shipped for use in Ant Farms, and each shipment is taken from the same colony. Ants from different colonies are not compatible and will often fight to the death.

JUMBO SHRIMP

While Uncle Milton had to delay shipments of ants if the weather was too hot or cold for fear that the ants would die during their trips to Ant Farm owners, Sea-Monkey pioneer Harold von Braunhut had no such worry. His critters actually came DOA. Well, they weren't really dead, but the fact that they appeared lifeless and then were instantly reborn was the very basis for his idea.

In 1957, one year after Milton Levine's life-changing picnic, Harold became fascinated with a species of brine shrimp known as *Artemia salina*. These amazing creatures are found in salt lakes and flats that are prone to evaporation. The tiny crustaceans adapt to their troublesome environment by gaining the ability to fall into a state of suspended animation known as "cryptobiosis." They remain in a protective cystlike casing, sometimes for

years, until water returns and them with it, seemingly from the grave. This phenomenon was hardly a secret in 1957, and for years the shrimp were harvested and sold to pet shops as aquarium food for fish. Harold's revolutionary idea was to turn the pet food into the pet!

Harold formed Honey Toy Industries (later spun off as Transcience Corporation) and worked with research scientist/marine biologist Dr. Anthony D'Agostino to perfect the chemical treatment needed to turn tap water into a purified habitat for crytobiotic brine shrimp. "We wanted them to grow to be large enough to be of interest, but also live long enough to be a pet," von Braunhut told me. "These goals took years to attain." After nearly three years of work, a successful

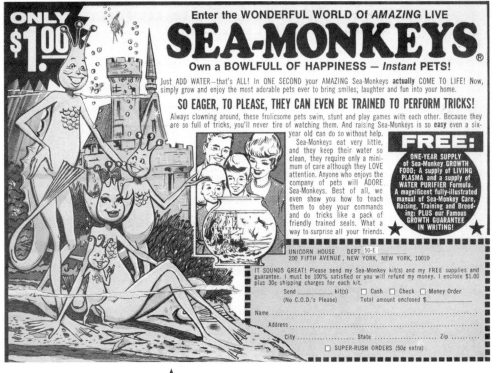

Early ads for Sea-Monkeys featured cartoon images of semi-humanoid creatures lounging together like royal families complete with antennalike crowns.

process was achieved and the product was dubbed Instant Life.

Far from an instant success, von Braunhut had trouble convincing stores to buy into his idea. Without a budget for TV or radio ads (a package of 10-20 sold for only 49 cents), he was forced to look elsewhere for a way to reach a young audience. He turned to the pages of comic books.

AD NAUSEAM

"Back then, a lot of companies looked down on comic books," von Braunhut said. "Everyone else in toys was buying TV time, but I bought comic book space. I bought tons of it." His ads were successful from the start and the more they worked, the more he spent on them. Starting in 1962, Harold von Braunhut unleashed an advertising assault on the realm of comics like none before or since. *Archie, Batman, Spider-Man*—it didn't matter. If you even browsed a comic book anytime from 1962 to 1975, you were introduced to von Braunhut's idea. "I think I bought something like 3.2 million pages of comic book advertising a year," he said. "It worked beautifully."

Stemming from his observation that these tiny shrimp grew "monkey-like" tails as they developed, Harold used the term "sea-monkeys" in his ads almost immediately. No, they weren't monkeys; they were brine shrimp. No, they didn't live in the sea; they lived in the saltiest of lakes. If this were marine biology these facts would matter, but this was marketing!

According to a classic ad from 1963, you could "... teach them to obey your commands like a pack of friendly trained seals." Another read, "playful tumbling sea-monkeys"

Today, Sea-Monkeys have tanks complete with built-in magnifying glasses.

Harold von Braunhut created Instant Life in 1959, renamed in 1962 as the American classic, Sea-Monkeys.

can "... chase each other in a playful game of hide and seek.... Watch them cavort singly or glide gracefully in formation...." Wow. *Glide gracefully in formation?* As if coming back to life wasn't amazing enough, now we're promised synchronized swimming? After reading those ads and seeing those images on the package, being a new Sea-Monkey owner could be a major letdown. True, it was amazing to see this magical dust spawn life, but as a gullible kid, I wanted to know why they weren't four inches tall and waving at me like in the ads. Combine this with the fact that the life span of the Sea-Monkeys in the early kits was notoriously short and you had the potential for marketing disaster.

Harold foresaw this and worked diligently to improve his creation. He offered a "Sea-Monkeys Life Insurance Policy" with every kit and studied the science of making his Sea-Monkeys grow faster, larger and live longer. By the late '60s, Sea-Monkeys were being sold in toy stores with sets like the Sea-Monkey Ocean Zoo and the Sea-Monkey Circus. If you were patient enough and followed the directions (important tip), you were rewarded with some neat little pets, even if they didn't really play hide and seek. They swam toward a flashlight beam and, when covered in darkness for a while and then exposed to bright light, they became frantic (or as the ads read: "danced about playfully"). They even swam against a current, as demonstrated in Sea-Monkey kits like Super Sea-Monkey Race and Deluxe Sea-Monkey Speedway, both introduced in the '70s.

Their most amazing tricks had to do with their biology and featured the kind of freaky things kids love. They are born with one eye, but grow two more when they reach maturity. They breathe through their feathery feet. They're translucent and able to reproduce sexually or asexually. What more could a budding biologist ask?

"The product we were selling in the 1960's is not the product we are selling now," Von Braunhut said. "Today it's far more advanced. Oh, yes." The species now grown in labs and widely used in today's Sea-Monkey kits are called *Artemia NYOS* (for New York Ocean Science). They are hybrid species of brine shrimp still within the genus *Artemia,* but you can just call them Super Sea-Monkeys.

I told my kids that we were going to hatch a batch and they became frantic (danced about playfully), at the astonishing possibility of growing their own pet. They were skeptical at first, but a few days into it and the proof is in the puddle—the one that holds their undying attention

and their growing Sea-Monkeys. "They're so cuuute!" the older one cries out. Then her little sister, with nose pressed against the plastic, says "Hey! They're chasing each other!"

Who's to argue?

Harold von Braunhut is also the inventor and mail-order maestro behind the classic X-Ray Spex glasses.

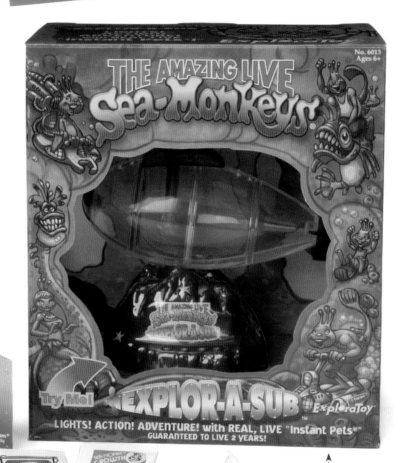

Sea-Monkeys are still produced and supplied by Harold von Braunhut's company, but marketed and sold by a California firm called ExploraToy.

Debut: 1959
Developer: Ruth Handler
  (1916-2002)
Company: Mattel

Predecessor: Bild Lilli (1955)
Illustrator: Reinhard
  Beuthien
**Inventors of the Bild Lilli
  doll:** Rolf Hausser and
  Max Weissbrodt

Barbie

BARBIE'S WORLD

I first realized that Barbie was from another world when I was six. My sister was seven, and to me, her Barbie was just another victim that my Super-Hero action figures could save . . . or kidnap, depending on who was looking. I didn't realize Barbie was different until the day my Grandpa Horan came over and saw Barbie lying naked on the floor. That's when he yelled (to no one in particular), "Will you get some clothes on that doll!?" I noticed he didn't say anything about The Incredible Hulk, who was also naked, having lost his purple pants. Somehow, Barbie's nudity made my grandpop's ears turn bright red.

In the toy biz, they don't get any bigger than Barbie. Her influence looms as large as her shoe selection—over 2 billion thus far. To gain a true appreciation for this pop culture icon, you have to look at the toy business pre-Barbie. Back then, most dolls were babies or

children. Toy makers believed that a girl played with dolls so that she could pretend to be a mother. Barbie changed all that. In 1959, plenty of dolls had the ability to burp or wet, crawl or cry, but Barbie possessed something that no other doll had: A figure.

Mattel conducted extensive market research before Barbie debuted in 1959. When mothers and daughters were shown the doll separately, all the girls loved her, but most mothers thought the doll was too "developed." This illustrates the Barbie dichotomy. On the one hand, it (not she) is a doll. It's not real, so what's all the fuss about? On the other hand, if we're going to give our daughters something new to idolize, then we want to know what it is. Who *she* is. Hold onto your high-fashion hats as more fuel is thrown on that polarizing fire: Barbie was inspired, at least in part, by a doll of ill repute.

In 1952 a cartoonist, Reinhard Beuthien, created a character named Lilli for a German tabloid newspaper called *Bild Zeitung.* In her book *Forever Barbie: The Unauthorized Biography of a Real Doll,* author M. G. Lord revealed this missing link that led to the introduction of the Barbie doll. According to Lord, Lilli was "a pornographic caricature" and "a gold digger, exhibitionist and floozy . . . [who] flung herself repeatedly at balding, jowly fat cats." The cartoon's

popularity spawned a doll, but certainly not one meant as a plaything for little German girls. In the summer of 1955, the Lilli doll met her lustful audience—adult men, who received her as a sexy souvenir at bachelor parties. Sold in tobacco shops and bars, Lilli was shipped all over the world for a brief time and came in 7-inch and 11-inch sizes. She was made in Hamburg, Germany, at first and later in Hong Kong.

Max Weissbrodt, a doll maker for the O.M. Hausser/ Elastolin Company, eventually got a patent on Lilli's limb construction. Her neck was too thin, her waist too wispy, and her legs too long. In other words, she was 100% consistent with her cartoon inspiration— complete with pouty, full lips, ample cleavage, arched eyebrows and a sensual sideways glance. She was bawdy and bad; nothing more than a gag gift. Amazingly, Barbie's developer viewed her differently.

One version of the story says that Ruth Handler first saw the Lilli doll in 1957 while visiting Lucerne, Switzerland with her husband, Elliot, and their two kids, Barbara and Ken. Oblivious to its bawdy roots,

Handler bought several Lilli dolls. Years before, she was intrigued by the way her daughter Barbie loved to play with paper dolls—specifically adult paper dolls. Handler observed as her daughter and friends role-played with these flimsy, paper cutouts. Could a plastic doll, made in the image of an adult woman, bring more realism to a little girl's dreams? Handler thought so. Discovering the Lilli doll confirmed that her vision was capable of being mass-produced.

Whereas many other inventors in this book started from scratch, Ruth Handler had an advantage. At the time of her chance meeting with Lilli, Handler and her husband ran a little toy company called Mattel. Ruth brought one of the Lilli dolls back to her designers. It took her some time to convince her husband and her all-male staff that if they built this doll, the little girls would swarm to it. Ruth Handler's dominant personality and steadfast belief eventually convinced them, and in 1958 Mattel bought the Weissbrodt/Hausser body design patent. After their market research and refinements to tone down the streetwalker appearance of Lilli, Mattel unveiled the fruit of its labor.

When the curtain finally rose on Mattel's new doll, it was evident that, visually speaking, the apple had not fallen very far from the tree. Mattel's doll wore a black and white

Intended as a sex symbol, the body of the Lilli doll was a deliberate caricature, faithful to Beuthien's cartoon creation.

striped, strapless bathing suit, cat's eye sunglasses and stiletto high heel shoes. Her facial painting was very similar to the Lilli doll, with a sideways glance under heavy makeup. Most noticeable were her measurements, which would equate to 38"-18"-33" had she been life-size.

But appearance is where the similarities stopped. For inspiration in naming the product, Ruth Handler looked no further than her daughter, Barbara. The image Mattel constructed for their new "Barbie" doll was one that carefully combined innocence and sophistication, attractive to girls as a role model and aspiration. Only time would tell if the retail community would buy it.

Barbie debuted at the 1959 International Toy Fair to mixed reviews. Many doll buyers refused to stock her, others worried that she was too mature. Yet on Mattel's reputation alone, some gave her a chance. Many parents had the reaction that the buyers had feared, but, to young girls, it was love at first sight. Mattel gambled on the girls winning over their parents, and won big. Over 350,000 Barbie dolls were sold in its first year.

Time magazine wrote about our country's increasing degree of affluence in 1959, declaring, "The new leisure is here." The ultimate symbol of commercialism, the shopping mall, first appeared that same year. Barbie not only came at the perfect time, she came with needs. Although she was much maligned by feminists (despite early careers as a registered nurse in '62 and an astronaut in '68), Barbie owned her femininity, along with clothes, cars, jewelry, jeeps, pets, shoes, and houses. She may or may not teach our daughters to be feminists, but she certainly preps them to be dutiful consumers. Just walk into any discount department store and look for Barbie's own pink aisle. It's the Rodeo Drive of Toyland with everything and anything Barbie's heart desires.

Shortly after her release, Barbie struck a nerve, Mattel struck oil, and the little girls of America were just . . . awestruck. No one had seen anything like her.

After just 10 years on the market, Barbie's dominance was unquestioned when she entered the '70s. The Barbie brand had expanded to include over 1,000 items, and she traveled all over the world. In 1971, Malibu Barbie looked us straight in the eyes for the first time, losing her coy, off-center stare. She also cracked her first smile and has had it ever since. Barbie made good career choices and gained a wide circle of friends under Mattel's guidance, including Ken, Midge, Allan, P. J., Stacey and Christie.

Barbie's boyfriend, Ken, was introduced in 1961.

Although these marketing decisions helped to soften Barbie's image, other choices reinforced Barbie's negative stereotypes. Consider 1978's Teen Talk Barbie. She said six phrases, one of which was "Math class is tough!" So much for that career as an astronaut.

In 1979 Barbie's shopping list included a safe for her fur and jewels, a convertible Super Vette Corvette and a Dream House—each sold separately. You could easily conclude that this was all in preparation for the selfish decade of the '80s, but as always, Barbie was not so easy to pin down. Instead, the new decade marked a period of purpose and empowerment for her. In 1980, the first African-American and Hispanic Barbie dolls arrived with skin tones, hair and facial features modified. By 1984 a new slogan, "We Girls Can Do Anything!" spoke of Barbie's change from fashion model to role model. Like never before, she enabled girls to imagine becoming anyone they wanted—a vision Ruth Handler maintained all along.

Ruth Handler posed with her creation in 1962. Here Barbie borrows Jackie Kennedy's popular bubble haircut.

Perhaps Barbie can be summed up as extreme, because in all aspects—whether it's her body, clothes, accessories or various careers—that word seems to define her. She's worked for NASA and has a medical degree. She ran for president of the United States twice (in 1992 and again in 2000). She's been an officer in the Army, Navy, Air Force and Marines, and has her pilot's license. Despite all this extreme empowerment, her shallow, bombshell reputation followed her. Barbie needed to gain a few grams of plastic before she could start to shed her negative persona.

It was news big enough for the *Wall Street Journal* when, in 1998, Mattel announced that they would begin selling a more anatomically "normal" Barbie. With a smaller bust, thicker waist, wider hips and flatter feet, the new Barbie promised to bring some realism to her role as a representative of the feminine ideal. In the eyes of millions of little girls, these changes may go unnoticed; more likely they'll become part of Barbie's influence on their collective subconscious—a place that parents should guard with great care.

When I asked my young daughters if they noticed any difference in the new Barbie, they both spotted some missing plastic flesh, but not in the area you might think. "She's got a belly button!" they shrieked. Change is good I suppose (it's an innie, by the way). At least my Grandpop Horan isn't here to see the navel ring that Barbie will surely be sporting next.

She's an inspiration to some and a distortion of femininity to others. She reinforces sexism to some; but to others, she represents the ultimate feminist by becoming anyone she sets her mind to be. Her reign as the biggest pop culture icon of the toy world, however, remains undebated. Mattel sells over 172,000 Barbie dolls *per day*. Numbers like that are sure to irritate her detractors and confirm what her fans already know: It's Barbie's world—we're all just living in it.

✦ Barbie's full name is Barbie Millicent Roberts.

✦ Elliot Handler formed Mattel in 1945 when he and Harold Matson (**Mat**son and **Ell**iot) started selling picture frames out of a garage. It evolved into a toy company by marketing dollhouse furniture. A few years later the Handlers bought out Matson. Musical toys dominated the first 14 years of Mattel's growth, until Barbie got Mattel singing a brand-new tune in 1959.

✦ According to Mattel, the typical girl between the ages of three and ten owns eight Barbie dolls.

The Barbie doll is the biggest selling toy in the history of proprietary toy manufacturing.

THE PLAYMAKERS
Toy Timeline

1950   **'55**   **'60**   **'65**   **'70**   **'75**

1948
• Spud Melin and Dick Knerr
form WHAM-O

1958
• **Hula Hoop**

1961
• **Slip 'N Slide**

1962
• The Limbo Party Kit
• Instant Fish

1957
• **Frisbee**

1964
• Monster Magnet

1965
• **Super Ball**
• Air-Blaster

1973
• The Magic
Window

1970
• SuperElasticBubblePlastic
• Water Wiggle
• Monster Bubbles
and Zillion Bubbles

1969
• Silly String

1968
• Whirlee Twirlee

1967
• Giant Comic Book

1966
• Super Stuff

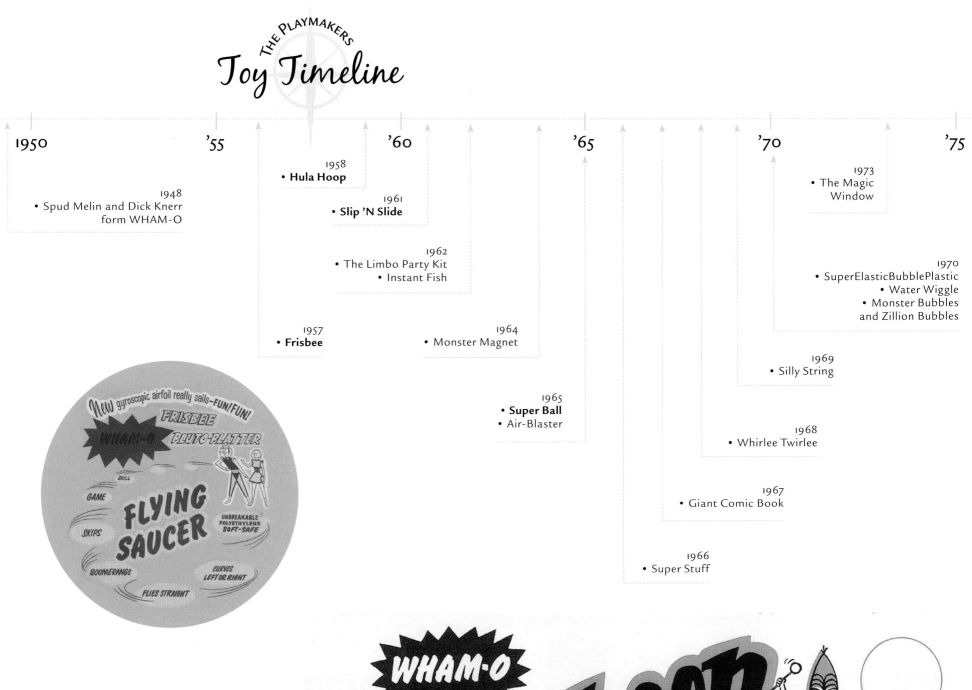

New gyroscopic airfoil really sails—FUN! FUN!

FRISBEE
WHAM-O PLUTO-PLATTER

FLYING SAUCER

UNBREAKABLE
POLYETHYLENE
SOFT-SAFE

SKILL
GAME
SKIPS
BOOMERANGS
CURVES
LEFT OR RIGHT
FLIES STRAIGHT

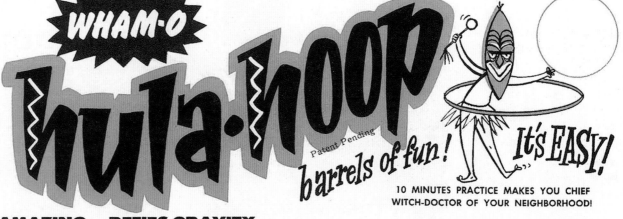

WHAM-O
hula·hoop
Patent Pending
barrels of fun! It's EASY!

10 MINUTES PRACTICE MAKES YOU CHIEF
WITCH-DOCTOR OF YOUR NEIGHBORHOOD!

AMAZING...DEFIES GRAVITY

WHAM-O

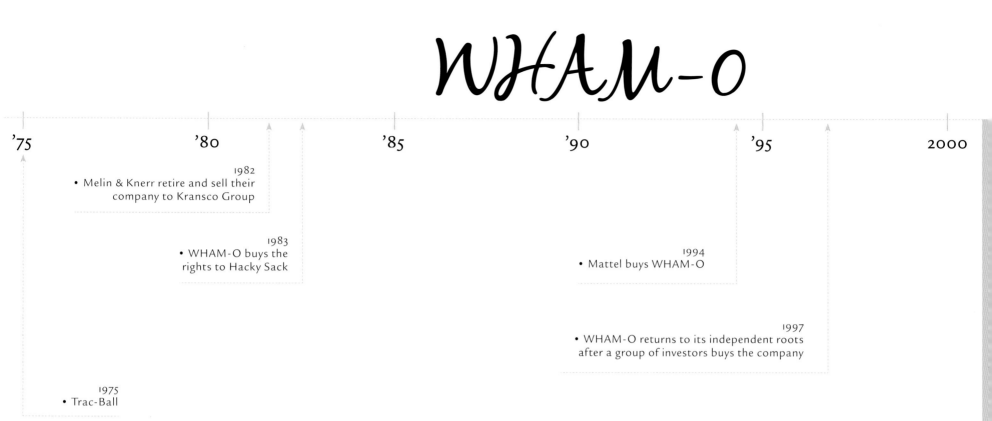

'75 '80 '85 '90 '95 2000

1982
• Melin & Knerr retire and sell their company to Kransco Group

1983
• WHAM-O buys the rights to Hacky Sack

1994
• Mattel buys WHAM-O

1997
• WHAM-O returns to its independent roots after a group of investors buys the company

1975
• Trac-Ball

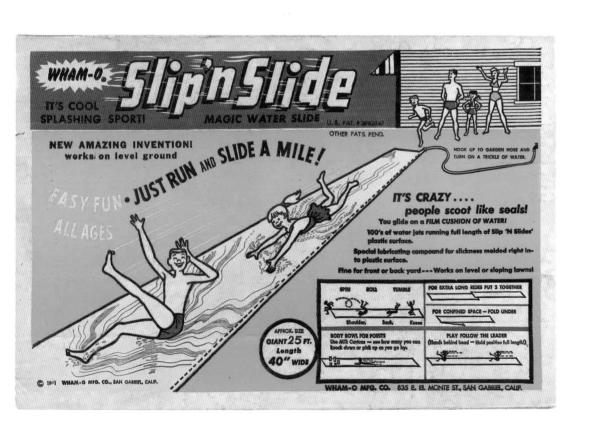

WHAM-O

INSIDE THE FAD FACTORY

It all started with flying meatballs.

Childhood friends Arthur "Spud" Melin and Richard "Dick" Knerr were attending the University of Southern California in 1948 when their hobby of raising and selling falcons took an unexpected turn. Using a homemade slingshot to launch meatballs into the air, Melin and Knerr were teaching their birds how to dive for prey when a man approached them offering to buy, not their falcon, but their slingshot. Thinking the man might be onto something, the two partners bought a band saw and set up shop in Knerr's parents' garage, making and selling the WHAM-O Slingshot, which they named after the comic book sound that resulted when you hit something with it.

The slingshot's success enabled them to move their business to the corner of an abandoned grocery store. There, WHAM-O's future in toys was prefaced by a paradoxical product line of slingshots, throwing knives, boomerangs, fencing swords and blow guns. It's sweet to know that it took the legacy of an 85-year-old pie bakery to save WHAM-O from a life of weaponry.

WHAM-O's start was in weapons, as indicated by these ads from the early 1950s.

Frisbee

WHAM-O

Debut: 1957
Predecessors: Flyin' Saucer
(1948), Pluto Platter
Flying Saucer (1955)
Inventor: Fred Morrison
Developer: Warren
Franscioni (1918-1974)
Companies: Pipco American
Trends, WHAM-O
Insider: Ed Headrick

PIE IN THE SKY

The legend begins in 1871 in Bridgeport, Connecticut, where a man named William Russell Frisbie founded a pie bakery. Upon his death in 1903, the family business passed to a second generation of Frisbies. By the end of 1905, Frisbies were flying off store shelves all over New England, foreshadowing what was to become of the family name.

With business brisk in 1915, Joe Frisbie built a new, larger bakery in Bridgeport where factory workers reportedly broke up their workday by having a game of catch with the pie tins. Sure it could be a bit dangerous—flying metal tends to be—but it was undoubtedly fun. The news of flying pie tins spread to nearby Yale University, where one can imagine the typical campus clamor of spring pervaded by a new sound; the noisy clang of metal pie tins hitting the ground. Cries of "Frisbie!" could also be heard, like the warning "Fore!" in golf, as errant throws sailed out of control.

College campuses in the Northeast embraced the new pastime. Along with Frisbie pie tins, other forms of flying disks emerged from everyday household items. Metal cookie can covers soared but were more than a little scary to catch. Cardboard ice cream container lids and woven paper plate holders weren't as dangerous, but both were so light they couldn't sail very far. These varied disks were fun to throw, but with some ingenuity a better design could surely be made. Leave it to two former Army Air Force pilots to make the idea fly.

Walter "Fred" Morrison and Warren Franscioni seized the marketing possibility of a flying disk in the mid 1940s. The two men agreed that the new post-war plastic was the perfect lightweight and durable substitute for the airborne metal of their youth. Deciding to become "Partners in Plastic," the two named their company Pipco. According to Victor Malafronte's book, *The Complete Book of Frisbee,* in Franscioni's California basement, the two men first took sheets of plastic and held them over a heater until they were soft enough to bend and form into crude disks. Their first plastic disk was dubbed, The Whirlo Way.

In July of 1947, rumor spread that the Air Force had recovered remains of a crashed "flying disk" near

ONE OF THE FLEET OF 200 TRUCKS, FRISBIE PIE CO., BRIDGEPORT AND HARTFORD, CONN.

In just a few years, the W. R. Frisbie Pie Bakery had become The Frisbie Pie Company, with a fleet of 200 trucks like the one pictured in this postcard from the 1920s.

WHAM-O

FRISBEE

Roswell, New Mexico. The "Roswell Incident" fueled our country's infatuation with UFOs, and in response, Pipco renamed their toy the Flyin' Saucer. According to written correspondence acquired by Malafronte, Morrison got some blocks of hard plastic and had a mechanic friend, who owned a lathe, turn out some models while Franscioni funded the start-up with $25,000. Using these early models, the first Flyin' Saucer molds were made sometime in 1948.

The Pipco Li'l Abner Flyin Saucer, launched in an effort to invigorate the company, ended up being Pipco's demise.

FLYIN' SAUCER PILOTS

Morrison and Franscioni quickly learned that after landing on a store shelf, their flying toy remained there. Like a UFO, the Flyin' Saucer had to be seen to be believed, so the entrepreneurs demonstrated it wherever they could find a crowd. Their first account was the local Woolworth's store in Glendale, California, where the two men dazzled shoppers with their remarkable skill at throwing and catching. Despite Morrison and Franscioni's proficiency, the store manager wasn't taking any chances—he had the men stand within a wire cage during the demonstration!

The sight of a sailing disk is so common today that it's hard to imagine the amazement that bystanders experienced when they first saw this new toy in use.

After Morrison and Franscioni moved their demonstrations to the great outdoors, they overheard an onlooker comment that "they must be using wires to fly the thing." Quickly, the two savvy salesmen incorporated the perceived deception into their sales pitch. "The Flyin' Saucer is free," they'd say. "But the invisible wire is $1.00."

They promoted the Flyin' Saucer in California and at Daytona Beach, Florida. They even landed orders from Disneyland, but despite their continued efforts, the "World Champion Flyin' Saucer Pilots" (as they hailed themselves) could not get their toy off the ground. With sales waning, they thought the recognition of a well-known license might provide the lift they needed.

In the spring of 1950, Pipco signed an agreement with Al Capp, the creator of the comic strip *Li'l Abner*. The men evidently overstepped the limits of their agreement with Mr. Capp in packaging Li'l Abner comics with the toys, because shortly after the disks hit the streets, Pipco was hit with the cancellation of the contract and a lawsuit. Having weathered four years of development and promotional efforts with little return, this threat of litigation proved too much for Pipco; they settled with Capp for $5,000, but the damage was done.

The Morrison/Franscioni partnership ended in late 1950 with Franscioni returning to active duty in the Air Force and Morrison taking a job as a building inspector for the city of Los Angeles. Both men continued to ponder the unrealized potential of their product, especially with the UFO phenomenon getting stronger. Morrison even continued to sell some Flyin' Saucers in his spare time. Franscioni attempted, unsuccessfully, to reunite with Morrison in order to have his former partner sign patent papers on their original disk design. Sadly, this is the point in the history of the Frisbee where Warren Franscioni fades into obscurity without his proper due as the co-developer of the first plastic flying disk. He died of a heart attack in 1974, relatively unknown to the Frisbee-loving world.

"When a ball dreams, it dreams it's a Frisbee."
—Dr. Stancil Johnson, Frisbee historian

SUCCESS ON A PLASTIC PLATTER

In 1953, Fred Morrison formed his own company called American Trends to sell a very similar design of the Flyin' Saucer made of softer, more durable plastic. Then, in 1955, he made an entirely new disk with a brand-new design. He called it the Pluto Platter Flying Saucer and fashioned it to look much more like a UFO with a raised cabin in the center, complete with portholes.

He sold the new disk via mail at first, but his big break came when he was demonstrating the Pluto Platter Flying Saucer in a Los Angeles store parking lot. A representative from WHAM-O saw the disk and brought word back to Spud Melin and Dick Knerr. With their hunting goods business shifting to sporting goods, the WHAM-O founders decided to take a chance on Fred's Flying Saucer. In 1956, Morrison signed a deal with the fledgling toy company that made him a wealthy man and his flying disk a household name.

The first WHAM-O disks had no reference to the name Frisbee anywhere on them. By this time, however, the game known as "Frisbie" was being played all over New England. The campuses of Princeton, Dartmouth and Yale were hotbeds for the emerging fad. There were at least six known companies making plastic disks from 1949 to 1959, but no matter what they called their disks—Space Saucer, Sky Pie, even the It Came From Outer Space Flying Saucer—players almost invariably referred to them as Frisbies, Frisbees, Frizbys, Frisbeys. It was as if the ghosts of W. R. and Joseph Frisbie wanted a legacy.

FRISBEE'S FIRST FLIGHT

Melin and Knerr were resourceful marketers, so after Knerr returned from a business trip with word of the "Frisbie craze" happening out East, WHAM-O adopted the classic business model: If you can't beat 'em, join 'em. They officially called their product a Frisbee, changing the spelling slightly so they could own the name.

The debate over whether the U.S. Patent Trademark Office erred in granting WHAM-O trademark

From Frisbie to Frisbee

It all depends what's in the bag. The Frisbie pie bag at left probably held its last pie in the mid-'50s. Sold in 1956, the Frisbie Pie Company closed its doors after auctioning off its equipment and inventory in 1958. That same year, WHAM-O filed their application for the trademark Frisbee, and inventor Fred Morrison received Design Patent No. 183,626 for his new

"flying toy." Shown here is WHAM-O's package right after they decided to start using the name "Frisbee." All references to "Pluto Platter Flying Saucer" soon ended and the name Frisbee became synonymous with fun instead of food.

Before WHAM-O began enforcing their trademark, other companies jumped on the fad too. Here's a package for a "Frisbee" made by Empire Plastic in 1959.

Giant **Frisbee** FLYING SAUCER

The New College Campus Craze!

SEE PLAYING INSTRUCTIONS
ON REVERSE SIDE OF BOX

No. 80

protection on a name that was arguably in the public domain, continues among Frisbee aficionados. The name stuck because, for nearly 30 years, that's the name that was embossed on every pie tin made by the Frisbie pie company. WHAM-O simply adopted the common name used for their product and filed the correct papers to make it exclusive to their flying disk. The year 1958 was also when a major explosion hit the WHAM-O plant. It was called the Hula Hoop, and it sold so well that production of

Frisbees (and virtually all other toys in the WHAM-O line) was cut to meet demand. But the fad died nearly as quickly as it was born, leaving WHAM-O with tons of excess raw plastic in inventory and no orders. In 1959, the Frisbee saved them, as their newly named disk began to soar; the plastic that was meant for Hula Hoops was formed into flying disks instead.

The Frisbee phenomenon hit full force in the dawn of the '60s, and WHAM-O shrewdly marketed it as a sport, introducing the first professional model in 1964. Its designer, Ed Headrick, also formed the IFA (International Frisbee Association) for WHAM-O, which boasted 112,000 members at its peak. By 1969, over 50 million Frisbee disks were sold and games such as Ultimate Frisbee and Frisbee Golf took the flying disk well beyond the backyard and the beach.

It's hard to imagine a summer without them. Adults throw them, kids marvel at them, dogs catch them. One look at a Frisbee floating on thin air or rising on a summer breeze is all it takes to make us want to catch one too. Today, it's estimated that over 200 million Frisbee disks have been sold since Fred Morrison and Warren Franscioni first began work on their fantasy of flight. What are the odds of creating a toy that sells that many units? About 200 million to 1 . . . a pie in the sky.

THE PLAYMAKERS
Now and Then

Australian Debut: 1957
U.S. Debut: 1958
Developers: Alex Tolmer
(1914-1998), Spud Melin,
Dick Knerr

Hula Hoop

DOWN UNDER AND ALL AROUND

If the odds of selling that many Frisbees were so infinitesimally low, then you may ask how the same company could market a second plastic plaything that would match Frisbee's sales. While you're at it, you might also ask how that plaything—a large ring that has been around in one form or another for thousands of years—could possibly become a hit toy. The answer to both questions is *no one knows.* Toy experts can identify trends within the toy industry but no one can predict a fad, and the granddaddy of all fads was the Hula Hoop.

Hoops have been around almost as long as the wheel. According to Charles Panati's *Extraordinary Origins of Everyday Things,* Egyptian tomb drawings dated 1000 B.C. show hoops in use, probably made from dried vines. In ancient Greece and Rome, adults exercised with hoops made of wood or bamboo. Historians note that the "hooping" craze swept England in the 1500s. The term "hula" was first used in association with hoops either by visiting missionaries to the Hawaiian Islands in the 1700s or British sailors who landed there in the 1800s. Whichever the case, the visitors noticed that the movements of the native hula dance were similar to the movements needed to keep these early playthings spinning in their gravity-defying manner. Primitive at best, but undeniably fun; it wasn't long before someone decided to mass-produce the humble hoop.

The bamboo hoop's path to plastic started in Australia. There, a Sydney schoolteacher reportedly taught her physical education students how to swing and sway a bamboo hoop some time in the mid-'50s. It's not clear whether she or another manufacturer began making and selling these bamboo hoops, but Australia's Coles department store began selling them with increasing success. The head toy buyer for Coles feared that the supplier would never be able to keep up with growing demand and called upon a legendary toy man, Alex Tolmer, to see if these bamboo or "cane" hoops could be mass-produced.

Tolmer was the founder of Toltoys, one of the first Australian toy manufacturers to make toys (trucks, sand buckets, shovels), out of a new unbreakable type of plastic. In the mid-50s, the new goo bubbled forth from laboratories all across the globe like lava erupting from the volcanoes in the Hula Hoop's motherland. This hot, gummy substance could be injected into a mold—or in the case of the Hula Hoop, extruded out of one—yet keep its flexibility even after it cooled and hardened. Polyethylene, a material stronger and less brittle than earlier plastics, was

Alex Tolmer, developer
of the Hula Hoop.

about to take the old-fashioned hoop into the atomic age.

The bamboo versions were heavy, expensive and plain, whereas Tolmer's new plastic version was lightweight, sold for less than two bucks and could be molded in any color under the sun. In 1957, Toltoys sold 400,000 plastic Hula Hoops. Their success was so great that Tolmer sent a representative over to the American International Toy Fair. "Toltoys was already producing toys made by WHAM-O and paying them royalties," Tolmer's son, David, told me. "So my dad had a relationship with them." WHAM-O deemed the hoop too generic to warrant a royalty. Instead, Melin and Knerr donated money to sponsor a bed at a children's hospital in Sydney at Alex Tolmer's request. The final deal that was struck would soon have the whole world hooping.

WHAM-O TAKES OVER

Melin and Knerr improved on the Tolmer design, and in the spring of 1958, began giving Hula Hoops away to trendsetting kids in southern California. Local news programs featured these hip-swinging hoopsters, and national TV exposure followed. After the toy appeared on *The Dinah Shore Show,* the spectacle began.

As WHAM-O struggled to keep up with demand, other companies were more than willing to help fill the void. Soon scores of imitation hoops inundated the market with names like Whoop-De-Do, Hooper Dooper, Wiggle-A-Hoop, Spin-A-Hoop and Hoop Zings. But don't feel too sorry for WHAM-O. They reportedly sold 25 million Hula Hoops in just four months, with the total number of hoops sold during the craze of '58 estimated between 80 and 100 million—all in a single year!

According to Jane and Michael Stern's *Encyclopedia of Pop Culture,* the Hula Hoop was a global hit of epidemic proportions. Doctors reported a spike in incidents of wrenched backs and torn abdominal

Spud Melin (skipping) and Dick Knerr (twirling) posed for this publicity photo in 1958, when the Hula Hoop put WHAM-O on the map.

As orders poured in, WHAM-O extended their production to a mind-boggling 20,000 Hula Hoops a day, but still couldn't fill the demand.

WHAM-O

HULA HOOP

Hula Hoop ad from 1959.

muscles, while the Russians condemned it as evidence of "the emptiness of American culture." In Indonesia, it was reportedly banned for use in public for fear of the sexual impropriety that would surely result from all those gyrating hips.

Back home, contests popped up everywhere. How long can you spin one on your waist? Neck? Arms? How many can you spin at one time? Kids seemed to be able to do it from birth, but the older you got (and the wider your girth) the harder it was to hula that hoop and keep it aloft. It turns out that there was more than just practice behind making the Hula Hoop do its thing.

The patent Melin filed on the Hula Hoop covered three key features: weight, diameter and shape. He discovered that the hoop's specifications had to be between 6 and 12 ounces with the diameter ranging from 30 and 40 inches so that the exertion needed to keep the hoop moving wasn't too intense. The shape of the hoop's interior surface contained ridges that helped keep the hoop up around the user's waist. Unfortunately for Melin and WHAM-O, by the time the patent was granted, the Hula Hoop craze was over.

Hula Hoop's bubble of popularity popped just ten months after it began. Not before or since has a toy sold so well so fast, only to stop so abruptly. Another amazing thing about the Hula Hoop craze is the fact that WHAM-O survived it. With thousands of dollars in raw materials on order and more in their warehouse, Melin and Knerr might have found themselves buried in plastic had they not been able to shift their inventory and orders to another fantastic toy of plastic, the Frisbee, which started to soar just as the Hula Hoop came rattling to the ground.

WHAM-O relaunched the Hula Hoop in 1965 with several ball bearings trapped inside its hollow tubing—which made a great sound as they raced around the hoop—and dubbed it the Shoop Shoop Hula Hoop. Today all Hula Hoops come with them, albeit without the Shoop Shoop name. As the hoop revolves, the ball bearings circle us like high-speed satellites—a reminder of how, one summer, the Hula Hoop encircled the earth.

Alex Tolmer was seriously wounded during World War II and earned Australia's Military Cross. He returned home a war hero, worked as a salesman, and in 1955, founded Toltoys. He was inducted into the Australian Toy Association Hall of Fame in 1998.

When Life magazine needed a cover image for its special edition on the era of the 1950s, they considered using the Hula Hoop or Elvis Presley. Both made hip gyrations hip, but it was Hula Hoop that made the cover.

Today's Hula Hoop comes in a variety of sizes for every waistline.

Slip 'n Slide

Debut: 1961
Inventor: Robert Carrier
 (1929-2002)
Developer: Mike Carrier

THE YELLOW SLICK ROAD

In 1961, WHAM-O introduced us to a young father's invention that made backyard belly flopping the summer silliness of choice. It all started the summer before, when Robert Carrier came home to see a most unusual sight. His 10-year-old son Mike and a friend had a hose running on their slick and painted Lakewood, California driveway, and both boys were sliding down it like otters. Mike Carrier told me the tale: "We lived with my grandfather at the time and his garage was carpeted so you could get a good running start. We'd get back in there and take off running and hit this driveway! Man, it went out and then down, so we'd slide along until we'd almost hit the curbing. My dad came home and said 'Jeez, you guys are going to kill yourselves doing this,' but we were having a blast, just kids with nothing better to do."

Jump ahead a few months and the Carriers have moved across town. "We had a patio out back at our new place and it had that same slick, painted surface," Mike laughed. "Pretty soon I was out back belly-flopping on that thing too." Mike's dad had seen enough.

Robert Carrrier was an upholsterer whose company made seats for the boating industry. He wasn't trying to create a hit toy when he brought home a big roll of Naugahyde (fabric coated with vinyl) from his workplace. He was simply trying to

The first Slip 'n Slide, 1961.

WHAM-O

SLIP 'N SLIDE

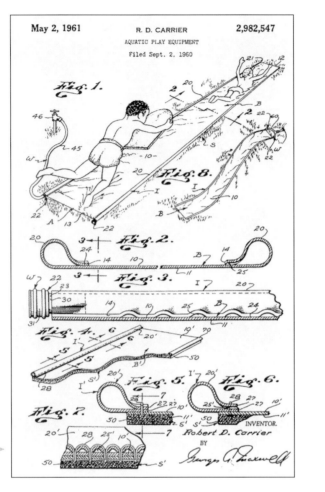

Robert Carrier filed a patent on his "Aquatic Play Equipment" on September 2, 1960.

give his son a surface safer than concrete on which to slide.

"He unrolled this thing in the front of our house. It must have been 50 feet long," Mike recalled. "Then he hosed it all down and the next thing you know he had every kid in the neighborhood in our front yard running and sliding, and he couldn't get them to stop. He told me that's when the light bulb went off."

Carrier took this long piece of ugly, beige fabric and looped one edge over a garden hose, sewed spaced stitches down the length of it and sewed the other end of it closed. When the water was turned on it filled the tube, and the resulting pressure forced the water out between the stitches, lubricating the slide's surface.

And the name? "He was trying to come up with a good one," Mike said. "So he asked himself, 'What are you gonna do with it? You're gonna slip and you're gonna slide—let's call it Slip 'n Slide.'" After showing it to the guys at work, Robert learned that his boss knew someone at a toy company up in San Gabriel. "After he heard that, he went through the process of patenting it," Mike said, "and took it to WHAM-O."

Spud Melin and Dick Knerr loved it. Needless to say, a 50-foot sheet of Naugahyde was not cost-effective, so WHAM-O released it as a 25-foot-long by 40-inch-wide strip of heavy-gauge, vinyl plastic. The package called it a "New Amazing Invention!" The WHAM-O Slip 'n Slide was first released at Toy Fair 1961. By September of that year, WHAM-O had sold 300,000 units with no end in sight.

From 1961 to 1992, over nine million Slip 'n Slide brand water slides were sold. Although Empire Plastics came out with a knock-off product called Crocodile Mile, which certainly ate into WHAM-O's market, it was the several serious injuries sustained by adults that took the Slip 'n Slide off the market in 1977 and then again in the early 1990s. Today it's back, but for kids only.

WHAM-O reports that for the past few years, their Slip 'n Slide line has been their biggest seller and consists of titles like Big Splash, Wave Rider, Super Geyser and Tropical Limbo. All Slip 'n Slides include inflatable

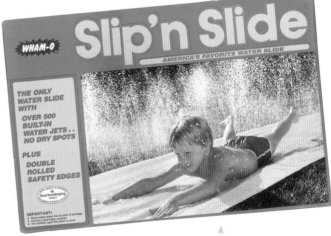

The 1984 version of "America's Favorite Water Slide."

Slip 'n Slide inventor Robert Carrier started his own aircraft interior business with the royalties from his invention. When the Slip 'n Slide was brought back by the new owners of WHAM-O in the mid-1980s, he negotiated a buyout of all his rights.

Like millions of kids who grew up in the '60s and '70s, we had countless hours of summer fun on Robert Carrier's invention. Our entire neighborhood lined up, slathered in the grassy muck that had collected at the end of the slide, with ample deposits of grass and mud in our hair and down our bathing suits. We didn't even notice. Up again and back in line we'd go, a never-ending stream of kids and water, running like an assembly line stuck at full throttle.

parts nowadays, making them sort of a cross between the original version and those classic inflatable pools. As a result, they are wetter than ever.

"My dad always told me that I was the inventor of the Slip 'n Slide because of what we did on the driveway," Mike Carrier said. "Of course, he was the real inventor . . . and a loving father."

Robert Carrier died in August of 2002, right before I finally tracked down his son. "It will be nice to give your father his proper credit," I said to Mike. "Oh yeah, I think so," he said softly. "It's just too bad you didn't call a month or two ago when he was still alive, because then you would really have heard some stories!"

Today's Slip 'n Slide toys are much more than they used to be. The Slip 'n Slide Tropical Limbo comes with two inflatable palm trees and an inflatable limbo pole, along with an 18-foot vinyl water slide.

Debut: 1965
Inventor: Norm Stingley
Company: WHAM-O
Insider: Ed Headrick

Super Ball

"It's Almost Alive!"

I miss my Super Ball. It was red and blue with swirls of yellow thrown in, just like the colors in Superman's costume and it really could leap tall buildings at a single bound. Of course it was eventually lost down the streetside sewer, or more likely, bounced to oblivion; but the memories of playing with it are as vivid as those colors. So, when I tracked down the man responsible for my favorite boyhood ball, I tended to call him "Sir" out of sheer appreciation and respect, but he would have none of it.

"First of all," he said in a friendly voice, "call me Norm." Unlike the high-bounding ball he created,

In 1963, Norm Stingley was chief chemist for Bettis Rubber Company in Whittier, California, when he invented the Super Ball.

Norm Stingley is incredibly down-to-earth. I gushed about how my "Superman" Super Ball (as I liked to call it) could bounce over our house, and he proudly replied, "Oh yeah—no trouble at all." Then he shared a story about how he had recently unearthed the past. He and his wife had just moved and he was tilling a garden in his new backyard. "I dug up what I thought looked like a ball and sure enough, it was a Super Ball, just like the one you're describing. It's still out there by the fence, but it's pretty bedraggled."

This is Norm Stingley, quick with a laugh and a story. And if you ask him, he will graciously share how 40 years ago, he had this idea.

"Bettis was in the oil industry," he said. "You've seen an oil well in the movies where they strike oil and it gushes? Well, you put one of our [rubber, molded] blow-out preventers on there and it won't do that, but that's another field."

The intersection of the oil field and the toy field describes the story of the Super Ball. As chief chemist for Bettis, whenever a company developed a new polymer, Norm was given first shot at trying to find

A super collection from 1965

applications for it. "One day they brought this material to me and after they left, I thought, 'I bet this stuff could sure make a good ball,'" Norm said. "I mean, you could cut a piece of it off the bale [the name for a block of rubber material after it was processed] and it would bounce like crazy, just in its raw state." He compressed the material to see if his hunch was right. Using a mold that Bettis had on hand to make part of an oil line valve, he took the auspicious leap into the toy field with explosive results.

"The first ball I made blew up!" Norm said with a laugh. "I compressed it under 2,500 pounds per square inch because that was the regular line pressure [Bettis used] for molding the valve parts. As soon as I opened the mold this stuff immediately tried to get out and tore itself to pieces! I later got patents on the molding procedure because you had to do it correctly by just barely filling the mold."

Amazed at the bounce the finished ball delivered, Norm took his invention to his boss at Bettis who called the ball "interesting," but questioned its commercial potential. "He had a young salesman there and he gave him a half dozen or so of the balls I'd molded and told him to take them out and try to sell them," Norm recalled. "But he couldn't interest anybody in them."

Despite the poor response Norm still believed in the ball, so he boldly sought a release from his employer. Bettis decided to focus on their business at hand and handed the rights to this new ball over to its creator. "Oh, I thought it would be big," Norm recalled.

THE TABLE TRICK

Through a friend in the toy business, Norm and his rubber ball were introduced to the guys at WHAM-O. "I went over there and met with Spud Melin. I bounced it first to show him and then he took it and bounced it too hard and it hit the ceiling!" Norm recalled. "But what really sold him

Bounce "Super Ball" so that it will hit on underside of table. "Super Ball" will return to you!

"There happened to be a low table there [at WHAM-O] and I threw it under the table and made it come back to me," Norm Stingley said. "Spud asked 'Can you do that again?!' and I said, 'Sure, I can do it every time.' So I did it again and he said 'Sold!'"

on it was the table trick." Eventually depicted on nearly every Super Ball package, Norm had discovered the nifty feat while throwing the ball under the heavy lab tables at Bettis Rubber (see caption above).

Although future WHAM-O packaging would show the ball flying over buildings, it started off as the ball that would fly apart, crumbling after too many bounces. Norm collaborated with WHAM-O's product development chief Ed Headrick on adding vulcanizing agents and making the ball more stable. "We worked on it over a period of three or four months," Norm said.

No. 278

WHAM-O MOST FANTASTIC BALL EVER CREATED BY SCIENCE!

SUPER·BALL

50,000 LBS. OF COMPRESSED ENERGY   PAT. PEND.

SUPER FUN!

PRICE 98¢

IT'S ALMOST ALIVE!

made of NEW AMAZING ZECTRON

MADE IN U.S.A.

...YOU CONTROL ITS SUPER POWER

Super Ball, the "most fantastic ball ever created by science!" really could bounce over a house!

WHAM-O

SUPER BALL

Once perfected, the WHAM-O marketing machine did the rest.

It was actually made of a polymer called polybutadiene, but they dubbed it "Zectron," a zingy, space-age "exotic material." It bounced so incredibly high that it seemed immune to the earth's gravitational pull. Beyond its ability to bounce back 92 percent of the height from which it was dropped, the Super Ball had what WHAM-O scientists called "an extremely high coefficient of friction." This meant that if you bounced a Super Ball to a friend 15 or 20 feet away, instead of sliding when it hit the ground at an angle, the Super Ball gripped the surface and picked up an incredible topspin. When it hit the ground a second time its rubbery spinning body acted like a tire on a dragster, propelling the ball forward, shockingly fast. Millions of kids soon had a love/hate relationship with the Super Ball's "second bounce." The accompanying

WHAM-O
SUPER MINI-BALL
PAT. PEND.
PRICE 98¢
50,000 LBS. OF COMPRESSED ENERGY
SUPER FUN!
6 times more bouncy
6 times more fun!
MADE OF NEW AMAZING ZECTRON
STOCK No. 2903
100s of games - super jacks, super marbles, super fun!

Sports and the Super Ball

The biggest game in professional football was once called the "World Championship Game." One day in 1969, Lamar Hunt, the head of the American Football League, recalled watching his daughter play with her Super Ball, and in that moment, renamed the contest "The Super Bowl."

In 1974, New York Yankee Greg Nettles was ejected from a game against the Detroit Tigers, after six Super Balls came out of his bat during a game. The slugger had illegally tried to "superfy" his bat with Zectron.

For promotional purposes, WHAM-O once had a Super Ball formed out of a bowling ball mold. "I mean, you can imagine a Super Ball that size!" inventor Norm Stingley shared with a laugh. "They bounced it in the hallway of a hotel and it broke through a wall. That was the end of that!"

welts they suffered while playing with this new leaping, lurching ball did nothing to slow the ball's sales.

Six million Super Balls were reportedly sold by the end of 1965, and kids everywhere had them—in their pockets, lunch boxes, junk draws and bedrooms.

"Oh, heck yes," Norm recalled. "My kids did. All kids did. In fact, I remember when the kids in our neighborhood found out who I was. We lived at the end of a cul-de-sac and many times they'd meet me as I pulled into it after work. They all wanted Super Balls. There'd be 10 or 12 of them yelling for me. I'd always have a few with me and I'd just throw them out the car window and let the winner take 'em."

With the Super Ball's bounding popularity it wasn't long before other manufacturers produced their own inferior imitations. Balls like Hi-Bouncer,

By the summer of '69, WHAM-O had extended the line to include "Mini" Super Balls, "Small" Super Balls, a Super Ball golf ball (for orbital blasts with Dad's 2-iron?), a Super Ball baseball, and even Super Ball Dice.

Jet Ball, Ski-Hi, and Zoomball, all cut into the original's action.

Over 20 million Super Balls were sold from 1965 to 1975. In '76, after several years of declining sales, WHAM-O updated the Super Ball by giving it "Bionic Bounce" in response to the popularity of *The Six Million*

Dollar Man TV show. By the end of the year, sales had declined so sharply that the Super Ball was taken out of the WHAM-O line.

In 1998, the bounce was back as WHAM-O reintroduced "The Original Super Ball," the only ball where "you control its super powers." Today it's still made from Zectron and it's still able to leap tall buildings at a single bound.

Norm Stingley and his wife have been married now for 63 years and they have three kids, five grandkids and six great-grandkids, all of whom know the fun of their grandpa's invention. "Oh yeah, everybody thinks I'm just wonderful," Norm says with modest sarcasm. But I soon found out that there's more truth to that statement than he's comfortable admitting. I got a lumpy brown envelope in the mail from him the other day. Along with a photo and press clippings he'd graciously sent was that dirty, bedraggled Super Ball discovered in his backyard garden. I don't know how he fit so much of my childhood into that envelope, but I do know that all I had to do to rediscover it was follow the bouncing ball.

THE WONDER OF A WHAM-O TOY

Beyond their abilities to spot new, exciting toys and their enviable marketing skills, Spud Melin and Dick Knerr knew something that allowed them to be the most successful summer toy maker that the toy industry has ever known. They knew that their next hit toy was probably going to come from outside the walls of WHAM-O.

In the book *Why Didn't I Think of That!* by Robert L. Shook, Richard Knerr explained the common denominator behind the success of Frisbee, Hula Hoop, Slip 'n Slide and Super Ball. "If a toy has magic, when people see it they say, 'Oooh! What is that?' A toy with that special ingredient makes an adult say . . . 'My gosh— look at that! It appeals to the kid in everybody.'"

In 1982, Spud Melin and Dick Knerr retired after 34 years inside the Fad Factory.

1970

1998

2001

THE PLAYMAKERS
Toy Timeline

1940   '45   '50   '55   '60   '65

1941
• Marvin Glass opens his toy design studio

1949
• Yakity-Yak Talking Teeth

1960
• Mr. Machine
• Super-Specs

1962
• Odd Ogg

1963
• **Mouse Trap**

1964
• **Hands Down**
• Time Bomb

1965
• **Operation**
• **Rock 'em Sock 'em Robots**
• **Mystery Date**
• Tip It

Marvin Glass

'65　　　　　　　'70　　　　　　　'75　　　　　　　'80　　　　　　　'85　　　　　　1990

1971
• Gnip Gnop

1970
• SSP Racers

1973
• Evel Knievel
  Stunt Cycle

1978
• **Simon**

1988
• Marvin Glass & Associates disband

1969
• **Toss Across**
• Dynamite Shack

1974
• Marvin Glass dies

1968
• Bucket of Fun

1967
• **Lite-Brite**
• **Ants in the Pants**

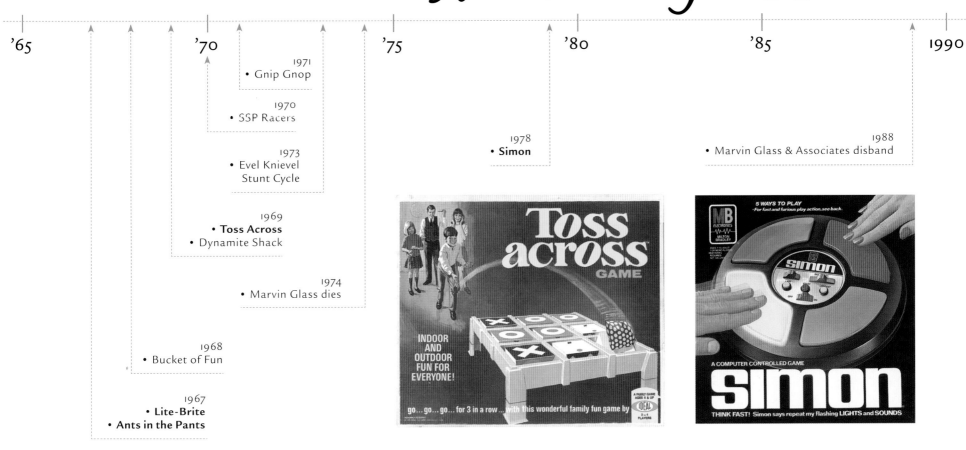

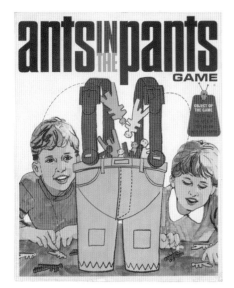

LASTING GAMES AND TRIVIAL PURSUITS

He could be greedy or generous. He was both an egomaniac and an insecure self-loather. He loved children's toys and sex, and to him the two were not mutually exclusive. Of his numerous traits, his greatest were his salesmanship, his work ethic and his uncanny ability to conjure forth the creative energies of those he employed, talents Marvin Glass learned early in his career.

After a failed attempt at making Christmas tree ornaments in the form of miniature stained-glass windows, Marvin plunged $300,000 in debt in the early 1940s. Others might have quit, but Glass was driven from an early age. He borrowed money from friends and started over, deciding this time to make toys and novelties for *others* to manufacture. Recognizing that he was more salesman than craftsman, Marvin was seeking a designer for his new enterprise in 1946 when he received a life-changing letter.

Eddy Goldfarb is one of the most respected toy inventors in the business today, but he was

Designer Marvin Glass talks toys with a colleague.

unknown and unemployed when he returned from World War II. Goldfarb sent a letter to twenty-five different companies within the toy trade. Glass got to him first and soon a profitable partnership formed around Marvin's salesmanship, Eddy's ideas, and a new way of manufacturing called injection molding.

GLASS AND PLASTIC

Plastic injection molding evolved from metal die casting, but whereas molten metals could easily flow into a mold, melted plastic had viscosity too high to be poured. Instead, a process was developed where great force was used to inject these "poly melts" into a hollow mold cavity. The technique meant that identical plastic parts could be produced inexpensively. "That was one of the exciting things about the toy business at that time," Goldfarb recalled. "You could take melted plastic, push it into a mold and then have that part. It was exciting."

Marvin sold Eddy's first two inventions, both made from molded plastic. The Busy Biddee Chicken and the Merry-Go-Sip cup (see *Kerplunk and Eddy*) became immediate hits after being introduced by Topic Toys at the 1948 Toy Fair. There, a bit of Marvin's sexual proclivities were revealed in his over-the-top promotion of the Merry-Go-Sip. According to the book *Toyland* by Sydney Ladensohn Stern and Ted Schoenhaus, " . . . Glass could not resist trying to boost sales at Toy Fair by handing out pictures of two nude models drinking from the cup."

As inappropriate as Marvin's marketing could be, the real beginning of the end for the Glass-Goldfarb partnership came earlier. "I got three jobs from those twenty-five letters I sent," Goldfarb shared. "The only one of the three that didn't pay me was Marvin Glass." By the time Marvin sold Eddy's third invention, the famed Yakity-Yak Talking Teeth, the partnership was nearing its end. "It didn't last long," Goldfarb says of his time with Glass. "We had two different personalities. I got married at that time and had a normal, happy marriage. Marvin was a different kind of a person. He should have gone to Hollywood."

Instead, Eddy left for California, while Marvin built his own toy empire in Chicago. Marvin Glass & Associates (MGA), and to a lesser extent Eddy Goldfarb & Associates, ushered in the era of big, plastic games, forever changing the genre. From 1962 to 1972, MGA introduced more than fifty games to the marketplace, an unprecedented number in such a short time. But the sheer volume wasn't as notable as the style of these playthings. Where board games were typically flat, MGA created bold, three-dimensional games. Some sat two feet high! They were loud, vibrant, and shook up the toy industry—just like Marvin Glass.

MARVIN THE MACHINE

Marvin's first big hit was Mr. Machine, a seventeen-inch-tall walking "robot" introduced by Ideal Toys in 1960. As demonstrated by Mr. Machine's release, plastics offered the prospect of updating old toys previously made from metal, wood or paper. Mr. Machine, a revision of the old tin robots of the 1950s, hit it big, earning Glass enough in royalties to turn MGA into a toy design dynasty.

Mr. Machine stands as a prime example of Glass's sense of the marketplace and his ability to predict what would sell. Inspiration could strike him anywhere—even while reading the paper. One of his biggest-selling inventions was inspired by some playful cartoons depicting, appropriately enough, inventions.

The original Mr. Machine was released in 1960 and was designed by MGA's Leo Kripak (a former watchmaker) and Burt Meyer. The toy became a part of Ideal Toys' corporate identity as the marching mascot who ended their commercials with, "It's a wonderful toy. It's Ideal."

Debut: 1963
Inventive Idea: Rube Goldberg
Inventors: Gordon Barlow, Burt Meyer
Companies: Ideal, Milton Bradley

Mouse Trap

MARVIN'S FIRST GAME

Rube Goldberg was a Pulitzer Prize-winning cartoonist, known for his "INVENTION" cartoons—crazy renderings of a series of outlandish props, pets, and people positioned together to form a contraption that accomplished the simplest of everyday tasks. The humor spoke to the fact that people are overwhelmed by the over-complication of their lives. Looking back, it's no wonder these cartoons appealed to something deep within the complex Marvin Glass.

"Marvin came up with the idea of doing a Rube Goldberg game and asked who'd like to do it," former MGA designer and partner Burt Meyer said. "Gordon Barlow [another MGA designer] was very new at the time and volunteered, but the engineering of the item got complicated and he was going to abandon it for another project." Meyer recognized the potential in the game and convinced Barlow to stick with it. Mouse Trap was revolutionary as one of the first truly three-dimensional board games, but also for the intricate way in which it was assembled by the consumer and ultimately, the way in which it "played."

In Mouse Trap, players move around the board, building the "trap" as they go. Mice tokens represent the players, all attempting to be the trapper and not the trapee once the apparatus is completed and it's time to turn the crank. The game came with 22 plastic parts, a rubber band, a steel marble, a plastic "bowling ball" and a spring, all positioned and connected to the board to create a trap that worked delightfully by domino effect.

Ideal introduced Mouse Trap at the 1963 Toy Fair and had an immediate hit that spring. A reported 1.2 million units of Mouse Trap sold before year's end. Marvin Glass & Associates was well on its way to becoming the center of the game development universe.

The game that put Marvin Glass & Associates on the map.

"Milton Bradley was first to see Mouse Trap but they passed on it," Burt Meyer, the game's co-inventor remembered. "We took it to Ideal next and when [company president] Lionel Weintraub saw it he said, 'This is it! This is the game that will put Ideal into the game business,' and he was right."

Burning wildly at MGA's center was its flamboyant namesake.

BURNING BRIDGES

Marvin could be very loyal to those in his inner circle but was paranoid and fearful of outsiders. According to Maynard Frank Wolfe, author of *Rube Goldberg Inventions,* in 1962 Marvin approached King Features, the company responsible for distributing and licensing Rube's work. When they asked for a royalty on Mouse Trap, which had plastic molded pieces virtually identical in style to Rube's cartoons, Marvin refused. No legal battle ensued; Rube was 80 years old at the time and retired a year later. The success of Mouse Trap inspired Marvin to follow it with two other Rube Goldberg style games called Crazy Clock and Fish Bait, introduced in 1964 and 1965 respectively. Neither credited Rube's influence. Marvin had burned another bridge, but as always, he never looked back.

"Marvin was a very strong, charismatic character," says former MGA designer and partner Jeffrey Breslow. "He could be very overriding and domineering on somebody. If you didn't stand up to him or have conviction in your ideas, he would steamroll you. That's how he operated."

Lyle Conway, another former employee, agrees on the two sides of Marvin Glass. "Marvin could be so cruel that you'd have to walk away from him because you couldn't stand to watch him be that abusive to someone. Other times, he could be so caring and generous. He was there for me when my mother died." Mel Taft, the longtime senior vice president of research & development at Milton Bradley says, "Marvin was a man that many people didn't like, because he could be quite tough-nosed, but if he liked you, he would give you the shirt off his back."

In 1960, a telling article in *The Saturday Evening Post* by Peter Wyden—appropriately titled "The Troubled King of Toys"—shed some light on Glass's personality. Born on July 14, 1914, to German immigrants, Marvin was short in stature (the article states he was five foot five inches as an adult, other accounts say he was five foot three). His tall father would wonder aloud why Marvin was so small. Marvin isolated himself from his father's verbal abuse and his parents' reportedly troubled marriage by inventing makeshift toys. He grew into a man tormented by a never-ending need to measure up. In his own mind, he never could.

In response to the success of Mouse Trap, Rube Goldberg licensed his cartoons to a model company called Multiple Products, Inc.

Debut: 1964
Inventors: Gordon Barlow
Companies: Ideal, Milton Bradley

Hands Down

SLAM-O-MATIC FUN

"The idea for Hands Down came from Marvin," Burt Meyer recalled. "He thought that a lot of old card and paper games could be done in plastic." Hands Down was an improvement on Slap Jack, a game where players had to be the first to slap a jack card when it appeared. Much of Hands Down's success can be credited to the gloriously loud Slam-o-matic, a big, blue plastic monstrosity that featured four brightly colored hands, all positioned palm-up and outstretched in "give me five" fashion (perfect for a game released in the mid-'60s). Four cards are dealt to each player, all seated within arm's length of the Slam-o-matic. On your turn, you draw a card and add it to your hand in an attempt to form a matching pair. If successful, slam down the nearest hand on the Slam-o-matic—with all other players following as fast as possible—then discard the pair and continue your turn. Beautifully engineered, the Slam-o-matic was durable and cleverly revealed who was the last to slam their hand down via an indicator in the center; slowest slap ended up with their color on top and lost a card, hoping to be faster next time.

Hands Down, shown here with its original 1964 packaging, introduced us to the classic "Slam-o-matic."

The best part of the game was the "fake." You'd start to go for the Slam-o-matic, but stop short in an attempt to get others to touch it. If they did, they had to give up a card to you. "Fakes" were often hysterical, with overacting, lurching and yelling all used in an attempt to fool the other players. The best fakers were proficient in the art of showmanship—an attribute that Marvin Glass possessed in spades.

SECRECY AND THE SHOWMAN

Legend has it that Glass's inventions arrived at Toy Fair via armored truck. Attractive models were commonplace at this, the biggest of all toy shows, but Glass's armed guards were altogether new to the industry. Glass got into the act too, sometimes carrying his inventions in a case handcuffed to his wrist. Large game prototypes traveled with the MGA designers, often strapped in a ticketed airplane seat next to their creator and never out of sight.

But was this all an act? Glass started MGA in nine rooms located on the ground floor of the Hotel Alexandria in Chicago. With success came renovation of a building at 815 North LaSalle Street in 1964, Marvin's very own fortress of secrecy and security. Surveillance cameras tracked people approaching the building and, according to former MGA designer Erick Erickson, "Marvin's office was double-walled and set to the inside of the building so that 'spies' couldn't eavesdrop from the Moody Bible Institute across the street."

Author Marvin Kaye described Glass's studio in his 1973 book, *A Toy Is Born:* "The 'fortress,' his Chicago headquarters, has no windows and is constantly patrolled by guards. Visitors are escorted up a staircase to Glass's office, and no farther. . . . Closed-circuit TV cameras keep watch over every doorway, and triple locks secure all portals. The locks are changed periodically, and only three full

sets of keys are ever maintained. Glass holds one set, while the owners of the other pair are unknown, even to each other." Oaths of secrecy, verbal and written, precluded designers from speaking about their projects with anyone, even their spouses. It was the Pentagon of Playthings.

Debate continues as to just how much of Marvin's obsession with secrecy was hype and how much was from actual fear of another toy maker stealing his ideas. Burt Meyer, for one, thought Marvin's obsession with secrecy was genuine. "You're dealing with a product that is worth your entire year's income . . . you need to protect it." While there's no doubt that the toy industry is cutthroat and competitive as any business, Marvin had reasons for security beyond the obvious. "Marvin was a man that had all kinds of phobias," says Jeffrey Breslow. "He was a great showman, but I think a lot of the secrecy was also based on his own paranoia."

An anonymous former employee cited Glass's carnal preoccupations as yet one more reason his studio was in a constant state of lockdown. "Everything was sexual with Marvin. There were frequent parties with belly dancers and other women. It was a strange, sealed-up place."

The '80s version of Hands Down promised "Slap-Happy Fun!"

Marvin Glass

HANDS DOWN

(L to R) Gordon Barlow (Hands Down, Mouse Trap), Leo Kripak (Mr. Machine), Burt Meyer (many MGA hits), and the man himself, Marvin Glass.

In *Toyland,* Stern and Schoenhaus describe him as "manipulative, predatory, and sexually voracious." He was married four times, twice to the same woman; one of his former wives was a Playboy bunny. His palatial estate in Evanston, Illinois, was built to equal the mansion owned by his friend and rival Hugh Hefner. Glass's home was even featured in a *Playboy* pictorial entitled "A Playboy Pad: Swinging in Suburbia." Mixed with photos of a naked masseuse in Glass's sauna and four nude frolickers in the bathtub Jacuzzi, the layout included some other adults (clothed, thank you) playing Funny Bones, a card game that MGA had created and sold to Parker Brothers. While most would find a family card game and nudity to be an odd (if not uncomfortable) pairing, mixing business with pleasure never seemed odd to Glass.

Sexuality aside, Glass's primary love was his work. "His main passion was the toy business and the men that worked for him," says Jeffrey

Breslow. "Marvin loved women, but he would give up anything for a meeting to talk about a new idea. If there was a long holiday weekend, he'd call us all up to his house for a meeting. If he had to spend three days alone without talking toys, he was a pretty unhappy guy."

Even when he was talking toys, Marvin showed regret. He is quoted in Wyden's article as saying "I consider myself a complete and utter failure." Despite his business' success, he bemoaned the fact that he never produced a hit doll and lamented over his stature. Part of his perverse charm was making others feel sorry for him, but deep down, there was truth to his torment. Both his generosity and his uncaring audacity masked deep insecurities. The resulting fallout on those close to him had a polarizing effect. "People loved him or hated him—there was nothing in between," says Breslow. Lyle Conway agreed. "As much trouble as I had with Marvin, I loved the guy. He fired me and then re-hired me three times . . . he was just totally off the wall." More than anything, he was passionate. "An idea session without a lot of shouting is a bad one," he was quoted as saying in *A Toy Is Born.* He challenged anyone and everyone, and seems to have enjoyed a good fight.

The Marvin Glass Logo

Marvin had the hits to back up his legendary ego. He was one of the few designers to have his company logo printed on the games his company created. "It was something that Marvin fought for and got because companies wanted to buy his products," former MGA designer Jeffrey Breslow says. "After Marvin was gone, the name just went away."

Operation

Marvin Glass

Debut: 1965
Inventive Idea: John Spinello
Developers: John Spinello, Gunars Licitis, Sam Cottone, Jim O'Connor
Insider: Mel Taft
Company: Milton Bradley

PLAYING DOCTOR

In 1962, John Spinello was an industrial design student at the University of Illinois when he was given the assignment to design a toy. He scored the highest grade in the class with his electric game where players took a metal probe and carefully inserted it into different holes within an electrified box without touching the sides of the metal-framed openings. If they failed, a bell would startle them.

"I showed the concept to my godfather, Sam Cottone, who was a top model maker at MGA," Spinello told me. "Sam was the one that convinced Marvin to see me. When I got there, Marvin said 'What is this piece of @#&!? Get it off my desk.' That was typical Marvin. But he tried it and when he touched the side, the bell went off. Marvin yelled and jumped back in his seat and said, 'I love it! I love it!'"

Glass gave Spinello a deal

Milton Bradley executives were fearful that the surgery theme of Operation was too grotesque. In the end, efforts like naming the patient Cavity Sam and giving him a light-up nose and humor-laced "body parts" won everyone over. Pictured here is the orignial game, released in 1965.

Marvin Glass

OPERATION

that he couldn't refuse. "He offered me $500, and better yet, a job upon graduation. I took it. He paid me in two installments of $250 dollars, but I never got the job. My wife and I got married in 1965, the same day I graduated. After our honeymoon, I called Marvin. 'Your studio isn't ready yet,' he told me. I got the runaround for about a month and half until finally I was told through his lawyer . . . that I was getting my name on the patent, but no job." Ironically, Spinello was eventually hired by MGA, but only after Glass's death. "Jeff Breslow hired me 10 years later, and of course, by that time Operation was a huge success."

At first, Spinello's game was called Death Valley (see below), a theme suggested by Cottone. The object was to insert an electric probe into a series of spaces, holes and channels as you progressed along a board designed to look like a desert. As you searched for water (presumably in the many holes) you tried to avoid touching the metal sides of the openings. By the time Milton Bradley released the game, its theme had dramatically changed. I asked Mel Taft, the

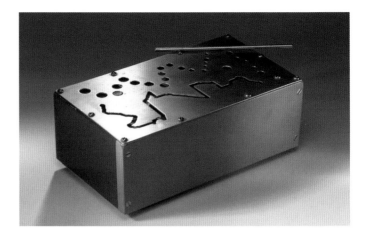

John Spinello's electric game—the prototype to Operation. Two plates, one a positive charge and the other negative, were positioned parallel to each other and only a ¼-inch apart. When the metal scribe touched the bottom and the top plate, the scribe completed the circuit and the 12-volt lantern battery set off a 6-volt bell. "It was over-engineered," John confessed. "It was loud!" But therein lies the fun of the game. Sparks flew, the bell rang and people jumped.

legendary gamesman at Milton Bradley, to shed some light on how the premise of the game went from the desert to the operating table.

"I saw the game at Marvin's studio," he said. "Every month I'd go out there and work with them on ideas." Taft liked the idea and took it back to Milton Bradley for further development. "One of my designers, Jim O'Connor, suggested to me that the game would be much better if we could have things in the holes and have the players take them out," Taft recalled. "I agreed, and so we altered the play from what Marvin had shown us." Instead of using an electric metal probe that players inserted, the now familiar electrified metal tweezers would be used by the players to remove objects. A buzzer sounded if the tweezers touched the sides of the openings, so the core of the game remained the same; the full conversion didn't happen until someone at Milton Bradley had the brilliant idea for the surgical theme and Operation was born.

Oddly enough, when Milton Bradley changed the game, a buzzer went off at the U.S. Patent Trademark office. The alterations MGA and Milton Bradley made

The patent for "a game utilizing an electronic probe" reflected its original theme. Once inside Milton Bradley, "Death Valley" became Operation.

to Spinello's game were significant enough to infringe on another patent held by a small toy company. Taft contacted that company and arranged to buy their patent on behalf of Milton Bradley, but still felt an obligation to MGA. "I insisted that we still pay Marvin Glass a royalty," Taft said. "My reasoning was that if I hadn't gotten the original idea from them, we never would have come up with the new idea." Taft fought hard for what he felt was right and finally convinced his boss to pay MGA. "Looking back, it was one of those things in my career that helped me enormously with Marvin," he said. "He cried when I told him that we were using another patent but that we were still going to pay him a royalty on the game. I had no regrets."

Milton Bradley didn't either. They went on to license many more games from MGA over the years, including Bucket of Fun, Dynamite Shack, Mystery Date and Simon, among others.

If Glass truly appreciated Mel Taft's integrity, it's a shame he didn't extend that same courtesy to John Spinello. "Anyone can look up the patent and see I created it, but what I really needed back then was a job," Spinello told me. He now owns his own successful trucking and warehouse company and has recently started to collect the many Operation spin-offs being produced, including pens, key chains and computer games, preserving his legacy for his grandkids. "I was wearing an Operation T-shirt one day and this older woman came up to me and asked me about it. When I told her that I had something to do with the game, she just gushed. She said 'My son became a doctor because of that game!' Her husband came over and they took my picture. They didn't want to leave me alone. So am I proud of it? Yes I am."

John Spinello, co-developer of Operation.

Except for the cigarette dangling from the surgeon's mouth on the 1965 box, the packaging for Operation has not changed in 38 years.

Rock 'em Sock 'em Robots

"THE BATTLE OF THE CENTURY . . ."

Forget Mr. Machine. If ever there was a game that epitomized Marvin Glass, it was this one. Marvin was a fighting robot. He worked 14 hours a day, battled with everyone, and if he got his block knocked off, he'd simply go again. He loved the action of the toy business and of all his company's toys, there was none more action-packed than Rock 'em Sock 'em Robots.

Recent reintroductions include a line of action figures, a Playstation game, a *Toy Story* version with Buzz Lightyear and Emperor Zurg slugging it out, and finally a reissue of the 1965 game, albeit on a much smaller scale. For many kids of the '60s, this game has no equal. The gear-like "whirrrr" of the Blue Bomber or Red Rocker's head popping up has the powerful ability to take us immediately back to the bouts of our youth. When our digits wore out, we used the palm of our hand to squash down the yellow plungers; you sacrificed mobility when you did this, but it always seemed to make your robot's jab all the more lethal. A loud game, it was inspired, fittingly, by a trip to the raucous fun of Chicago's penny arcades.

"Marvin and I used to go to the arcades and check out their games," Burt Meyer shared. "One day we found this two-player boxing game. We thought it was fun, but

In the days before Nintendo, Rock 'em Sock 'em Robots was the game that gave us sore thumbs. Pictured here is the 1965 original.

it was this great big clunky thing. It was very cumbersome with figures that were covered with rubber so they looked somewhat real. We started working on a game, but the mechanism was bad. We were having trouble getting some realistic motion in it which would allow the figures to fall over." Despite the design challenges, Glass and Meyer were ready to move

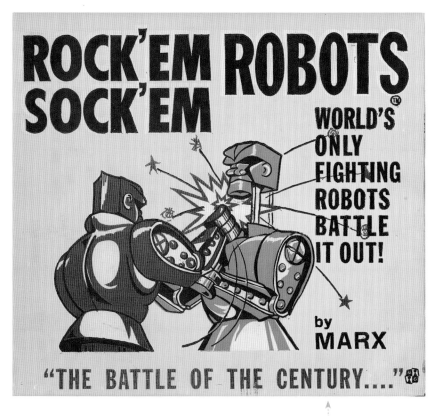

ROCK 'EM ROBOTS SOCK 'EM

WORLD'S ONLY FIGHTING ROBOTS BATTLE IT OUT!

by MARX

"THE BATTLE OF THE CENTURY...."

Making the boxers robots lowered the complexity of the engineering. "All we have to do is make their heads pop up or something," Burt Meyer excitedly told Glass. Marvin agreed, and the newly named Rock 'em Sock 'em Robots was put back into development.

forward with the development of the game until an unforeseen tragedy halted development.

On March 21, 1963, boxer Davey Moore died shortly after fighting for the world title in Los Angeles and a dark cloud hung over the sport. Suddenly, creating a boxing game was out of the question. "Marvin said 'We're going to drop it. The engineering is too hard and no one will do it with this stigma of death in boxing,'" Meyer recalled. The idea was shelved until Meyer had the ingenious idea of making the combatants robots.

Judd Reed and other designers at MGA worked on the look of the robots and how they would function. But when the patent was issued on February 15, 1966,

the list of inventors on the official document was topped with the name Marvin I. Glass.

MARVIN I. GLASS: INVENTOR

Although Marvin's name is on the Rock 'em Sock 'em Robots patent, he had little to do with the true invention and engineering of the game itself. Stern and Schoenhaus say in *Toyland:* "Ironically, Glass, who . . . left his name on what became the preeminent design firm in the country, never invented a single toy, but he was the only toy 'inventor' ever to achieve recognition outside the industry. He managed to take credit for everything . . ." Marvin was an egotist, and since his name was on the company letterhead it also found its way onto many of the company's patents, whether he deserved the credit or not. But Marvin was creative. "To say he never invented anything is an exaggeration," Meyer says. "Many times he would define something. 'Let's make this boxing game. Let's make some giant sunglasses.' He did invent. No question about it."

Jeffrey Breslow agrees. "He was the spark. He was the motivation behind many, many ideas. The fact that he didn't physically make the thing is irrelevant. He had the people to do that. Marvin was the driving force in the company."

Although Marvin Glass & Associates was certainly the dominant player in the business of toy and game design, they had no monopoly on ideas. Just as toy companies relied on MGA and other design houses for new concepts, MGA needed outside help from time to time too—although Marvin was reluctant to admit it.

According to former MGA designer Erick Erickson, Marvin Glass found himself at a dinner party listening to a bespectacled, self-absorbed bore, when he envisioned the man's glasses growing until they were as wide as his shoulders. The result was the Glass-designed Super-Specs. Self-absorbed bore sold separately.

Marvin Glass

ROCK 'EM SOCK 'EM ROBOTS

Mystery Date

FUN COMES KNOCKING

What would you get if you crossed Barbie in all her high-fashion glory with 1965's biggest game show, *Let's Make a Deal?* Marvin Glass did just that and got Mystery Date. In this classic game, the question became *"Who's* behind door number one?" The anticipation of who would come calling crested on every turn of the game's little blue doorknob.

"Mystery Date was Marvin's idea, but Henry Stan created it," Burt Meyer said. Girls started the game not knowing where they were headed or with whom they were going. Each player collected two pieces to an outfit and one corresponding accessory and then hoped that her date matched the destination for which she had planned all game. Gather your things for a nice trip to the beach and you might open the door on an admirer who's planning to take you to a formal dance. No match and the paper hunk was history. The neat door mechanism (or "random selecting device" as the patent calls it) is what created such great antici- pation and made the game a sleepover favorite throughout the late '60s. The five possible bachelors were pictured one per card and stacked within the plastic

door frame. Depending on the turn of the doorknob, the players would cause the back side of the doorknob to catch a

Meet your secret admirer!

Is your date behind this door?

Mystery Date is one of the most sought-after games from the '60s. An original like the one pictured here can sell for $150 -$200 to collectors nostalgic for suspense and all those secret admirers.

different tab on the stack of die cut cards, revealing a different guest when the door was opened. Simple, yet ingenious—the mark of a Marvin Glass design.

The game was updated in 1972, but was discontinued sometime in the late '70s. For the game's 35th Anniversary in 2000, Milton Bradley reintroduced it as "the classic mystery game for girls . . . updated for the new millennium." With three kinds of mysteries to solve and 24 boys to vie for, girls can lose themselves in this modernized dating game.

The original Mystery Date featured the hunky beachgoer, the athletic skier, the fab formal date, the bowler, and of course, the dreaded dud. Today, more than a few girls would pick the dud over the bowler, but times and appearances have changed.

Life with . . .

When I asked Norman McFarland, a former designer for MGA and the co-inventor of Toss Across, if he had any stories of Marvin Glass that he'd like to share, a laugh erupted from my phone's earpiece. It was a response I would hear time and again when interviewing those who knew this one-of-a-kind toy king.

"Oh, there are many, many stories," McFarland said. He told me of the time Glass decided out of the blue that he wanted to go to Mexico, and roped McFarland into making the trip with him. McFarland's recount was something out of *Planes, Trains and Automobiles*. "Every time we'd get to the plane he'd panic and back out," McFarland said. "I think that happened two or three times. So he said 'If we go by train, I'll be okay.' I think we got as far as Joliet [from Chicago] and he got off. Then he said 'Well, maybe we could drive down.' So he contracted with a driver from Mexico City to drive up to the border and meet us. Marvin's personal driver drove us from Chicago all the way to the border, but when we got there, Marvin just couldn't give up his car, so here we are—two Americans with two cars and two chauffeurs driving down to Mexico City. We got down there and Marvin was convinced that he was dying, so we had to turn around and make this mad dash back. We drove all night to get back to the States. That was life with Marvin." He laughed. "On the drive back he asked me if I had a good time, and I said 'It was very luxurious Marvin, like sitting on a gold tack.'"

Marvin Glass

Debut: 1967
Inventor: Burt Meyer
Company: Hasbro

Lite-Brite

PAINTING WITH PEGS

Bright lights, big city. During the Toy Fair bedlam of 1966, Glass, Henry Stan and Burt Meyer were walking down Fifth Avenue in New York when inspiration struck. The trio stumbled upon a window display featuring hundreds of different colored lights. They stopped and Meyer noticed that other pedestrians had also slowed for a second look. "All three of us had the same thought," Meyer recalled. "'Boy, a kid would love to play with that!'"

The men speculated that such a toy would be unsafe, impractical and too expensive to make with individual lights. They were about to continue walking when Meyer had a brainstorm. "I bet you could get the same effect with

one light and a bunch of pegs," he said. But when Glass questioned the cost and Stan wondered aloud how they would block out the light from where the pegs weren't placed, the idea was dropped. "Later, I thought; well hell, just a piece of black paper would block

Burt Meyer, inventor of Lite-Brite and many other Marvin Glass hits.

A light-filled window display in Manhattan inspired Burt Meyer to invent Lite-Brite, a way for kids to "create beautiful pictures with . . . LIGHT." Pictured here is a first edition from 1967.

out the light," Meyer said. "So I went back to the shop and started working on a model."

The original prototype Meyer created had two thick plastic panels with an identical series of holes in each. He used a small injection molding machine in the MGA studio to make pegs out of polystyrene and sandwiched black paper in between the panels to block out the light from where the pegs weren't placed. When these translucent-colored pegs were plugged into the holes, they perforated the paper blocking the light and appeared to magically "turn on." The effect was so dramatic that Glass immediately invited the head of Hasbro to come to Chicago for a demonstration.

"I brought Merrill Hassenfeld into our conference room," Meyer shared. "I dimmed the lights and plugged it in. As soon as I put a peg in it, the peg lit up. After he tried it himself, he sat back and said 'That's my item!' Marvin and Merrill inked a deal within an hour."

TOY TRIP

It is a testament to the influence and power of Marvin Glass that toy companies almost always flew to Chicago to see him and his toys and rarely the other way around. Ideal, Schaper, Kenner, Lakeside, Parker Brothers and others benefited from his studio's prolific output and trekked from all over the country to see what MGA was doing next. Of course, Marvin's fear of flying may have had something to do with it, but ask anyone who was fortunate enough to see inside and they'll tell you—Marvin's studio was worth the trip.

The exterior was drab and grey with all the style of a prison, but the inside gleamed with opulence and sophistication. Chandeliers, sculptures of nude females and original paintings by Dali graced the interior. An on-staff Chinese chef prepared daily gourmet lunches for the partners and any visiting

Hasbro engineers initially thought Lite Brite couldn't be done for the right price and still work safely. Merrill Hassenfeld insisted that they keep at it, and eventually the common household light bulb—used creatively two years earlier in Hasbro's Easy Bake Oven—became the solution. Pictured here is Hasbro's original prototype packaging for Lite-Brite, first displayed at Toy Fair in 1967.

dignitaries. Toy ideas were presented in state-of-the-art conference rooms, complete with dramatic lighting and long, comfortable couches. Presenters in white lab coats would roll in the products on cloth-draped carts, all in the name of salesmanship and theatrical suspense.

Few outsiders saw the design section, but it rivaled the office in appearance. "It was the most incredible shop you'd ever seen," Erick Erickson said. "There were milling machines and this bank of lathes that were all set at angles and painted toy colors like Willie Wonka, you know? Orange, blue, green. They were definitely intended to be a toy producer's fantasy, even though very few people were ever allowed back there."

Lyle Conway recalls one celebrity piercing Glass's corporate veil. MGA had designed a stunt cycle for Ideal that was all the rage in 1973. "I remember Marvin walking Evel Knievel through. He was a showman with an ego just like Marvin. He was fascinated by all the machinery we had there more than the toys."

Debut: 1967
Inventor: Jeffrey Breslow
Company: Schaper Toys, Milton Bradley

Ants in the Pants

FINGER-FLICKIN' FUN

Of the many games Jeffrey Breslow has worked on in his 36-year career, his longest-selling one was also one of his simplest. "We were going through names and clichés, looking for any that could be turned into a game," he said. "We had pages and pages of sayings like 'bird in the hand,' 'ants in the pants,' etcetera. Schaper [Toys] had Don't Break the Ice out at the time. It wasn't very involved or difficult. Ants in the Pants started with a name, which is not typical. Typically you start with a concept and then struggle to come up with a good name."

Just like its name, Ants in the Pants was irresistibly cute. It brought the classic play of Tiddly Winks to a younger audience. The original game featured wood or plastic Winks that were often difficult for little fingers to control. With Ants in the Pants, kids flipped the plastic ants with just a flick of the finger. However, learning to control their crazy trajectories was another story and a big part of the fun. One look at some kids trying to arch those classic springy bugs into those big blue overalls is all you need to understand why this game has lasted nearly four decades. The game was a huge success for Schaper Toys, second only to their Cootie game in popularity.

Jeffrey Breslow began working for Marvin Glass in 1967, the same year his first big invention, Ants in the Pants, was released.

Ants in the Pants continues today (along with Cootie and Don't Break the Ice), as the core of Milton Bradley's preschool line.

Toss Across

Marvin Glass

Debut: 1969
Inventors: Norman McFarland, Burt Meyer
Companies: Ideal, Tyco, Mattel

TIC-TAC-TOSS

Ants in the Pants updated an old favorite into three dimensions. The same can be said of Toss Across. The best ideas make us say, "Why didn't I think of that?"

The spark of the idea for Toss Across came from Norman McFarland, a professor of design at the University of Illinois, who worked for Glass on and off for over 20 years. Burt Meyer worked with McFarland on it until the two had devised a clever way to give the old game of Xs and Os an ingenious upgrade. Imagine playing a game of Tic-Tac-Toe where you could erase the X your opponent wrote down or turn it into an O—or even mark two or more Os on a single turn. Toss

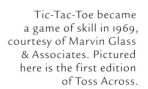

Tic-Tac-Toe became a game of skill in 1969, courtesy of Marvin Glass & Associates. Pictured here is the first edition of Toss Across.

Marvin Glass

Toss Across

Norm McFarland, co-inventor of Toss Across.

dropping a beanbag from its mouth. Today, Mattel sells Toss Across to a new generation of families.

Out of the Game

On July 8, 1973, Glass suffered a stroke that began a dramatic decline in his health. "Marvin was not someone who took care of himself," Jeffrey Breslow said. "He smoked three packs of cigarettes a day, drank twelve cups of coffee, and got little sleep." Sadly, no matter how many hours he worked, how many women he had, or how many millions he made, he never seemed to find happiness. He eventually succumbed to cancer and died in January of 1974, at the age of 59.

"He was the most brilliant guy I ever knew and the most unusual man I have ever run into in my life. I regret that I only spent seven years with him," Breslow says. Mel Taft added, "There are few people I would put this nametag to, but Marvin, he was a genius."

Across allowed you to do all of the above . . . if you had the aim.

By turning the familiar Tic-Tac-Toe grid into nine targets, McFarland and Meyer introduced a skill factor to the game. They devised a triangular shape for each target that would rotate within each space on the grid. "The trick was in engineering them to rotate 60 degrees and remain face up when they stopped," McFarland recalled. When the team finally found the solution, Toss Across found a home at Ideal Toys. It was released in 1969 as a "new" game that the entire world already knew how to play. The new twists were demonstrated in TV commercials by a boy who nails two in a row with a sidearm throw, followed by a dog scoring the deciding mark by

"Everybody loves it—" Ideal's 1967 catalog said of Toss Across. ". . . young and old, at parties, on the beach, anywhere!"

Simon

Marvin Glass

Debut: 1978
Inventors: Ralph Baer,
    Howard Morrison
Developer: Lenny Cope
Company: Milton Bradley

FOLLOW THE LEADER

In 1977 the toy industry witnessed the phenomenal success of Atari's Video Computer System. As games like Pong and Centipede were being played on TV sets across the country, Space Invaders erupted within American arcades. Marvin Glass had recognized and embraced the plastic revolution within the game industry in the post-war years; now Jeffrey Breslow, Burt Meyer and the other surviving partners in MGA saw the new writing on the wall: electronic games are here to stay.

MGA was certainly no stranger to the electronic game market. After all, by the time Atari made their splash, Operation and Lite-Brite had both been selling for over a decade. Although those games were electric, their nonelectric components comprised a very big part of their play-value. To bridge the gap separating games powered by electricity from games where the fun was in the electronic programming itself, MGA called upon the man who invented the video game.

Ralph Baer was chief engineer at Sanders Associates, a military electronics development and manufacturing company, when in 1966 he conceived of playing games on a standard TV set. Over the next six years, Baer worked towards producing the first video game system, succeeding with the release of Magnavox's Odyssey in 1972, the game that led to Pong. Soon after Odyssey's release, Ralph sent a letter to MGA touting his expertise. The timing was perfect for both parties and a great partnership was struck. Of the many games he

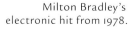

Milton Bradley's electronic hit from 1978.

Marvin Glass

SIMON

Ralph Baer was MGA's "outside electronics capability," and the co-inventor of Simon.

made for MGA, his biggest hit was inspired by a trip to a trade show.

Baer first saw a new Atari arcade game called Touch Me at the Music Operators of America show in 1976. It was a large, coin-operated cabinet game with four buttons facing the player. After depositing a quarter, the buttons lit up in random sequences while emitting corresponding sounds. Your goal: repeat the sequences of lights and sounds by pressing the correct buttons. The game was a flop, probably because most coin-op arcade games were based on action, not memory. Despite its poor performance, Baer and MGA partner and designer Howard Morrison agreed that the concept of Touch Me warranted a closer look.

Jeffrey Breslow remembers well the first time the idea was explained to him. "Howard came into my office and said 'Grab a pencil and follow me.' I had a glass there and he tapped the glass, so I tapped the glass. Then he tapped the desk and I followed." Morrison added an additional target each time, making the

game progressively more challenging. Breslow agreed that the idea had merit, so Morrison and Baer set out to turn the concept into an electric handheld game. Morrison dubbed it Follow Me.

Baer and his "software guru," Lenny Cope began writing code in early 1977, embarking on what would prove to be a two-year journey with lights and sounds. Cope encoded and re-encoded the game to the specifications laid out by Baer and Morrison. Baer designed the rest of the game and credits a subtle portion of its development as the key to the game's longevity.

Simon started with four buttons that needed to emit four distinct tones that sounded well together in whatever order they played. "It was a nontrivial matter," Baer contends. "The tones define the game's character." He was looking through a children's encyclopedia for an instrument that could play tunes with only four notes when he discovered the lowly bugle. It could play G, C, E and G in any order and still sound somewhat pleasant. "If you're gonna have four tones associated with four buttons you might as well pick those," Baer said. "They sound consonant and they don't grate on your ears."

Mel Taft from Milton Bradley saw the game first and loved it; however, Simon went through many revisions before the rest of the game world got to play. As Baer and Cope produced a working model for approval, followed by a microprocessor version, Milton Bradley's marketing team tried out potential names. It was called Follow Me, then Tap Me, then Feedback, before being aptly named Simon after the children's game of Simon Says.

Although the development of Simon was a tedious process, the timing of its release could not have been better. Baer

Howard Morrison, co-inventor of Simon.

and Morrison finally filed for the Simon patent in July of 1977. That same summer, Steven Spielberg's *Close Encounters of the Third Kind* was released to theaters. In the film, the circular alien spacecraft communicates via tones and lights. The fortuitous similarities between Spielberg's spaceship and Simon, and the amazing box office success of the movie, propelled the game's popularity. By the end of 1982, after just four years on the market, Simon had sold over 10 million copies.

The earliest models of Simon were monsters, requiring two "D" batteries and one 9-volt battery to power its lights and sounds. There were four skill levels to choose from and three separate games to play. The four large buttons in bright primary colors lit up and sounded off when the game started. It was your task to press the same buttons in the same sequence as Simon. If you pressed correctly, Simon added one more to the sequence, and so on and so on. As the game progressed, the sequence quickened, adding suspense and pressure. Repeat the sequence incorrectly and a horrible "RAZZ" announced your mistake, but make it to the end of a level and Simon rewarded you with a six-signal salute.

"Other companies marketed cheaper versions, but they completely forgot that part of the charm of the game is the proper selection of the tones," Simon co-inventor Ralph Baer said. "That's certainly one of the psychological reasons why the copy cats became also-rans and Simon is still selling today." Today, the new Simon 2 (which was released in 2000) comes with two playable sides and "seven brain baffling games!"

THE END OF AN ERA

In 1988, Marvin Glass & Associates disbanded. For Marvin Glass, the legacy of his name is assured in the playthings that he helped create. Decades from now children will still be trapping that mouse, flipping those ants and creating art with all those bright plastic pegs. It's sad that Glass never took lasting joy from that fact. After giving so much fun, so much delight and so much excitement to so many, the success, approval and love that he endlessly searched for was right there all along.

Marvin Glass was a genius. It's a shame he wasn't smart enough to figure that out.

Marvin Glass & Associates wasn't the same without its figurehead, yet the firm survived not only his passing but a terrible tragedy as well. Two years after Marvin's death a disturbed designer roamed the offices, killing three people and wounding two others before turning the gun on himself.

Many former MGA designers launched their own successful toy design companies. The two most prominent are Meyer/Glass, formed by Burt Meyer, and Big Monster Toys (formerly Breslow, Morrison, Terzian & Associates), formed by Jeffrey Breslow, Howard Morrison and Rouben Terzian.

"Marvin was such a good salesman that he could sell an item to a manufacturer one evening only to have the guy wake up and say to himself the next morning 'What the hell did I just buy?'" Eddy Goldfarb said with a chuckle. "Then he'd have to call Marvin that following day and back out of the deal. That happened all the time."

Marvin Glass was inducted into the Toy Industry Hall of Fame in 1984.

The author with Simon (and his little sister, anxiously waiting her turn), Christmas morning, 1979.

Marvin Glass

SIMON

THE PLAYMAKERS
Toy Timeline

1960 — '61 — '62 — '63 — '64 — '65 — '66 — '67 — '68 — '69 — '70

- **Trolls**
- **Lego**
- Stratego

- Wal-Mart, Kmart and Target stores are all established
- Mille Bornes

- **Etch A Sketch**
- **The Game Of Life**
- Play-Doh Fun Factory

- **GI Joe**
- Mighty Tonka Dump Truck
- General Mills buys Rainbow Crafts

- Snurfer, predecessor to the Snowboard

- **Twister**
- Barrel of Monkeys

- **Spirograph**
- **Kerplunk**
- Skip-Bo
- General Mills buys Kenner

- **Big Wheel**
- **Nerf**

- General Mills buys Parker Brothers

120 PIECE SET

LEGO Building Toy

Etch A Sketch

HOURS OF fascinating FUN FOR THE ENTIRE FAMILY
DRAW LINES WITH Etch A Sketch in any direction
DOODLE DIALING FUN ALL
PRINT write DRAW
Just SHAKE TO ERASE
unlimited design possibilities
SKETCH · ERASE AND SKETCH AGAIN

G.I. JOE ACTION SOLDIER
by HASBRO
America's movable fighting man
MOVE G.I. JOE INTO ACTION POSITIONS

THE GAME THAT TIES YOU UP IN KNOTS
Twister
MILTON BRADLEY COMPANY
SPRINGFIELD MASSACHUSETTS 4645
FOR AGES 6 TO ADULT
A STOCKING FEET GAME
OBJECT

THE GAME OF LIFE
A FULL 3-D ACTION GAME
MILTON BRADLEY 100th ANNIVERSARY GAME

1960s–1970s

'70	'71	'72	'73	'74	'75	'76	'77	'78	'79	1980

• Boggle

• The Little People, predecessors to Cabbage Patch Kids

• Stretch Armstrong

• **Uno**
• Alabe Crafts is bought by Ideal Toys
• Odyssey, predecessor to Pong
• Milton Bradley buys E. S. Lowe for the rights to Yahtzee
• Othello

• Pong
• Connect Four

• Binney & Smith buys the rights to Silly Putty
• Magic Cube, predecessor to Rubik's Cube

• Pente
• Shrinky Dinks
• Dungeons & Dragons

• Mastermind
• Whizzzer

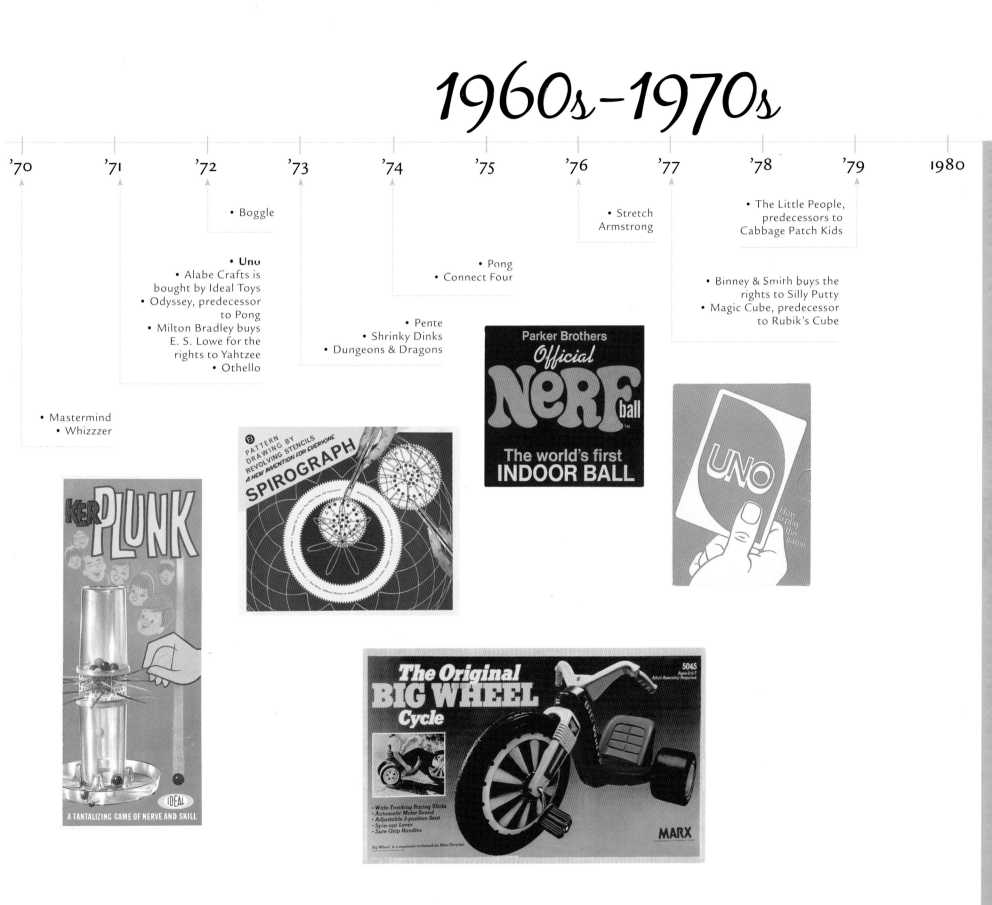

Debut: 1959 as Telecran in
France
U.S. Debut: 1960
Inventor: Arthur Grandjean
Developer: Paul Chaze
Insider: William Casley
Killgallon
Company: Ohio Art

Etch A Sketch

LINE ART

This simple drawing device has captured our imaginations for 44 years. A lot has changed since 1960, but thankfully the success of the Etch A Sketch has been as continuous and unbroken as the little black line that I can't . . . make . . . curve . . . *the way I want!* Shake and start again, I say. Had I invented the toy, it would have been called the Dump A Drawing. Thank goodness Bill Killgallon had a better idea.

William Casley Killgallon was the man who named our favorite drawing toy. In 1959, he was working for a toy company called Ohio Art as its director of development when he received a call from a toy agent. The agent was representing a Frenchman named Paul Chaze who had developed this amazing new drawing toy called "L'Ecran Magique," or Magic Screen. After hearing about the device, Bill was intrigued enough to want a firsthand look and soon found himself on a plane to New York. Meanwhile, the agent informed Mr. Chaze, who spoke very little English, that the prestigious Ohio Art company was sending someone to review his new toy. What Paul Chaze, his agent and Bill Killgallon didn't know, was that Ohio Art had already turned down the Magic Screen.

Original Etch A
Sketch, 1960.

OHIO ART

A dentist named H.S. Winzeler founded Ohio Art in 1908. Over the years the company made wonderful tin toys and Disney play sets, which are coveted by collectors today. By 1959, Winzeler had passed the reins to his son, Howard "Howie" Winzeler. An active president, Howie Winzeler made yearly treks to all the major Toy Fairs. In 1959, several months before Bill Killgallon's fateful trip to New York, Howie attended the International Toy Fair in Nuremberg, Germany, where he stumbled upon this amazing drawing device. The owner wanted

$100,000 for the rights, so Winzeler declined. One hundred thousand dollars is a lot of money today, but in 1959 it was a small fortune.

Paul Chaze wasn't a greedy man, but he believed he had a hit toy. He was a garage mechanic who owned a tool shop near Paris. A talented employee of his named Arthur Grandjean had invented a drawing device that required no batteries, had no pieces that could get lost or components that would wear out. Chaze brought it to Nuremberg with high hopes and a hefty price tag. Like Howie Winzeler, every toy company executive that saw L'Ecran Magique passed once they heard what Chaze wanted for it. Undaunted, but perhaps a bit more humbled, Chaze hired an American agent to arrange for a U.S. tour after the Nuremberg fair in the hopes of attracting a U.S. manufacturer. When Bill Killgallon saw L'Ecran Magique for the first time in New York, he was impressed by its intricate construction and simple mechanical function. It was a stroke of engineering genius. He immediately called his boss, Howie Winzeler, who listened as his director of development excitedly described what he had seen. Soon the picture was clear. "I saw that in Nuremberg!" exclaimed Winzeler. Was it fate? Winzeler thought so. If he and his head of development had both independently seen this toy at opposite ends of the world, and both independently liked it, then it warranted a second—or in this case, a *third* look. Killgallon convinced Chaze and his agent to come to Bryan, Ohio, and after a more reasonable (but still steep) advance of $25,000 was agreed upon, Howie Winzeler and Paul Chaze signed a one-page contract that agreed to pay Chaze royalties over time. That humble, handwritten deal turned out to be worth millions.

After months of development (it seems relatively simple today, but in 1960, the manufacturing of such

This '70s ad called the Etch A Sketch ". . . one of the nicest childhood memories anyone can have."

a complex toy was no easy task) this 9-inch by 8-inch device received its now famous moniker. Although Magic Screen is still a part of its name, most of us just call it the Etch A Sketch. Production began in earnest on July 12, 1960, and soon thereafter Ohio Art introduced it to American toy lovers with a national television campaign.

The first commercials featured a little girl named Pernella who was reduced to hiding under a basket with her Etch A Sketch because everyone wanted to play with it. Once she came out, however, she proudly proclaimed "It's magic! I'm not using pencils or crayons or chalk . . . and look! No mess!" The ads were such an immediate success that by Christmas of that year, Ohio Art had trouble filling all the orders. They frantically pushed their production to its limits, all the way up till noon on Christmas Eve. At that point, production stopped so that they could get shipments out to West Coast stores in time for Christmas morning.

PLASTIC, POWDER, AND PULLEYS

Our magical tour of the Magic Screen begins inside its plastic casing. There, a static-charged concoction of aluminum powder and plastic beads awaits its first shake off the assembly line. Once in motion, static electricity causes the powder to stick to the underside of the glass screen, giving the Etch A Sketch surface its silvery appearance. Next, the white knobs act to move two rods (which are connected to a stylus) by a system of pulleys threaded with nylon string. Twisting one knob controls horizontal lines and twisting the other controls vertical lines by dragging the tip of the stylus across the underside of the screen. The powder drops to the bottom of the casing and—tah dah—a black line or "etch" appears. Turning the screen over and shaking it scatters the powder over the etch, erasing it.

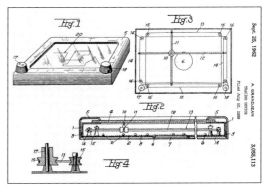

1960s–1970s

Etch A Sketch

How many December 25ths have seen the unwrapping of a brand-new Etch A Sketch? It's been called the first laptop, but requires no power source other than fingers. Who can forget sitting with it and twisting away on a rainy afternoon? Remember the soft sounds of tension against the nylon string when you turned the knobs? How about the telltale shaking sound? Were you in that group of curious ones who just had to clear the entire screen, or at least a small window, in order to see what marvels were hidden inside? If so, your patience was rewarded with a shadowy view of the stylus and rods. They looked like relics in an archaeological dig, partially covered by all that silvery sand lying underneath the glass.

Persistence was all it took to clear the screen, but drawing anything identifiable required practice. Something like a staircase was simple enough to render because straight lines were a snap (or a twist), but getting a line to *curve* where you wanted was another story. The ultimate test of your etch a skill? Drawing a circle. You had to continuously twist both knobs one way and then try to smoothly reverse direction with each knob *at the exact same speed but at different moments.* Anyone who has ever attempted the maneuver would have to consider professional Etch A Sketch artist, Nicole Falzone, the Monet of the Magic Screen. There are a handful of talented Etch A Sketch aficionados out there, but Falzone has attained a measure of deserved mainstream attention; her remarkable etches of celebrities like John Lennon and Louis Armstrong

Etch A Sketch artist Nicole Falzone creates images that are nothing short of amazing.

Shake It!

This classic TV spot with a catchy jingle ran in the '70s and encouraged all ages to draw (and shake) their Etch A Sketch, anywhere they wanted!

Etch A Sketch!
Turn the dials and you'll see what I mean
Yeah, your fun time starts with Etch A Sketch!

A line appears magically
Shake it upside down, it's fun you'll see!
O-HI-O ART! Etch A Sketch!

Draw anything
Your mind can see
Anywhere you have to be
O-HI-O ART!
Etch A Sketch!

Sketch Appeal

The Etch A Sketch line now includes pocket versions, "Jelly" colored versions (like the Travel Etch A Sketch shown here), and even the Etch₂o Etch A Sketch, featuring a frame filled with liquid glycerin and glitter.

Perhaps a part of the Etch A Sketch's multi-generational charm lies in the fact that it has remained unchanged to parents who grew up playing with it in the '60s, '70s and '80s. In its 44 years on the market, the Etch A Sketch has never utilized a licensed character to help sell it . . . until now. Sababa Toys recently released the Hello Kitty Etch A Sketch, with amazing results. The toy doubles as a purse, and has drawn a huge crowd of little girls.

have appeared on *Late Night with David Letterman* and other national TV programs. Envious of her unusual skill, I asked for some tips and discovered that she is also an ambidextrous, dyslexic drummer. Okay, mystery solved.

Innate abilities aside, the two big secrets Falzone shares with other Etch A Sketch pros out there are planning and a good power drill. The trick in making your Etch A Sketch art permanent is to drill holes in the back of its casing and carefully drain the aluminum powder. With no powder left to threaten your fine art, it's now suitable for hanging, already in a frame of red.

In 1977 the Killgallon family bought Ohio Art from the Winzelers, and today William Killgallon's son William Carpenter Killgallon runs the company. When I asked him why Etch A Sketch has lasted so long, he had a simple response: "It's magic!" Then he added, "The secret to the Etch A Sketch is that it engages a child, allowing them to input their own creativity while playing. It can be challenging, too, so there's a sense of satisfaction when you create a nice picture."

After learning how it works, am I a better Etch A Sketch artist? Nope. I take consolation in knowing that erasing my mistakes is half the fun. After a little shake my slate is wiped clean and another silvery canvas calls out.

Arthur Grandjean filed for a French patent on his device on May 28, 1959. Gradjean was working for Paul Chaze, and the two had presumably signed a common agreement where anything invented by an employee becomes the property of the employer. That is why the U.S. patent granted on Sept. 25, 1963, named Arthur Grandjean as the inventor and assignor to Paul Chaze.

Since we etched our first sketch in 1960, over 100 million Etch A Sketch toys have been sold in more than 70 countries.

In 1971, Ohio Art released Etch A Sketch with "Cool Blue" and "Hot Pink" colored frames, but classic red remains the best seller.

Debut: 1860
Inventor: Milton Bradley
(1836-1911)
Company: Milton Bradley &
Company

The Game of Life

LIFE'S WORK

Milton Bradley was born and raised in Vienna, Maine. In 1856, he started out on life's highway with a dream of using his substantial drawing skills to launch a career as a draftsman. After being awarded an amazing lithograph reproduction of a drawing he had rendered, Bradley was determined to find his future in lithography, unaware that he would soon put his hand to work for a future president and eventually the most important benefactors of his work—generations of children.

Today, lithography is known as "offset" printing. It was revolutionary at the time because it allowed an image to be reproduced at a higher quality and quantity than ever before imagined. According to the 1960 book, *It's All in the Game* written by James Shea, Bradley bought a lithography press in Providence, Rhode Island, and after learning how to use it, brought it back to Springfield, Massachusetts, and formed Milton Bradley & Company in 1860.

Not long afterwards, a prominent man in Springfield contracted Bradley to produce a lithograph of a politician running in the 1860 presidential election. The candidate was a thin-faced and beardless Abraham Lincoln. Bradley reportedly produced thousands of lithographs of "Honest Abe" and sales were brisk. By the time Lincoln won the presidency, however, he had grown a beard. Demand for Bradley's lithograph of a clean-shaven Lincoln abruptly stopped, with some customers even requesting a refund. Bradley was considering what to do with the scores of Lincoln lithographs that no one wanted when the Civil War broke out, seemingly marking his business for failure. Instead, Bradley hit upon the idea of putting

Milton Bradley's first game—an 1866 version of The Checkered Game of Life. The game box and components date to the 1870s.

his idle presses to work making games, and in 1860, set out on what would be his life's work.

It seems prudish today, but in Puritan New England in the 1860s, games were taboo. They were associated with the wickedness of gambling and the wastefulness of seeking idle pleasure (a trivial pursuit if there ever was one). Bradley's solution was an instructional game on morals, wherein the goal was to reach 100 points and "Happy Old Age." The game was designed on a checkerboard, with alternating squares representing either virtue or vice. Players who landed on spaces such as "HONOR" or "HAPPINESS" gained points and moved further toward contented senior citizenship. Others who landed on "IDLENESS" or "CRIME" moved backwards. Since dice were considered the devil's instruments and cast only in sinful games of chance, Bradley used a teetotum in his game; a numbered top that, after being "twirled," came to rest with a number "remaining uppermost" on the top's hexagonal surface. In *It's All in the Game,* it's evident that naming the game was pivotal in Milton Bradley's mind. Shea writes:

> Studying the checkered pattern of the game on his rolltop desk, he [Milton Bradley] thought that it was like the design of his life and the life of nearly everyone he knew: checkered, hazardous, uncertain in its outcome. Life was like a game, and a game—a good game—must be like life itself. You subscribed to fixed rules, you recognized the element of chance, and you exercised all the skill and judgment you possessed to win it. He would call it "The Checkered Game of Life."

With no dice and a strong moral lesson throughout its play, the new game avoided controversy and attracted buyers. According to Shea, Bradley hand

Milton Bradley was a draftsman, lithographer, publisher and educator. He founded the company that bears his name in 1860.

made several hundred copies of The Checkered Game of Life and set off for New York City to try and sell some of them to shop owners. With a steamer trunk full of games and a belief in what he had created, Bradley boarded the succession of three trains that carried him on the long trip from Springfield, Massachusetts to New York City. When he returned from his successful trip, his trunk was empty. Back in New England his games sold just as fast as he could produce them.

"He sold games by traveling around New England with his horse and buggy," says Mel Taft, the longtime senior vice president of research & development at Milton Bradley. "He sold 40,000 games. At that time—well, even today, that's one hell of a lot of games!"

The game was updated in 1866, in the 1870s, and then again around 1911, the same year that Milton Bradley died. As times changed and the popularity of board games grew, more game companies ventured into the realm of entertainment, forsaking the moral lessons that early games preached through play. With the phenomenal success of Monopoly, a game where the goal was to bankrupt all opponents and emerge wealthiest, the era of "fun" games officially arrived. Suddenly The Checkered Game of Life, with its overt ethics, didn't seem all that

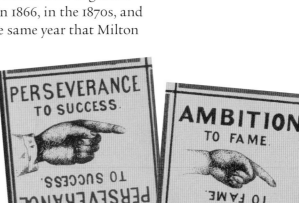

The success of The Checkered Game of Life can be credited directly to Milton Bradley's perseverance and ambition—not coincidently, two virtues also featured in his game.

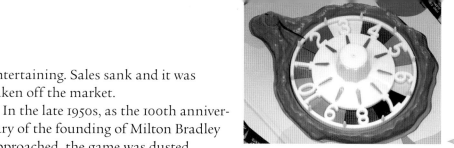

The Game of Life was one of the first games to discover plastic's potential. Today the spinner in The Game of Life remains one of the most recognizable sounds in all of games.

1960s-1970s

Debut: 1960
Predecessor: The Checkered Game of Life (1860)
Inventor: Bill Markum, Ruben Klamer
Developer: Art Linkletter
Company: Milton Bradley

entertaining. Sales sank and it was taken off the market.

In the late 1950s, as the 100th anniversary of the founding of Milton Bradley approached, the game was dusted off and updated for an entirely new audience. When The Game of Life was unveiled, it was apparent that times had certainly changed!

Puritan principles and the 1960s. Some things just don't mix. The Checkered Game of Life needed a total revamp to fit the new times,

and the Milton Bradley Company hired game inventor Reuben Klamer to work on the update. Klamer knew TV personality Art Linkletter, who was the host of *two* TV game shows in 1960, *People Are Funny* on NBC and *House Party* on CBS. Sensing huge promotional potential, Klamer, Linkletter and the Milton Bradley Company inked a deal that funneled royalties through Linkletter's company, Link Research Corporation, in exchange for promotional endorsements. According to Mel Taft, who was in charge of the project at Milton Bradley, a talented designer named Bill Markham who worked for Klamer, actually designed most of the game. "He [Markham] decided to make the game three dimensional," Taft said. "It had roads raised up with elaborate buildings. I'll tell you it made your mouth water it was so beautiful, but we had to take it and make it cost-effective. Geez, we had a terrible time."

Taft's dilemma defined the very thing that gave the new game its visual appeal, for Markham and Klamer had created the first three-dimensional game board using plastic. Over the years, the term "plastic" would also come to mean something marked by artificiality; the surreal world of The Game of Life fit that description.

The goal in The Checkered Game of Life was happiness through moral choices as viewed through the lens of the 1860s. The updated version, released for Milton Bradley's 100th anniversary in 1960, gave kids a new goal: "the player with the most money WINS THE GAME."

Called "A Full 3-D Action Game," the wonderful rolling hills, tall plastic buildings and the classic "Wheel of Fate" spinner delivered on that box-top billing. The only thing laid on thicker than the 1-inch-high plastic board elements was the '60s kitsch of gambling found in this "swinging" new version. Dean Martin's Rat Pack was at the height of their popularity when the game was released, so perhaps it's no accident that the spirit of the 1960 version emits a *Viva Las Vegas* vibe.

Looking for some fun, my family and I gathered to play the 1960 version of the game, the one with Art Linkletter's face on every $100,000 dollar bill. In the world I have entered, plastic is just about everywhere. All my children are made of plastic. My plastic wife sits next to me in our plastic convertible. It's the latest model and everyone in our town has one just like it. We cruise through the days of our lives on our hunt for fortune. It's really a perfect, plastic little world . . . but then the soap opera starts. All of a sudden there are lawsuits and everyone's having *twins.*

My uncle goes to jail for God knows what, and then my mother is put on probation. *MOM?!* Everyone seems to have just returned from the races, Vegas or Monte Carlo. In the Life I'm in, my best friend sells me a phony diamond and takes me for $10 grand, but fortunately one lucky landing on a space marked REVENGE and he's gotta cough up $100,000. This version of Life (like revenge) is sweet.

To be fair, we also had a ton of fun playing this old classic. Who could forget that spinner? If you spun it too hard, it would pop out of its hillside home and take out half the neighborhood. That's an indelible memory from my boyhood days of playing the game. But what The Game of Life really gave us kids was the chance to play grown-up. While Monopoly provided the adult thrill of financial decisions, The Game of Life gave us money choices and more. The rules told us, "You start out on Life's highway, just out of high school, with a car and $2,000." Right from the start you had a decision to make. *Should I buy car insurance or drive on the edge? Should I be patient and go to college or take*

All my girls were named "Peg," my boys, "Rod."

The many gambling references in the 1960 version of The Game of Life are ironic considering that gambling led to ruin in The Checkered Game of Life. Today's version of the game has no mention of bet making.

the quicker route and join the work force right away? For kids, this newfound responsibility was liberating and the fantasy, downright fun. Money changed hands on every spin of the wheel and parents liked the counting and subtracting the game taught. Exposure to the adult world of insurance, stocks, taxes and bank loans sprang up along the game's winding path.

In the 1990s, The Game of Life was politically corrected. Life tiles were added that were "all about family activities, community service and good deeds!" Now instead of collecting $50,000 from a weekend in Las Vegas, you earn it after finding a solution for pollution, saving an endangered species or finding a new energy source. The revenge spaces are gone and players hand over money to other players based on the careers chosen and services rendered. For instance, if you're an accountant and someone lands on a taxes due space, you get paid. Medical

expenses are paid to the person who chose a career as a doctor. And if you're a computer consultant, you get paid anytime another player twirls the spinner off its track.

Milton Bradley would be amazed at how his game has evolved over the years. Ambition may move you forward in all versions of the game, but the fun lies in the journey taken. Maybe Milton knew that all along. After 144 years, that seems to be the lesson learned. Win or lose in Life, it's how you play the game.

The Game of Life has been translated into 20 languages.

Recently, Hasbro has introduced themed versions of The Game of Life including one based on *Star Wars: Attack of the Clones* and the animated film *Monster's Inc.*

Kids still love to play grown-up with today's version of the Milton Bradley classic.

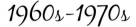

Debut: 1956
U.S. Debut: 1961
Inventor: Thomas Dam
Companies: Dam Things
   Establishment—Dam
   Trolls, Uneeda Wishniks,
   EFS Manufacturing,
   Norfin Trolls, Playmates

Trolls

SHORT ON LOOKS, LONG ON LUCK

Art is a funny thing. When it's bad, it's just bad, but when it's *really* bad, it starts to look . . . good. Likewise, grape juice needs to turn a little before it is wine. As it is with the finest of things, so it is with the haute couture of play figurines, the troll doll—so very ugly, and yet—so cute. The French may be famous for their art and wine, but the Scandinavians were the ones that gave us trolls.

It all began in Europe, where the weaving of scary troll tales was a Nordic tradition. Gigantic, mean and flesh-eating aren't the typical adjectives used in describing trolls today, but that's the way trolls came into the Old World. As the stories evolved, trolls lost their great size and strength but not their malicious behavior. In the old tales, tiny trolls kidnapped babies and seduced unsuspecting women. Only sunlight or hearing their own name, as in the story of Rumplestiltskin, could kill a troll.

Over time, these creatures achieved a more benign reputation much like their cousins, the elves and dwarves. Eventually, trolls were not only perceived as good, but actually as good luck charms. A few thousand years and some creative P.R. can really polish an image!

The troll dolls that took the world by storm in the '60s were known as Dam Trolls. Thomas Dam (pronounced Dom), began his working career as a baker. After World War II, the factory that supplied Dam with the flour he needed to run his bakery closed and he went bankrupt. He shoveled snow for money, and although it was certainly a devastating period in his life, Dam would later quip, "It was the greatest bankruptcy ever. I never got up early again [as bakers do] and it got me carving more." Thomas Dam's idle carving soon changed his luck.

Dam's son Niels was five years old when his father put his considerable wood carving skills to use. Today Niels runs the company his father formed in Gjol, Denmark. "My father was not a big man, so throwing snow,

Forty years of good luck. A 2001 Totally Troll stands beside her forefather, an original 12-inch Dam Troll from 1961.

his only other option at the time, was not a good one," Niels told me. "My father came from a home where you don't sit with your hands doing nothing. Even back when he was baking, he would carve at night by the fireplace, cutting funny figures. It was my mother that convinced him to go and try to sell his carvings in Alborg."

Alborg was the city nearest to Gjol, and it was there that Thomas Dam began selling his figures door to door. On his first trip, he sold all the figures he had brought, which was all that he could carry. Niels laughed when he told the story. "He soon realized that he could make two or three times what he could make throwing snow, plus he could sit by the fire and carve, which he loved doing!"

Dam soon had customers in Alborg asking him to come to their house first so that they could have best choice of his new characters. He carved animals and caricatures of funny old men and women. One of his best customers owned an amusement park and loved Dam's work so much that he hired the sculptor to create some monsters for his haunted-house attraction. Dam first designed and sculpted the creatures in clay. Next a gypsum cast was made and used to mold them

in a flexible, lifelike rubber. Thus Dam discovered a means of producing his figures much more quickly than hand carving each one individually. Plus, he found that rubber was a much better medium than his original wood for conveying the detailed facial features of his work.

Word got around about the talented sculptor. In 1956, Dam was contracted by a large department store in Sweden to create a two-story Santa figure for their Christmas display. It was a huge project, made mostly of metal but with Dam's honed sculpting skills providing the figure's rubber face and hands.

The Santa store display was such a hit in Sweden that the owner of a local shop in Alborg hired Dam to construct a life-size Santa for his store. Only after he completed the figure did Dam notice that it was too big to be seen effectively from outside. That is when he thought of the window display that would turn passersby into customers.

THE TROLLS SPRING ONTO THE SCENE

Niels remembers vividly his father's first step toward toy immortality. "My father took mattress springs and made the body of the first troll dolls. He sculpted the hands and face from rubber and the spring was the body, which was hidden by a dress, like a hand puppet." Dam attached a row of these springy Christmas trolls to a long plank which was displayed in the window of the toyshop. "A simple mechanism that turned slowly around would lift up one end of this wood and drop it again and again," Niels recalled. "The trolls were standing there waving, jumping up and down and their heads were rolling. That was all it took."

Thomas Dam adjusts the beard on his giant Santa troll. The sculpture, created by Dam in 1956, became the Christmas link that led to the creation of Dam's troll dolls.

What happened next was very much like the story of Joshua Cowen's first Lionel train. The trolls were just part of the Christmas display, but the shop owner was confronted with people wanting to buy the display! Niels said, "The shopkeeper, of course, he told my daddy, 'You've got to make more of these because the people are totally crazy. They come in here and say they want to buy them!' and you know every one he made sold before Christmas even came." The first troll craze had begun.

Production of the first Dam Trolls started in 1956. They were made with their spring bodies at first and met with great success despite their high price. The springs were expensive, so Dam gambled that people liked his trolls because of their cute and whimsical appearance and not their bouncy antics. By 1957, he replaced the spring bodies with rubber ones that were then stuffed with wood shavings. Dam realized that his figures needed to become more than just Christmas trolls, since that season came only once a year. Dam's wife and daughter helped him fill demand as best they could, but they couldn't make the "Dam Things" fast enough. On May 11, 1959, they broke ground on a small factory, and formed Dam Things Establishment.

The labor and handwork required to make those first rubber trolls was intense, consisting of many parts that had to be hand-glued. By the end of 1961, the increasing demand for the Dam Trolls necessitated a change. Rotational molding arrived just in time for Thomas Dam and his family business. The process, where plastic is heated and then put into a rotating mold so that the finished, hollow plastic part has a consistent and uniform thickness, allowed for high quality dolls to be made from the plastic known as polyvinyl chloride or PVC, the same plastic used today.

Dam's creations were bowlegged, potbellied and wrinkle-faced. They had wide heads and a crooked, toothless smile. Their pointy ears were huge and their "deer in the headlights" eyes stared longingly, as if searching for some affection. Their arms spread open, offering a hug, with hands that each ended in four stubby little fingers. But the most memorable element of these dolls was their wild "penny in the light socket" hair.

By 1962, Thomas Dam added factories in New Zealand and Florida to keep up with the growing craze. The year 1964 marked the high point of the Troll craze in the United States, with over a million trolls sold under the Uneeda Wishniks brand. In the doll world

The Dam Trolls' unforgettable hair was called mohair, but was actually dyed wool. At the height of the Dam Trolls popularity in 1964, Thomas Dam purchased Iceland's entire harvest of wool.

The idea behind their appearance was simple, yet profoundly connected to their use as good luck charms. "They were so ugly," Thomas Dam once explained, "that when you looked at them you couldn't help but laugh, and when you laugh, luck follows you."

TROLLS

At their height, the Dam Trolls seemed to be everywhere. There were troll pencil toppers, carrying cases for collections and scores of other troll paraphernalia like this book from 1965.

Trolls, Acme Trollkins, HYI Fairy Tale Trolls, Galoob Monster Trolls; even Hasbro got into the game with Battle Trolls. All of them owe a piece of their good fortune to Thomas Dam.

A new law allowed Dam Things Establishment to regain their rightful copyright on the Trolls in 1996. The Dam family's new company, Troll Company ApS., continues to ship Dam Trolls all over the world. Even 40 years after their first appearance, you still can't keep a good luck troll down.

their sales were second only to Barbie. Hippies dug the trolls, kids dug the trolls, even the First Lady, Lady Bird Johnson, professed to love the Dam Things.

Being as ugly as they were, the Dam Trolls didn't receive many compliments, but they certainly received the sincerest form of flattery. By 1964 scores of imitators (not to mention counterfeiters) entered the market. Many of these knockoff trolls were unmarked to avoid identification of the maker, but some companies were bolder. A company called Scandia House introduced their own troll dolls—virtual replicas of the ones made by Dam Things Establishment. Thomas Dam sued, and the two companies settled their differences—joining forces in 1967. Other imitators popped up, and by the mid-1970s the market was so flooded that the sales of Dam Trolls were but a fraction of their 1964–1967 heyday.

In 1989, without warning, the trolls returned. Revitalized by a nostalgic public, the Dam Trolls (and their imitators) were back at the top of the toy world. In the early 1990s more troll dolls were shipped than in the initial craze of the 1960s—almost 2 billion dollars worth in '91 and '92 alone. Only a small fraction of those sales were official Dam Trolls (licensed as Norfin Trolls by EFS Manufacturing this time around). The other notable '90s troll dolls included Russ Berrie Russ Trolls, Applause Magic Trolls, Ace Novelty Treasure

In Dutch folklore, the Jule-Nissen or Christmas Troll, stayed with every Dutch family for the 12 days of Christmas as a good luck charm. Children who were kind and nice caused the Troll to stay and fill the house with kindness and peace.

The first commercial troll dolls were made in 1952 by Helena and Martii Kuuskoski of Finland.

Under an agreement with Playmates Toys, the original Dam Trolls entered the 21st century as the newly-named Totally Trolls in 2000.

Lego

PLAY WELL

Debut: 1958
U.S. Debut: 1961
Predecessor: Self-Locking Building Bricks (1949), Automatic Binding Bricks (1949)
Inventor: Godtfred Kirk Christiansen (1920–1995)
Companies: LEGO, LEGO Systems, Inc., The LEGO Group

Wooden building blocks have long been praised for their open-ended play that allows a child's imagination to run free. But as anyone who's ever built a tower out of wooden building blocks will attest, the bigger they come, the easier they fall. The legendary LEGO brick revolutionized building play by giving kids even more possibilities. They coupled together, enabling even the youngest architects to create elaborate and semi-permanent buildings, quite literally in a snap.

Out of the small town of Billund in Jutland, Denmark, Ole (pronounced Oh lee) Kirk Christiansen first started making wooden toys to supplement his line of wooden stepladders and ironing boards. The toys promptly outsold the tools, so the company shifted to playthings exclusively and took the name "LEGO," a contraction of the Danish expression "LEg GOdt," which means "play well." Specializing mostly in wooden toy vehicles and pull toys, LEGO soon earned a sterling reputation. Each toy received three coats of paint and was finished to exacting standards, a fact that made mass production of the toys impossible. To build

his business, Ole Kirk Christiansen needed something he could manufacture in volume while still adhering to his high standards of quality.

As fate would have it, and as Ole Kirk Christiansen would later learn, the word "LEGO," a term chosen for its Danish meaning, meant something entirely different in Latin. It meant "I assemble," or "I put together."

Deluxe LEGO set from the 1950s.

Master carpenter Ole Kirk Christiansen founded the company that became LEGO in 1932.

THE BRICK IS BORN

Like anything well made, LEGO had a foundation on which to assemble a toy empire. In 1939, Self-Locking Building Bricks were patented by plastics pioneer, Hilary Fisher Page, founder of the Kiddicraft Company. By 1945, he improved his building blocks by adding channels, which according to the patent, held "thin members which may represent windows, doors or the like." It was these early, plastic-injected building bricks and their accompanying doors and windows that influenced Ole Kirk Christiansen's son, Godtfred Kirk Christiansen, the man who gave the world the LEGO building system.

Kiddicraft introduced their Self-Locking Building Bricks in 1949. According to The Plastics Historical Society, LEGO introduced their "Automatic Binding Bricks" the same year after acquiring rights to the

Kiddicraft design. Released only in Denmark, LEGO's Automatic Binding Bricks had no fastening mechanism underneath their hollow frames and were prone to shrink and crack, a problem that often affected their ability to fit and stay together. In addition, these early sets were not colorfast and over time they faded. Despite their flaws, they sold well enough to establish a new direction for the LEGO company. By the mid-'50s, the quality of these new polymers had dramatically improved and plastic toys accounted for half of LEGO's product line. Although LEGO still made many plastic toy vehicles and wooden playthings, their little plastic brick would not be denied.

In 1953 the Automatic Binding Bricks were renamed LEGO bricks, a move that reflected their importance in

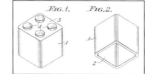

In 1939, Hilary Fisher Page applied for a British patent on his "Improvements in Toy Building Blocks" that featured familiar studs protruding atop each hollow brick.

Rare examples of Automatic Binding Bricks from 1949 line the top row. The bricks were renamed LEGO bricks (middle row) in 1953. A year later and the new logo appeared (bottom row). Slots are for doors and windows like the one pictured at lower right.

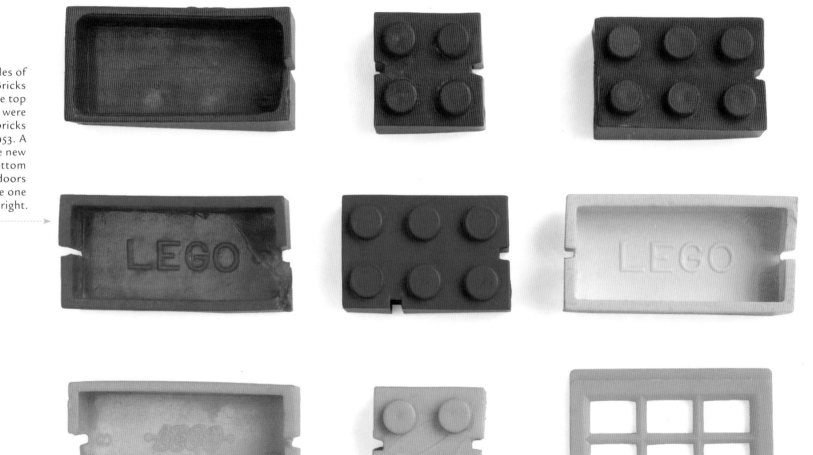

Godtfred Kirk Christiansen filed his patent on a "stud-and-tube coupling brick" on July 28, 1958. The new design created greater play possibilities, with two eight-stud bricks able to be combined in 24 different ways.

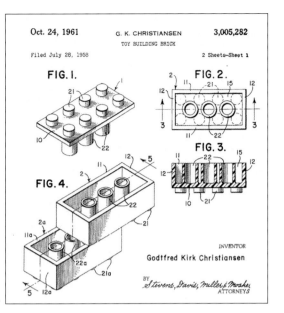

and allowed the studs to grip adjoining blocks more securely and in more ways than ever before.

The introduction of LEGO vehicles demanded that little plastic people exist to operate all the planes, trains and automobiles. The first LEGO figure was released in 1974. With a LEGO mother, girls could build a house and then "play house" after they were done. Boys could construct a castle and then storm it with a group of LEGO knights. LEGO figures gave the fun a human face and connected a snap-together world with the kids who shaped it.

the overall LEGO business. Even the vehicles that the company continued to produce in wood and plastic as stand-alone toys were now being offered as a part of LEGO sets. Vehicles had been demoted to mere props within the broader LEGO play. In 1955 "The LEGO System of Play" was introduced and entire towns could be created with these amazing little bricks, beams, doors and windows. The LEGO "Town Plan" line included 28 building sets and 8 vehicles, along with assorted plastic trees, road signs and lamp posts for play on a cardboard map that featured roads and walkways in a thriving downtown setting.

The company offered the first lighted brick in 1957, but it was the invention of their patented "stud-and-tube system" the following year that represented their greatest advancement. Godtfred Kirk Christiansen created a hollow tube within the formerly empty underside of the LEGO brick that flexed

Wheels were added in 1962 and marked the start of the company's inclusion of a diverse variety of shapes beyond the rectangle and the square brick.

A Chip in the Block

The LEGO company will always be synonymous with the basic building brick, but innovation and use of the latest technical advances have always marked their products. As they diversified to reach older kids, the toy went high-tech. Just 40 years after Godtfred Kirk Christiansen added a simple plastic tube to a basic building brick, LEGO designers inserted something almost unimaginable: a microchip.

In 1998, with the help of scientists from MIT, LEGO created a computerized building system called LEGO Mindstorms. Using a home computer to program the microcomputer hidden inside the RCX LEGO Brick, kids could construct robots that performed specific functions. The Mindstorms line continues today as kids fantasize about a future where their LEGO robot takes over their chores and a bunch of bricks makes their bed.

LEGO continues to innovate. The "parts" in their new Bionicle line form an ever-expanding universe that takes players on an adventure integrating comics, internet games and "webisodes," all telling a vast backstory. The Bionicle storyline features the "Toa," legendary heroes who seek the "Kanohi," also known as The Masks of Power, on the island of "Mata Nui," in order to defeat the evil "Makuta." Post-pubescent tongues may be twisted, but kids love mastering the strange names. (The Bionicle website features an entire lexicon of over 200 new words created just for use in the Bionicle story lines.) All this content, synchronized across multiple media platforms, has made Bionicle one of LEGO's biggest success stories. There are trading cards, video games, board games, pens, a sneaker made by Nike and a full-length feature film coming direct-to-video in 2004.

If all this cutting-edge stuff makes you long for the old school days, take heart, LEGO lover, and know that some things never change. Whether they're basic bricks or Bionicle components, LEGO parts are still stepped on by parents, sucked up into vacuums and lost under couch cushions everywhere. That's everywhere. It's been estimated by the company that *203 billion* LEGO parts have been manufactured since the first Automatic Binding Brick popped out of the mold in 1949. LEGO play sets are sold in approximately 115 countries, making it one of the most widely distributed toys ever created. Long live LEGO.

Bionicle, a futuristic line of parts that fit together in new and exciting ways, goes far beyond the mere connection of plastic to plastic. LEGO Technic (introduced in 1977), gives kids the ability to make models that move with the help of motors and gears.

Denmark's LEGOLAND Billund, a LEGO theme park which opened in 1968, welcomes almost 1.5 million visitors a year.

The miniature Port of Copenhagen in the Denmark LEGOLAND is LEGO's largest single exhibit, made from over 3.5 million individual bricks.

DUPLO bricks, LEGO's larger bricks for little hands, came out in 1967.

Early sets featured bricks of white and red, with only a handful of different building elements. Today's LEGO artist has a vast palette of colors, and over 2,000 different shapes from which to choose.

GI Joe

THE UNMOVABLE MAN

He arrives at toy stores with a conspicuous scar on his right cheek. If you get the sense that this guy has seen the front line long before the checkout line, you're right. Back in 1963, before GI Joe entered into a single conflict or launched a single mission—heck, before he even had his name—he earned his stripes in some hard-fought battles. He overcame corporate fear of gender typing and prevailed over the lack of funding for his military operation. He proved himself more masculine than a Ken doll, then had to travel over 8,000 miles to reach Rhode Island and the home of the company he ended up saving, Hassenfeld Bros. Inc., better known as Hasbro.

This fighting man's story of conflict and triumph starts in 1963, but curiously, not at Hasbro.

One version of the story has Larry Reiner, a designer for the Ideal Toy Company, in a brainstorming meeting for Ideal's popular Tammy doll line. According to G. Wayne Miller's book *Toy Wars,* Reiner's mind drifted off as talk turned to making older relatives for young Tammy. When someone suggested making Tammy's father a fireman and her uncle a policeman, Larry got a big idea: a soldier doll. Not a soldier like the little green army men that were frozen in a single position, but more of a military mannequin that could be posed holding weapons and equipment. He allegedly told his boss, Lionel Weintraub, about his concept after the meeting and was told flatly "boys will never play with a doll." Shortly after the 1963 Toy Fair, Reiner reportedly met with licensing agent Stan Weston, who was not so quick to dismiss the idea.

1960s–1970s

Debut: 1964
Inventive Idea: Stan Weston and Larry Reiner
Developers: Don Levine, Sam Speers, Hugh O'Connor, Janet Downing (Taylor), Jerry Einhorn
Insider: Merrill Hassenfeld
Company: Hasbro

". . . EACH SOLD SEPARATELY."

Another version of the story begins with Stan Weston working on his own soldier concept based on something Mattel's co-founder, Elliot Handler, had once told him. The success of his Barbie product, Handler said, was due to the "razor–razor blade" approach Mattel used in marketing the doll. Barbie was the "razor" and her myriad outfits and accoutrements were the "razor blades"—the accessories that Barbie fans couldn't do without. It took little imagination to see how this concept would work in an armed forces universe of military uniforms and equipment.

In John Michlig's book, *GI Joe: The Complete Story of America's Favorite Man of Action,* considered by many to be the definitive history of the product, Weston recalled a conversation with Larry Reiner wherein Reiner suggested that the soldier be poseable. Weston felt the suggestion had enormous value; he promised Reiner that, if the concept sold, he'd "be in for a piece of the action." As a licensing agent, Stan Weston had pitched TV and movie properties to numerous toy companies and had connections in the business. He decided to take this soldier doll concept to Don Levine, creative director at Hasbro.

Don Levine, who joined Hasbro in 1959, the same year that Barbie debuted at Mattel, grasped the accessorizing potential of this soldier doll concept. Although the comparison to Barbie was easy enough to draw, there was another example of collateral sales success much closer to home; Hasbro had released Mr. Potato Head nearly 10 years prior and had been accessorizing the spud profitably ever since. The real question was whether this soldier's potential could outweigh the many obstacles and "nevers" he would soon face.

The realism and detail that the toy commanded would require overseas manufacturing, something that Hasbro had *never* attempted. The cost of producing the kind of line that would discourage copying and establish their soldier as the first of its kind would necessitate an amount of up-front money that Hasbro

Licensing agent Stan Weston is credited as the man that brought the GI Joe concept to Hasbro.

had *never* before spent. The time frame was very tight—less than a year before Toy Fair 1964—which meant a turnaround time that Hasbro had *never* tried with such an expansive project. Finally, there was the industry belief that "a boy will *never* play with a doll."

NEVER SAY NEVER

Don Levine was the man who would have to champion the idea past all those early minefields. Development actually began while Hassenfeld was out of the country; Levine feared that his boss might reflexively squelch the project, and so he pushed his team to get far enough along on the concept to win over Hassenfeld upon his return. Next, Levine decided to banish the word "doll" when describing this soldier. They were building an articulated combatant, in the most generic terms, an "action figure." Yes, the deadline was tight but not impossible to meet. And the overseas production? Mattel and Marx, two of Hasbro's biggest competitors at the time, had both moved toward supplementing their domestic factories with Far Eastern manufacturing sources prior to 1963. If Hasbro were to compete, they would have to follow suit very soon—why not now?

But by far the nastiest "never" Levine and his team faced was the daunting amount of money Hasbro would have to venture to make their soldier a reality. By itself the investment would be a formidable hurdle, but coupled with the money that Hasbro had lost in 1962 ($2.7 million according to Miller) *and* what they were currently hemorrhaging in '63, it was a risk that could bankrupt the company.

Over the years several people have

Don Levine, the co-developer of GI Joe.

taken credit as "inventor" of GI Joe. Given his unusual start and passage from Weston and Reiner to Levine, all three men have been called (or called themselves) the father of our hero. All agree, however, that it was one man in particular who made the idea a commercial reality.

"Merrill [Hassenfeld] was the guy that said 'Let's do it,'" Don Levine told me. "It was a tremendous gamble! If he had said 'No,' GI Joe would not exist and you and I would not be talking about it 39 years later. It was Merrill's decision, plain and simple." Merrill Hassenfeld was the son of Hasbro's founding father, Henry, who formed the legendary company in 1923 with his brother Hillel. Now the future of Hassenfeld Brothers, Inc. hinged on Merrill's intuition. Levine was pitching a project with an unprecedented $15 million dollars in anticipated development costs at a time when the fortunes of Hassenfeld Brothers, Inc. teetered on the brink. Levine's faith in the concept was such, however, that he lobbied Hassenfeld constantly

with the materials his small team had clandestinely constructed while his boss was out of the country.

Finally, with everything on the line, Merrill tapped his formidable intuition and bravely green-lighted the project. He met with his bank contacts and jumped through extraordinary hoops to secure financing; the weight of his company's fate now lay on the shoulders of an $11 \frac{1}{2}$-inch plastic man.

Of course plastic can't *feel* pressure. Getting Joe ready for deployment became the responsibility of Don Levine and his group of talented artists, designers and engineers. Nearly everything except the plastic body was to be made in Japan (later in Hong Kong). The cast of characters included "Ace" the fighter pilot, "Skip" the navy frogman, "Rocky" the marine paratrooper, and a yet-unnamed army soldier, each a "movable fighting man."

Hasbro's original hand-carved GI Joe prototype, shown here with several of the early packaging mock-ups.

Hasbro's advertising agent suggested to Levine that they needed a single name to represent the entire line. Hasbro staff artist Janet Downing suggested GI Joe, a term that had been around since World War I. A toy legend was born. During World War II, the name represented the enlisted infantryman, the common, everyman soldier. The generic-ness of the name "GI Joe" left room for a boy's imagination, yet made the fun official.

Levine and his team provided plenty of accessories to spark the imagination. Marketing man, Jerry Einhorn secured real uniforms and weapons to use as reference in designing the entire line of 75 different items, all meticulously detailed. The collecting of dress

The classic toy's name could have been inspired by the GI Joe comic books published in the '50s by Ziff Davis Publishing. Others credit this 1945 movie, starring Burgess Meredith and Robert Mitchum.

uniforms, field radios, tents, machine guns, life rafts and parachutes all took place just months before GI Joe's Toy Fair introduction. Like a well-drilled platoon driven by Levine, the Hasbro development team assembled everything quickly and quietly all very much under the radar.

Hasbro was so concerned over their idea leaking out, that they undertook stringent security measures. Among themselves, they referred to GI Joe only as "the Robot," and promised to speak to no one—not even their spouses—about him. The military nature of the toy certainly lent itself to the "secret mission" that Levine's team was undertaking, but the grave monetary risks involved kept it from becoming a joke. Their jobs were on the line. If a competitor like Mattel or Marx beat them to the punch, Hasbro would be in a hole so deep that even Mr. Potato Head wouldn't be able to pull the company out.

"We were very lucky because Hasbro was a very small company at the time," Don Levine told me. "We were in a small town and nobody in the industry really paid that much attention to us. Still, we were very secretive of it. When we finally showed GI Joe in 1964, [legendary toy designer] Marvin Glass saw it in our showroom and he said, '@$%! I thought of this two years ago!' But we did it first. We were there when fate struck and we took advantage of it."

THE MILITARY MAN STRIKES . . . A POSE

The only other adult male toy figure at the time was Barbie's boyfriend, and as just one of Barbie's many fashion accessories, Ken didn't have to be very flexible. GI Joe rode in Jeeps, kneeled in life rafts, wore boots, scuba fins and eventually snow shoes. He needed the bendable knees and ankles that Ken lacked. But just as important as Joe's ability to get into position was

To dissuade competitors from coming up with a pilot figure in response to their foot soldier, Hasbro made the shrewd (and overwhelming) decision to release figures representing the four branches of the military all at once.

his ability to *hold* that position. GI Joe had to stand on his own two feet, and therefore his limbs needed to be held together tightly while remaining flexible enough to endure the rough play he would certainly face.

Michlig learned that the engineering behind GI Joe's revolutionary design came from the skilled hands of Hasbro's VP of product development, Sam Speers, and their VP of mold procurement and design, Hugh O'Connor. Using a single elastic braid hidden within the figure's body and tight rivets or balls for all the joints, Speers and O'Connor created a figure that would hold fast its position, just like any good soldier.

A month before Toy Fair, and the frenzy to complete the line hit fever pitch. Janet Downing and a group of freelance artists worked around the clock to make the packages for display, while Merrill Hassenfeld fretted over the stigma of GI Joe being a "doll for boys." With millions of dollars already invested, they were well past the point of no return.

Word was spreading among buyers as to how much Hasbro was spending and their reactions were divided. Retail giant Woolworth's supported the line, which forced other retailers to follow reluctantly. Other chains predicted that the line would be the downfall of Hasbro. Orders were modest leading up to GI Joe's release, as most in the toy industry took a "wait and see" approach. In the summer of 1964, the wait was over.

Hasbro ran expensive television ads, first in New York and then across the nation. The spots featured a stirring marching song sung to the chorus of the popular World War I tune *Over There:* "GI Joe, GI Joe fighting man from head to toe! On the land, on the sea, in the air!" The song got kids humming and parents buying. The first ads ran in the summer, an unprecedented time to launch a toy. But as the holiday season approached, GI Joe was selling so well that Hasbro had to limit quantities available to order. The company purchased new molds and expanded production. They started the Official GI Joe Club to connect all the fans of the toy and enlist them to collect all the GI Joe accessories. By the end of the year, over 150,000 kids had joined the club and over two million GI Joe action figures were sold.

Hasbro quickly added to their line. The year 1965 saw the first African-American GI Joe figure released, along with new gear for new adventures as a "Deep Sea Diver," duty on the "Ski Patrol," and others. With all the GI Joe accessories Hasbro was selling, kids needed a place to put it all, so the classic GI Joe footlocker appeared. The GI Joe line helped Hasbro gross $23 million before the end of 1965, making him their true soldier of fortune.

WAGING WAR

In 1966, as GI Joe sales skyrocketed, the war in Vietnam continued to escalate. By the end of that year, the United States had over 184,000 troops in Asia and the backlash back home spilled onto the streets and eventually into the toy trade. With the horrors of battle continually broadcast into American living rooms, parents had had enough. While war protesters on Pennsylvania Avenue in Washington were a regular occurrence, the protesters on Fifth Avenue during Toy Fair of '66 seemed oddly out of place. Their banners read "Toy Fair or War Fare?" and their fervor was pointed directly at Hasbro's super soldier.

Sales of the GI Joe line declined as rapidly as they had risen and Hasbro's competitors jumped on the opportunity by producing non-military action figures. Mattel released an astronaut figure called Major Matt Mason in 1967, but the real threat to Joe came in the form of Captain Action, developed for Ideal by GI Joe's concept team of Stan Weston and Larry Reiner. Whereas GI Joe was limited to his military persona, Captain Action could take on heroic adventures via masks and disguises as Spider-Man or Batman. (see Insider Profile on page 202.)

In 1967 and 1968, sales of GI Joe figures and accessories plummeted. To climb back up, Hasbro's articulated hero would need a major makeover.

A year after his introduction GI Joe faced James Bond. Marvin Glass licensed the idea to Gilbert, who released a 12-inch Bond doll with the label "Action Figure," perhaps coining the phrase in the process. Even though the line was powered by the hit movies *Goldfinger* (1964) and *Thunderball* (1965), 007 couldn't dethrone Joe.

In 1969, the GI Joe Action Soldier became a "Man of Action," the Action Pilot became an "Air Adventurer," the Action Marine was replaced by the "Land Adventurer," and the Action Sailor was reintroduced as the "Sea Adventurer." GI Joe was suddenly more about "daring expeditions" than "deadly missions," but the fun remained. He led a team in search of sunken treasure, captured gorillas and traveled to dangerous and exotic places.

The reconfigured GI Joe sold respectfully from 1969 to 1972, increasing in sales each year as the memory of Vietnam faded. However, 1972 witnessed the release of the first in a series of action figure lines that triggered GI Joe's second and ultimately lethal decline in sales.

Again, Stan Weston entered the picture. In 1972, still representing rights for a slew of comic characters, he pitched Mego on an update of the pulp-hero idea that his Captain Action tested five years earlier. The World's Greatest Super-Heroes line was for a younger audience than GI Joe, and Mego shrewdly introduced them in an 8-inch size for smaller hands.

For the first time Hasbro was demoted to mere follower within a category they had invented and led for over a decade. Instead of setting the trends, GI Joe reacted to them. As the popularity of martial arts surged, Hasbro responded in the mid-'70s by giving GI Joe a rubbery "Kung Fu Grip." In 1975, with *The Six Million Dollar Man* TV show a huge hit, GI Joe became part machine with the release of Mike Powers—Atomic Man. When Mego's super-hero line continued to do super-human numbers, GI Joe added the flying, leotard-clad Bulletman in 1976. Their fatal mistake came in 1977 when they shrunk their Joe down to match Mego's 8-inch size and, worse, removed the "GI" from his name. The ill-fated Super Joe did not live up to his name.

The trend of shrinking action figures came to a head in 1977 when the skyrocketing price of oil forced the price of raw plastic through the stratosphere. At the same time, the movie *Star Wars* took the world by storm. Kenner introduced a line of 3-inch action figures to make the spaceships they rode in a manageable size. Their immediate and colossal success was a light saber through GI Joe's heart. Having endured four straight years of declining GI Joe sales, Hasbro decided to retire their man of action. He remained out of production for nearly five years, while the *Star Wars* sequels in 1980 and 1983 turned Kenner's line into the most successful series of action figures of all time, with 300 million total units reportedly sold. The industry was awestruck. Never again would an action figure line come close to those sales numbers.

GI Joe's Adventure Team medallion featured an overlapping "A" and "T" icon. It resembled the '60s peace symbol, possibly a subconscious good-will offering aimed at concerned parents.

SEA ADVENTURER ™

WITH **LIFE-LIKE HAIR** AND **BEARD**

In 1970, GI Joe grew more hair, distancing himself further from his former military appearance.

Never Say Never . . . Again

GI Joe's triumphant return in 1982 came within the window of opportunity that stood open after *The Empire Strikes Back* and just before *Return of the Jedi.* Ronald Reagan had taken office in 1981, and the timing seemed right for a renewed appeal to patriotism. Hasbro had no blockbuster movie tie-in, but the repositioning of GI Joe came with the launch of a Marvel comic book series.

A new marketing regime at Hasbro (led by Merrill's son, Stephen Hassenfeld), reintroduced GI Joe at the new 3-inch standard size, which allowed for a vast, cost effective world of accessories. Taking a page from the book of *Star Wars,* the new line featured a good-versus-evil back story with an "evil empire" known as Cobra set up as GI Joe's antagonist. The hero found purpose and flourishing sales. GI Joe was now the code name for an elite force whose members were given names like Short Fuse and Snake-Eyes.

According to *Toy Wars,* Joe's comeback resulted in sales of $51 million dollars in 1982, and by 1986 the number had grown to nearly $185 million. The GI Joe Club was relaunched, and this time the licensing pool that Hasbro had only touched upon in the 1960s was transformed into an ocean of opportunities. In the 1980s, GI Joe lunch boxes, walkie-talkies, board games, video games and sneakers all fueled the toy's popularity, but the pinnacle of GI Joe fame came in 1983 when he got his own Saturday morning cartoon. It ran until 1987 and helped create a buying frenzy for GI Joe action figures that still reigns supreme.

The November 2002 issue of *Toy Fare,* a magazine dedicated to action figures, celebrated the 20th anniversary of the reintroduction of Hasbro's classic hero by declaring: "The GI Joe: A Real American Hero line conquered toys, television, comics and kids' imagination in the '80s in a way that has never been replicated. Nothing—not *Star Wars,* not *He-Man,* not even *Transformers*—could touch Joe's popularity at its apex." From 1982 to 1987, Hasbro created over 500

figures and nearly 250 vehicles and playsets. It was the biggest comeback in toy history.

In 1990, GI Joe was re-released in his original 11 $\frac{1}{2}$-inch glory. With Operation Desert Storm under way, this retro-size Joe came outfitted in desert camouflage and was introduced exclusively at Target stores for a limited time as Duke: Hall of Fame GI Joe (named after a 3-inch GI Joe). The figures sold out immediately; Duke's success told Hasbro that the larger format still had enormous appeal, and a new generation of kids met GI Joe, just as their fathers had decades

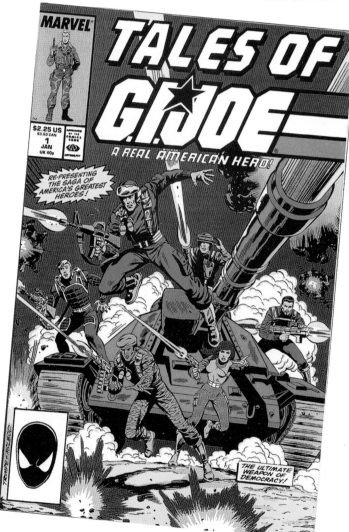

The subtitle of the 1982 Marvel comic was shared by the accompanying toy line, and "A Real American Hero" was reborn.

before. Eventually the line grew to include real-life heroes like astronaut Buzz Aldrin, Colin Powell and even George Washington, as the father of our country met the father of the action figure.

GI Joe has earned his stripes. After his deployment and early success, he would fight for his very survival against public boycotts, Super-Heroes and Jedi Knights. In the end, this "movable fighting man" remains very *unmovable,* his position secure atop the action figure universe.

Today's GI Joe might represent "The Real American Hero" in your neighborhood.

Meetings with overseas lawyers led Don Levine to add a distinctive scar to GI Joe's face, a legendary trademark. To protect the body from pirates, Joe's right thumbnail was etched where his thumbprint should have been—a miscue that could be checked if Hasbro's tooling was ever illegally duplicated. A few years later that very thing happened and Mego's Fighting Yank—a direct rip-off of GI Joe, thumbnail and all—was taken off the market after Hasbro successfully sued.

Legend has it that on the eve of GI Joe's debut, Hasbro had still not negotiated a compensation agreement for agent Stan Weston and his silent partner, Larry Reiner. Merrill Hassenfeld eventually offered a 1% royalty, but Weston declined. After a $75,000 buyout was raised to $100,000, Weston took the deal, and split the one-time payment with Reiner.

In 2003, the original GI Joe prototype (shown on page 197) was purchased by comic book distributor Stephen Geppi for $200,000.

THE WALT DISNEY OF ACTION FIGURES

Stan Weston is credited with conceiving three action figure lines *after* spawning GI Joe in 1964. In 1966 he developed Captain Action for Ideal (with Larry Reiner, who was still employed there), and in the process created the first line of superhero action figures. In 1971, he topped himself by bringing Mego the concept and characters for The World's Greatest Super Heroes line. Weston represented properties from rivals DC and Marvel comics, and in an amazing feat, struck the deal that placed DC legends like Batman, Superman and Wonder Woman, *in the same line* with Marvel icons like Spider-Man, Captain America and Iron Man–something that would be unheard of today. Finally in 1973, he created the Lone Ranger action figure line for Gabriel.

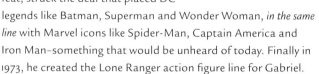

Twister

1960s–1970s

Debut: 1966
Inventive Idea: Reyn Guyer
Predecessor: King Footsie
　(1964)
Inventors: Neil Rabens,
　Chuck Foley, Reyn Guyer
Insider: Mel Taft
Company: Milton Bradley

KNOTS AND STITCHES

In Twister, you're always one call away from winning or being out of the game. Hear "Right Hand Red" when you're hoping for a "Left Foot Blue," and you're going down. Here's the twisted tale of shoe polish, shower curtains, celebrity intervention and the one call that would have ended the game, but never came.

Reyn Guyer is blessed with seven offspring: four girls, a boy, Twister and Nerf. Guyer is a toy inventor, one of the most famous of all time due to his two youngest inspirations. Beyond heading the company that developed a couple of the most recognizable icons of the toy world, he is also songwriter, song publisher, painter, sculptor, and the co-developer of a multisensory phonics reading system. Before all this he was a packaging designer like his father, who after amassing over 125 patents, founded his own company in 1957. Creativity obviously ran in the family.

Reyn joined his father in the business shortly after its inception, and soon they boasted a client list that included Pillsbury, Kraft Foods, and 3M.

One day Reyn came up with a back-to-school promotion for a brand of shoe polish made by another client, Johnson Wax. The promotion evolved into a mat game called King Footsie, wherein the players themselves were the play pieces. Players strategically stood and moved on a mat featuring colored spaces while blocking their opponents from doing the same. The idea was pitched to 3M (who made games beginning in the 1940s) but it was rejected. Regardless of their rocky start in the game business, Reyn convinced his dad to stick with the new direction the company was taking. "To his credit, my dad underwrote the entire development," Reyn said. Next, Guyer hired two talented game developers named Chuck Foley and Neil Rabens, to add to his team of designers. Foley had a toy background, having worked for Lakeside Toys, and Rabens was an artist who had worked for a toy pool company called Doughboy Industries. Together they devised several games around the "human play piece" idea.

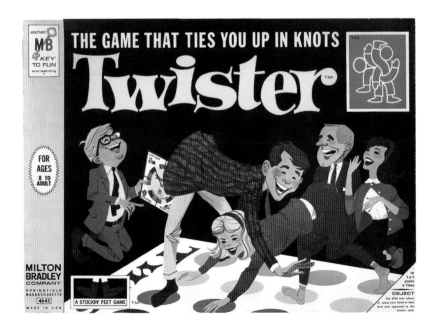

The 1966 version of "The game that ties you up in knots."

Rabens refined a game that he dubbed "Pretzel," and when Foley suggested rearranging the colored dots on the mat so that players became more entwined, the game really took shape. The subsequent subtitle they chose was perfect: *The game that ties you up in knots.* It took about a year and a half from the initial idea to the point where the team had developed a handful of other mat games with names like "Safari," "Pantomimic," and "Bump." With prototypes of these concepts in tow, the fledgling toy company went to where games were born: Springfield, Massachusetts, home of Milton Bradley.

Milton Bradley executives saw the concepts in the fall of '65. Mel Taft, senior vice president of research & development singled out "Pretzel" after watching it played by some of the Milton Bradley office staff. Beyond the game's play-value, he admired its simplicity; it consisted of a large vinyl game mat and a spinner. Players added their own pieces (themselves)

and a caller, who hit a spinner that was separated into one of four limbs (right hand, right foot, left hand, left foot), each with four colors. Players stood on a mat covered with rows of corresponding colored circles and tried to place their hands and feet according to what was spun. They twisted, reached and balanced until the one left standing (or more accurately, the one with elbows, knees and butt off the mat) won. The game had progressive play—easy at the start, but as the game wore on, the players wore out and often collapsed in fits of laughter.

The only snag was the name. "Everyone at Milton Bradley liked the name 'Pretzel' a lot, but their trademark lawyers found a toy dog with that name so we had to steer clear," Reyn shared. "I didn't like the name Twister at

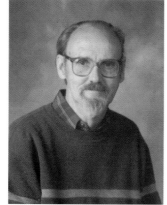

Chuck Foley (above) and Neil Rabens (right) contend that they are the sole inventors of Twister.

all, but in the end, the name of a game matters little. It's the play."

Ah, the play. Twister had its critics before it debuted, some decision makers at Milton Bradley among them. In 1965, the idea of being in such close proximity to someone— especially someone of the opposite sex—was socially unacceptable. "I was getting so much flack in-house that I took the thing home," Taft remembered. "We had three other couples over and as soon as we started, I got to laughing so hard that I damn near had appendicitis. I knew this thing was worth its weight in gold . . . if adults could have that much fun with something, somehow we had to get it in the hands of consumers." Mel Taft championed the game internally and MB scheduled it for Toy Fair, the largest and most important of the toy industry trade shows.

Twister was intended to be an adult party game from the start, as evidenced by the illustrations on the cover of the original package depicting cartoon versions of adults playing. The sexual innuendo that grown-ups projected onto the game sashayed in on the heels of its introduction. Neil Rabens was disappointed. "Watch kids play it and its nothing but innocent fun," he said. "The rules are exactly the same, no matter who's playing—it's adults that twist everything around." Chuck Foley offered the best explanation of Twister's often-contradictory allure: "Dirty mind, dirty game. Clean mind, clean game."

Suggestive overtones weren't the only hurdle Twister faced. Another dilemma surfaced when Milton Bradley had trouble sourcing the game's components before the crucial Toy Fair deadline. The challenge was

A STOCKIN' FEET GAME

Milton Bradley called Twister "a stockin' feet game," an expression they would eventually trademark—ironic given the game's shoe polish origins.

finding a company that could produce vinyl sheets in a size big enough for Twister mats. Foley thought of a not so obvious source: a producer of shower curtains. "I was helping the buyer for Milton Bradley source components and we thought we had it licked until Mel called and told me, 'If you want to see Twister at Toy Fair, you had better get up here. We're having problems with General Tire,'" Foley said. General Tire was a big producer of rubber and vinyl and one of the few companies Foley found that had a Roto Gravier, the only machine at the time that could print on vinyl at the size they needed. Foley had to persuade the rubber company to make room in their production schedule for Twister mats. He recalled, "When the CEO asked me, 'Why should General Tire stop printing shower curtains to print game mats?' My reply was, 'Because in one year, you will print enough Twister mats to stretch from Massachusetts to California'—and I was right!" Though Foley's confidence in the game would one day prove prophetic, Twister slipped coming out of the gate.

Twister hit the scene as a totally original game. Consumers didn't "get it" when it first appeared on store shelves and some retailers refused to even stock it. Sales were so slow for the four-month period after Toy Fair that Milton Bradley decided to cut the rope on the game that tied you up in knots.

"Late in April, I got a call from Mel," Guyer told me. "He said, 'Bad news Reyn. We're not going forward with it. It's too risqué and Sears won't touch it. We're pulling the advertising.' Well, Sears was such a key retailer back then that their decision could make or break a game. Twister was dead."

Anxiously, I asked him, "But then what about Johnny Carson? How did that happen?"

"Well, that's the thing," Guyer continued. "Milton Bradley had hired a PR firm to pitch Twister and when they decided to discontinue it, they called their ad agency and pulled the TV spots and they called me to tell me it was finished. But for some reason, *no one*

called the PR firm. All of a sudden, they booked it on *The Tonight Show,* and you know the rest."

The rest is Twister history. On May 3, 1966, Johnny Carson invited his guest, the glamorous and shapely Eva Gabor, to try out this new game with him. Ms. Gabor proved to be a good sport, which proved to be *very* good luck for Twister. The hilarious sight of a slightly embarrassed Johnny Carson and the refined Eva Gabor on all fours sent Johnny's studio audience into hysterics.

Mel Taft was seated in the front row that momentous night. "I'll never forget it," he said. "Ruth Millard from the public relations firm that had booked it was sitting next to me." Taft told me how nervous he was that Johnny would ridicule the game and that the result would be the nail in Twister's coffin. "You never knew what Johnny was going to do. No one did. We were unsure until they began playing and we heard that roar of laughter from the audience," he said. Soon after the show, it was apparent that the home audience had the same reaction. "They were standing 50 deep at Abercrombie

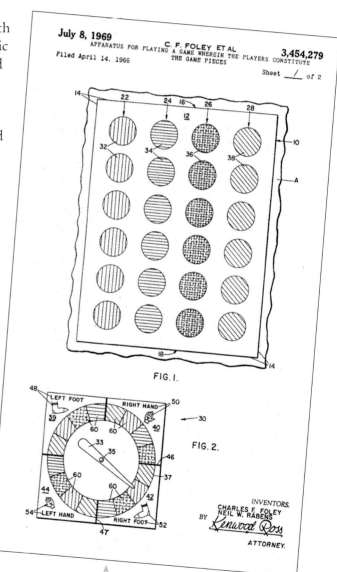

Foley and Rabens filed for their patent on Twister on April 14, 1966, but at the time it looked like it was all for naught.

Helping soap let you play safe hour after hour. This is Monsanto today.

Monsanto

During the height of its popularity in the late '60s, Twister appeared in movies and was used in the advertising of other products, like this soap ad from 1966.

competitors released scores of similar games.

Millions of people have played Twister since its introduction, but usually only 2–4 players at a time, as the rules state. But that didn't stop the students at the University of Massachusetts in Amherst from setting a world record in 1987 by positioning hundreds of mats together and having 4,160 students participate in the largest Twister game ever played. News of the campus happening prompted others to give it a try and sales surged once more.

Like the Frisbee, Twister has had more than its share of college-age enthusiasts over the years. Yet, unlike the famous flying disk and the Hula Hoop that preceded it, Twister demands no acquired skill. Although some flexibility surely helps, Twister remains a game for just about everyone.

So if you know your left from your right and your primary colors, you can join in on the contortive fun too. Unfold that vinyl mat (the smell is sure to take you back) and grab some friends. Soon you'll be ready to twist, reach and laugh all over again—because after 35 years, Twister still ties us up in knots and keeps us in stitches.

& Fitch the next day," Guyer recalls. "They were the only store in New York that still had any left!" Sears changed their minds and the Roto Gravier machine at General Tire ran in double shifts to keep up.

Over three million sets were sold in 1966, after this TV ad and jingle encouraged people to play on a polka-dotted mat:

Singers: Milton Bradley has the hot one—
It's a Twister.
Spin the spinner and call the shot.
Twister ties you up in a knot.
That's Twister, yeah Twister

Caller: Right foot blue—left hand red!

Singers: Get Twister—from MB!

Announcer: Twister, the action game from Milton Bradley

During the Twister craze of '66 and '67, the game was played a second time on *The Tonight Show* and then on *The Mike Douglas Show.* Its popularity continued throughout the '70s even as Milton Bradley and their

The game that ties you up in knots.

Twister

LEFT FOOT

RIGHT HAND

RIGHT FOOT

It's marketed exclusively to kids today, and with over 70 million games sold and counting, Twister shows no sign of falling out of favor.

Debut: 1965
U.S. Debut: 1967
Inventor: Denys Fisher
Companies: Denys Fisher (Engl.) Ltd., Kenner Toys, Hasbro

Spirograph

SWOOPS AND SWIRLS

When it came out in 1967, a cursory glance made it easy to assume Spirograph put the "work" in artwork. The various components came in a box with a segmented plastic tray, positioned according to size, laid out like sterile surgical instruments. The box cover blandly promised, "Pattern drawing by revolving stencils." Invented by an electrical engineer, its look said "drafting tool" more than "drawing toy."

But then something magical happened. You played with it for the first time and marveled at what you could create. You! The one who couldn't draw a straight line now ruled because there were *no straight lines in Spirograph!* Daring designs! Amazing arrangements! The more you filled the page with those colorful repeating swoops and swirls the more you were filled with awe and fascination.

For years prior to Spirograph's release, British engineer Denys Fisher was fascinated with unlocking the key to hypocycloids or, as the dictionary puts it: "The plane locus of a point fixed on

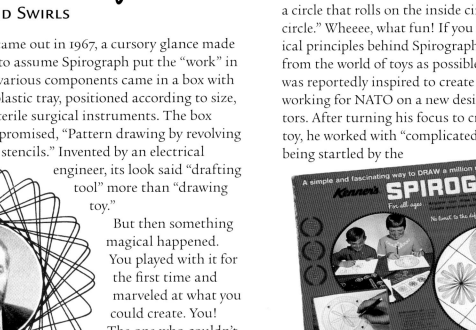

Spirograph inventor Denys Fisher, as he appeared in a booklet within the original 1965 version of his drawing toy.

a circle that rolls on the inside circumference of a fixed circle." Wheeee, what fun! If you think the mathematical principles behind Spirograph are as far removed from the world of toys as possible, you're right. Fisher was reportedly inspired to create Spirograph while working for NATO on a new design for bomb detonators. After turning his focus to creating a drawing toy, he worked with "complicated mechanisms" before being startled by the

Spirograph, 1967

simplicity of the final result of this toil, something he called "a new use of the wheel."

Spirograph debuted at the Nuremberg Toy Fair in 1965 where it received the attention of representatives from Kenner Toys. By that time, Kenner had several hits with "contraption toys" like the Give-A-Show projector in 1959 and the classic Easy-Bake Oven in 1963. These playthings required a great level of interaction between the user and the toy itself. They allowed for the creation of something, and resisted classification into any easily defined toy category. In other words, Spirograph fit Kenner like a swirl-patterned glove.

Today's Spirograph and Denys Fisher's original 1965 version.

Before Spirograph

B ack in 1907, a device called The Wondergraph was patented and produced, but never took off. In the early 1930s a toy called Hoot-Nanny, the Magic Designer, was released and sold moderately well for several companies before leaving the market sometime in the late 1950s. In 1949, yet another similar toy was produced called the Dizzy Doodler. It too turned out designs identical to those produced by the Spirograph, but quickly faded from sight. Why has Spirograph endured when others could not? A good guess would be timing,

that critical factor which repeatedly curses or blesses a product upon its release. Spirograph was released in the late '60s, when psychedelic pop art was in vogue. These previous drawing devices may have been all right toys, but Spirograph proved to be the right toy at the right time.

By 1967, psychedelic art was all the rage. Concert posters from artists like Wes Wilson established a new direction for pop illustration and promoted acts like The Grateful Dead and Bob Dylan. Spirograph, with its psychedelic patterns and mesmerizing kaleidoscopic images, hit toy shelves at the ideal time. It won the coveted Toy of the Year award in 1967 and was joined by a junior version called the Spirotot in 1968. Spirograph was one of the biggest selling toys in the United States during its first two years on the market.

The original Spirograph came with twenty-seven pieces, including gear wheels, gear rings, gear racks, a dozen or so push pins and four ballpoint pens in green, red, blue and black. A handful of glossy paper sheets were included, along with a booklet of designs and a thick piece of cardboard on which to pin the paper canvases. The box said "for all ages" and heralded it as "a simple and fascinating way to draw a million marvelous patterns." With a little patience some truly stunning designs could be created. There were snowflakes, flowers, twisted triangles, wheels, mesmerizing tunnels and stained-glass windows.

A spin around the ring with your pen in the center of a small gear and you could make some easy designs, but things got trickier when you placed the pen in a really off-centered hole and tried to control the gear (and more importantly your pen). Many of us felt Spiro-*spastic* when we ruined our masterpieces with just a slip of those tiny teeth. We used those long tongue depressor-like gears or "racks" with often torturous results. With no outer frame to press against, you had to force your gear inward or risk sending the pen point off on a wild streak. Remember how a pin would pop out, sending the gear sliding under the ring and you back to the drawing board? In retrospect, perhaps these frustrations added to the sense of accomplishment when you finally turned out a perfect pattern.

Old-school swirlers hardly recognize today's basic Spirograph set. It includes only a fraction of the gears found in the original, but with some noticeably un-Spirographic stencils added. Not all changes are bad though. The new gear templates feature a molded edge

Spirograph continued to keep kids mesmerized in the '70s and '80s.

1960s–1970s

SPIROGRAPH

that prevents gears from popping out. Plus, the teeth on both the gears and templates are much bigger and set wider, virtually eliminating the previously standard Spirograph slippage.

Safety regulations have banished the classic pins from newer sets. I missed them at first, but my nostalgia faded when I pulled out an original set to draw with once again. I pinned the paper to the cardboard backing and managed to pierce my thigh in the process. Then I remembered that it's cardboard, paper, *gear ring,* and *then* pin. My tetanus shot is Thursday.

Since the day Kenner Toys introduced us to Denys Fisher's brainchild, people all over the planet have spent countless hours lost in the sweet solitude of their Spirograph.

Twenty-seven million sets later and the fun still sneaks up on you. You don't really believe that the fantastic patterns on the box can come from your hand, until you're magically drawn into that receding tunnel you just created. Around and around you go, toward the overlapping colors, psychedelic symmetry and the rhythm of all those turning gears.

The new Spirograph Studio includes tons of gears, colored pens, felt-tip markers, several color-change markers, a highlighter and colored paper all in a cool carrying case.

Debut: 1967
Inventor: Eddy Goldfarb
Companies: Ideal, Mattel

Kerplunk and Eddy

MARBLES, TEETH AND TOPS

Eddy Goldfarb has created over 750 products in his 57-year career as an inventor. Although his ideas range from high intensity flashlights to a housing for computer fans, most of his 300 some-odd patents are for games and toys. His list of playthings is astounding and begins in 1948, when Eddy first cut his teeth as an inventor of novelties.

Eddy knew from the start what he was going to be when he grew up. "From my earliest memory I was taking things apart and putting them back together," he told me. "I've always loved inventing." He volunteered for submarine duty during World War II and even then dreamed of what he would do when the war ended. "I had a lot of time to think. We'd go out to sea for two months at a time . . . so I would read, invent and plan." After returning home in 1946, he sent a letter to twenty-five different companies touting his ability to make inexpensive models by using a flexible plastic molding process he had developed. "I got three jobs from those twenty-five letters. I thought that was a pretty good start."

Things only got better. He sold his first two inventions to Topic Toys of Chicago, after partnering with fellow toy inventor, Marvin Glass (see Marvin Glass). His Busy Biddee Chicken was a plastic hen that laid five white marbles (one at a time) when pressed down; the Merry-Go-Sip was a novelty cup topped with a tiny carousel that spun when a child drank through the cup's straw. Both items were created in a corner space he rented within a plastic fabrication factory.

Next was the pop culture icon and unlikely hit known to many as chattering false teeth, the last item Eddy licensed through Marvin Glass (see Yakity-Yak Teeth side bar). After the three-year partnership of Goldfarb and Glass ended, Eddy left Chicago for California and formed Eddy Goldfarb & Associates. "We had two different personalities, Marvin and I. He was a great hard-sell salesman," Eddy shared. "I was soft-sell."

AN IDEAL PARTNERSHIP

Goldfarb's first introduction to Ideal Toys was at Chicago Hobby Show, where he was turned away at the front door because he was an inventor and not a buyer. Having flown from Los Angels to the show, the tenacious Eddy would not be denied. He found a back door which led him into a dimly lit area. "I wandered around back there until I found what I thought was a door," Eddy laughed. "I pushed it open and knocked over a big part of Ideal Toy's

Eddy Goldfarb

1960s–1970s

KERPLUNK AND EDDY

display area. I did get in though and they didn't call the guards." Ideal Toys became an important client for Eddy, eventually licensing a noisy marble game that has entertained millions of kids all over the world.

Kerplunk. What a great name for a game. It's onomatopoeic, imitating the sound and the action of the game, and like Kodak

Original Kerplunk, 1967

and Kleenex, it makes your tongue do that clickety-click thing which, for some unexplainable reason, is a big plus in the trade of trademarking. Kerplunk was billed as "The Tantalizing Game of Nerve and Skill" when it was released by Ideal Toys in 1967, but it was more a game of "Nerve and Noise." To play, the 11-inch clear, plastic tube was shish-ka-bobbed with dozens of flexible sticks through its many-holed midsection until the center of the tube looked like a bird's nest. Kids then gleefully emptied thirty-two marbles into the top of the tube until they all came to rest against the crisscrossed sticks, suspended above a hard plastic base. The object was to "skillfully pull out Skinny Sticks and drop as few marbles as possible." A few would drop at the start, but eventually one unlucky player would cause an avalanche of cat's eyes. The polystyrene plastic was hard and the sound of the glass marbles crashing against the bottom would be loud by itself, but then the sound traveled up the megaphone-like tube and became a cacophony. Kids couldn't get enough of the racket, the game, or the fun.

A year after Kerplunk, Goldfarb and Ideal had another hit game called Battling Tops. Kids sat ringside for "The Bout of the Century," which pitted 2 to 4 tiny plastic tops against each other in a spinning, colliding, last-one-standing battle, with tops knocked completely out of the ring on most occasions. Though only four could play at once, the game came with six spinning combatants; Dizzy Dan, Twirling Tim, Tricky Nicky, Smarty Smitty, Super Sam and Hurricane Hank. The game was relaunched in the late '70s as Battling Spaceships in the wake of the *Star Wars* craze, but the original was the best.

Along with former partner Marvin Glass, Eddy Goldfarb helped establish this emerging game category. "We did a lot of skill and action games," Goldfarb recalled. "Lionel Weintraub was the president of Ideal Toys in those days and we had a great relationship." By the time Ideal was sold to CBS in 1982, the legendary game company had marketed an astonishing run of fifty-seven games created by Eddy Goldfarb and his team of designers.

Although he had a great rapport with Ideal Toys, Eddy's ideas were not exclusive to them (he told me that Battling Tops was rejected by Milton Bradley before landing with Ideal). Eddy was one of the first inventors to license his ideas to more than one company. This was unprecedented in the '40s and '50s, as it was typical for an inventor to have an arrangement with just a single toy company. After discovering all he had invented and talking to him on several occasions, I got some insight as to how he was able to do this. His many ideas were *that* good, and the man—*that* likeable.

A further study of his creations over the years reveals him as an innovator of product trends as well. For instance, Mattel's Vac-u-Form was invented by Eddy in 1962 and influenced the creation of Thingmaker and Creepy Crawlers. And before Beanie Babies and the entire crop of bean-stuffed animals that followed, Eddy created Baby Beans for Mattel in 1970. In the twisting and turning toy business, Eddy Goldfarb was always ahead of the curve.

Mattel recently introduced Electronic Super Kerplunk, a bigger, battery-operated version of his timeless tower of sticks and marbles. Just like the game he made famous, Eddy Goldfarb remains an American classic. "I still work every day," this 81-year-old kid told me. "I've been very fortunate to do what I love." He always knew what he was going to be when he grew up. Fortunately for us, Eddy Goldfarb never did.

Toothy Toys

Yakity-Yak Talking Teeth were a bit freaky when they came out in 1949 and they're still just as humorously unsettling today. "I saw an ad for this thing called 'The Tooth Garage' or something like that. It was a container in which you put your false teeth at night," Eddy recounted. "Anyway, it struck me as being very funny and that's where I got the idea." Eddy licensed his clicking creation through Marvin Glass & Associates to the H. Fishlove & Company novelty business, and that company's successor (appropriately called Fun, Inc.) still sells them today as The Original Talking Teeth.

Eddy created several joke items with a toothy theme. His favorite was a fake tooth he molded onto a fake plastic toothpick. "After you ate dinner you'd secretly pop this in your mouth, then you'd yell, pull it out and scare everyone," he confessed with a chuckle. "Now listen, I'm not very proud of these items, but I do have a sense of humor."

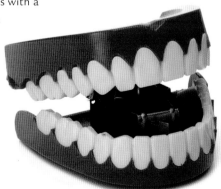
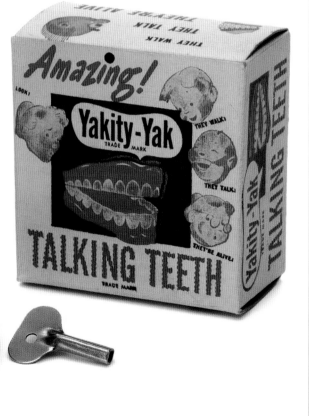

1960s–1970s

KERPLUNK AND EDDY

Eddy's son, Martin, joined his dad in 1980 and the company was renamed Eddy & Martin Goldfarb & Associates.

One of Eddy's most successful toys was Stompers, a line of miniature, battery-operated vehicles that were released in 1980 by Schaper Toys. Stompers have been sold by numerous companies over the years, including Tyco, Dreamworks and Peachtree Playthings. Today, Tinco Toys continues to sell these powerful 4x4s overseas, and at 200 million reportedly sold, Stompers just might be the best-selling battery-operated vehicles in toy history.

Eddy Goldfarb was the first American to receive the I.D.I.O.T. (International Designers & Inventors of Toys) award from his peers within the European toy industry and was inducted into the American Toy Industry Hall of Fame in 2003.

The recent wave of fighting tops, including Hasbro's Beyblades can be traced back to Eddy Goldfarb's Battling Tops game of 1968.

Big Wheel

1960s–1970s

Debut: 1969
Inventor: Ray Lohr
Companies: Marx Toys, Empire Plastics, Alpha International

SELLING DOUGHNUTS

It's the summer of '70, and I am six years old. My older sister is selling lemonade from our family's suburban driveway. Her friends are there too, and in an attempt to impress them, I decide to sell some doughnuts.

Twenty feet from her stand, the handlebars begin to vibrate in my hands. The distinctive rumbling of plastic on pavement is so loud that it threatens my sister's fledgling enterprise. I pick up speed, my bony little knees pumping frantically. When I'm ten feet from the stand, I hit the brake. Simultaneously, and with timing I've perfected over months of practice, I turn the wheel on my Big Wheel. The chubby back tires begin their perfect arch amidst the pebbles and debris in our driveway. Then, with the hollow sound of scraping plastic still in my ears, my ride comes to a grinding halt. "Check out the doughnut!" I boast. Granted, it's hard to appreciate coolness when there's dirt sprayed into your lemonade, but I think somewhere deep inside they all longed to be me.

Okay, maybe not.

It's not hard to put your finger on the appeal of Big Wheel. It was visceral. When you rode one, every bump and imperfection in your path instantly transferred through the shuddering plastic to your various appendages. Whether skidding to a sliding halt or leaning into a 180° spin,

Big Wheel, 1977

the application of the brakes sent a reverberation up your backbone that turned your spinal column into a tuning fork. Big Wheel nirvana.

Peeling out in Big Wheel was cool too. Zero traction meant that when you tried to take off from the starting line, you pedaled hard before you actually moved even an inch forward. With all your weight resting over the back wheels, the front wheel would grind away. Drag racing was big back then, and peel outs in a Big Wheel could make even the littlest kid feel like "Big Daddy" Don Garlits. It's no wonder so many Big Wheels had holes worn in all three tires—the designers of the toy learned something that kids of the early '70s knew from watching car chase scenes on TV shows like *Adam-12* and *Hawaii Five-O:* Traction was overrated. Bring on the screeching stops, doughnuts and peel outs!

Although this book is a celebration of those marvelous playthings that were invented by people *not* associated with major toy companies, the fact is that Big Wheel meant too much to me to leave out. So it's an exception, a contraption invented within the hallowed halls of Marx Toys—at the time, one of the biggest toy companies in the world.

Founded in 1921 by brothers Louis and David, Louis Marx & Company climbed to the top of toydom with Louis Marx as its monarch. Known as "The Toy King," Marx was to the toy industry what Henry Ford was to the automotive industry. From 1955 through 1966—before Mattel, before Hasbro—Marx Toys ruled.

Throughout the company's meteoric rise, a man named Ray Lohr designed toys in the shadows. Lohr joined Marx in 1933 and didn't retire until 1976. In those 43 years, he was responsible for scores of toys, all designed in and around the Marx plant in Erie, Pennsylvania. As the company's chief designer, Lohr headed the team that conceived and developed Big Wheel.

According to his friend, Jay Horowitz, Lohr often took his work home and tinkered with designs in his basement. "Ray told me that he got the idea from something he did when he was a kid," Horowitz said. "He'd take his tricycle and remove the seat and then invert the frame. After putting it back together, he'd sit over the back axle and pedal."

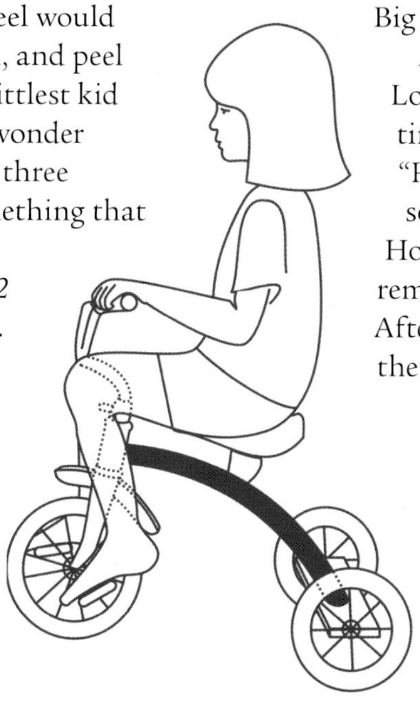

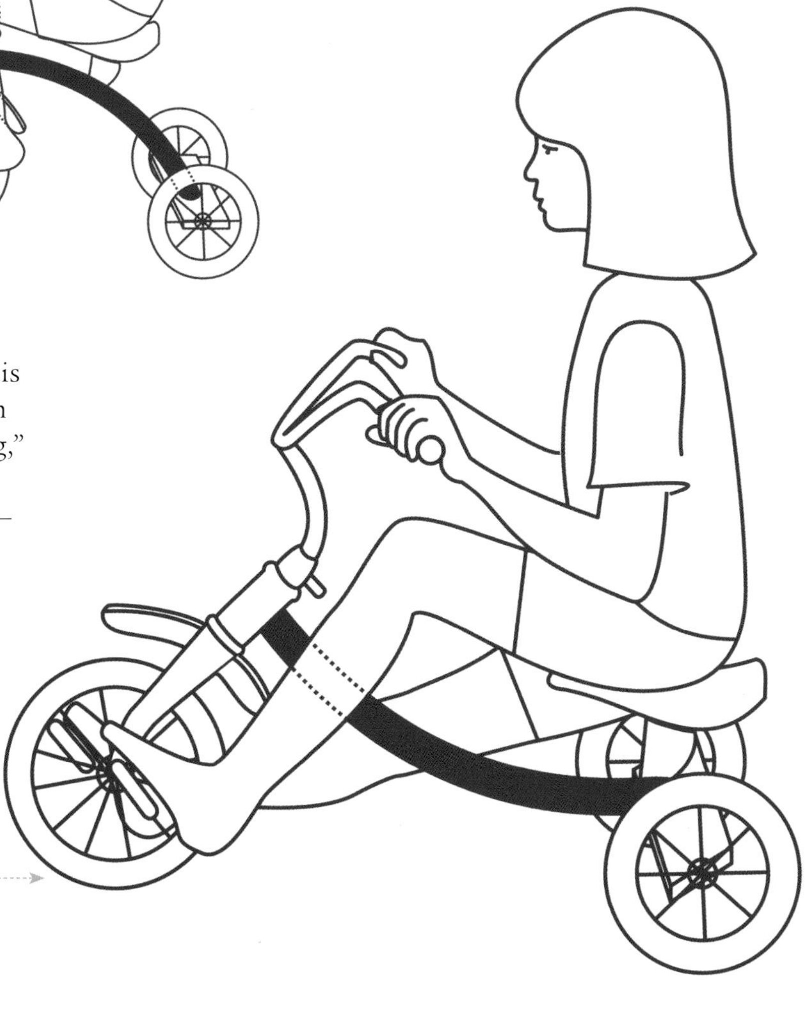

This illustration shows how tricycle frames were inverted during the Depression. "It was really a matter of extending the life of a toy for purely economic reasons," said toy historian Allan Miller. Some thirty years later, this conversion inspired Ray Lohr to invent Big Wheel.

This anecdote was confirmed by Allan Miller, a toy historian and curator of The Krueger Street Toy & Train Museum in West Virginia. "I spoke to former employees of Marx Toys and they relayed stories of Depression-era resourcefulness that inspired the Big Wheel. In the early 1930s, no one had any money, so you weren't going to get a new bicycle when you outgrew your tricycle. With a little tinkering, people figured out how to invert the tricycle frame and have kids sit down low over the axle."

It was as if a tricycle had morphed into an adrenaline-filled cross between a low rider and a chopper. Big Wheelers held their handlebars high, but sat low to the ground where the perception of speed was heightened. It was easy to ride, so it was a "bridge vehicle," appealing to kids who were too old (or too cool) for a preschool ride-on, but not quite ready for a two-wheeler.

As we aged, many of us found it a hard toy to give up. Even after mastering a bicycle, we came back to Big Wheel—it was that much fun. Remember taking the seat off so you could still fit in it? We'd ride it down hills, crouched low like a catcher, in the spot where the seat should have been. Or we'd use it like a scooter, and our weight (certainly much more than factory specs allowed) caused the body to sag and scrape along the pavement.

For many, Big Wheel was the one childhood toy they played with until it disintegrated beneath them. It was difficult to pedal once the front tire began to split, but we still did. In fact, the sound of gravel tumbling around inside that hollow plastic wheel remains vivid today. I remember filling a cracked back wheel with the dry dirt from under our tire swing so that when I rode it down the sidewalk the dirt sprayed out in a cloud of dust, which

Riding . . . Churning?

For some strange reason, when we were done selling doughnuts we sold ice cream. In a phenomenon that ranks as one of the wonderful mysteries of childhood, many a Big Wheeler turned his or her ride upside-down and cranked the pedals with their hands while screaming "Ice Cream!" at the top of their lungs. There was no ice cream. There were no patrons. These kids were too young to remember churning anything, yet thousands did it. On a warm summer evening when the lightning bugs were just starting to flicker, if you were selling doughnuts and ice cream with your Big Wheel, you just knew that all was right with the world. Years later, I would meet more than a few Big Wheel fans and we'd share that bizarre bond. "ICE CREAM!? You did that!? I did that, too!"

looked (to me anyway) like smoke from a squealing tire.

Marx sold nearly 3 million Big Wheels in 1971 *and again* in 1972, making it the runaway hit of both years. In 1972, at the height of Big Wheel's popularity, Louis and David Marx sold their company to Quaker Oats for $52 million. Many believe that they would not have received close to that amount had it not been for Big Wheel, which went on to become a landmark toy of the '70s.

The first Big Wheel, 1969

A company called Empire Plastics had a Big Wheel knockoff product called Hot Cycle, and competition from them and others caused Big Wheel's heyday to pass. In the early '80s, Empire bought all the rights to Big Wheel and upgraded it into the world of licensing. Many young professionals today can recall their *CHiPs* Big Wheel, *Dukes of Hazzard* Big Wheel, or *Knight Rider* Big Wheel. Empire brought the fun to girls with lines featuring '80s icons like Smurf, Cabbage Patch Kids and Strawberry Shortcake. Boys didn't want to admit it, but the doughnuts on these Big Wheels were just as sweet.

Today, competitors with hot licenses have overtaken the original Big Wheel. A company called Processed Plastics makes Mighty Wheels and a Big Wheel-inspired vehicle for girls called the Speed N' Style Cycle. Neither are true Big Wheels, but they're emblazoned with the Hot Wheels and Barbie logos, so they make for stiff competition. Big Wheel now is owned by Alfa International, the company that took over many of the Empire Plastics trademarks. Christmas 2001 was the first year since 1969 that Big Wheel was not available.

Marx came out with the Green Machine for older kids in 1975. Although it had a cool name and "stick-shift steering" it just couldn't match our beloved Big Wheel.

But there is hope. For Toy Fair 2003, Alpha International announced "The Big One is Back!" Slated for a reintroduction in the spring, Big Wheel will make its triumphant return and a new generation of kids will experience the original spinning, sliding, riding sensation. Doughnuts anyone?

When Disney Imagineers designed Disney's Pop Century Resort in Orlando, Florida, the icon they chose to represent the 1970s section of the 5,760-room, 20-building mega-plex was Big Wheel. Disney plans to build a 22-foot-high replica of the original ride-on slider at the front entrance of the new resort.

Razor USA, the company behind the folding Razor Scooter, released what they called "A contemporary spin on an old favorite." The Scream Machine is a new interpretation of the Big Wheel featuring an all-steel frame and a rubber front tire. Not to be outdone, Huffy Bikes has introduced an "extreme" version of the Green Machine featuring a strong steel frame construction that can hold up to 180 lbs!

On the left is a Big Wheel ad from 1974. By '81, when the ad on the right ran, Marx was pitching Big Wheel's fun to girls too.

Nerf

Debut: 1969
Inventor: Reyn Guyer
Developer: Will Kruse
Insider: Bill Dohrmann
Companies: Parker Brothers, Hasbro

AN INSIDE THE HOME, HOME RUN

Moms have rules. One of the biggest is: *Don't throw the ball in the house.* After I broke our front room window with something as harmless as a plastic water pistol, I decided it's a good rule. I could only imagine the destructive force of a basketball. I later learned that this was pretty much a universal household rule—until 1969. That's when inventor Reyn Guyer's Nerf ball was released much to the chagrin of Moms everywhere. Guyer wasn't anti-authority or even trying to cause trouble. He was just trying to finish the Caveman game.

In 1966, Reyn Guyer was working at his father's sales promotion company when he had the idea for a promotional game that eventually became Milton Bradley's Twister. After inspiring one of the biggest games of the '60s, Guyer was trying to duplicate that ever-so-rare feat. His creative team, now branched into the toy business, was hard at work one day in 1968 perfecting a new Stone Age-themed game. This meant that he and his learned colleagues (five or six engineers) spent the day whacking each other with rocks. Some would call it insanity; in the toy biz, it's called "play testing."

Caveman consisted of fake money, paper stepping-stones and rocks cut from mattress foam. It was something of a cross between musical chairs and the *Flintstones;* players jumped from one stepping-stone to another, under which could be found counterfeit cash. The Caveman object? Protect your loot while fending off your opponents with the "rocks," which were so lightweight (made from "open-celled" polyurethane)

that they bounced harmlessly off walls and heads. Reyn Guyer was struck with a rock and then with an idea. A big idea.

Guyer shared the moment. "One of my team members, Will Kruse, began bouncing a foam rock. 'That's it!' we all said. 'Indoor ball.' We got rid of the stepping-stones right then and there." Quite by accident, Guyer and his team had discovered something far better than the original game idea—a soft, safe ball that could be thrown and kicked indoors with no fear of knocking over a lamp or breaking a window. But would the new ball's blessing also be its curse?

"We thought that if it was too light to knock over a vase, then it

When Reyn Guyer was struck by foam "rock" (and then the idea for an indoor ball), the Nerf ball was born.

Official Nerf Ball, 1969

would be too light to be sold in a store," Guyer said. "We didn't think a toy company would do it as a ball, so we devised a ton of fun games you could play with it." For lack of a better name, his team dubbed it the Muffball. The pitch to game manufacturers was simple: Classic outdoor favorites like basketball and volleyball could now be played indoors. Guyer took the line of games to Milton Bradley first, since they had a hit with his company's Twister game. After tinkering with it for a while, they passed on the concept. Milton Bradley's key competitor was next, and as toy history would have it, Parker Brothers didn't make the same mistake as its rival.

Ironically, when the Parker Brothers' product development team (Henry Simmons, Bill Dohrmann, Arthur Venditti, David Laughridge and others), first saw these foam spheres, they envisioned exactly what Reyn Guyer originally had; not a line of new sports, but a new ball. *The world's first indoor ball!*

THE NAME GAME

The New Dictionary of American Slang defines the word "nerf" as a verb used by hot rod fans. To "nerf" means "to bump a car out of one's way." Others in the auto racing world referred to the "nerf bar"—metal tubing mounted loosely to the frame of a race car—used mostly for visual effect. "The term 'nerf' has been used in racing since the 1940s and probably well before that," author and hot rod enthusiast Don Montgomery told me. "Then in the 1960s, the hot rod and muscle car crowd picked it up." By 1969, when hot rods, surfing and the California beach scene were all the rage, Parker Brothers happened to be searching for a name for their new ball. Bill Dohrmann thought Nerf was perfect because it somehow conveyed a feeling of softness and fun, but at the same time, conveyed nothing (or at least nothing outside racing circles). "At the time, we didn't

The world's first indoor ball began as mattress foam cut to look like rocks for an ill-fated game called Caveman. After inspiration struck, the rocks were cut into more spherical round balls of foam and painted bright orange. Pictured here is the original Nerf ball prototype.

know if this thing was going to ever go beyond just this one ball, but as it turned out it went way beyond it," Dohrmann said. "Nerf started as a nonsense word and turned into an umbrella word." To Parker Brothers, the word Nerf became synonymous with warm, soft toys and cold, hard cash.

In its first year on the market over four million Nerf balls were sold. The original 4¼-inch cube package featured a smilelike window that revealed one of the four original Nerf balls in yellow, orange, red or blue. The rounded Nerf letters were classic '70s and the box copy boasted of the things you could and couldn't do with this wonderful new ball . . .

> SAFE! The Nerf Ball is made of incredibly soft and spongy synthetic foam. Throw it around indoors; you can't damage lamps or break windows. You can't hurt babies or old people.

Good to know.

To their credit, Parker Brothers, primarily a game company at the time, produced and promoted the Nerf ball well, and was rewarded handsomely for it. "When we first showed the Nerf ball to our customers, they laughed at us." Bill Dohrmann remembered. "They said stuff like, 'You guys have got to be kidding. You're a game company. This thing is woefully overpriced.

When Neil Armstrong took that giant leap for mankind on July 20, 1969, it almost influenced Parker Brothers to name their new foam sphere Moon Ball. Other names in the running included Orby and Falsie. From the beginning, a number of Parker Brothers executives claimed credit for coming up with the now classic name, Nerf.

The soft, safe, floating, whirling, dipping, darting object for inner space.
Spongy and harmless for home fun, it's a flying disk with a flick of your wrist.

And don't forget Parker's Official Nerf Ball, for great games of Wastebasketball, Sock soccer, Nerfminton, Soft softball, and like that.

© 1970 Parker Brothers, Inc., Salem, Mass. 01970. Made in U.S.A.

The Nerf disk was released in 1970. Legendary Mad magazine artist Jack Davis provided the artwork, which depicted hounds, hippies, house-wives and others, all enjoying the foam fun.

Forget it.'

But after it started selling big elsewhere they called us back. They had to, it was a hit."

Nerf bounced beyond a ball to become a brand. Parker Brothers released a slew of Nerf products just as Reyn Guyer's team had originally pitched. Nerf Soccer, Nerf Golf, Nerf Ping-pong, Nerf Basketball (called Nerfoop), Nerfminton, Nerf Fencing and even Nerf Pool all reached store shelves. An independent inventor came to Guyer and pitched an idea for a vehicle. Guyer took it to Parker Brothers and the result was the classic Nerf-Mobile. If you didn't feel like driving, you could fly as Nerf Man (complete with cape), or take off in a Nerf Glider. Many Nerf brand items came and went, but one in particular established the brand as a toy for generations.

The Nerf football arrived in 1972, after Parker Brothers successfully tackled the job of creating a denser ball. Realizing that the polyurethane foam of the original Nerf ball was too light to kick or throw

very far, the engineers at Parker Brothers consulted with a manufacturer of foam armrests for the automotive industry and conse-quently perfected their new foaming process. Where the original Nerf ball was cut on a lathe with hot wire (and later knives), the Nerf football was made from liquid foam that was poured into a heated mold. When finished, this new ball had a "skin" or durable outer covering that made it suitable to punt, pass or kick. True, it was much softer and smaller than a real football, but it was definitely *not* for indoor use. Mom's rule was reestablished as Nerf moved outside with the big boys.

Nerf was so big throughout the '70s and early '80s that Parker Brothers lent its name to playthings beyond the realm of foam. There were Nerf pencils, a line of Playmobile-like plastic characters called Nerfuls and even Nerf chewing gum. Clearly the popularity of Nerf had transcended the original foam ball, but few

Shortly after its release, teenagers and college students across the country made the Nerf football what it is today, the biggest selling football of all time.

could have predicted the kind of new product line that blasted its way into Nerfdom.

FIRING FOAM

While some kids dreamed of being John Elway, others wanted to be Arnold Schwarzenegger. The new promotional copy called it "Nerf to the Next Power!" While it was once a ball for the passive peacekeeper, the new weaponized Nerf boasted of its firepower. There were names like the Nerf Bow, the Chain Blaster, the Rip Chord Mega Blitz, Bazooka Pump 150, and the Triple Strike Blaster. These new guns, or "launchers" as they were called, fired foam balls, disks or darts. Clearly some mad scientist (a.k.a. toy developer) had mixed testosterone with the polyurethane foam.

One such scientist was Dr. Lonnie Johnson, the man that invented the Super Soaker water gun (see Super Soaker). Johnson thought of using pressurized air to make toys that shot foam projectiles. "My initial idea was to improve upon Nerf's spring loaded models and take market share away from them by going to another toy company," Johnson shared. "But Tyco Toys

The SuperMaxx 750 Dart Blaster shoots foam-shafted darts with suction cup tips, using pressurized air technology provided by Dr. Lonnie Johnson, the inventor responsible for Super Soaker water guns.

had already tried that and Hasbro countered with the campaign 'Nerf or Nothing.' From then on, all Hasbro's competitors were 'gun shy,' so to speak." So Johnson took his ideas to Hasbro and the result were new models like the Wildfire Automatic Blaster, an automatic weapon that fires 20 Nerf darts.

Today the Nerf blaster line emphasizes the plastic gun more than the foam projectile. Recent years have seen the line decline, probably due to teenagers migrating toward the popular paint ball games. Through the rise and leveling off of Nerf blasters, Nerf's ball line has continued to fly. Today, a new generation of Nerfers is busy dreaming of being the next Peyton Manning. He endorses the new Vortex Spin Devil football with his right arm, the only "gun" he needs.

Nerf basketball hoops still sell like gangbusters and the Nerf line has attracted more than its share of imitators. It's not often that an entire *category* of toys can be credited to a single idea. The competition that Nerf faces is proof that the business of foam toys, launched with Reyn Guyer's little foam ball, is still alive and well.

One of Nerf's "farthest flying footballs!"

Rock Box

In 1989, Nerf ball inventor Reyn Guyer was invited to Toy Fair for the Nerf ball's 20th anniversary. "The Parker Brothers executives knew that I had kept that first foam ball we had hand cut with scissors and asked me if I'd bring it with me to show the press," Guyer said. "Well, we didn't have anything to carry it in, so my son Tom had this mahogany box made. It was hinged, with velour inside—you'd think it was the Hope Diamond in there. Every year we dust the box off and use that first Nerf ball as an ornament on our Christmas tree. It's become a Guyer family tradition."

Uno

Debut: 1971
Inventors: Merle Robbins (1912-1984) and Ray Robbins
Developers: Marie Robbins, Bob Tezak, Ed Akeman
Insider: Pete Voit
Companies: Uno Games, International Games, Mattel

ONE IN A BILLION

In 1971, if you were to wander into Merle's Barbershop in Arlington Heights, Ohio, you'd be able to get a trim, a shave or an Uno game. Some customers probably took all three. Although you could probably get the same haircut anywhere in the city, if you wanted to pick up the new card game you'd heard people talking about this was the only place in town. It was a humble beginning for a game that has sold over *150 million* copies. If Monopoly didn't have a 36-year head start, Uno would be the biggest selling commercial game in the world.

A few years earlier, Barber Merle Robbins and his son Ray created this simple card game as an alternative to Pinochle and as a twist on the popular game of Crazy Eights. Merle and his family (his wife Marie and their grown kids Myrna, Gerald, Ray, and John) were lovers of games and used the extra bedroom on the first floor of their modest home to play cards. There in the Cincinnati suburb of Reading, the game that became Uno was born over a family debate.

One night some time around 1970, the Robbins family gathered with some friends to play. One of their old favorites was a game where you had to get rid of your cards as turns passed "neighbor to neighbor." It was played with two full decks of cards, with the picture cards all signifying a command.

A king reversed play, a queen was a skip, aces were wild, etc. When a friendly argument began over which picture card meant what, the Robbins family resorted to writing down the commands on each card with a magic marker. It was suggested that Merle write out the rules, so he did. Next, he found himself buying two blank decks of cards and writing out the commands on each card so they'd be easier to read. Finally, the fun just took over and Robbins thought about the next logical step—actually printing copies of the game.

After getting production quotes, the Robbins family set out to make 5,000 sets of their new card game at a cost of $10,000. There were ten people involved and the plan was for each to invest $1,000. Perhaps it was the stress over the money involved ($10,000

Uno now and how it looked in 1978.

Barber Merle Robbins (at left) and his son Ray pooled $10,000 to produce 5,000 Uno games in 1971.

would equate to over $42,000 today), but soon arguments over the exact rules and the style of the artwork caused this business start-up to shut down. Some relatives and family friends bowed out, leaving Merle, his son Ray and their wives to figure out how they were going to come up with the rest of the money.

John Robbins shared with me a pivotal phone call he received one day from his strong-willed mother, Marie Robbins. "I'll never forget her call. Six people had dropped out of the venture so my parents and brother Ray were left about $6,000 short of the $10,000 they needed. She called to tell me that she and my dad were going to sell their house and move into a trailer so that they could make this card game. I couldn't believe it!" John Robbins was 23 years old at the time, yet *he* was the voice of reason. "I told her that I was totally against that, but we talked for a long while that night and she said, 'Johnny, I really think we have something here. We're gonna go ahead and chance it.' I never discouraged them from then on."

Merle and Ray finalized the game play and settled on the name that Ray had suggested: Uno. Spanish for "one," Uno had a nice sound to it and described the moment of play when a player had but one card left and was about to win—or get nailed with a command card. The name was also reminiscent of Bingo, where the rules (like Uno) required the players to yell out the name of the game—a smart marketing touch. The object of Uno was to get rid of the cards in your hand by laying down a card matching the color, number or word on the card played by the previous player. It was fast-paced and quite possibly perfect in its design for family play. Kids could play it with adults without feeling overmatched. Adults could play it and have a blast without feeling foolish. Uno was destined to go beyond the barbershop.

ROAD TRIP

After the house in which Uno was conceived was sold to pay for the production of the first games, Merle and Marie planned their next step. With the money from the sale, they bought an old car and a camper trailer. They had signs made up that read "Uno—Best Card Game in America," and with these homemade billboards attached to the sides of their trailer, Merle and Marie Robbins hit the road.

In the summer of 1971, The Who toured the major cities of the United States while the much lesser hyped "Uno North American Tour" started in Cincinnati and then headed south. Merle and Marie visited parks and campgrounds with their new game literally in tow. They pulled their dream through Texas and Florida, showing anyone who'd listen how to play the game. In

Merle the Marketer

Forget for a moment that today it is sold in nearly every mass-market retailer in the free world. Imagine Uno as it began, for sale exclusively in Merle's Barbershop on the corner of Carthage Street and Glenrose Avenue in Arlington Heights, Ohio. If you wanted a copy, you could buy it there for $3.49, and if you wanted to play it, you could always go next door to Lichty's Tavern. There, patrons could often be heard shouting "Uno!" while they waited for their number to be called.

John Robbins shared a great story that illustrates just how innovative Merle Robbins was. "My father set up an intercom system between his place and Lichty's next door. You'd come in to his barbershop and if he was busy you'd just grab a number. Then you could go next door and shoot the bull with your buddies and have a beer, even play Uno. He'd call your number over the intercom when his chair was free and you'd go on over and get your haircut. He was very creative."

those days many trailer parks had a clubhouse, and within these humble amphitheaters of the road, Merle and Marie Robbins put on their show and won over many Uno fans.

By the time they returned to Ohio, just before Christmas, they had enough orders to ship their entire inventory of 5,000 games and enough confidence to make 10,000 more. Soon, with his son Ray's help, Merle placed Uno in retail stores throughout Cincinnati. Don Vonderhaars was a family friend who sold the game in his butcher shop. Because of his business, Don knew many distributors who serviced grocery stores. He became the Robbins' first outside salesman by enlisting food distributors to place the game in food stores across Cincinnati. Word began to travel about this new game and soon Uno began to show up in popular Cincinnati department stores like Shillito's and Pogue's. Not that there's anything wrong with cutting your teeth in barbershops and butchers' markets, but Uno was beginning to move up the retailer food chain! Less than a year after its introduction, it swelled beyond Cincinnati and even beyond Ohio. Then one fateful day, Merle got a call from a very interesting man named, Bob Tezak.

Tezak was in his family's funeral home business in Joliet, Illinois. Already a mover and shaker in local politics, Tezak was just 24 when he was introduced to Uno. He was so enthralled by it that he contacted the Robbins family to buy several copies. Much to Merle's surprise, he called back a few weeks later wanting to buy not just a few more games, but the entire company.

Uno Goes International

Tezak and several friends had decided to pool their resources and take a stab at the game business. As unpretentious as Uno was, it needed someone with the salesmanship of P.T. Barnum and the brass of Donald Trump to take it to the big time. Bob Tezak had those qualities in spades. He flew to Cincinnati and met with Merle and Ray, and after a few phone calls over the

following week the deal was done. The Robbins family agreed to a payment of $50,000 and royalties of 10 cents per game sold.

In 1971, Tezak, his brother-in-law Ed Akeman and several other relatives and friends formed a company called International Games, Inc. to promote the Uno card game.

While Bob Tezak was the company figurehead, Ed Akeman ran day-to-day business. International Games started in Akeman's Lockport, Illinois apartment, and since the game was not available in many stores outside of Cincinnati, Ed took write-in orders directly from Uno fans and shipped games from his apartment-turned-warehouse. Slowly, store orders trickled in as the game started to take off. "I would pass cases of Uno out the first floor window of my apartment, directly to the UPS man," Akeman remembered. "That was how we began."

Part of the purchase from the Robbins family included inventory, and after they sold out of the remaining original "pea-soup" green Uno games, International Games (or IGI as they were known) made several changes. "I spent about a year playing the

The original Uno game made by the Robbins family had 112 cards and a khaki green color scheme.

game . . . and completely overhauled the rules and re-copyrighted the game," Bob Tezak wrote in a letter to me. "The original cards were changed to bridge-sized cards which were much easier to handle and more economical to print." Finally, the original game's color scheme was scrapped in favor of the familiar bright red packaging millions now recognize.

After some modest success, the fledgling game company moved shop out of Akeman's apartment and into a small room in the back of a florist in Joliet. There, Akeman manned the phones and held together the illusion that "International Games" was indeed a worldwide player, even though reality (and the smell of freshly cut flowers), told him otherwise. "I would answer the phone 'International Games,' and no matter what department they asked for, I'd put them on hold, and then pick the phone back up and disguise my voice," Akeman laughed. "It was all an effort to make us look bigger than we really were."

In the mid-'70s Pete Voit was hired as IGI's national sales representative. He later went on to form a game company called Fundex around another hit card game called Phase 10. Akeman credits Voit's salesmanship as one of the key factors that launched Uno. "We had no game experience. I was a banker, Bob was a funeral director, but Pete knew games—and that made all the difference." Soon, word of mouth marketing from fans helped spread Uno farther, even down to the Missouri-Arkansas border. "I remember when Wal-Mart first ordered," Akeman recalled. "They're in the middle of nowhere and I had one heck of time getting all the way down there. I met with their buyer in the lobby of their headquarters and for whatever reason, he wasn't going to buy. So there I was packing up, thinking it was a

long, wasted trip when this guy in overalls comes up and starts asking me questions. Needless to say, I was not in a good mood. He asks 'Are you the outfit with that Uno game?' And I said 'Yeah, that's right,' then he asks 'You're a family corporation aren't you?' and again I said 'That's right.' Then this guy turns to the buyer and says 'Buy a couple gross from the young man.' Come to find out, it was Sam Walton! True story—Sam Walton put Uno in Wal-Mart!"

As IGI flourished it became evident that America was in love with Uno. "We sold over 11 million games in 1980 and [then again] in 1981," Tezak shared. At the game's peak, Uno cards were printed around the clock by plants in Hong Kong and Belgium. The success afforded the original owners of the company many luxuries; Tezak, for example, enjoyed a private company plane and several homes. But it was International Game's new Joliet office that became the symbol of Uno's success.

The address was "1 Uno Circle." The reason behind the street address was obvious enough, but the shape of International Game's new Joliet headquarters was harder to put your finger on. From the ground it was a curvy, unidentifiable oddity. From the air, it looked much like the tilde mark "~" which meant, "approximately equal" in mathematics. It was state of the art and finished in cut stone. That's why the cost to build it in 1981 was "approximately equal" to 2 million dollars. Today it houses a land surveying firm, but still draws stares and more than its share of questions. To many in Joliet, it remains the house that Uno built.

From '81 to '91 video games boomed, busted and boomed again, but good ol' fashioned card games never

Pictured here in 1986, Uno co-developer Ed Akeman holds the 50 millionth Uno game produced by International Games.

Forget "Draw Two," Uno Attack is, as its name suggests, an ambush of cards when you least expected it. The game was invented by Big Monster Toys (formerly Breslow, Morrison and Terzian) of Marvin Glass fame.

Uno Stacko was released in 1994 in response to the popularity of Jenga and was an immediate hit. If the fun and flexibility of Uno's play could allow a card game to be morphed into a plastic stacking game, then anything was possible. Uno Attack was next, where a plastic card-dealing gizmo spit cards out to unsuspecting players. Uno Blitzo, Uno for Gameboy and Uno on CD-ROM all helped to take the game high-tech.

From the late '90s to today, the power of using mega-popular brands helped deal Uno cards to new audiences. Fans were rocked by the Elvis Edition of Uno and got in 'toon with versions of Uno based on *The Simpsons* and *SpongeBob SquarePants,* to name a few. A deal Mattel recently signed with Sababa Toys promises to result in an avalanche of Uno games based on licenses as diverse as The Care Bears and Spider-Man.

went south. With the colossal success of Trivial Pursuit and Pictionary, traditional games enjoyed high times, with Uno leading the pack in card games.

Western Publishing and Parker Brothers both tried to purchase International Games in 1986, but Tezak refused. IGI's leader had the Midas touch, with success following him wherever he turned. In 1991, he bought part of the race team that won the legendary Indianapolis 500. Arie Luyendyk was the driver of a cherry red Chevy sponsored by RCA and a powerful little card game. When Luyendyk crossed the finish line before anyone else in 1991, his car was sporting a rather large Uno logo.

In 1992, Mattel bought International Games. The acquisition gave the toy giant a long desired foothold in the game business as they gathered Uno and another IGI card game called Skip-Bo into their fold of products. Masters at toys like Barbie and Hot Wheels, Mattel had struggled with marketing games prior to the deal. With Uno, they got not just a game but a franchise.

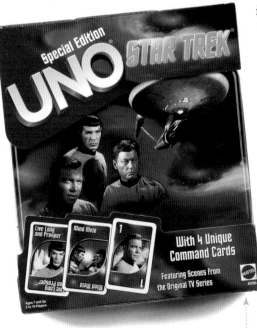

Merle Robbins passed away in 1984, but not before he saw Uno become a colossal hit. This simple game of matching numbers, colors, or words has lasted 30 years. With 150 million copies sold in 80 countries, it's conceivable that over *a billion* people have played the game. Now *those* numbers are hard to match. Many card games have come and gone since the launch of "America's Favorite." There are games, but there's only one Uno.

Over the years, licensed editions of Uno have taken the humble game light-years from its beginning at Merle Robbins' hometown barbershop.

THE PLAYMAKERS
Toy Timeline

1980	'81	'82	'83	'84	'85	'86	'87	'88	'89	'90

• **Tonka buys Kenner/**
Parker Toys
• Koosh ball

• **Trivial Pursuit**
• My Little Pony
• Sequence
• Phase 10

• **Pictionary**

• Hasbro buys Ideal Toys
• Tyco Toys buys Schaper Toys
• Coleco buys Selchow & Righter
• Balderdash
• Outburst

• Hasbro buys Milton Bradley
• Hallmark buys Binney & Smith

the original **RUBIK'S CUBE** over three billion combinations... just one solution.

IDEAL

ASSEMBLED IN HAITI   PACKAGED IN U.S.A.
No. 2164-2   © IDEAL TOY CORPORATION 1980, NEWARK, N.J. 07105

• **Jenga**
• **Cabbage Patch Kids**
• CBS buys Ideal Toys
• Nintendo Entertainment System

• Hasbro purchases Coleco's assets
• Tyco Toys buys View-Master/Ideal Toys
• Polly Pocket
• Scattergories

• **Rubik's Cube**

Trivial Pursuit®

MASTER GAME - GENUS EDITION

The Perpetual Challenge

JENGA

A game for all ages, requiring a keen eye, a steady hand and nerves of steel

Application Card for Free Membership of the International Jenga Club enclosed.

PICTIONARY®
THE GAME OF QUICK DRAW®

Contains one Cabbage Patch Kid™ doll.

Cabbage Patch Kids

The Cabbage Patch Kid™ shown is one of the many 'Kids' available for adoption. The special 'Kid' that you've adopted has arrived.

Ages 3 & up

I'm one of a kind. I'm adoptable.

© 1983 Cabbage Patch Kids™ is a trademark of and licensed from Original Appalachian Artworks, Inc., Cleveland, GA U.S.A., All Rights Reserved

1980s–1990s

'90   '91   '92   '93   '94   '95   '96   '97   '98   '99   2000

•Hasbro buys
Larami

•Tickle Me
Elmo

•Mattel buys WHAM-O
•Hasbro buys Western Publishing's game line
•Blurt!

• **Beanie Babies**
• Upwords
• Magic the Gathering

•Mattel buys Tyco Toys

•Mattel buys International Games
•Guesstures

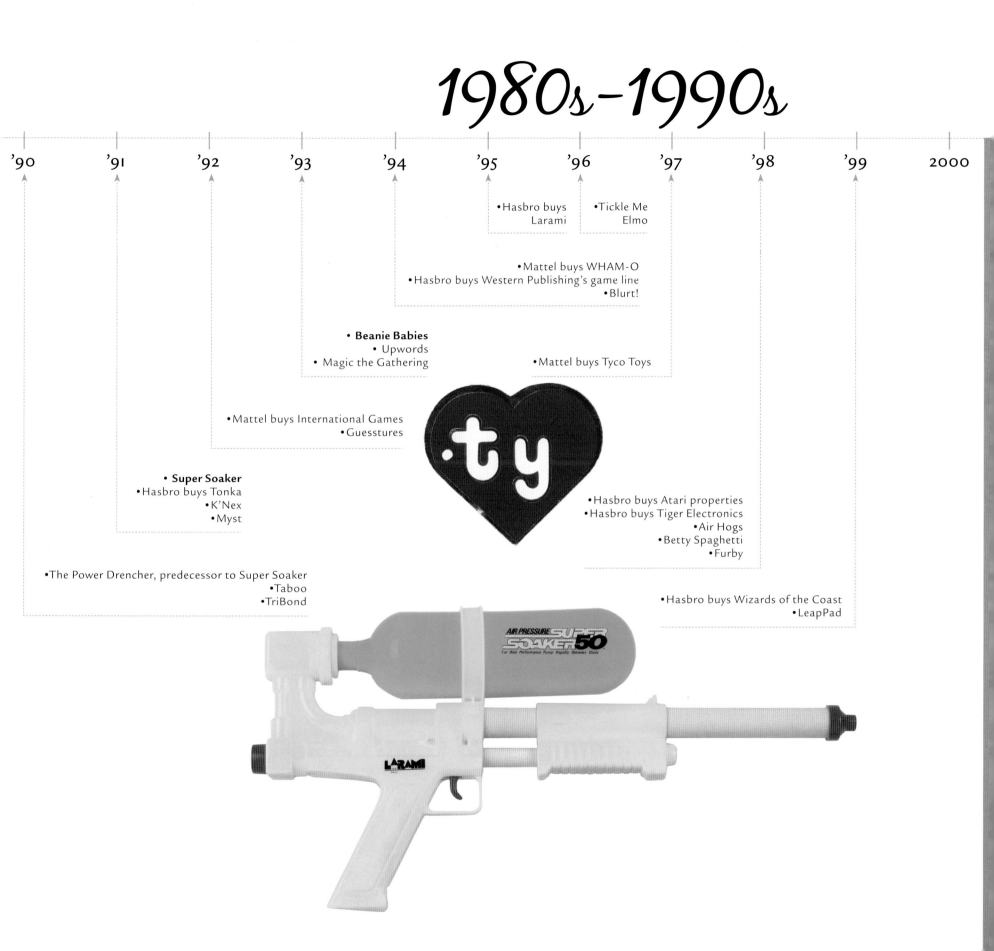

• **Super Soaker**
•Hasbro buys Tonka
•K'Nex
•Myst

•Hasbro buys Atari properties
•Hasbro buys Tiger Electronics
•Air Hogs
•Betty Spaghetti
•Furby

•The Power Drencher, predecessor to Super Soaker
•Taboo
•TriBond

•Hasbro buys Wizards of the Coast
•LeapPad

Debut: 1977
U.S. Debut: 1980
Inventor: Erno Rubik
Developers: Tibor Laczi,
    Tom Kremer
Insider: Stewart Sims
Companies: Konsumex,
    Seven Towns, Ideal Toys,
    OddzOn, Milton Bradley

Rubik's Cube

ERNO'S ENIGMA

Every cube starts its journey in a perfect state of color-coded calm—each side a different hue and in perfect harmony with each other. Don't touch it, don't twist it. Step away from the puzzle! Curiosity killed the cubist—or at least his spirit. A closer look reveals that each side is divided into three columns and three rows, with each column and row able to turn 360°. Just a few innocent twists of a few rows and a few harmless turns of a few columns, and the colors begin to run. The object then is to twist and rotate the individual rows and columns and arrange all six sides of the cube back to their original state. Oh, and by the way, there are 43,252,003,274,489, 856,000 (that's 43 quintillion) wrong arrangements and one correct one.

How could one of history's most difficult puzzles also be history's most popular? How could professors fail to solve the infuriating thing, while the first record holder, who was only 16 years old at the time, mastered it in just 22.95 seconds? How can something so elegantly simple be so amazingly complex? Welcome to Erno's enigma, Rubik's Cube.

This puzzle of puzzles was conceived during the spring of 1974 in the most unlikely of places: communist Hungary. Rubik was a 29-year-old professor at The Academy of Applied Arts and Design, and his humble living space was filled with cardboard figures and wooden models. With a passion for geometry and an innate creativity, Rubik fashioned a sort of movable cube sculpture from stacks of wooden blocks he'd attached together with elastic string. As he twisted and turned them, he was amazed at the way the individual blocks began to rearrange themselves in perfect rows and columns. So it didn't matter when the elastic finally snapped and sent the blocks flying, for Rubik had seen something in all that turning that turned him into a puzzle maker.

In his 1986 article entitled, "The Perplexing Life of Erno Rubik," *Discover* magazine writer John Tierney described how Rubik built his prototype of the new design by meticulously assembling each of the sculpted, wooden blocks into the final cube shape. He distinguished each side of the cube with adhesive paper of a different color and started to twist. Quoting from Erno's autobiographical manuscript (the unpublished *Rubik on Rubik)*, Tierney shared the moment when the professor discovered that his moving sculpture had turned into something more.

Erno Rubik

> It was wonderful [Erno wrote], to see how, after only a few turns, the colors became mixed, apparently in random fashion. It was tremendously satisfying to watch this color parade. Like after a nice walk when you have seen many lovely sights you decide to go home, after a while I decided it was time to go home, let us put the cubes back in order. And it was at that moment that I came face to face with the Big Challenge: What is the way home?

Not knowing if it was even possible to get "home," Rubik worked to see if he could get the colors to choose sides. The key, he assumed, was to first line up the eight corner blocks correctly with the center blocks on each face, since those center blocks were the only ones that did not change in respect to one another. After more than a month from when he first began his journey, an obsessed Rubik solved the puzzle in the summer of 1974. Little did the he know that his mania over the Cube would soon spread across the globe.

Buvuos Kocka (Magic Cube) first appeared in Hungary in late 1977. It had taken some time for the toy-making cooperative in Budapest to agree to produce it and then figure out how to make it.

Engineers worked for almost three years turning Rubik's handmade, wooden prototype into a durable, plastic puzzle that could be mass-produced. When their achievement finally appeared in stores, Hungarians did not feel the magic at first. Eventually pockets of fans throughout the country came under its spell, but it could very well have remained a local diversion had a key figure in the future of the Cube not stopped for lunch at a certain Hungarian café in November of 1978.

Dr. Tibor Laczi lived in Vienna but was born in Budapest, and he made frequent business trips back to his homeland. Laczi discovered the cube in the hands of one of the café's wait staff, who was not sure what to make of this new puzzle he had acquired. Being a mathematics enthusiast, Laczi was intrigued and asked to see it. A few twists later, he bought it from the puzzled waiter. Laczi was so convinced of the Cube's potential that the next day he visited Konsumex, the state trading company. Asking for permission to sell it outside of Hungary, Laczi was denied at first, but eventually Konsumex consented. Laczi's next step was to request a meeting with the Cube's inventor.

The first thing Laczi learned from Erno Rubik was what everyone wants to know: The Solution. Convinced that demonstration of the Cube was the key to its success, Laczi set out to unlock the door to the West. His first stop was the International Toy Fair in Nuremberg, Germany. Even without a stand or booth in which to display it, he attracted crowds in the aisles with his twisting and solving of the puzzle. One amazed bystander was British toy man Tom Kremer, whose successful London based company, Seven Towns Ltd., enjoyed a great reputation for spotting hit toys and taking them to the rest of the world. Kremer also had Hungarian roots and felt an immediate bond with both Laczi and Rubik, but more importantly, he shared their belief in the potential that remained hidden within those twisting colors. The three agreed to take this Hungarian invention beyond the Iron Curtain. It proved to be a tough sell.

In 1979, the toy industry was still swimming in the wake of Atari's Video Computer System, which had been released two years prior. Pong was on TV screens across the country and Space Invaders erupted in arcades. Handheld electronic games like Milton Bradley's classic Simon and Mattel's Electronic Quarterback took the industry by storm. In short, if it didn't plug in or eat batteries, a toy was deemed dead in '79.

Beyond its low-techiness, Magic Cube faced other daunting hurdles. Bill Dohrmann, Parker Brother's then-head of research and development, was one of many that rejected the Magic Cube. "A friend of mine, who was a professor at MIT, gave me one as a present in '78. I thought it was too expensive, impossible to manufacture and impossible to solve. Next thing I know

it's on the cover of *Newsweek*." Dohrmann laughed. "I stared at that thing for a year and a half sitting there on my desk at Parker Brothers, not knowing it was going to be one of the greatest puzzles of all time." But Tom Kremer knew something that the American toy companies did not. Back in Budapest, the Magic

Ideal Toy's 1980 catalog read: "Already a phenomenon in Europe, Rubik's Cube comes to America as Ideal's sensational new puzzle challenge." It was first released in an upscale, plastic cylinder, shown here.

Mathematics with a Twist

The popularity of Rubik's Cube reached virtually every demographic, but it was within the higher echelons of academia where this "toy" really turned heads. No other plaything has ever had such an immense impact outside of the toy industry as Rubik's Cube had on the study of mathematics.

Group theory is an area of abstract mathematics that looks at the ways you can turn, rotate, or stretch a group of related elements back onto itself. It was developed in the 19th century as a study of the algebra behind symmetry and transformations. Rubik's Cube made the investigation of these principles real in a tangible sense. MIT established "Cube-ins" for its professors and students, and to this day it remains a key element in many a group theory curriculum.

$$a \bullet x = b \bullet x$$
$$(a \bullet x) \bullet x^{-1} = (b \bullet x) \bullet x^{-1}$$
$$a \bullet (x \bullet x^{-1}) = b \bullet (x \bullet x^{-1})$$
$$a \bullet e = b \bullet e$$
$$a = b$$

Theoretical physicists also discovered that move sequences of a Rubik Cube form groups or states that are similar to that of particles. Fractional twists of the Cube in different directions were compared to a quark, a meson (quark-anitiquark pair), and a baryon (a quark triplet).

All these academic revelations became my source of relief. No wonder I could never solve the thing. "My meson was not aligned with the, uh . . . algebraic baryon therefore . . . My cube must be broken."

DISSOLVING RUBIK'S CUBE
The Ultimate Solution!

If you can't crack it, whack it. This 1982 book by Ken Lawless spoke to millions of frustrated cubists who could never find the answer.

A mind-blowing 100 million were reportedly sold in this relatively brief time period, which equates to an average of more than 91,000 sold *per day!*

It became the fastest selling and most popular puzzle in history. It inspired songs, a plastic hammer called The Cube Smasher, scores of books teaching how to solve it (*Mastering Rubik's Cube*), live with it (*How to Live with a Cubaholic*) or kill it (*101 Uses for a Dead Cube*). One solution book reportedly sold 1.5 million copies.

Countless cheaters took it apart and put it back together in order to "solve" it, while others resorted to buying a complete set of colored stickers offered

Cube was starting to take off. It was now being played in public, on trams and in parks. He realized that the sight of people from all walks of life, ages and socio-economic status, equally mesmerized by the Cube, had to be seen to be believed. He convinced Stewart Sims, the vice president of marketing at Ideal Toys, to come to Budapest.

The immense risks for Ideal Toys included a huge investment in inventory and a patent problem. Because both Konsumex and Erno Rubik failed to patent the puzzle outside of Hungary within the required year from the date of their own filing, the puzzle was left unprotected when Ideal Toys acquired rights to sell it. Their consolation was that they could at least file and own a trademark. Magic Cube was deemed too generic, and so the name Rubik became famous. As it turned out, Ideal needn't have worried about having too many puzzles in the warehouse.

From 1980 to 1983 Rubik's Cube gripped the planet earth like no other puzzle before or since. Millions were produced by Politechnika, a Hungarian state manufacturing plant, and were sold all over the world by Ideal Toys. When it became evident that Poletechnika couldn't make even a fraction of what was needed, a Hungarian import/export company was brought in to help Ideal contract with other plants in the United States, Hong Kong, Taiwan, Costa Rica, Brazil and the Caribbean. The Cube caused rioting in Japan and sold 2.5 million in Germany alone.

THE PLAYMAKERS
Now and Then

The return of Rubik's Cube as a Milton Bradley puzzle and how it looked in 1980, after Ideal Toys was forced to create an inexpensive, mass-produced package when the puzzle's popularity reached epic proportions.

by some opportunistic company who knew when to capitalize on a mega-fad. There was even a Saturday morning cartoon called *Rubik the Amazing Cube.*

By 1983, the pirated versions of Rubik's creation almost outnumbered the authentic Ideal Toy versions, and with the market saturated, Rubik's Cube faded away. But Tom Kremer never lost his belief in the classic status of the puzzle. In 1985, Seven Towns quietly acquired worldwide rights to Rubik's Cube, believing that in time it could be re-released to a new audience. Seven Towns began that process in 1991 with distribution in foreign countries. Then in 1995, they signed a deal with OddzOn, Inc. (the company behind the Koosh ball), who reintroduced history's best-selling puzzle. Hasbro bought OddzOn in 1998 and today, Rubik's Cube is sold by Milton Bradley. Now in its second incarnation, the marvel that was created by Erno Rubik nearly 30 years ago is available once again.

Over 15 different puzzle products currently bear the Rubik name. Milton Bradley boasts that over 250 million Rubik's Cubes have been sold around the world, and it's estimated that one-eighth of the world's population has held one, begging the question: Did we take hold of the cube or was it the other way around?

A PUZZLE APART

How the rows or columns of blocks could move independently of one another and yet not fall apart proved to be the billion-dollar question for Erno Rubik. So elegantly brilliant was the engineering involved in his answer, that today many consider the internal design of the cube a greater achievement than the puzzle itself. Reportedly inspired by the sight of some water-worn pebbles in the Danube River, Rubik had an epiphany. To facilitate movement, the internal construction of the cube had to be rounded, but still interlocking. Every block acts like a capstone in an archway, yet they move! Pop just one out and the whole thing falls apart.

Trivial Pursuit

1980s–1990s

Debut: 1981
U.S. Debut: 1982
Inventors: Chris Haney, Scott Abbott
Developers: Chris Haney, Scott Abbott, John Haney, Ed Werner
Insiders: Linda Pezzano, Richard Gill
Companies: Horn Abbot, Selchow & Righter, Parker Brothers, Hasbro Games

IN PURSUIT

I t's the story that launched a thousand games: Two Canadian journalists create a trivia contest so popular that they soon retire multimillionaires. Trivial Pursuit inspired others to try their hand at the game trade, but while Chris Haney and Scott Abbott's game went on to be wildly successful, countless imitators failed in their wake—adrift in a sea of sameness. In 1984 alone, the opportunists included Trivia Fever, Rock 'N Roll Trivia, Solid Gold Music Trivia, *Time* [Magazine]: The Game, *TV Guide* Trivia Game and The Ultimate Trivia Game presented by *Newsweek*."

It's fitting that the game which inspired so many others was itself inspired by a game. If it hadn't been for a few missing Scrabble tiles, Trivial Pursuit may have never set sail.

On December 15, 1979, Chris Haney and Scott Abbott decided to challenge each other in a friendly game of Scrabble. Haney discovered several tiles missing from the game. After returning from the store with a new set, he complained to Abbott that the game had cost him a pretty penny and that it was one of numerous replacements he had bought over the years. Abbott reportedly said that he too had purchased his share of Scrabble sets over time and quipped, "These guys must be making a fortune."

Scrabble lit the light bulb,

and the two friends set out to invent a game of their own.

But what kind of game? Scrabble had been invented by a man with an unbridled obsession for the frequency with which letters appeared in words, while Monopoly found its start in the mind of a woman with deep-rooted beliefs regarding the evils of land ownership. Neither Haney nor Abbott had any profound passion suitable for the sole focal point of a game. However, the men decided to turn what might seem a

weakness into a strength. They may not have known a lot about any one thing, but they knew more than a little about a lot of things.

Trivia: *(plural noun)* Insignificant or Unimportant Matters

At the time, Haney was a photo editor for the *Gazette* of Montreal and a movie buff. Abbott wrote sports for the Canadian Press news agency. As journalists they were trained to look for the "who, what, where, when and why" of a story, and the same mode of thinking produced interesting trivia questions. In Matthew Costello's book *The Greatest Games of All Time,* Scott Abbott is quoted as saying, "We sat down—then and there—and started doodling a game board. The whole thing was done in 45 minutes." That oft-cited quote has helped foster the belief that Trivial Pursuit was an instant success. While the design may have shaped up quickly, the developing and marketing of the game took its inventors on a four-year journey toward financial ruin and mental anguish, before finally reaching its successful finish. If Trivial Pursuit was an overnight success, then it was one long night.

After considering several ideas Haney and Abbott settled on an elegant, round play path with six "spokes" radiating from its center. The shape was reminiscent of a ship's helm and the game was christened Trivia Pursuit, until Haney's wife, Sarah, suggested that the word "Trivial" with an "l" sounded better. The wheel shape carried over to the playing pieces, which acted as both markers (tokens that identified your space while moving) and scorekeepers (containers in which you placed your "scoring wedge" upon answering a question correctly).

With a rough sketch of the game, the partners recruited help from Chris's brother,

The original Trivial Pursuit game board was sketched out by Chris Haney and Scott Abbott on a scrap piece of cardboard. It was later framed with the footnote "Montreal, December 15, 1979."

E	Who directed Lawrence of Arabia?
SN	What species is man classified as? *not in two border*
G	The Khyber Pass joins what two countries?
L	Shaw's Major Barbara is a major in what army?
H	Who was Sitting Bull's right-hand man?
SR	Where were the 1940 Olympics held?

Genus

E	David Lean
SN	Homo Sapien
G	Afghanistan and Pakistan
L	Salvation Army
H	Crazy Horse
SR	They weren't

Cards from the prototype of Trivial Pursuit.

categories of Geography, Entertainment, History, Arts & Literature, Science & Nature and Sports & Leisure. The questions were read aloud. The player who answered a final question after filling his or her token with all six scoring wedges won.

THE FIRST 1,100 STEPS ARE THE HARDEST

The components of the game were not as simple. The elaborate folding game board had never been done before. One thousand cards had to be cut from large printed sheets, collated and sorted into decks. This all cost more money than the four entrepreneurs had personally committed to the project. Eventually, thirty-four investors saved the day and the game. They were all friends or co-workers who scraped together as little as $1,000 each for an investment in Horn Abbot. Some just rendered free services in exchange for shares in the start-up, like artist Michael Wurstlin, the graphic designer who helped create the look of the first Trivial Pursuit game.

Wurstlin was an unemployed, 18-year-old, starving artist when Horn Abbot contacted him. "I gave them a figure of a thousand dollars for the entire project," he recalled. "They had a very specific idea of what they wanted. They had pencil drawings and clearly wanted it to be a game for adults." With a very small budget, Wurstlin designed the now famous Trivial Pursuit logo and the graphic elements for the cards and game board. After several months, when the project was nearly done, the artist heard the infamous pitch.

"They hemmed and hawed about paying me. At that time a thousand dollars represented four months rent to me," Wurstlin said. "They were saying, 'Why don't you take some shares?' and I said 'because I need the money!' Their final argument was classic. They

John Haney, and their friend, attorney Ed Werner. In January of 1980, the four friends formed Horn Abbot Limited, named by combining Chris's nickname "The Horn" with Scott's last name (minus a "t"). With their pursuit of fun under way, the entrepreneurs pooled what money they had, wrote questions and fleshed out just how the game would play.

The rules were straightforward. A player collected scoring wedges to place within his or her token by correctly answering questions in the six color-coded

"I had to generate images that would reflect the world, but there was no budget . . . so I found some archival books with some rather archaic images, like the guy with pole in his mouth," artist Michael Wurstlin said. "The old clip art was partly out of necessity—we had no money."

G	Zimbabwe
E	Darling
H	The zipper
AL	Postscript
SN	Benjamin Franklin
SL	Take a card

The original Trivial Pursuit was one of the most costly games ever produced. It required tooling to make plastic pieces consisting of 6 tokens and 36 scoring wedges, a foil-stamped game board, 1,000 game cards with four-color printing on both sides, a two-color printed storage bag and even a wax paper insert to protect the quad-fold board from scuffing!

accused me of being a typical, risk-averse Canadian. That really stung me because I had always railed against our passivity as a nation. So that was it—I took the shares instead. I thought I'd never see them again."

He almost didn't. After nearly two years of toil and deal making, Trivial Pursuit became a reality in the fall of 1981. Thereupon the entrepreneurs promptly lost their shirts. The gamesmen had spent a reported $75 per game to produce 1,100 copies of Trivial Pursuit,

due to all the up-front costs. Yet, the most they could hope to wholesale the game for was $20, which in turn would force the game to sell at retail for $39.95. That was an exorbitant price for a game in 1981, yet Trivial Pursuit found some success, landing in a few game shops and book stores in Canada and the United States.

That momentum was lost when the partners ventured into the world of trade shows. Trivial Pursuit debuted at the Canadian Toy Show in Toronto, followed by Toy Fair in New York. It was a humbling introduction to the toy industry, a fashion business where companies tend to move in herds towards whatever is hot for the moment—and at that moment, video games were on fire.

The Screen vs. the Board

It was the beginning of 1982. Nintendo's Donkey Kong had just been released and was an instant hit in arcades, while Pac Man, which had been launched as a coin-operated game just two years prior, continued to eat everything in sight, including the disposable income of kids looking for entertainment through games. Trivial Pursuit, on the other hand, was downright Victorian in its simple call to gather around the table. "An old-fashioned paper game will never sell in today's high-tech retail climate," the industry experts said. After Toy Fair 1982, Trivial Pursuit was dead.

The rejection took a personal toll on Chris Haney. His savings were gone and he had sold most of his photography equipment to help finance what was turning out to be a very trivial pursuit indeed. With both trade shows terrible disappointments and the failure of the game almost certain, he was stricken with ever-increasing bouts of anxiety and had to take a sabbatical to recover.

Then in the summer of 1982, the impossible started to happen. People slowly began to gravitate toward the game and the social interaction it produced. Encouraged by reorders from shops that had been carrying it, Scott Abbott took a $40,000 loan from his father. According to Costello, this influx of cash enabled Horn Abbot to secure an additional $75,000 line of credit. Throwing caution to the wind, they printed 20,000 copies of Trivial Pursuit: Master Game-Genus Edition.

That strange word in the subtitle was "Genus," as in a class or group, not "Genius," as in what many thought you had to be to play the game. Trivial Pursuit was challenging, but the reason was clear in the rules; as long as a player answered correctly he or she maintained control of the die. If the questions had been too easy, a single player could monopolize the game very quickly. To many, the difficulty level made the game gratifying. The sense of satisfaction when one answered a particularly difficult question correctly was a wonderful payoff and made the fun of Trivial Pursuit addictive. A keen listener had a distinct advantage in the cleverly written game because hints to the answer were often hidden within the question.

Despite the varying opinions over the questions in the game—perhaps in part because of them—sales picked up with word of mouth. Nearly all 20,000 games sold by the end of 1982. Then Trivial Pursuit caught the eye of game giant Selchow & Righter, makers of Parcheesi and Scrabble.

In the late '70s, when electronic games began to flood the market, the family-owned Selchow & Righter had been making traditional board games for over 100 years. Richard Selchow, the grandson of the company's founder, was the new president. In an article in the February 1981 issue of *Game Merchandising* magazine, a year before Trivial Pursuit would become a Selchow & Righter game and transform the toy industry in the process, Richard Selchow spoke prophetically:

> One hears a lot of debate in the industry about the future of games. Are electronics the wave of the future? Will board games survive? We feel these discussions are somewhat irrelevant. There should be no dispute about whether the future of games lies in microcomputers or small wooden game pieces. There is ample room for both if the games involved are fun to play.

When the video game balloon of popularity burst in 1983, Selchow & Righter was more than content to let the microchips fall where they may. Trivial Pursuit was about to become the fastest selling game the world had ever seen.

Star Search

In 1983, while Atari shipped over a million unwanted video game cartridges to a landfill in New Mexico, Selchow & Righter introduced Trivial Pursuit to the United States. They hired a New York PR firm headed by marketing guru Linda Pezzano, who ingeniously sent out samples of the game to toy buyers, but also to nearly every celebrity that appeared within the game's questions and answers. The unorthodox campaign worked magic. In 1983, *Time* magazine reported that the entire cast of the hit movie *The Big Chill* "became addicted to the game, playing it night and day." With stars like Glenn Close, William Hurt, Jeff Goldblum, and Kevin Kline unintentionally endorsing it, Trivial Pursuit promptly sold over a million copies in the States and over two million in Canada. Any concerns over traditional board games surviving against Pac Man and his computer-generated compatriots were vaporized.

Horn Abbot emerged from debt and the partnership of Haney, Abbott, Haney, and Werner finally breathed that sigh of relief that comes after a long, hard, risk-filled ride. But the trip was not over. Trivial Pursuit's success in 1983, which would have been huge news in any other year, was somewhat overshadowed by the craze of the Cabbage Patch Kids. As the media scrambled to cover the riots and unprecedented publicity generated by all those soft, little adoptees, Trivial Pursuit's success went relatively unnoticed. But not for long.

TRIVIAL TRIUMPH

After facing the electronic barrage of the "interactive" game market, America embraced Trivial Pursuit for the human-to-human interaction it provided. Even though trivia was not a unique idea (Authors quizzed kids beginning in the 1860s and Go to the Head of the Class was released in 1938), what was different about Trivial Pursuit was its intended audience. The sides of the box read "Age–Adult." The baby boomers (that vast group of kids who were raised on board games) were now credit card-carrying adults. After discovering this chic game, grown-up gamers couldn't get enough. When sales of Trivial Pursuit increased even after the Christmas buying season, Selchow & Righter sensed what 1984 would bring and wisely called on a legendary gamesman to help feed the frenzy.

"I was a printing broker and my niche was game cards," Joe Cornacchia told me. "I started by sourcing just the card decks, but as time went on and the demand outgrew the capacity in Selchow's plant, I secured more outside suppliers. I lined up plastic manufacturers, boxes, dice, everything. In the early part of 1984, we were making a million Trivial Pursuit games a week."

Trivial Pursuit developers (L to R) Scott Abbott, Chris Haney and John Haney pose for a 1984 publicity photo. Their ship had set sale.

SMOKING!

Before the end of 1984 a brain-busting 20 million Trivial Pursuit games were sold in the United States. Black market games appeared. Original sets were being sold for $50, even $60, but no one seemed to care. The prestige of owning the game outweighed its hefty price tag.

Selchow & Righter took full advantage of the game's popularity and the exploding mass-media culture of the times. Trivial Pursuit Silver Screen Edition was released in 1984, followed quickly by an All-Star Sports Edition, Baby Boomer Edition and a Young Players Edition.

The first country to sell Trivial Pursuit outside of Canada and the United States was Australia. From there, non-English speaking countries followed suit and the entrepreneurs soon learned that keeping control over their brainchild was no trivial matter. Richard Gill, the man who would eventually help license Trivial Pursuit around the world, shared how controlling the game's destiny overseas was like trying to lasso a runaway train.

"In the beginning, it was selling so fast that licensees did whatever they wanted," Gill said. "In France it was called Remue Méninges, which translated into 'Brainstorm.' In Holland it was called Triviant. Companies launched it without getting the questions sanctioned." Horn Abbot finally had to put their foot down.

Ed Werner had shrewdly formed an offshore company in Barbados to manage the worldwide rights to Trivial Pursuit outside of North America. Determined to control their game's destiny across the globe, Horn Abbot International canceled many of the licensing contracts that were formerly granted and formed a company called Sans Serif to exclusively license the game to foreign game companies and control the final product.

Richard Gill became Sans Serif's group commercial director in December of 1985. "After six months we were rolling in cash," he recounted. "We sold a million Trivial Pursuit games in the UK that year. In '86 it was 1.2 million units in the UK and 2.5 million units across Europe. Through the balance of the '80s we were

The card in the image reads:

G
E
H
AL
SN
SL

What's the largest island in Europe?

What bandleader always carried a Chihuahua under his arm?

What restaurateur kicked the bucket in 1980?

Who's the most-translated English author after Shakespeare?

How many matches are there in a standard book of matches?

What drink is mixed with scotch, sweet vermouth and angostura bitters?

"The biggest problem was figuring out how to mass-produce all those cards," game broker Joe Cornacchia said. "Federal Paper was the largest producer of that type of card stock. When I started placing the orders, they couldn't believe it. They told me that I was the largest single-user of their paper—20% of their mill! That was amazing considering they produced cigarette cartons for every tobacco maker in the country. Twenty million games times 1,000 cards equals *20 billion cards.*"

doing well over 3 million units a year." Trivial Pursuit was officially a global phenomenon.

It has sold over 70 million copies. Other than Monopoly, a more influential game than Trivial Pursuit would be hard to find. It established the adult game category and catapulted the careers of Linda Pezzano (who went on to form the P.R. firm behind Pictionary and Outburst) and Richard Gill, the man who would lead Pictionary's international success. It unleashed Joe Cornacchia's entrepreneurial streak and inspired a group of Selchow & Righter salesmen to form The Games Gang (the successful sales team for Pictionary and Balderdash). Trivial Pursuit even inspired two friends of mine and me to create a game called TriBond.

THE MONEY GAME

Life changed for the people behind Horn Abbot Limited. Even the minority investors earned back hundreds of thousands of dollars from their initial

In turning Trivial Pursuit into a brand, Selchow & Righter invented the refill card market for games, selling numerous card sets to supplement the original game.

investment. "As I recall the first dividend check I received was for $800," artist Michael Wurstlin shared. "I thought, 'Holy smokes, that's fantastic! That's almost all the money they owe me!' I thought that would be the end of it, but the checks kept coming . . . and they kept getting bigger." Richard Gill recalled another investor in the Trivial Pursuit pipe dream. "One of our guests in Barbados was the mail room guy from the *Gazette,* who, for all of his sins, had bought two shares [of Horn Abbot] . . . When I met him he had flown to Barbados in a private jet from somewhere in South America."

And the original partners? The inventors of Trivial Pursuit now own two golf courses north of Toronto, thoroughbred horses, a hockey team and a very, very big part of game history.

Our mass media culture, the ever-changing world of politics and our continual infatuation with celebrity will insure that the next edition of our favorite quiz game is just over the horizon. After 20 years, the pursuit goes on.

✴ Coleco purchased Selchow & Righter in 1986, but filed for bankruptcy two years later (see Cabbage Patch Kids). Hasbro bought Coleco's assets in 1989, but Parker Brothers was the high bidder for the rights to Trivial Pursuit. Ultimately, the game became a Hasbro brand when the toy giant bought Kenner and Parker Brothers in the Tonka deal of 1991.

✴ In Steven L. Kent's book, *The Ultimate History of Video Games,* Ray Kassar, the former president and CEO of Atari is quoted as saying, "In 1982 we shipped 12 million Pac-Man cartridges. It was a record. I mean, to ship 12 million of one product at a retail price of $25.75 was

After "sweeping the country" in 1984, Horn Abbot set out to sweep the world in 1985.

extraordinary." Little did he know that just two years later, Selchow & Righter would sell 20 million copies of Trivial Pursuit at a retail price of $29.95.

The game that shunned the electronic gaming world eventually joined its ranks. Trivial Pursuit has been turned into an electronic handheld game, a desktop computer game, a CD ROM game, an online web-based game and even a television game show starring Wink Martindale.

THE PLAYMAKERS
Now and Then

When Hasbro released the 20th Anniversary Edition of Trivial Pursuit in 2002, they dubbed it "the last 20 years in a box." According to the NPD Group, Inc., a firm that tracks retail sales, it was the best-selling game that year and the fifth best-selling item in the entire toy industry.

JOE CORNACCHIA

Pictionary inventor Rob Angel called him, "The entrepreneur of the century." His uncanny ability to broker not just printing, but incredibly profitable business deals, is the stuff of gaming legend. He was paid on every Trivial Pursuit game he made for Selchow & Righter and put together the deal that paid him on every Pictionary game sold by his sales force, The Games Gang (see Pictionary).

When another supplier overproduced five million Trivial Pursuit games after the craze fizzled, it was Cornacchia who was paid to destroy them. "They would have been sold eventually but instead . . . they became roof shingles," he said. "Selchow & Righter was being sold to Coleco at the time and they needed to liquidate the dead inventory before the deal closed. Dick [Selchow] sold me 5 million games for a buck. He got a $25 million dollar tax write-off and I think I cleared about $150,000, which was nice money."

THE PLAYMAKERS
Insider Profile

At the apex of his venture in the game business he owned two Saber 40 airplanes, one named Trivial Pursuit and the other Pictionary. After helping to build two game dynasties, he set his sights on horse racing. He won the Kentucky Derby twice, first in 1991 with his horse Strike the Gold, and then again in 1994 with Go for Gin. Two years later, his horse Louis Quatorze won The Preakness Stakes.

Debut: 1974
U.S. Debut: 1983
Inventor: Leslie Scott
Developers: Robert Grebler, David Grebler, Paul Eveloff
Insider: Hal Ross
Companies: Irwin Toy (Canada), Schaper Manufacturing Company, Milton Bradley, Hasbro

Jenga

BRINGING DOWN THE HOUSE

If ever there was proof that no one can predict what will be successful in the toy industry, this runaway hit of 54 wooden blocks is it.

A single Jenga block holds no immediate allure. It measures approximately 3 inches by 1 inch by $\frac{1}{2}$ inch, each humble hunk of wood from the game unrecognizable from any other. But stack 54 of them up, 3 to a row, 18 rows high, and they're transformed into a surprisingly suspenseful and addictive game.

Since Jenga's breakout year in 1986, it's become one of the most popular games in the world, at times second only to Monopoly in global sales. With such an amazing following, you might think Jenga was launched with a multimillion dollar TV campaign by a major U.S. toy company. But in fact, this stacking game had a much quieter debut over 30 years ago in Africa.

THE GAME FROM GHANA

Leslie Scott was born in Tanganyika and raised in Kenya, East Africa, before moving with her family to Ghana in 1972. In 1974, just before the 18-year-old was about to graduate from high school, her parents brought home a set of children's building bricks they had purchased from a wood craftsman in the nearby city of Takoradi. Wood was plentiful

Milton Bradley's 1986 edition of Jenga.

and inexpensive there and the bricks, a simple gift meant for Scott's little brother, changed her life.

"I don't remember when we first started playing with the bricks as a game," she says. "The bricks were slimmer back then and we stacked them three across, spaced apart from each other." The rules were fairly basic at first. Everyone simply took turns removing bricks from somewhere in the middle of the tower until a player made it collapse. The Scott family named their game Takoradi Bricks after the city in which it was made. "My family had many more sets made in Takoradi over the years to give to friends," Scott said. "I even took a set with me to England."

Scott enrolled in Oxford to pursue a degree in teaching. She later dropped out and started a career in marketing, working first for a fledgling company called Intel and later for a business that made trade show booths. During those five years, Scott introduced her game to friends and colleagues. She improved upon it by adding a rule where removed blocks had to be placed on the top of the tower. Now as play proceeded, the tower grew increasingly tall and more unbalanced. The new rule added even more fun and suspense to the game, which by then Scott had renamed "Jenga."

"I grew up speaking Swahili in East Africa—it was my family's second language," Scott said. "We would often give our pets or things that were special to us a Swahili name. The word Kjenga means 'to build.' Jenga is the imperative, which means 'Build' or 'Build it!' So it's a strong name."

In 1982, after further encouragement from her friends and colleagues at the trade booth company, Scott decided to market Jenga. "We had a carpentry shop there and I asked one of the joiners if he could

Jenga inventor Leslie Scott and her towering success.

help me come up with a way to produce the Jenga bricks in a more mass-produced way," Scott recalled. "We designed a template that could be attached to a machine that would produce them much faster."

BANKING ON THE BRICKS

She copyrighted the rules and commissioned Camphill Products (a workshop that provided handicapped workers with employment) to produce and package 500 games in time for the London Toy Show. "At that stage I took samples to the bank to get a loan," Scott shared. "I had quit my job, which was just so incredibly optimistic!" Scott credits her "naive enthusiasm" and the British government's willingness to subsidize banks that helped small businesses, as two crucial points in Jenga's journey.

"You can't go to a bank today and tell them 'I've got this idea,' and show them a pile of wooden bricks and get a loan," Scott said. "I thought that I'd take these games to the show in London and then have hundreds of thousands of orders. Of course it doesn't work like that. By the end of it I owed the bank quite a lot of money."

Leslie Scott sold the very first commercially produced Jenga games (like the one pictured here) in Harrods, the historic English department store.

Made in the UK
Leslie Scott Associates 7 Bath Street St Clement's Oxford OX4 1AY
UK Trade Mark Application No. 1184464
UK Patent Application Nos. 8227004 & 8231160

The Perpetual Challenge

JENGA

A game for all ages, requiring a keen eye a steady hand and nerves of steel

★ ★ ★ ★ ★ ★ ★ ★ ★ ★ ★ ★
Application Card for Free Membership of the International Jenga Club enclosed.

JENGA
THE Perpetual Challenge

This exciting and elegant game requires a keen eye, a steady hand and nerves of steel! Using a set of irregular hardwood blocks a tower is constructed from which players have to remove loose pieces without causing the structure to tumble. Difficult at all times, impossible after a bottle of wine! Selected by many of the best London Stores, and played throughout Britain, *Jenga* makes an unusual and lasting gift for children and adults alike.

NEW FROM ENGLAND!

Send to:
Leslie Scott Associates, P.O. Box 22444, Lexington, Kentucky, 40522

Please send _____ sets of the game *JENGA* at $20 each (inclusive of postage)   Total $ _____

Please send _____ sets of the game *SWIPE* at $10 each (inclusive of postage)   Total $ _____

Kentucky Residents add sale tax   Total $ _____

Enclosed is a check/money order payable to Leslie Scott Associates $ _____

Name _____

Address _____

City _____ State _____ Zip _____

If not satisfied, return in good order within 10 days for full refund.

In 1983, Scott placed ads for Jenga in *Smithsonian* magazine and *The New Yorker*. After selling only a handful of games, she abandoned her U.S. marketing and turned her focus back to England.

"I spent two or three weeks in December leading up to Christmas exhibiting the game in one of Harrods rather busy halls," Scott recalled. "It would fall down and I'd be crawling around in this crowd picking up stray bricks." The demonstrations worked and Harrods sold hundreds of Jenga games. With that success, Scott set her sights on America.

"At the time Europe was less accessible than other English speaking countries. Also, America was easier because I had a brother living over there and he and his wife were happy to keep stock in their house for me," Scott said. She ran ads in several prestigious U.S. magazines, but received a lukewarm reception. Convinced that more stores would buy Jenga if she had a line of games, Scott did the unimaginable.

"I sold my house to keep Jenga going, but also to expand the business. It was a huge risk I realize now, but when you're younger you don't think negatively," she recalled. "I created a mail order catalog with a whole line of games including Jenga."

Despite some success, Scott's mail order business was just getting by and Jenga seemed destined to remain a small-time venture. She still owed the bank a considerable amount of money and was reluctant to borrow more. As if on cue, an oil baron came calling.

SNACKS AND STACKS

In 1983, Robert Grebler had a fledgling health foods distribution business that sold natural seed, nut and vegetable oils. He also had a sister, Gillian, who was a close friend of Leslie Scott. "Leslie had come to the U.S. to sell her game and visited my family in California, leaving behind a copy of the game," Robert Grebler said. "I remember seeing it sitting on the windowsill of my parents' house. It looked so boring, just a pile

Robert Grebler demonstrated Jenga in natural food stores as it stacked up next to dried fruit and tofu. Here he is in Montreal, 1985.

of wood." However, something in Jenga was different enough to leave an impression on the entrepreneur.

The following year Grebler was living in Montreal, selling his oils and all-natural snacks to health food stores. Looking to expand his offerings, he remembered Scott's game. "It was made of wood, I recalled, and being that my accounts were natural food stores, I thought it might fit their mix of products." He contacted Scott and learned that she still had some games in the United States. After buying her remaining inventory, Grebler hit the health food circuit throughout Montreal. "I'd have people gathering around and the excitement would build," Grebler recalled. "So often I did that and it literally drew a crowd. That's when I knew this thing was going to work. Jenga created excitement."

The entrepreneur was so encouraged by the reaction to the game that he convinced Scott to sign a deal making him the exclusive distributor for Jenga in Canada and the United States. "When I met Robert I had already had the game on the market for three years," Scott said. "I figured, what did I have to lose?" A deal was struck and the importer of food was now officially an importer of fun.

As sales began to build, Grebler invited two cousins, David Grebler and Paul Eveloff, to become partners with him in Pokonobe Associates in 1985. They branched out from exclusively health food stores, to gift shops, toy stores and eventually some department stores. Jenga's success prompted them to acquire the worldwide rights from Scott in exchange for a royalty. "I think because of the family relationship we had, Leslie knew that she could trust me," Robert Grebler said. "We were lucky."

In February of 1985, Robert arranged a Jenga tournament in the Cavendish Mall in Montreal as a benefit for the Heart Foundation. He gave out samples of an all-natural ice cream bar he was selling to anyone who entered the Jenga tournament. "It must have been a slow news day in Canada," Grebler surmised. "We had a local news crew, a national TV show and a radio station all show up. It was just phenomenal coverage. Everyone bought one."

Response from the promotion encouraged Grebler to contact the major department store chains, including Zellers, one of the biggest retailers in Canada. The buyer at Zellers liked the game and showed it to a toy industry veteran named Hal Ross, a salesman at Irwin Toy, the same Canadian Toy company that had launched Slinky and Etch A Sketch in Canada.

"When I saw Jenga, I flipped," Ross recalls. "It was so easy to understand and to play. With promotion behind it, I could see it being a huge hit, so I brought it back to Irwin." Grebler knew that Zellers would buy Jenga if a larger manufacturer stood behind it. "Plus, Hal really championed it at Irwin," Grebler said. "The timing was right to hand it over."

Speakin' Swahili

The Swahili language has pervaded our culture in several not-so-subtle ways. Disney's animated classic *The Lion King* featured several Swahili words including simba, meaning "lion," rafiki, meaning "friend," and the expression for "no worries," or hakuna matata —words that any parent of young children has heard sung over and over again. Not to be outdone, Milton Bradley ran TV ads for Jenga where grown adults chanted "JEN-GA! JEN-GA!" The commercial was a hit (Scott told me, "Well, I was right about the name wasn't I?") and as word of mouth took over, the game became a standard

everywhere from hospital gift shops to mass-market drug stores, making the Swahili word for "build it" a part of our collective vocabulary.

A GAME BY ANY OTHER NAME

Irwin Toy believed in the game and promised Grebler and Scott that they'd promote it on television across Canada. But first there was the issue of the name.

"We hated it!" Hal Ross shared. "We said 'What the hell is 'Jenga?!' It means nothing!'" Jenga conjured no associations (for English speakers, anyway) and had no real appeal other than its short, punchy sound. Scott, who still had creative control, remained adamant. "The name was the one thing I was absolutely unmovable on," she said. "I told them that they couldn't have it if they weren't going to call it Jenga. That was quite difficult for me to say because I very much needed them to take it!" In the end, Irwin decided that "Jenga" could mean whatever anybody wanted it to mean, as long as it translated into fun.

Irwin became the worldwide master licensee to Jenga and the respected toy company put it on television as promised. The campaign was an immediate success, prompting sales of over 100,000 games—a huge number for Canada. Irwin Toy searched for a U.S. firm to duplicate their success and chose Schaper (formerly Schaper Toys), the company behind Cootie and Ants in the Pants.

"Milton Bradley wanted Jenga from the moment they saw it," Grebler said. "But Irwin was committed to Schaper." Milton Bradley was owned by Hasbro and they too had seen the game's potential. "Stephen Hassenfeld, who controlled Hasbro with his brother Alan, played Jenga at Irwin's showroom during the Canadian Toy Fair in January 1985," said Grebler. As fate would have it, the Hassenfelds would get their chance to build Jenga soon enough. Schaper was put up for sale and Tyco Toys took over most of their game line, but Jenga slipped through the cracks. "Stephen thought that Jenga could become a classic and he championed it at Hasbro once he got the license," Grebler said. In 1986, Jenga was relaunched under Hasbro's Milton Bradley banner, and its success soon had game players, not to mention the game industry, under its spell.

COPYCAT STACKERS

While millions of players tried to avoid knocking Jenga over, game companies couldn't seem to avoid knocking it off. Unoriginal manufacturers have given Jenga the dubious honor of being one of the most copied games ever. Its colossal success has inspired the release of Taka-radi, Tumbling Tower, Jumbling Tower, Timberrr, Krazy Tower, Stack-Attack, Uno Stacko and countless others.

"The story of Jenga's origin has been distorted by these imitators who try to claim they didn't copy

Schaper produced this rare version of Jenga in 1985, but stumbled financially shortly after the deal was put together. When the dust settled, Jenga was a Milton Bradley game.

Jenga," Robert Grebler contends. "Jenga came from Africa in that Leslie's family was living there at the time she created it, but it is not an African game." Grebler has searched the game archives at the British Museum in London and elsewhere and has yet to find a single historic game similar to Jenga. But the misconception persists. "I have had people say that it's a game they think they've played or must have played when they were younger because it's such an obvious game," Scott said. "But then they realize they didn't. Thank goodness it occurred to me to put it on the market, because it's also such an original game."

HOW I LEARNED TO STOP WORRYING AND LOVE THE BLOCKS

I'll admit that when I first saw Jenga, the fun it promised was far from obvious. I stopped thinking "its just 54 pieces of wood" a long time ago and surrendered to all its engaging suspense. In doing so, I joined a legion of fans in over 40 countries and accepted the fact that Jenga simply is what it is—a block party on a global scale.

You don't even realize you're holding your breath until a sigh of relief marks the end of your turn. Jenga lives up to its claim as "edge-of-your-seat-fun."

After Jenga became a hit it was sometimes hard to find. "I remember being in a store with my sister once and we saw a lady pick up the last Jenga game on the shelf," Leslie Scott shared. "We were just watching her when my sister blurted out, 'This is my sister and that's her game!' Without missing a beat the woman said 'No, I picked it up first,' and walked off."

Debut: 1983
Predecessors: The Little
People (1976)
Inventor: Xavier Roberts
Insider: Roger Schlaifer
Companies: Original
Appalachian Artworks
(OAA, Inc.), Coleco,
Hasbro, Mattel, OAA,
Inc.

Cabbage Patch Kids

BABY BOOM

Call them funny looking or even ugly, but don't call them "dolls." Cabbage Patch Kids may have a certain homely allure, but it was the elaborate fantasy surrounding them—the pretense of their being real—that drove their popularity from the start. While other dolls crawled, ate, cried, slept or mimicked some other human bodily function in an effort to create realism, Cabbage Patch Kids sustained an illusion that was bigger than anything the dolls themselves could do. They weren't for sale; they were "available for adoption." They weren't found in any stores, only at "Official Adoption Agencies." They weren't made, they were "born" in a hospital staffed by women in white nurses' outfits and a man with no medical degree named Dr. Roberts.

Xavier Roberts, the

Coleco's 1983 version of the Cabbage Patch Kids.

"doctor" behind the adoptees, was born the last of six children in rural Cleveland, Georgia. After his father died in a car accident when Xavier was five, he was raised by his mother, Eula, in a loving but impoverished home. In order to feed her family, Eula Roberts made and sold beautiful quilts to supplement her meager earnings at a local textile company.

Xavier Roberts grew up despising the poverty that surrounded him and vowed to escape. He struggled through high school and, with no money for college, retreated into his own world of art. First he worked in clay, selling pots and figures at local craft shows. There he learned that his salesmanship matched his artistic skills. After months of struggle, he decided to set himself apart from the many artists working in clay and found a new medium.

Roberts encountered the old folk art known as soft sculpture. He worked with his mother to learn how to form fabric. Then, after experimenting with soft sculpture plants, wall hangings and animals, he began creating fabric figures in human form. Using his newly-found skills—and his nieces and nephews as models—Roberts created predecessors of the Cabbage Patch Kids in 1976. He called them The Little People.

Handmade versions of The Little People were true works of art.

In the book, *Fantasy: The Incredible Cabbage Patch Phenomenon* by William Hoffman, Roberts is quoted as saying, "I couldn't believe the expressions I got with stitching. A tuck here, a pucker there, and the whole face took on life." Roberts showed off his creations at the craft shop where he worked and was surprised when a patron inquired how much the dolls cost. The artist reportedly responded with a now-famous comment: "They're not for sale . . . but you can adopt them."

The idea was part ingenious marketing plan and part preservation of his hard work. Fearful that children would turn his handmade treasures into a pile of rags in short order, Roberts conceived the idea of having "adoptive parents" sign an adoption certificate and pledge to take care of his or her "kid."

The legend Roberts created told of his offspring emerging from an "enchanted cabbage patch," but the truth was much more expensive. His creations

In 1978, Roberts formed Original Appalachian Artworks, Inc. to produce his "kids" in greater quantities.

were handmade from stretch fabric, stuffed with soft filling and painstakingly handstitched or "sculpted" with threading. The faces also included handpainted eyes and eyebrows, and on those that had it, yarn hair. Airbrushed highlights were added to the entire doll (not just the face), as well as stitched dimples, fingers, toes and even a belly button. Roberts dressed his creations in clothes and shoes purchased at local flea markets and yard sales, which gave The Little People even more realism. The artist even handsigned and numbered the bottom of each kid. Roberts also printed one thousand authentically detailed "birth certificates."

Roberts took his sculpted offspring (and their official paperwork) on an arts and crafts show tour of the southern United States and quickly created a demand that far outpaced his ability to produce. He sold bald babies for $30 and those with hair for $40, a steep price for a doll in the late '70s, yet he couldn't make them fast enough. Even after recruiting his mother and sisters to help pump up production, Roberts knew he needed more help.

Today, Babyland General Hospital still greets 250,000 visitors a year.

In 1978, Roberts and five high school friends formed Original Appalachian Artworks, Incorporated (OAA, Inc.). To infuse further realism into the world he was creating, Roberts envisioned a "hospital" where none existed. He found the ideal place in an old abandoned medical clinic in his hometown of Cleveland, Georgia.

According to Hoffman, the Neal Clinic was founded in 1919 when Dr. L.G. Neal settled in Cleveland. More home than hospital, the little clinic was the birthplace of thousands of real babies as it served the people in this remote Georgia town for nearly 50 years. In disrepair since its doors closed after Dr. Neal's death in 1969, the clinic was the perfect birthplace for The Little People. Again, Roberts had more imagination than money and struck a deal with Dr. Neal's daughter, who agreed to allow them the use of the clinic in exchange for their services repairing it. After much hard work Babyland General Hospital was in the business of birthin' babies . . . and from the start, business was good.

FLOATING ON PLASTIC AND QUILTS

Business, however, has its rules. Not everything OAA, Inc. needed could be found at flea markets, created by Roberts's skillful hands or secured in exchange for hard work. Capital was needed to create inventory and not everyone in Roberts's small town shared his eccentric sense of optimism. In *Fantasy* Roberts is quoted saying, "The townspeople couldn't believe that a hospital for soft sculpture babies would be successful. The banks couldn't believe it either. We got one small loan by putting our personal cars up for collateral, but mostly we had to do business with plastic—a Visa Card. With that, I could order up to $700 worth of fabric, thread, and stuffing a month, and there were times we couldn't have kept going if it hadn't been for my mother's quilts. Whenever the pinch got bad she would sell a quilt and give me the money."

With Eula's help, the five friends made it to their first trade show in Atlanta, where the full Roberts-created fantasy was witnessed for the first time. In a white lab coat with "Dr. Roberts" on his lapel, this twenty-three-year-old spun elaborate tales about his various "kids"—what they liked to eat, what scared them, what their favorite TV show was and, most of all, what they all longed for: adoption into a loving home. Many of the specialty market buyers who came to Atlanta that year perceived the dollars behind the nonsense and bought into the whimsy, turning their gift shops and toy stores into Little People Adoption Centers.

By the summer of 1979, Babyland General Hospital employed over fifty fulltime "doctors and nurses." The price for these individually crafted works of art had increased to $80–$100 and still Roberts and his friends could not meet the demand. Word of mouth had boosted the babies well beyond Georgia and now their success—and the wonderful fantasy that surrounded them—was too much for the press to resist.

THE LITTLE PEOPLE MEET "REAL PEOPLE"

The forerunner of all magazine-style shows that followed it, by 1980 *Real People* was a major TV hit. The show traveled America in search of stories that were offbeat, heart-warming or just plain odd. Babyland General Hospital was all these and more. *Real People*'s story on Xavier Roberts and his Little People aired just before Thanksgiving in 1980 and featured the fantasy in full bloom. One of the most crucial aspects of the Cabbage Patch Kids phenomenon was the length to which people would extend themselves into the imaginary world Roberts had created, and in this early coverage viewers across America got their first glimpse of just how deep the rabbit hole ran. Seeing Roberts and his employees traipsing around in medical attire was one thing, but hearing folks not associated with OAA, Inc. *believe* that these dolls were real was enough to launch The Little People into nationwide popularity.

From 1980 through 1982 OAA, Inc. garnered incredible press coverage in *Time, Newsweek,* the *Wall Street Journal,* and many other publications in the United States and Europe. With sales topping well over a million dollars, Roberts had the tiger by the tail. At the time, early editions of his Little People were being re-adopted (resold within the doll collector community) for thousands of dollars. Yet the phenomenon was restricted to mostly high-end collectors. Roberts sought a way to translate his incredibly successful concept into the mass market.

Enter Roger Schlaifer, the owner of Atlanta-based advertising agency Schlaifer Nance & Company. Schlaifer had seen firsthand the hold Roberts's Little People could have over fans when his wife and young daughters became infatuated with the babies. Roberts had no need for advertising, as his company could barely fill demand for their creations. Instead, Schlaifer pitched a licensing program for The Little People that promised to put their likenesses on everything from their own clothing line to lunch boxes and backpacks. Roberts was impressed, and Schlaifer Nance & Company became the licensing agent credited with putting together the Coleco deal.

Cabbage Patch Kids
inventor Xavier Roberts.

THE CONNECTICUT LEATHER COMPANY

Coleco is remembered as a high-tech company because of their home video game systems Telstar and ColecoVision and the ill-fated Adam computer. However, the original company founded in 1932 made leather components for shoes as the COnnecticut LEather COmpany. Equally ironic, the Cabbage Patch Kids will be remembered for taking the toy industry's focus off the computer craze of the early '80s and returning it, temporarily, to the traditional doll business. However, the Cabbage Patch Kids were much more high-tech than most people think. In fact, Coleco's expertise with sophisticated manufacturing was precisely why the deal was ultimately struck.

Roberts and Schlaifer knew that the appeal of The Little People rested in their individuality (no two had the same look or name), realism (adoption papers, birth certificates, etc.) and unique appearance. The duo also believed that these elements needed to be retained in order for a mass-market toy maker to duplicate OAA, Inc.'s success. Coleco's experience with computerization convinced everyone involved that the look of each kid (they were still never referred to as dolls) could be randomly altered by changing clothes, eye color, the number and location of dimples or freckles, hair style and hair color. Much easier were the computerized production of the birth certificates and the generation of distinct double names (like

The enchanted cabbage patch had been an integral part of Babyland General Hospital to begin with, so the new name, Cabbage Patch Kids, was approved by all.

Della Sarah), which OAA, Inc. had ingeniously established to allow for a greater combination of naming possibilities (while also fitting their rural southern roots).

Early in the Coleco deal it was decided that dolls would be made smaller and with vinyl heads so that adoption fees could be around $30. Another big change came when Schlaifer suggested renaming The Little People as the more distinctive Cabbage Patch Kids, possibly due to a trademark issue over Fisher-Price's Little People miniature dolls line, which had been on the market since 1959. In the summer of 1983, the Cabbage Patch Kids were born.

It was the most successful first-year launch of a doll in the history of the toy industry. Three million Cabbage Patch Dolls sold—and Coleco could have sold more had the company been able to keep up production. By December of 1983, the Cabbage Patch Kids

To add to the fantasy, Coleco sent all registered Cabbage Patch Kids a birthday card (in care of their adoptive parents, of course) on the one-year anniversary of their adoption.

accompanying article said, "Cabbage Patch Kids, this year's most frantically sought-after Christmas present, prove that looks aren't everything, but hype sometimes is . . . [They] should be good news for retailers except that they're afraid of being trampled in their own stores."

It was ugly. In Pennsylvania a woman broke her leg in a scuffle over the dolls. Riots broke out at stores in New Hampshire, Illinois and elsewhere after hundreds of consumers waited in long lines for hours only to be turned away when supplies ran out. In Milwaukee, a radio station played a prank by announcing that (impossibly) some Cabbage Patch Kids would be dropped from a B-29 bomber over the Milwaukee Brewer's County Stadium. Gullible fans showed up in freezing temperatures for naught.

Schlaifer Nance & Company used this success to place the Cabbage Patch Kids on over 250 products made by 70 manufacturers throughout the United States alone. Coleco rode the wave for four years, but didn't know when to get off. An article in *The Atlantic* in 1986 reported that from 1983 until 1985, the Cabbage Patch Kids brought in $1.2 *billion* for Coleco. The article went on to say, "Last spring analysts were predicting that Cabbage Patch sales for 1986 might decline by as much as 35 percent . . . [from 1985]. Since Coleco's 1986 catalogue is still weighted heavily toward Cabbage Patch, the company could be in serious trouble." Coleco lost over $100 million in 1986 *and* in 1987. In 1988, they filed for bankruptcy.

Roberts had no problem finding another mass-market toy maker to fill Coleco's shoes. After all, by then over 60 million Cabbage Patch Kids had been adopted. Hasbro bought Coleco in 1989 and produced

the Cabbage Patch Kids until 1994, most notably reducing the size of the dolls for a younger audience. In 1994, Mattel became OAA, Inc.'s official licensee, leading Xavier Roberts's creation into their 15th anniversary in 1998. Today, Cabbage Patch Kids continue to be adopted across the country, although pop culturalists tend to look at them as a phenomenon specific to the '80s.

Coleco is often given the credit for making the Cabbage Patch Kids a craze, thus many have written them off with Coleco's demise in 1989. But while Coleco filled the pipeline, it is clear that Xavier Roberts and his band of baby lovers primed the pump. They created a unique doll with a very original marketing concept. After developing this twofold approach of originality and adoption, Original Appalachian Artworks, Inc. garnered incredible national press coverage—long before the Coleco deal happened.

In 2002, it was announced that Toys R Us stores would be exclusive "adoption centers" for Cabbage Patch Kids. Xavier Roberts, for one, couldn't be happier. Dr. Roberts, chief of staff at Babyland General Hospital, remains in the business of birthin' babies and business is still quite good.

In 1995, the Cabbage Patch Kids received the kind of notoriety they didn't want. The Cabbage Patch Snacktime Kid simulated chewing and swallowing when a pretend piece of food was inserted into its mouth. Unfortunately, the Snacktime Kids ate anything that came their way, including the long hair of their adoptive parents.

Throughout his deals with Coleco, Hasbro and Mattel, Xavier Roberts retained the rights to create his handmade original Cabbage Patch Kids, and has continued to do so for adoption fees ranging from $190 to $400.

Debut: 1985
Inventor: Rob Angel
Developers: Terry Langston, Gary Everson (1950-1995), Richard Gill
Insiders: Tom McGuire, Joe Cornacchia, The Games Gang
Companies: Angel Games, Pictionary, Inc., Western Publishing/Cornacchia Press, Milton Bradley (U.S.), Mattel (Worldwide outside U.S.)

Pictionary

PICTURE PERFECT TIMING

Just outside the revolving door of Seattle's Lake Union Café stands a majestic pedestal clock. Timing is a curious thing. As a waiter at the café, Rob Angel walked past that clock hundreds of times back in 1984. He was 24 years old when he ventured into the game business at precisely the right time.

In 1981, Angel graduated from college and moved into a cramped house in Spokane with some high school buddies. There the beginnings of a game formed around a most unlikely plaything—a dictionary. In the beginning, it was half classic charades and half drawing charades, where a player picked a word from the dictionary and whispered it to the player doing the "charading." There were no rules and no board, only the dictionary passed from player to player. Although unmarketable in this early form, Angel worked on the game briefly by organizing some rules and starting a word list, all scratched out on a yellow legal pad. However, earning money to eat tends to derail even the best entrepreneurial dreams. He filed that pad away and as he put it "did nothing with it for three years."

THE LAUNCHING PAD

In February of 1984 Angel moved to Seattle and unpacked his future in the form of that forgotten yellow pad. "I was surprised I had even saved it," he recalled. "But from the time I unpacked it, I couldn't stop thinking about the game. We played with great fun out of a dictionary, but I knew people just wouldn't do that." He found a solution that summer in the form of a hugely successful question and answer game. "When I saw all those words on cards, I thought 'That's it—a card based game.' The next day I went into the backyard and started reading the dictionary, pulling out words."

Rob Angel watched along with the rest of the world as that game he encountered— Trivial Pursuit—became a sensation. Like scurrying mice, the rest of the toy business brought out trivia games of their own, trying desperately to get even a little crumb of the Trivial Pursuit pie. The market became saturated with mentally challenging games for adults, setting the stage for a less-cerebral party game to reach this massive, growing audience. Angel's game was dubbed Pictionary and its timing, picture perfect.

The object was to identify a word by looking at sketched clues or drawings made by another player. It was fun and boisterous, and when an "All Play" word was picked, real pandemonium resulted as a sketcher from each team drew frantically, while everyone else raced to guess the word first by yelling out possible answers.

With the play figured out, Angel needed an artist to design the look of the game. He found one in a fellow waiter and friend at the Lake Union Café, Gary Everson, a part-time graphic artist and the first partner to join Rob's new company, Angel Games, Inc. With no money, the best he could offer in payment was a piece of the profits if Pictionary took off. Everson bravely took the leap. Rob offered a similar deal to other friends, but couldn't find any other takers until one fateful night of play testing.

Terry Langston had a good job as a CPA when he was first introduced to Rob and his game. "We met at a party at a mutual friend's house," Langston recalls. "They began discussing this game. I wasn't into games, but we decided to just go ahead and play it anyway. The game cards were just index cards that had been cut in half. There was some difficulty reading the words Rob had scrawled on them and the game board was sketched out on a brown paper bag." Langston was partnered with Angel. "We lost, as I recall . . . badly," he shared. "Our relationship started over the game that night and we've been partners ever since." Langston joined the Pictionary team a few weeks later. When I asked him why he agreed, he said, "I had such a good time that night . . . and I hated games! I figured if I could be won over, then others could too."

THREE'S A CHARM

The addition of Langston made Angel Games a balanced (if undermanned) trio. "Gary created our logo, designed all the graphics for the game and knew how the printing process worked," Angel explained. "Terry was a perfect fit because of his accounting skills, but he also turned out to be one hell of an entrepreneur." Angel was the salesman and also devised the unique trifold board, which dictated Pictionary's distinctively shaped box.

With $35,000 start-up capital borrowed from his aunt and uncle, and a Seattle Yellow Pages in hand, Rob set out to find suppliers for the Pictionary components. The team demanded an elegant, well-made game, so when they couldn't afford to mold their own plastic game pieces, Gary Everson came up with the ingenious idea of using blank dice of different colors. They were elegant, functional and cheap. Nine companies committed to supplying all the parts needed to make the first 1,000 games in time for a launch party set for June 1, 1985. With invitations sent and the wheels of production turning, Pictionary— The Game of Quick Draw was ready to meet the world.

(L to R) Rob Angel, Gary Everson, Terry Langston. Of their team, Angel said, "There's no question that it took all three of us to make Pictionary a success."

But just eight days before the party, Rob learned that the company hired to cut and collate the game cards had misquoted the job. They needed more time and much more money. Rob was furious, but resolute. Drastic measures were needed to get Pictionary back on schedule. The consummate playmaker, he went to the phone book one more time.

Rob's apartment became an assembly line. Everything he owned was crammed into his bedroom to make space for the eight rented banquet tables, 170 shoe boxes, and *half a million* game cards. The printer had agreed to cut them, but not collate them. As a result, 1,000 decks were hand sorted by Rob, Terry, Gary and various Seattle friends. For six days straight, sixteen hours a day, they sorted cards between beer runs and pizza deliveries. They stopped briefly to swap out the shoe boxes for the first Pictionary card boxes, which finally arrived from the printer. They finished two days before the party.

After spending $1,000 dollars for the caterer, after sending out the invitations, after hand sorting half a million cards, they sold . . . *forty-two games.* To top it off, in the midst of all the chaos over the cards, they had forgotten to invite the press. With such a dismal start, you'd think Rob Angel would have quit then and there. Instead, he quit waiting tables and started selling Pictionary full-time.

The first store he landed was the campus bookstore at the University of Washington, but the pivotal step came when Pictionary entered Nordstrom stores.

That fall, the three entrepreneurs went to various Nordstrom locations and stood for hours on end, accosting shoppers by literally placing the pencil and pad in their hands. The results became known as Pictionary pile-ups—20 or 30 people all playing at once, with the guys acting as ring masters, yelling and passing games over the crowd to purchasing customers. "The managers ended up calling other managers down the West Coast and that's how we spread to other stores," Langston shared. "Our marketing mantra was 'get the pencil in their hands.'" Once people played Pictionary, they were hooked.

Angel Games threw a second launch party at the Lake Union Café (the press were invited this time) and soon the buzz in Seattle was that Pictionary was more fun than Trivial Pursuit. They sold all 1,000 games and were now consumed with trying to figure out how to make 10,000 more before Christmas.

No bank in Seattle agreed to loan them the $80,000 they needed.

Once again, Langston and Angel took that long

One of the original 1,000 Pictionary games produced by Angel Games in 1985. The cards were oversize and the inventors couldn't afford to have the box bottom printed, so they shrink-wrapped the black and white insert at right, to the bottom of the package.

drive to visit Rob's aunt and uncle. "It was a pressure meeting," Langston shared. "Sure we needed to keep this dream going, but the real pressure was self-imposed. We had already committed to the next print run! I don't know what we would have done if they'd said 'No.'" Angel added, "I borrowed some money from my aunt and uncle in the past and had paid it back, so they knew I was trustworthy. But more than anything, I think they agreed because they saw this unrelenting enthusiasm from us."

By Christmas of 1985, the entrepreneurs had sold nearly their entire second printing of 10,000 games. The pressure to keep up with the success of Pictionary became paramount. For Langston, those early days required many late nights of moonlighting. One particular late night of Pictionary paper-work drove him to make a decision. "I crashed, exhausted, but then woke up in a cold sweat an hour later," Langston shared. "The next day I drove into work and gave my two weeks notice." Meanwhile, 3,000 miles away in New York, another instance of picture-perfect timing was about to provide Pictionary with a national sales force.

Just outside the revolving door of the Toy Center on Fifth Avenue in New York stands another majestic pedestal clock. Tom McGuire walked past that clock hundreds of times in 1986, when he was the West Coast manager for Selchow & Righter. He was 58 years old and about to be fired.

Selchow & Righter had made Trivial Pursuit a household name a few years earlier, and then the legendary game company was purchased by Coleco in 1986. As a forced retirement loomed, McGuire heard about an opening for a national sales manager

position at this upstart game company in Seattle. After meeting with Rob, Terry and Gary, McGuire took a few games back to New York with him. Proof was in the playing, he thought. As he watched his three grown daughters play Pictionary for the first time, he was convinced that Pictionary could be the Trivial Pursuit phenomenon, all over again.

Back in Seattle, Rob, Terry and Gary looked at McGuire's impressive track record with Scrabble (another Selchow & Righter legend) and of course, Trivial Pursuit and knew he was their man. McGuire joined the newly named firm of Pictionary, Inc. in mid-1986, and brought with him four other Selchow & Righter veterans named Hudson Dobson, Tom McGrath, Bill Napier and Kevin McNulty. Before long, the company had sold 45,000 Pictionary games with the help of their new independent sales force. The burgeoning success of the game brought with it even greater risks. Filling the pipeline with games meant raising big bucks. The entrepreneurs decided that the only way they could get Pictionary into millions of homes was to license it to a larger game company. The talk of the toy trade was that Pictionary was about to erupt. Right on cue, the courters came calling.

Terry Langston invented "Pic-packs," which were small promotional handouts that included several Pictionary game cards, rules, paper, and a golf pencil. The "sampling" had begun.

Worlds of Wonder had the number 1 toy of 1985 with a talking bear named Teddy Ruxpin. A few months later, when they began wooing Pictionary Inc. for the rights to their game, the toy company had the hit of the 1986 summer season with Lazer Tag. "Four of their top executives came out to Seattle to meet with us, but they wanted worldwide rights for a 5% royalty and anything we invented in the future," Langston shared. "We didn't have much trouble saying no to them." Turning down Milton Bradley wasn't as simple. The game giant flew Rob, Terry and Tom McGuire to their headquarters in Springfield, Massachusetts. "The meeting went smoothly and by the time we left, we had a deal all worked out with a contract to be sent later," Langston told me. "Rob and I were grinning ear to ear, but Tom still wanted us to take a meeting with Western Publishing."

The guys agreed to schedule a talk with the Wisconsin-based printer, but couldn't stop thinking about Milton Bradley and what that deal meant for their game. The contract from MB arrived, but the game giant had reconsidered some of the terms. "We called and questioned them on it, but the arrangement they offered was so far away from what we had agreed upon that we just said 'No,' and hung up," Langston recalled. The entrepreneurs waited, but Milton Bradley never called back. Fortunately, Western Publishing remained a possibility.

In 1986, Western Publishing was one of the biggest children's book publishers in the world, but not a game company. If the deal were to go through, it would be a very unique arrangement within the business. Weeks before the meeting, Tom McGuire had introduced the guys to a friend of his named Joe Cornacchia. He was a print broker who had handled production of Trivial Pursuit for Selchow & Righter, and was uniquely qualified to spearhead the production of Pictionary (see Trivial Pursuit.)

"Tom asked me to take a look at the game," Cornacchia shared. "I said, 'Okay, but I'm really not interested. I just spent three years of my life chasing a game, making all this money and I don't want to lose it.'" After playing the game, Cornacchia (like Tom McGrath before him), became a believer in the possibility of lightning striking twice. Once again, timing played a big part in convincing a key person to join the Pictionary venture. "After Trivial Pursuit sales faded, I ended up with two or three million dice. One of the reasons I got interested in Pictionary was because it had a die in it!" Cornacchia said with a laugh. "At the time, I had also taken over about a half million dollars worth of blank card stock." Both the dice and the card stock would be used in the production of Pictionary.

Cornacchia was the man that ultimately got the deal done by putting his reputation and his own money on the line. "Western Publishing didn't want to do it, but when I threatened to do it without them, they finally agreed to partner with me," Cornacchia said. Pictionary's future was now hitched to a joint licensing agreement between Western Publishing and the print broker's own Cornacchia Press. Joe's experience managing inventory combined with such a huge commercial printer gave this new venture the ability to make as many Pictionary games as needed. Before long, they would need millions.

ENTER THE GAMES GANG

McGrath, Dobson, Napier, and McNulty, the ex-Selchow & Righter salesmen, had renamed themselves The Games Gang. Their line consisted of one item, Pictionary, but it was all they needed. The word of mouth had been spreading east from Seattle, so when supply finally met demand, Pictionary met the world. In 1987, over three million games were sold. The toy business was still in shock over Trivial Pursuit when Pictionary surpassed it as the most popular game in America.

Pictionary Junior, Bible Pictionary and Travel Pictionary were introduced with great success. An unbelievable nine million Pictionary games were sold in North America in 1988, making it the biggest hit in the toy business two years in a row.

Kevin McNulty recalls when Pictionary erupted. "Toy Fair of '88 was insane. We were sold out of Pictionary the second day of the show. Kmart came into the showroom and wanted 50,000 games *a month.* It was incredible." Success was sweet for The Games Gang, a group of industry veterans whose average age was nearly 60, especially after being discarded from the company for whom they'd all worked for decades. "We were all fired from Selchow two weeks after the Coleco buyout," McNulty told me. "Pictionary came just in time for us."

Pictionary, Inc. then set their sights on the rest of the world. In 1987 they licensed their game to a company called Sans Serif in London, which made Pictionary the top game in the United Kingdom, winning the Game of the Year award in '87 and '88 at the British Toy Fair. By the following year the game appeared in France, Spain, Australia and several Scandinavian countries. "Terry and I were running ourselves ragged, flying overseas four and five times a year," Angel recalled. "We knew we needed help to make Pictionary a global game."

Angel and Langston first met Richard Gill across the negotiation table. As the man who licensed Pictionary from them for San Serif, they knew him to be a tough negotiator. Rob recalled his next serendipitous meeting with Gill at the '89 Toy Fair. "We were getting on the elevator and he was getting off," Angel recalled. "We basically dragged him back on and made him go to lunch with us." The story didn't make *Playthings*

Celebrating the three millionth Pictionary game sold in 1987 are (L to R) Mike Simpson of Western Publishing, Rob Angel, Joe Cornacchia and the Games Gang: Tom McGuire, Mike Gasser, Kevin McNulty, Bill Napier, Hudson Dobson, Tom McGrath, Frank Martin, and Angelo Longo.

magazine, but Richard Gill, the man who was responsible for licensing Trivial Pursuit all over the world, had just been kidnapped.

After leaving his job as an employee of Horn Abbot International, Gill became a partner in Pictionary, Inc. Unlike Trivial Pursuit, Pictionary was relatively easy to translate into foreign editions. But the real plus for Pictionary Inc. was that Gill had contacts within game companies all over the world. In just 8 years, he secured licensees and distributors that put Pictionary in over 70 countries.

In 1994, Pictionary became a Milton Bradley game when Hasbro, its parent company, bought Western Publishing's game division for a reported $105 million. The legendary company finally secured the U.S. and Canadian rights to the game they had missed out on nearly a decade before.

Boosted by Milton Bradley's expertise, Pictionary sold big numbers. Today, The Game of Quick Draw continues to pervade pop culture. It's been referenced in novels, TV shows and movies. Its influence on the rest of the game world has been undeniable. Trivial Pursuit may have kicked the door open for board games marketed to adults, but Pictionary permanently knocked it off its hinges. Charade games like Taboo and Guesstures owe a debt of gratitude to Pictionary, while Cranium and other games with "drawing play" owe it a lot more than that. As Gary Everson once said, "If imitation is the sincerest form of flattery, then we've been flattered many times over."

In 1995, Gary Everson died from complications related to AIDS. In the 10 years that he helped make Pictionary a success, he became a brother to Rob Angel and Terry Langston in every sense of the word.

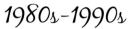

THE PLAYMAKERS
Now and Then

"The loss of Gary is still a struggle for us professionally, as well as personally. We were family," Angel said.

There's no wondering what Gary would have thought had he lived to see Pictionary become a television game show in 1997. Hosted by actor Alan Thicke, the syndicated show was nominated for an Emmy award the year it debuted. Everson, the artist, the co-developer of Pictionary, would have been proud.

Timing is a very curious thing indeed. Rob Angel rediscovers his game idea right on the heels of Trivial Pursuit. Tom McGuire and the other Selchow & Righter salesmen are fired just in time to re-form as The Games Gang. Rob and Terry agree to meet with Western Publishing right before the Milton Bradley deal falls through. Joe Cornacchia just happens to have millions of dice and tons of card stock waiting to be used. And after Pictionary takes off, Richard Gill becomes a partner just when the game is ready to conquer the world. These events in time are all enough to make you think Pictionary was destined to succeed. But while Father Time may have smiled on the game's developers, it was their tenacity that put Pictionary in the position to achieve something special. Once there, the fun took over.

After nearly 20 years, Pictionary still draws a crowd. That's the real reason it has sold over 31 million copies in 42 languages all over the world. It's a great game. Still, when I asked Rob why he and the guys sold their company to Mattel in 2001, he simply said, "The timing was right."

RICHARD GILL

As the group commercial director of Sans Serif, Richard Gill helped sell nearly 4 million Trivial Pursuit games in 1986. In 1987, he was hired by Trivial Pursuit's international arm to run the

parent company out of Barbados. "I was 28 year old and they flew me to Barbados on the Concorde!" he said incredulously. After working for Horn

Abbot International for nearly three years, Gill became a partner in Pictionary, Inc., securing licensees for The Game of Quick Draw all over the globe. "We ran a tournament at the university in Istanbul when we launched the game in Turkey," he said. "To see all those boxes with our trademark 'Pictionary' in English and then everything else in these Turkish symbols—that's when I knew Pictionary had really made it."

After Pictionary Inc. sold to Mattel in 2001, Gill became a principal investor in Sababa Toys, a company that was quick to make its mark. Through a deal with Mattel, Sababa has created licensed versions of the Magic 8 Ball and over 25 versions of the Uno card game, featuring licenses as diverse as The Hulk, Muppets, Care Bears and Peanuts. Most recently, Gill helped Sababa create licensed versions of Ohio Art's classic Etch A Sketch, featuring Hello Kitty and *The Simpsons*.

Debut: 1991
Predecessor: Power Drencher (1990)
Inventor: Lonnie Johnson
Developer: Bruce D'Andrade
Insiders: Myung Song, Al Davis
Companies: Larami Corporation, Hasbro

Super Soaker

PUMP UP THE VOLUME

It was the water fight to supersede all others and six-year-old Aneka Johnson couldn't wait. In her hands she held a strange contraption made from a collection of plastic parts attached to a two-liter Coke bottle. To her water fight opponents, the thing might just as well have been attached to a fire truck. Aneka's friends had doubted her prideful claims about her daddy's invention, but now *they* were the ones who were all wet. The soggy lesson learned? When it comes to water fight firepower, never doubt the daughter of a nuclear engineer.

Lonnie Johnson already had quite a résumé when he conceived the idea of engineering a pressurized, high-performance water pistol. He had advanced degrees in mechanical engineering, nuclear engineering and stints with the U.S. Air Force and Strategic Air Command. He was even an astronaut candidate, but it was his mind that was always in the clouds, the mind of an inventor.

In 1982, a few months before Aneka's famed water fight, an experiment in Johnson's bathroom led to a water pistol epiphany and a new career in toys. The engineer had been working on a heat pump that cooled itself with pressurized water vapor instead of ozone-depleting Freon. To test the apparatus, he attached it to his bathroom sink via some rubber tubing and turned on the water. The pressure shot out a stream of water so powerful that its air currents ruffled the shower curtain. Johnson said, "When I saw that I thought, 'you know, a high performance water gun would make a great toy.'" He dismissed his idea as folly at first, but then reconsidered. "I said to myself musingly, 'Well I'm a nuclear

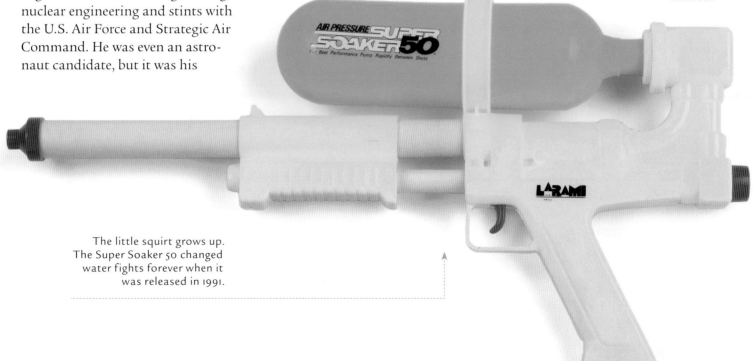

The little squirt grows up. The Super Soaker 50 changed water fights forever when it was released in 1991.

Aqua Man. Dr. Lonnie Johnson invented the Super Soaker and many other inventions that fall in the realm of fluid dynamics. He holds over 80 patents.

weeks of tinkering it was time to put the toy to the test with his six-year-old daughter and her friends.

"The first one I built, I gave to her and it worked great. It was one of those things that when you see it work for the first time you just say, 'Wow!' Her friends never even got her wet. They couldn't get close enough to her," Johnson recalled with a laugh. He called it the Pneumatic Water Gun, but Aneka and her friends just called it fun.

After further neighborhood testing (the toy proved to be a hit with adults as well as kids), Johnson approached manufacturers. "I tried to get that toy into production over a number of years," Johnson recalled. "I went to a plastic products company in Omaha first and they couldn't do what I needed at the price I needed. From that point, I started to talk to toy companies. First was Daisy."

According to Mark Rich's book *Toys: A to Z*, the Daisy Manufacturing Company (known for its air-powered BB guns) was the first company to introduce a metal water gun in 1913. It was called the Daisy Liquid Pistol, No. 8 (see ad on page 267.) Making a second breakthrough in water pistols, 70 years after introducing the first metal one, would have been a great PR story and possibly a marketing bonanza for Daisy, but the deal was not meant to be. For two years, Johnson worked with several Daisy engineers, only to be interrupted by one company reorganization after another.

Next he contacted Entertech and even signed a deal with the maker of battery-powered water guns, but the company never produced the finished product and went out of business in 1987. Five years after Johnson had conceived his Pneumatic Water Gun he still had nothing to show

engineer, I should be qualified to design a toy water gun.' From that point it was just a matter of engineering."

Johnson's two criteria presented an engineering challenge. First, the toy had to be highly pressurized by its user. Secondly, he wanted a small child to be able to use the toy. Logic dictated that these two conditions might contradict each other. Johnson thought otherwise.

Using PVC pipe, Plexiglas, and parts he had to envision and then construct, Johnson went to work. "I had a small hobby lathe in my workshop," he said. "With it I could make parts out of plastic and soft metal. I machined all the parts and super glued them together. I went to the hobby store and picked out just the right springs and O rings. I made my own check valves. Everything had to be hand made." After a few

Dr. Lonnie Johnson's Super Soaker prototype, hand made in 1989.

for all his hard work. In 1989 he decided to travel to Toy Fair.

"I was walking the halls [at the Toy Center] looking for someone to talk to. It was Toy Fair—I figured I'd find somebody," Johnson laughed. "I asked some people I'd met in the hall where they thought I should take an idea for a water gun and they sent me down to talk to Larami."

Larami Corporation was founded in 1959 by Al Davis and Myung Song. Johnson met with Davis during the busy rush of the industry's largest trade show. "I told him [Davis] that I had a high performance toy water gun and he said 'Well, that sounds interesting. If you're ever in the Philadelphia area, why don't you drop in and see us," Johnson recalled. "Then at the end of our conversation he added, 'Don't make a special trip, but if you're in the area . . .' In hindsight what he was

saying was 'We look at a lot of stuff. Don't put yourself out because no matter what you've got, the probability that we would be interested is very low.'"

THE TRIP

"I went home immediately and started working," Johnson said. He made a few revisions to his initial design, most notably placing the water bottle on top. "After a couple of weeks I had a working model." Johnson's drive was as impressive as his invention. He called Al Davis and then his travel agent, planning to do exactly what Al Davis had asked him not to. He made a special trip to Larami.

In an article in *Black Enterprise,* writer Caryne Brown described the moment when Larami knew they had found something super. "A guarded Johnson showed up carrying a battered pink Samsonite suitcase. He walked into the room, opened the suitcase, and pulled out the prototype—a handheld pump apparatus of PVC tubing, Plexiglas and a plastic soda bottle. A split second later, he fired a giant stream of water across the room. The reaction was dramatic." Johnson heard a familiar word from Larami's president. "Wow!" Myung Song said. "It was clear to me from that point on that Larami really wanted to do it," said Johnson.

Larami's in-house engineer was Bruce D'Andrade, the man who would eventually share several water gun patents with Johnson. His job was to figure out how to cost-effectively manufacture Johnson's sophisticated design. "Bruce took a functional model that I provided," Johnson noted, "and then changed it so that it could be injection molded and put into production."

After extensive tooling and testing, Larami released Johnson's toy as Power Drencher in 1990. The toy sold well from the start and drew its share of attention from the industry. After a trademark

9929-0

"The appearance and shape of the prototype really did resemble the finished product," inventor Lonnie Johnson said. The finished product was Power Drencher, released by Larami in the fall of 1990.

infringement claim by a rival water gun maker, the Power Drencher's name was changed to Super Soaker in 1991. "My [Myung] was accountable to Larami's holding company and because of Power Drencher's success he was getting a lot of pressure to put it on television," Johnson said. "It was going to cost over a million dollars and Larami hadn't done anything like that before. It was a very stressful time for him."

Song and Davis decided to risk it, despite the gnawing fear that consumers would never spend $10 for a "water gun." The TV ads showed that Super Soaker was no mere squirt gun. The newly named toy was seen shooting a stream of water 30 feet! The rules of water warfare were officially rewritten. In its first three years on the market, over 27 million Super Soaker water guns were sold.

In 1992, the Super Soaker 100 was released, featuring a secondary water tank, also designed by Lonnie Johnson. "1992 was our biggest year," Johnson recalled. Soon models like the 25 (made smaller to fit into a belt holster), the 200 (made bigger to hold more water) and the 300 (made bigger still and worn like a backpack) turned Larami's investment in Super Soaker into very liquid assets.

WATER WEAPONS?

Success brought wider distribution and with it, some controversy. In 1992, gang members in Boston and several other cities filled Super Soakers with bleach and ammonia and used them as weapons. As a result, some politicians sought to ban the toys.

In the book *Toy Wars* by G. Wayne Miller, Hasbro's then CEO, Alan Hassenfeld is quoted

This ad from 1916 shows the "Daisy No. 8," the first metal water pistol, invented by Charles Frederick Lefever. It reads in part, "When dilute ammonia is used, it makes a very effective weapon against vicious men or animals." Ironically, three-quarters of a century later the Super Soaker would be temporarily banned in some cities after being misused in that precise manner.

as saying, "I find it fascinating—absolutely fascinating—how we can legislate toys and toy guns but we can't legislate real guns . . . I just think it's wonderfully hypocritical." Miller adds that, "He [Hassenfeld] considered the much publicized efforts of politicians to ban squirt guns in several cities an absurd commentary of modern life." Not surprisingly, Lonnie Johnson agrees. "The politicians behind it had taken a draft of a bill or something that proposed to ban real guns and used it as a template to write their proposed Super Soaker ban. It said things like 'No one can carry a gun loaded between play areas.' Things like that. No toys between 'play areas'? It was ridiculous."

In 1994, the unbelievable success of Johnson's invention prompted Hasbro to plunk down a reported $100 million for Larami. In an article in the *Los Angles Times* in 1999, writer Greg Miller noted that, "Ten years ago, the squirt gun market was still largely the province of 29-cent plastic pistols that could barely douse an insect. Squirt guns weren't even tracked as a separate category by the industry analysts. Today it is a $215-million-a-year business in the United States, and Larami owns 90% of it."

Over the years, Larami and Hasbro have produced well over 125 different Super Soaker toys, making the brand a summertime mainstay. "I made an attempt to keep one of every model, but somehow over the years

THE NEW DAISY LIQUID PISTOL, No. 8

Designed after the latest automatic pistol and would readily be taken for one. Made from steel, blued finish. Simple to load and discharge—no rubber bulb to get out of order.

Great sport for boys and girls, as it throws a fine stream of water a distance of 25 feet. When dilute ammonia is used, it makes a very effective weapon against vicious men or animals. Length, 5½ inches; weight, 5½ ounces, each in carton, packed one gross in a case. Retail price, 25 cents.

An old and popular toy brought up to date in design and operating on a new principle. It is bound to become one of the best selling 25-cent articles on the market.

my kids pilfered them away," said Johnson, a father of three. Seventeen Super Soaker models are out for 2003. There's the Max-D (Maximum Distance) 2000 for ages 5 and up and a personal favorite, if in name only, the Splashzooka featuring a CPS (Constant Pressure System) for ages 8 and up. Any question over Super Soaker's popularity with teens and adults is put to rest when you witness the water wonder that is the Super Soaker Monster XL (Extra Large). It's also marked for 8 and up, but at a length of over four feet and a water holding capacity of 1.25 gallons, it's hard to imagine an eight-year-old lugging it very far. When full it weighs over 16 pounds!

STILL SOAKIN'

To those water gun warriors who grew up *pre*-Super Soaker, Johnson's invention seems like a technological leap of epic proportions. Maybe that's why adults loved Super Soakers from the start. A 35-foot stream of continuous water tends to impress us more than kids who never had to suffer the indignities of our "ray gun" water pistols with a "squirt" range that peaked at a whopping three feet. Sort of makes you want to pick a water fight with someone, doesn't it?

If so, beware. At an estimated 300 million Super Soakers sold, it's probable your opponent will be armed and aqueous as well. After 15 years, Super Soaker still delivers the water and the promise: "Don't get wet . . . get soaked!"

Water fight, anyone? A '60s water pistol faces off against the Super Soaker Monster XL.

THE BLUEPRINT FOR SUCCESSFUL SOAKAGE

All Super Soakers feature a reservoir partially filled with water, leaving a void for air to enter. By using a pump attached to the squirt gun, the user compresses air into the void within the reservoir, pressurizing the water in the process. In early models, the gun's trigger released a pinch valve, opening a tube that fed to the nozzle of the squirt gun. The built-up pressure (which could reach a maximum of 35 ppi due to a release valve), forced the water out in a stream. "Still later,

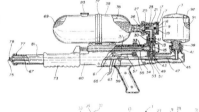

with new models, we were constantly trying to minimize the pressure drop as the water flows inside the gun," Johnson said. One solution was invented by Johnson in 1992. The Super Soaker 100 featured a secondary reservoir which stayed pressurized even while the primary reservoir lost pressure. The result? A stream of water reaching over 40 feet. Most recently, Super Soakers with a

Constant Pressure System (CPS) used a bladder within the reservoir to minimize the loss of pressure even further.

Debut: 1993
Inventor: H. Ty Warner
Company: Ty, Inc.

Beanie Babies

A Mountain of Beans

The first nine were a lobster, a killer whale, a moose, a dog, a frog, a dolphin, a platypus, a pig, and a bear. They were just playthings—polyester plush, filled with polyvinyl chloride pellets. Over 10 years and 300 species of Beanie Babies later, they're all still just fabric and filling. There's no need to get all emotional about them, right? *I mean pull yourself together will you people?!*

To the uninitiated, the Beanie Babies craze looks like madness. It's enough to make you think some evilly-addictive substance hidden within these little animals causes people to buy them, collect them, and *crave* them. Look beyond the polyester and pellets and you begin to feel it.

The best toys move us. "Beanies," as they were quickly dubbed, aren't just "stuffed" like most plush toys; they're under-stuffed, which makes them floppy and vulnerable. Their shifting pellets make a wonderfully comforting sound and allow them to be posed (somewhat) and hugged (definitely). There are touches of brilliance in the way they're made, but it's the marketing genius of the man behind the Beanies that turned them into one of the biggest collector crazes in history.

After an 18-year stint as a salesman for Dakin, a toy plush manufacturer, H. Ty Warner formed Ty, Inc. in 1986. His first plush animals included some Himalayan cats named Smokey and Peaches that had feet filled with plastic pellets. After dabbling in

Brownie and other early Beanies became difficult to find with their original swing tags. That's because parents, unaware of the collectible frenzy to come, would routinely cut the tags off before giving the plush toys to kids who actually played with them!

1980s–1990s

Beanie Babies

The starting nine for Ty Warner were (clockwise starting with the Crustacean) Punchers, Splash, Chocolate, Spot, Legs, Flash, Patti, Squealer, and Cubbie.

collectible plush with his 1991 line of Annual Bears, Warner combined the cute names, the collectibility and the pellets to create Beanie Babies in 1993. Reportedly convinced that no quality plush toy existed that was also affordable, Warner launched his well-made menagerie for the retail price of around $5—or, as he stated, "allowance money." The very first Beanie Babies were a bear named Brownie and a deep fuchsia-colored platypus named Patti. Then in 1994 Brownie was rechristened Cubbie and Patti lost her rich color as both joined the original line of nine.

Warner released the Beanie Babies Collection in the Chicago area that same year and the exclusive nature of the toys hinted at the brilliance in his marketing plan. He sold them only to specialty gift and toy shops, even after their popularity soared and the line expanded. No store was shipped the entire assortment, which sent eager collectors all over the Windy City looking for the entire line (which by year's end had multiplied into a collection of 36 distinctive animals).

TAG YOU'RE IT

Beanie Babies came with a two-sided, heart-shaped "swing tag" that provided only the animal's name at first, but later opened like a book to include a date of birth and a four-line poem about the critter's origin. As scarcity became evident to collectors, a pristine tag on a rare Beanie signified a badge of purity (and profit).

Their popularity grew steadily throughout their introductory year. According to Becky Estenssoro, author of several Beanie collectors' guides and the owner of the authentication service known as True Blue Beans, it was a series of events during '96 and '97 that really set the stage for the Beanie explosion.

"Because the Olympics were taking place in the summer of '96, Ty produced a teddy bear named 'Libearty' with an American flag embroidered on his chest," Estenssoro explained. "In anticipation of the November elections that fall, he also introduced an elephant named 'Righty' and a donkey named 'Lefty' which also came with American flags." All three garnered positive press, which added fuel to a fire that had been smoldering for nearly three years.

The final catalyst was the first public announcement of a line retirement. "Libearty, Righty and Lefty were what really triggered the craze. Ty announced that they [along with six other Beanies] would be 'retired,'" Estenssoro said. "The race was on to find them all."

THE YEAR OF THE BEANS

Ty Inc.'s first retirement announcement came in January of 1997. It was a familiar toy company warning: "Get them before they're gone." But in this case, the warning came from a company that had severely limited the distribution of the plush toys. Fearful that there was some truth to the warning, Beanie fans panicked, setting off a buying frenzy.

"Another significant bit of timing was the fact that the Internet was starting to really explode at that time," Estenssoro contends. "Beanie websites appeared as collectors from all over the world began to sell and trade." A secondary market emerged with determined collectors buying rare or retired Beanie Babies for 10, 20, or even 100 times their original cost.

Warner stuck to his plan of limiting the assortments shipped to each store and refused to sell to any mass-market retailers. Forgoing the quick buck and striving for longevity, Warner was rewarded for his patience. Fans of all ages camped out for hours in front of Hallmark stores and gift shops just on the rumor that a shipment was to arrive. Because the craze never went to the mass market, Beanie Babies never had to

Hang in there!

Dear Friends:

Thank you. You've made TY a huge success! Because of your unparalleled enthusiasm, both consumers and retailers alike, *Beanie Babies®* are the largest success story in the history of the toy and gift industries. Our other plush categories are experiencing similar growth and success as TY becomes the brand of choice. We are very grateful for your support.

However, unprecedented growth such as this brings tremendous challenges and we are doing our best to meet them ... but it takes time. We are aware of the frustration that many of our loyal customers have felt recently when searching for TY products. We want you to know that we are doing all that we can to alleviate the delays and provide increased shipping in the next few weeks. Although we can not control the effect that the economics of supply and demand have on retail prices, we are making every effort to satisfy the supply in a timely manner so that the demand can be met.

Loyal customers are what makes a company strong. We thank all of you for your loyalty, support, determination, and patience, and we look forward to sharing our success with you for a long time to come.

Sincerely,

Ty Warner

© Ty Inc.
www.ty.com

On August 8, 1997, Warner took out this full-page ad in *USA Today*.

face the rioting adults behind kamikaze shopping carts that scarred the Cabbage Patch Kids craze. There were some altercations reported as zealous fans fought over a rare spotless Spot or a wingless Quackers, but overall Beanie Babies collectors displayed decorum and an air of sophistication that could be traced back to the inventor of the collection . . . whoever he was.

SHY AS A FOX

The man behind the craze shunned the press, adding an aura of mystery and aloofness to his line. A *People* magazine article called Ty Warner "a

Beanie Babies inventor Ty Warner has the goods. Paul Roche, Warner's former boss at Dakin, was interviewed for a *People* article entitled "Bean There Done That." In it he called Warner, ". . . the best salesman I ever met."

mediaphobic marketing whiz who rarely grants interviews." But don't mistake savvy for shyness. Estenssoro's book *Beanie Mania II,* co-authored with Becky Phillips, includes a rare interview with Ty Warner (by reporter Joni Blackman), which reveals more about the man behind Beans.

A former actor, Warner moved to Los Angeles after graduating with a degree in drama from Kalamazoo College. When his dream of a career in Hollywood ended in 1968, he followed in his father's footsteps and became a salesman for Dakin, where his flair for the dramatic ignited. Warner took on the role of an eccentric millionaire (prophetic) and arrived at meetings in a white Rolls Royce, wearing a fur coat and top hat and carrying a cane. He told Blackman, "It was all to get in to see the buyer. I figured if I was eccentric-looking . . . people would think, 'What is he selling?'"

After Warner left Dakin to form Ty, Inc. and his marketing plan changed from flashy showmanship to standoffish exclusivity, his sales skill remained intact.

Beanies traveled all over the world, one specialty shop at a time, restricted from ever setting foot or paw in any mass market retailer. However, in April of 1997, Warner's exclusive little animals landed an unlikely promotion with the biggest restaurant chain on the planet.

BEANIES AND BURGERS

The McDonald's campaign contradicted Warner's avoidance of mass-consumerism, but exposed Beanie Babies to millions of new potential customers. McDonald's enjoyed ("endured" might be a better word) the most successful Happy Meal promotion in the company's history. The fast food chain featured miniature Beanie Babies (called Teenie Beanie Babies) in their children's meals and was flooded with crazed fans who

Since Teenie Beanie Babies were smaller, cheaper and available only through McDonald's, Warner avoided alienating his specialty accounts who continued to carry the exclusive, high-end line of originals.

drove from one McDonald's to another, searching for them all. Many restaurants sold out on the first day of the promotion, and before it ended an estimated 100 million Teenie Beanie Babies were purchased by fervent fans.

Ty and McDonald's repeated the promotion the following year and the result was almost as insane. Shortly after it began the *Wall Street Journal* reported that "almost overnight about 80 million toys were gobbled up, leaving a string of unhappy children, piqued parents, exhausted restaurant employees and stories of customers throwing away Happy Meals they had just bought for the toys." McDonald's ran the promotion every spring for four straight years.

HARD PRESSED

The media had always been good to Warner, even after he decided to ignore their requests for interviews. In her six years of intimately covering Beanie Babies for her magazine *Beanie Mania,* and her current job as owner of True Blue Beans, Becky Estenssoro has met Ty Warner only once and has never interviewed him, despite numerous requests. "You can't get to him," she explained. "You can talk to everybody else there [at Ty, Inc.], but never him."

The eccentric entrepreneur's maneuvering came to a head in the fall of 1999. On September 1st, as the world stockpiled water and tuna fish for Y2K and the start of the end the world, an abrupt announcement appeared on the Ty, Inc. website that read: "All Beanies will be retired by the end of the year." Then, in a move that surely added to the apocalyptic worries for Beanie collectors, the website was blacked out. Both the company and the man behind it weren't talking. As fans rung their hands, the website returned, but with an addition. A new Beanie bear, teasingly named "The End," was up for sale. The media backlash was immediate.

"Beanie Move Giving Rise To Skepticism," the *New York Times* reported, with an article stating that consumers were "outraged" and that "Ty, which does not advertise and instead relies heavily on marketing gimmicks, was simply engaging in a corporate game of 'gotcha' to drive sales . . ." Even the *Economist* in London ran a story entitled "You've Beanie Had." Just a few months after the announcement, Warner relented, and in yet another media ploy, put the fate of the Beanie Babies in the hands of the fans who were charged fifty cents (which went to charity) to vote for the outcome of the line on the Ty, Inc. website.

Warner faced stiff criticism, but not from fans. If giving some money to a worthy cause was all the penance it took to have their beloved Beanie Babies back, they were willing to pay. The media, on the other

Don't Kill the Messenger. The infamous bear that marked "The End" of the line for Beanie Babies in 1999.

hand, couldn't let it go. *Advertising Age* said that "it is surprising that toymaker Ty's brazenly manipulative marketing ploy . . . did not backfire in its face. Ty should come clean to Beanie fans about the story behind the 'retirement' story." Ty Warner never would, and the entire incident only added to the eccentric allure of the man behind the mania.

COUNTING ON THE BEANS

Many of the most valuable Beanie Babies are ones that were made for only a short time before a mistake or an inadvertent trademark infringement forced a change in color or name. For instance, Peanut the elephant was originally released with a very light blue color. A subsequent limited run of royal blue Peanuts were produced before the mistake was caught and the color corrected. In 1994, Pinchers began arriving with the name misspelled "Punchers." The typo was corrected, but not before several thousand Punchers hit the market. Nana the monkey and Sparky the dog had to be renamed Bongo and Dotty respectively after their names infringed upon other company trademarks.

So, if you want to buy a retired Bear named Brownie or a discontinued Lobster named Punchers, you'll need hundreds of dollars. And if you want a royal blue Peanut the elephant, you'll probably need thousands of dollars—especially if she is authenticated and comes MWMT—Beanie-speak for "mint with mint tags."

If all you have to spend is allowance money, you can still buy one of the *new* Beanie Babies. But if Ty Warner were the talking type, he'd probably warn you to get one now, before they're gone.

Warner has always been a charitable CEO. In 1998, Princess the royal purple bear helped raise $10 million for the Diana, Princess of Wales Memorial Fund.

In March 2000, Becky Estenssoro founded the authentication service, True Blue Beans in response to all the counterfeit Beanie Babies entering the market. "Counterfeits from Asia were coming in by the hundreds of thousands," she said. "Collectors were tired of getting ripped off." Today, she continues to authenticate around 15,000 Beanie Babies a year.

According to a 2001 article in *Forbes* magazine, Ty Warner bought the Four Seasons Hotel in New York, the Four Seasons Resort near Santa Barbara and California's San Ysidro Ranch for a total of $472 million. He is the sole owner of Ty, Inc.

"Marching across the dusty ground,
You'll hear me from miles around.
My trunk is swinging to and fro,
Listen to my trumpet blow!"
—Pounds the elephant

Acknowledgements

After I co-invented the TriBond game in 1989 (and survived the three-year push to make it successful), I lost the fun of simply walking into a toy store and browsing the aisles. Looking at the latest plaything, no matter how cool it was, made me wonder who invented it, what the tooling cost, how it worked or why they chose *that* color box.

Similarly, after two and a half years on *The Playmakers,* I will forever be unable to browse a bookstore without thinking of the authors, and with admiration, the long and lonely hours they must have spent with their fingers resting on a keyboard. When I envisioned this project, I had no idea how much searching, interviewing, designing, collecting, costing,

hauling, hunting, photographing, sleuthing and phoning there was in "writing a book." I do now. With that knowledge, comes the overwhelming desire to thank some people.

Inventive people have a certain mind-set. They like to create things, not necessarily talk about creating things. Thank you to all the inspired **inventors and developers** who generously gave of their time to talk toys with me: Ed Akeman, Rob Angel, Ralph Baer, Jeffrey Breslow, Chuck Foley, Richard Gill, Eddy Goldfarb, Robert Grebler, Charlie Groschen, Reyn Guyer, Betty James, Lonnie Johnson, Terry Langston, Don Levine, Milton Levine, Norman McFarland, Burt Meyer, Neil Rabens, Bill Rhodenbaugh, Leslie Scott, John Spinello, Norm Stingley, Bob Tezak, Harold von Braunhut and Kay & Bob Zufall.

THANKS TO:

Mike Carrier, William Darrow, Niels Dam, Steve Levine, David J. Mullany, Stephen Mullany, Tom Guyer, Robert Pasin, Paul Pasin, Joe Rhodenbaugh, John Robbins, David Tolmer, Yolanda von Braunhut, Joni Gruelle Wanamaker, Mary Wenkstern—the **relatives of inventors and developers** who shared their family legacy and their stories

George Atamian, Bradd Bowen, Peggy Brown, Dennis Callaghan, Laura Chase, Rebecca Colter, Jeff Conrad, Lyle Conway, Joe Cornacchia, Tracy Dudkiewicz, Donna Durant, Bill Dohrmann, Julius Ellman, Hank Emerson, Erick Erickson, Kent Gass,

David Grebler, Linda Hill, Jay Horowitz, Bill Killgallon, David Laughridge, Lloyd L. Laumann, Lindsay Martinez, Zicel Maymudes, Kevin McNulty, Ed Muccini, Philip Orbanes, Cara Lynn Orchard, Calle Østergaard, the people at Patch Products, Vic Reiling, Hal Ross, Margaret Strong, Peter Sgromo, Diana Sparrow, Kate Stec, Mel Taft, Irene Vega, Helen Van Tassel, Ron Weingartner, Michael Wurstlin, Dave Yearick—the **toy industry insiders** who helped me tell the stories of these marvelous playthings

Ralph Anspach, Tina Bamert, Mary Brooks, Kim Bunner, Martha Clyde, Jeff Eger, John Michlig, Patricia Hall, Kate Lippincott, Victor Malafronte, Don Montgomery, Joan Palicia, Will Shortz, Terry Stokke, Jennifer Strobel, Maynard Frank Wolfe, Travis Westley— the **writers, librarians, archivists and sleuths** who shared the fruits of their digging and whose generosity in sharing their stories and contacts, helped fill in the blanks of this book

Richard Biddle, Paul Fink, Thomas Forsyth, Richard Learn, Joseph Mania, Dennis Martin, Dalia Miller, Allan Miller at The Krueger Street Toy & Train Museum, Ron Morris, David E. Richter, Debby Stowell and Eric Lamboley at Circle Books in Sarasota, Mary Ann & Wolfgang Sell at the National Stereoscopic Association, Rich Sommer, Francis Turner at The Official Marx Toy Museum, Kelly Weeks at Gulf Coast Model Railroad in Sarasota—the **shop owners, historians, collectors and museum curators** who graced me with their enthusiasm, pictures, stories, knowledge and collections

Herb Booth at Booth Studio for taking great pictures; Giles Hoover and Amanda Smith at *osprey*design for their fine design; Marcia Fairbanks and John Michlig for their editing expertise; Dana Lutz for her thorough proof reading; Luke T. Murphy for his excellent photo editing; Wendy and Kevin Alex for their awesome indexing—all **pros, friends and colleagues** who held my hand through this two-and-a-half-year journey.

SPECIAL THANKS TO:

Sarah—for putting up with my childish tendencies and loving me in spite of them

Kate & Emma—for making it all worthwhile

Mom and Dad, who taught me how to play hard, follow the rules, dream big and most of all, to have fun

Jesus. The First, the Last and the Ultimate Playmaker.

Credits

Photography

All photographs were taken by Herb Booth of Booth Studio unless otherwise noted (www.boothstudio.com). Photo editing by Luke T. Murphy.

All toys, ads, postcards, catalogs, books and associated literature pictured within *The Playmakers* are from the author's collection unless otherwise noted. Neither the author nor the publisher claim any copyright to the objects pictured herein.

Flexible Flyer
p. 4 Samuel Allen courtesy of Westtown School, Westtown, PA

Lionel trains
p. 2 Lionel package courtesy of Joseph Mania
p. 8 Joshua Lionel Cowen courtesy of Lionel LLC

Teddy Bear
p. 2 teddy bear courtesy of National Museum of American History Smithsonian Institution Behring Center Political History Collection
p. 16 Clifford Berryman cartoon courtesy of National Museum of American History Smithsonian Institution Behring Center Political History Collection
p. 16 Teddy Roosevelt, Time Life Pictures/Getty Images

Crayola
p. 20 Edwin Binney and C. Harold Smith courtesy of Binney & Smith
p. 21 artwork by Kate Walsh
p. 21 American Gothic courtesy of The Art Institute of Chicago. Grant Wood, American, 1891-1942, American Gothic, 1930, oil on beaverboard, 74.3 X 62.4 cm, Friends of American Art Collection, All rights reserved by The Art Institute of Chicago and VAGA, New York, NY 1930.934 " The Art Institute of Chicago. All Rights Reserved.
p. 22 artwork by Emma Walsh

Erector
p. 26 A. C. Gilbert, George Karger/Time Life Pictures/Getty Images

Crossword Puzzle
p. 27 Arthur Wynne from the collection of Will Shortz
p. 28 *New York World* and the first crossword puzzle courtesy of the Library of Congress
p. 29 *The Cross Word Book* courtesy of the National Puzzle Museum at www.puzzlebuffs.com
p. 30 Crossword bathing suit, Hulton Archive by Getty Images

Lincoln Logs
p. 33 Lincoln Logs set from the '40s courtesy of Hasbro

Radio Flyer
p. 3 Liberty Coaster Wagon, p. 35 Antonio Pasin, p. 35 Coaster Boy, p. 37 Radio Flyer # 18 model, p. 37 Streak-o-lite wagon, and p. 36 the kids around the Radio Flyer wagon, courtesy of Radio Flyer, Inc.

Raggedy Ann
p. 38 Johnny Gruelle courtesy of The Johnny Gruelle Raggedy Ann and Andy Museum
p. 41 FAO Schwarz photographed by author

Monopoly
p. 46–7 The Landlord's Game photograph courtesy of Thomas E. Forsyth, game from the collection of Thomas E. Forsyth
p. 48 Early Atlantic City, Library of Congress, Prints and Photographs Division, reproduction number LC-D401-72995
p. 49 round Darrow board courtesy of The Forbes Collection, New York © All rights reserved
p. 50 Patterson printed board courtesy of William Darrow, photographed by author
p. 50 Charles Darrow courtesy of William Darrow
p. 50 Marven Gardens sign photographed by author
p. 51 white box edition scanned and edited by author
p. 51 rejection letters courtesy of William Darrow, photographed by author
p. 53 Bargain Day game from the Alex G. Malloy collection
p. 53 The Landlord's Game courtesy of Richard L. Biddle, game from the collection of Richard L. Biddle
p. 56 Esther and Charles Darrow courtesy of William Darrow

Photography

Photography

Nerf
p. 219 Reyn Guyer courtesy of the Guyer family
p. 220 Nerf prototype courtesy of the Guyer family
p. 222 Nerf prototype courtesy of the Guyer family

Uno
p. 224 Merle Robbins and Ray Robbins courtesy of John Robbins
p. 226 Ed Akeman and the 50 millionth Uno game courtesy of Ed Akeman

Rubik's Cube
p. 231 Erno Rubik, Hulton Archive by Getty Images

Trivial Pursuit
p. 236 original Trivial Pursuit board courtesy of Hasbro
p. 237 card prototype courtesy of Michael Wurstlin
p. 240 Scott Abbott, Chris Haney and John Haney, Hulton Archive by Getty Images
p. 243 Joe Cornacchia courtesy of Joe Cornacchia

Jenga
p. 245 Leslie Scott, p. 245 original Jenga and p. 246 Jenga ad courtesy of Leslie Scott
p. 246 Robert Grebler courtesy of Pokonobe Associates

Cabbage Patch Kids
p. 252 Babyland General Hospital courtesy of Original Appalachian Artworks, Inc.
p. 253 Xavier Roberts courtesy of Original Appalachian Artworks, Inc.

Pictionary
p. 257 Rob Angel, Gary Everson, Terry Langston courtesy of Seattle Games
p. 258 original Pictionary courtesy of Rob Angel
p. 261 Games Gang courtesy of Kevin McNulty
p. 263 Richard Gill courtesy of Seattle Games

Super Soaker
p. 265 Lonnie Johnson, p. 265 Super Soaker prototype and p. 266 Power Drencher courtesy of Johnson Research & Development

Beanie Babies
p. 271 Ty Warner, Kevin Horan/Time Life Pictures/Getty Images

The Making of *The Playmakers*
p. 299 All photos by Dawn Butters and Debra Lindsey

Bibliography

Books:

Amende, Coral. *The Crossword Obsession.* New York: Berkley Books, 2001.

Angel, Robert S., Langston, Terry R. and Everson, Gary. *The Official Pictionary Dictionary: The Book of Quick Draw.* New York: The Putnam Publishing Group, 1989.

Anspach, Ralph. *The Billion Dollar Monopoly Swindle.* Palo Alto: American Printing, 1998.

Auerbach, Stevanne. "Dr. Toy." *F.A.O. Schwarz Toys for a Lifetime: Enhancing Childhood Through Play.* New York: Universe Publishing, 1999.

Brady, Maxine. *The Monopoly Book.* New York: David McKay Company, Inc., 1974.

Cordry, Harold. *The Everything Crossword and Puzzle Book.* Avon: Adams Media Corporation, 1998.

Cossman, E. Joseph. *How I Made $1,000,000 in Mail Order (And You Can Too).* New York: Fireside, 1964.

Costello, Matthew J. *The Greatest Games of All Time.* New York: John Wiley & Sons, Inc., 1991.

Cross, Gary. *Kids' Stuff: Toys and the Changing World of American Childhood.* Cambridge: Harvard University Press, 1997.

Dennis, Lee. *Warman's Antique American Games 1840-1940.* Radnor: Wallace-Homestead, 1986, 1991.

Dorling Kindersley Limited. *The Ultimate LEGO Book.* New York: DK Publishing Inc., 1999.

Epstein, Dan. *20th Century Pop Culture.* New York: Carlton Books Limited, 1999.

Fatsis, Stefan. *Word Freak.* New York: Houghton Mifflin Company, 2001.

Fennick, Janine. *The Collectible Barbie Doll.* Philadelphia: Courage Books, 1999.

Frey, Tom. *Toy Bop: Kid Classics of the 50's & 60's.* Murrysville: Fuzzy Dice Productions, Inc. 1994.

Geary, Richard. *Pez Collectibles.* Atglen: Schiffer Publishing Ltd., 2000.

Goodfellow, Caroline. *The Ultimate Doll Book.* New York: Dorling Kindersley, Inc., 1993.

Gruelle, Johnny. *Raggedy Ann Stories.* Joliet: The P. F. Volland Company, 1918.

Hall, Patricia. *Johnny Gruelle Creator of Raggedy Ann and Andy.* Gretna: Pelican Publishing Company, Inc., 1993.

———. *Raggedy Ann and More: Johnny Gruelle's dolls and merchandise.* Gretna: Pelican Publishing Company, Inc., 2000.

Harry, Lou. *It's Slinky! The Fun and Wonderful Toy.* Philadelphia: Running Press, 2000.

Hockenberry, Dee. *Steiff Bears and Other Playthings Past and Present.* Atglen: Schiffer Publishing, 2000.

Hoffman, David. *Kid Stuff: Great Toys from Our Childhood.* San Francisco: Chronicle Books, 1996.

Hoffman, William. *Fantasy: The Incredible Cabbage Patch Phenomenon.* Dallas: Taylor Publishing Company, 1984.

Hollander, Ron. *All Aboard!* (Revised Edition). New York: Workman Publishing, 2000.

Johnson, Dana. *Matchbox Toys 1947 to 1998.* Paducah: Collector Books, 1999.

Johnson, Stancil E.D. *Frisbee: Practitioner's Manual and Definitive Treatise.* New York: Workman Publishing Company, 1975.

Kaye, Marvin. *A Toy Is Born.* New York: Stein and Day, 1973.

Kent, Steven L. *The Ultimate History of Video Games.* New York: Prima Publishing, 2001.

Korbeck, Sharon, Stephan, Elizabeth A. *2002 9th Edition Toys & Prices.* Iola: Krause Publications, 2001.

Lee, Laura. *The Name's Familiar.* Gretna: Pelican Publishing Company, Inc., 1999.

Levy, Richard C. and Weingartner, Ronald O. *Inside Santa's Workshop.* New York: Henry Holt and Company, Inc., 1990.

Lord, M. G. *Forever Barbie: The Unauthorized Biography of a Real Doll.* New York: William Morrow and Company, Inc., 1994.

Mack, Charlie. *The Encyclopedia of Matchbox Toys: Revised & Expanded 3rd Edition.* Atglen: Schiffer Publishing, 2002.

Malafronte, Victor A. *The Complete Book of Frisbee.* Alameda: American Trends Publishing Company, 1998.

Malloy, Alex G. *American Games: Comprehensive Collector's Guide.* Iola: Antique Trader Books, 2000.

Maniera, Leyla. *Christie's Century of Teddy Bears.* New York: Watson-Guptill Publications, 2001.

Mayer, Roy. *Inventing Canada: One Hundred Years of Innovation.* Vancouver: Raincoast Books, 1997.

Bibliography

McClary, Andrew. *Toys with Nine Lives: A Social History of American Toys.* North Haven: The Shoe String Press, Inc, 1997.

Michlig, John. *GI Joe: The Complete Story of America's Favorite Man of Action.* San Francisco: Chronicle Books, 1998.

Miller, G. Wayne. *Toy Wars: The Epic Struggle between G.I. Joe, Barbie, and the Companies that Make Them.* New York: Times Books, 1998.

Millington, Roger. *Crossword Puzzles: their History and their Cult.* New York: Thomas Nelson Inc., 1974.

Morreale, Marie T. *Pez! A Little Collectible Book.* Kansas City: Andrews McMeel Publishing, 2001.

Mullins, Linda. *Teddy Bear Centennial Book.* Grantsbille: Hobby House Press, 2001.

Orbanes, Philip. *The Monopoly Companion.* Holbrook: Adams Media Corporation, 1999.

Palicia, Joan. *Flexible Flyer and Other Great Sleds for Collectors.* Atglen: Schiffer Publishing, 1997.

Parker Brothers. *90 Years of Fun: The History of Parker Brothers 1883-1973.* Parker Brothers, 1973.

Pasin, Robert and Paul. *My Little Red Wagon: Radio Flyer Memories.* Kansas City: Andrews McMeel Publishing, 1999.

Peterson, Shawn. *Collector's Guide to PEZ.* Iola: Krause Publications, 2000.

Phillips, Becky and Estenssoro, Becky. *Beanie Mania II.* Naperville: Dinomates, Inc. 1998.

Polizzi, Rick and Schaefer, Fred. *Spin Again: Board Games from the Fifties and Sixties.* San Francisco: Chronicle Books, 1991.

Rich, Mark. *100 Greatest Baby Boomer Toys.* Iola: Krause Publications, 2000.

——. *Toys: A to Z.* Iola: Krause Publications, 2001.

Rinker, Harry L. *Collector's Guide to Toys, Games & Puzzles.* Radnor: Wallace-Homestead, 1991.

Rushlow, Bonnie B. *A Century of Crayola Collectibles.* Grantsville: Hobby House Press, 2002.

Santelmo, Vincent. *The Complete Encyclopedia to GI Joe.* Iola: Krause Publications, 2001.

Scarpone, Desi. *Board Games.* Atglen: Schiffer Publishing, 1995.

——. *More Board Games.* Atglen: Schiffer Publishing, 2000.

Scholl, Richard J. *Matchbox Official 50th Anniversary Commemorative Edition.* New York: Universe Publishing, 2002.

Sell, Mary Ann & Wolfgang, with Van Pelt, Charley. *View-Master Memories.* Self-published, 2000.

Severin, Gus. *Teddy Bear: A Loving History of the Classic Childhood Companion,* Philadelphia: Courage Books, 1995.

Shea, James J. *It's All In The Game.* New York: G.P. Putnam's Sons, 1960.

Shook, Robert L. *Why Didn't I Think of That!* New York: Signet, 1982.

Skolnik, Peter L. *Fads: America's Crazes. Fevers & Fancies.* New York: Thomas Y. Crowell Company, 1972.

Sommer, Robin Langley. *"I Had One of Those" Toys of Our Generation.* New York: Crescent Books, 1992.

Souter, Gerry and Janet. *Classic Lionel Trains.* St. Paul: MBI Publishing Company, 2002.

Stern, Jane & Michael. *The Encyclopedia of Bad Taste.* New York: Harper Collins, 1990.

——. *Encyclopedia of Pop Culture.* New York: HarperPerennial, 1992.

Stern, Sydney and Schoenhaus, Ted. *Toyland: The High-stakes Game of the Toy Industry.* Chicago: Contemporary Books, Inc. 1990.

Sutton, Robert. *Weird Ideas that Work: 11 1/2 Practices for Promoting, Managing, and Sustaining Innovation.* New York: The Free Press, 2002.

Tabbat, Andrew. *The Collector's World of Raggedy Ann and Andy.* Annapolis: Gold Horse Publishing, 1996.

Van Dulken, Stephen. *Inventing the 20th Century: 100 Inventions that Shaped the World.* New York University Press, 2000.

Wadsmith, John. *Stereo Views: An Illustrated History and Price Guide.* Iola: Krause Publications, 1991.

Watson, Bruce. *The Man Who Changed How Boys and Toys Were Made.* New York: The Penguin Group, 2002.

Wolfe, Maynard Frank. *Rube Goldberg Inventions.* New York: Simon & Schuster, 2000.

Whitehill, Bruce. *Games: American Boxed Games and Their Makers 1822-1992.* Radnor: Wallace-Homestead Book Company, 1992.

Wright, Frank Lloyd. *Frank Lloyd Wright: An Autobiography.* New York: Duell, Sloan and Pearce, 1943.

Wulffson, Don L. *Toys! Amazing Stories behind Some Great Inventions.* New York: Henry Holt and Company, 2000.

Zellnik, Miriam. *Inside the Magic 8 Ball: The Complete User's Guide.* Philadelphia: Running Press, 2002.

Magazine, Newspaper and Internet Articles:

For reference purposes, the author used numerous editions of the toy trade publications *Playthings* and *Toy Book.*

Allphin, Willard. "Who Invented Monopoly?" *Games & Puzzles,* 3/75.

Associated Press. "Stretching a Buck: Silly Putty going on 50 but still bouncing along." *Florida Times Union,* 07/16/98.

Barrs, Jennifer. "To some, she's a living doll." *Tampa Tribune,* 12/8/95.

Blackman, Joni. "Beanie-mania." *People Weekly,* 7/1/96.

Brady, Diane. "Highly Profitable Pursuits." *Maclean's* (Toronto edition), 2/20/93.

Brown, Caryne. "Making Money Making Toys." *Black Enterprise,* 11/93.

Canedy, Dana. "Beanie Move Giving Rise To Skepticism." *New York Times,* 7/2/99.

Courant Staff. "Silly Putty: It's 45! It's Still Silly! And it Still Sells!" *Hartford Courant,* 8/2/95.

Dana, Mark. "After 30 High-Flying Years, The Frisbee Still Soars." *Sports Illustrated,* 5/11/87.

Dunstan, Keith. "Obituary: Alexander R. Tolmer, Toy Man." *Melbourne Age,* 4/7/98.

Efnor, Claude. "Tonka, The Toy Giant, and How It Grew." *Industrial Supply Expediter,* 11/53.

Eliot, John. "Magic 8 Ball Keeps Selling and Selling." *Cincinnati Post,* 12/5/73.

Emery, Dave. "Dad Idea on Popular Slip 'N Slide." *Long Beach Press-Telegram,* 9/14/61.

Emmerman, Lynn. "A peek at the wizards of ahs in Marvin Glass' house of toys." *Chicago Tribune,* 2/13/83.

Farmer, Bill. "St. Paul Twister Parlor Game Has Nation in Gyrations." *St. Paul Pioneer Press,* 12/18/66.

Finnegan, Helena. "Bye, Bye Beanies." *Sarasota Herald Tribune,* 12/30/99.

Gibson, Richard. "At McDonald's, a Case of Mass Beaniemania." *Wall Street Journal,* 6/5/98.

Goodman, Walter. "The Doll That Put the Sex in Success." *New York Times,* 6/11/98.

Green, Lee. "The Wiffle Effect." *Atlantic Monthly,* 6/02.

Griswold, Wesley S. "Can You Invent a Million-dollar Fad?" *Popular Science,* 1/66.

Hamilton, John. "500,000 hoops going round." *Melbourne Age,* 7/4/67.

Haim, Alan. "Play-Doh Shaping Up: 20 Millionth Can Filled For Kiddies By Four-Year-Old Firm." *Cincinnati Enquirer,* 2/26/59.

Hobart, Randall. "Detroit Far Behind Tonka Toy Trucks." *Minneapolis Star,* 3/8/63.

Johnston, Theresa. "Mrs. Stanford and the Netherworld." *Stanford Magazine,* May/June 2000.

Klein, Frederick C. "On Sports: Backyard Classic." *Wall Street Journal,* 4/16/93.

Klein, Michael. "It is rocket science that helped create Super Soaker gun Inventor of kids' water weapon designed 3 NASA space probes." *Florida Times Union,* 8/20/98.

Leonard, Dorothy Harvey. "Generic Atlantic City Monopoly." *Game Researchers' Notes AGCA,* August 1990.

Leibowitz, Ed. "Macho in Miniature." *Smithsonian Magazine,* 08/02.

Lithgow, Adrian. "Astonishing Secret behind the World's Most Famous Toy." *Mail on Sunday,* 7/26/87.

Lobo, Erik. "He invented Sea-Monkeys and X-Ray Spex." *Planet X Magazine,* 2002.

Maxim Staff. "The Novelty Toy Hall of Fame." *Maxim,* 4/01.

McFarland, Patrice E. "My Search For Elizabeth Magie Phillips." *Game Researchers' Notes AGCA,* August 1990.

Moonan, Wendy. "A Perfect Toy for a Nation of Inventors." *New York Times,* 12/13/02.

Morgan, Philip. "Ant Farms Reap Profits for Diligent Entrepreneur." *Tampa Tribune,* 4/6/96.

Miller, Greg. "Little Squirt Turns Big Shot." *The Los Angeles Times,* 7/29/99.

Miller, Russel. "Still on the Farm, 200 Million Ants Later." *New York Times,* 12/19/91.

New Yorker Staff. "Here to Stay." *The New Yorker,* 8/26/50.

Owen, David. "Where Toys Come From." *Atlantic,* 10/86.

Palmer, Ann Therese and Tresniowski, Alex. "Bean there, Done that." *People Weekly,* 7/20/99.

Petrik, Paula. "The House that Parcheesi Built: Selchow & Righter Company." *Business History Review,* 1986.

Pritchard, Michael. Creators of A.C. Version of Monopoly to get Recognition." *Press,* 09/10/89.

Raine, George. "Fad Factory Wham-O Finds Itself Back in Style." *San Francisco Chronicle,* 5/6/01.

Reid, Emma. "The fad that won't fade hits the big Five-O." www.exn.ca/stories/2000/03/02/54.asp 03/02/00.

Root, Steve. "Uncle Ant." *Los Angeles Times Magazine,* 5/89.

Shrieves, Linda. What Goes Around, Comes Around - The Hula Hoop is Back." *Orlando Sentinel,* 3/22/88.

Shortz, Will. "Ephemera Offers a Clue to Crossword Origins." www.ephemerasociety.org/article-shortz.html

———. "How to Solve the New York Times Crossword Puzzle." *New York Times,* 4/08/01.

Sindrich, Jackie. "Nostalgia Sells: Old Toys Reappear in Stores." Reuters Limited, 2001.

Solis-Cohen, Lisa. "Forbes Corners Early Monopoly Games." *Maine Antique Digest,* 1/94.

Staff writer. "Young Enterprise." *Cincinnati Pictorial Enquirer,* 11/58.
——. "Gnus Nix Zax Tut" *Time,* 7/20/53.
——. "A Playboy Pad: Swinging in Suburbia." *Playboy,* 5/70.
——. "Business: You've Beanie had." *Economist,* 07/4/99.
——. "The Gang that Got Away." *Inc. Magazine,* 9/1/88.
——. "Bad Beanie." *Advertising Age,* 7/13/99.
——. "Obituaries: Mrs. Elizabeth Magie Phillips." *Arlington Sun,* 3/5/48.
——. "Oh, You beautiful Dolls!" *Newsweek,* 12/12/83.
——. "Monopoly." *Fortune,* 12/35.
——. "Let's Get Trivial." *Time,* 10/24/83.
——. "Selchow & Righter." *Game Merchandising,* 02/81.
Steck, Robert N. "The Checkered Game of Life." *D&B Reports,* Sept./Oct. 1992.
Sullivan, Patrick. "Extra! Extra! Great "Monopoly" Seizes All Boston." *Boston Sunday Post,* 2/16/36.
Thomas, Jr., Robert McG. "Solved! Prof. Plum and Cohorts in the Clear." *New York Times,* 12/01/96.
Tierney, John. "The Perplexing Life of Erno Rubik." *Discover,* 3/86.
Troxell, Margaret. "Game of Monopoly Originally Devised by Arlington Woman." *Arlington Sun,* 1937.
UPI. "Toy Designer Kills Three in Chicago Plant Shooting." *Chicago Tribune,* 7/76.
Wallace, Robert. "Little Business in the Country." *Life,* 12/14/53.
Warshofsky, Fred. "Rubik's Cube: Madness for Millions." *Reader's Digest,* 5/81.
Watson, Bruce. "Hello Boys! Become an Erector Master Engineer!" *Smithsonian Magazine,* 4/99.
Wickland, John A. "$$$ by the (Toy) Truckload." *Minneapolis Tribune,* 11/22/53.
Williams, Elisa. "There Goes the Neighborhood." *Forbes,* 10/1/01.
Wells, Melanie. "Cult Brands." *Forbes,* 4/16/01.
Wolfe, Burton H. "The Monopolization of Monopoly." *San Francisco Bay Guardian,* 1976.
Wyden, Peter. "Troubled King of Toys." *Saturday Evening Post,* 3/5/60.

Videos:

Our Favorite Toys. Termite Art Productions, 1997. (videocassette)
Baseball: A Film by Ken Burns. The Baseball Film Project, Inc. 1994. (DVD)
The History Channel: History of Toys and Games. A&E Television Networks, 1996. (videocassette)

Miscellaneous:

Spirograph booklet, copyright 1965 Denys Fisher, Ltd.
Flexible Flyer: The First Hundred Years, copyright 1997 Pacific Bicycles (Roadmaster Corporation).
A History of the Flexible Flyer, written for the Smithsonian Museum. Copyright 1986 Blazon-Flexible Flyer.
Important Robots and Antique Toys from the Estate of F.H. Griffith, copyright 2000 Sotheby's.
"Brief History of the Cube," Copyright 1998 Rubik/Seven Towns at www.rubiks.com

Interviews:

Ant Farm and Sea-Monkeys
Atamian, George, president, ExploraToy. Telephone interviews, 5/20/02, 5/23/02.
Levine, Milton, inventor of the Ant Farm. Telephone interviews, 5/17/02, 6/10/02.
Levine, Steve, president, Uncle Milton Industries. Telephone interview, 6/10/02.
von Braunhut, Harold, inventor of Sea-Monkeys. Telephone interview, 7/18/03.

Beanie Babies
Estenssoro, Becky, owner of True Blue Beans. Telephone interview, 5/6/03.

Big Wheel
Hill, Linda, former Marx employee. Telephone interview, 3/14/02.
Horowitz, Jay, author. Telephone interviews, 3/21/02, 3/29/02.
Miller, Allan, curator of The Krueger Street Toy & Train Museum. Telephone interview, 4/19/02.

Cabbage Patch Kids
Strong, Margaret, director of corporate communications, OAA, Inc. Telephone interview, 7/18/03.

Candy Land
Taft, Mel, former senior vice president of research & development, Milton Bradley. Telephone interviews, 1/21/02, 6/13/03.

Crossword Puzzle
Shortz, Will, editor, the *New York Times* crossword puzzle. Telephone interview, 10/09/02.

Etch A Sketch
Killgallon, Bill, president, Ohio Art. Telephone interview, 2/21/02.
Falzone, Nicole, Etch A Sketch artist. Telephone interview, 2/27/02.

Flexible Flyer
Palicia, Joan, author. Telephone interviews, 5/28/02, 6/3/02.

Brooks, Mary, archivist, Westtown School. Telephone interview, 5/30/02; E-mail correspondence, 9/12/02.

GI Joe

Michlig, John, author. Telephone interviews, 9/28/02, 10/1/02; E-mail correspondence, 11/18/02, 3/12/03.

Levine, Don, co-developer of GI Joe. Telephone interview, 10/09/02.

Jenga

Grebler, David, co-developer of Jenga. Telephone interviews, 1/27/03, 1/28/03.

Ross, Hal, former vice president of sales, Irwin Toys. Telephone interview, 2/1/03.

Grebler, Robert, co-developer of Jenga. Telephone interview, 3/13/03; E-mail correspondence, 5/29/03.

Scott, Leslie, inventor of Jenga. Telephone interview, 5/22/03; E-mail correspondence, 5/28/03.

Kerplunk and Eddy

Goldfarb, Eddy, inventor of Kerplunk, Battling Tops, etc. Telephone interviews, 6/14/02, 8/19/02, 9/20/02.

Lionel

Mania, Joseph, model railroad enthusiast. Telephone interview, 3/28/03; E-mail correspondence, 6/4/03.

Hollander, Ron, author. Telephone interview, 4/11/03.

Marvin Glass

Taft, Mel, former senior vice president of research & development, Milton Bradley. Telephone interviews, 1/21/02, 1/24/02, 6/13/03, 7/05/02.

Erickson, Erick, former designer, Marvin Glass & Associates. Telephone interview, 6/10/02.

Spinello, John, co-developer of Operation. Telephone interviews, 6/11/02, 6/19/02, 7/25/03; Personal interview, 7/19/02.

Meyer, Burt, former designer, Marvin Glass & Associates. Telephone interviews, 6/12/02, 8/27/02; E-mail correspondence 8/24/03.

Goldfarb, Eddy, former partner with Marvin Glass. Telephone interviews, 6/14/02, 7/12/02, 9/20/02.

Breslow, Jeffrey, former designer, Marvin Glass & Associates. Telephone interviews, 6/20/02, 7/30/02.

Conway, Lyle, former employee, Marvin Glass & Associates. Telephone interview, 6/20/02.

Baer, Ralph, co-inventor of Simon. Telephone interview, 6/26/02; E-mail correspondence, 7/27/02.

McFarland, Norman, former designer, Marvin Glass & Associates. Telephone interview, 7/5/02.

Wolfe, Maynard Frank, author. Telephone interview, 7/19/02.

Monopoly

Biddle, Richard, Georgist historian, educator, economist, and game collector. Telephone interview, 7/18/03; Written correspondence, 7/21/03.

Darrow, William, son of Monopoly inventor Charles Darrow. Telephone interviews, 12/4/02, 12/11/02; Personal interview, 6/26/03.

Forsyth, Thomas, game collector and historian. Telephone interviews, 12/18/02, 6/11/03.

Learn, Richard, Monopoly collector and historian. Telephone interview, 12/18/02.

Orbanes, Philip, former senior vice president of research and development, Parker Brothers. Telephone interviews 1/6/03, 1/15/03.

Patterson, Lytton, son of Charles Darrow's printer. Telephone interview, 12/18/02.

Patterson, Betty Lee, wife of Lytton Patterson. Telephone interview, 12/18/02.

Utterback, Mary, early Monopoly player. Telephone interview, 12/11/02.

Anspach, Ralph, author. Telephone interviews, 8/4/01, 12/23/02, 12/24/02, 12/27/02, 12/28/02.

Mr. Potato Head

Ellman, Julius, former partner, The Lernell Company. Telephone interview, 4/4/02.

Martin, Dennis, Mr. Potato Head collector. Telephone interview, 4/10/02.

Nerf

Guyer, Reyn, inventor of Nerf ball. Personal interview, 11/7/01; Telephone interview, 4/23/02.

Laughridge, David, former designer, Parker Brothers. Telephone interview, 11/6/01.

Dohrmann, Bill, former employee Parker Brothers. Telephone interview, 5/6/02.

Montgomery, Don, hot rod enthusiast. Telephone interview, 5/6/02.

Pictionary

Angel, Rob, inventor of Pictionary. Telephone interviews, 3/19/02, 4/11/02, 3/14/03.

Langston, Terry, co-developer of Pictionary. Telephone interviews, 3/19/02, 4/5/02.

Gill, Richard, co-developer of Pictionary. Telephone interviews, 3/20/02, 5/1/02, 3/13/03.

McNulty, Kevin, former partner, The Games Gang. Telephone interview on 3/26/02.

Cornacchia, Joe, owner, Cornacchia Press. Telephone interview, 3/14/03.

Play-Doh

Rhodenbaugh, Joe, president, Kutol Products Company. Telephone interviews, 9/26/02, 10/31/02.

Rhodenbaugh, Bill, co-developer of Play-Doh. Telephone interviews, 10/30/02, 10/31/02, 11/5/02, 11/18/02.

Zufall, Kay, co-developer of Play-Doh. Telephone interviews, 10/30/02, 10/31/02, 11/05/02.

Bibliography

Raggedy Ann
Wanamaker, Joni Gruelle, granddaughter of Johnny Gruelle. Telephone interview, 5/22/03.

Radio Flyer
Pasin, Robert, CEO, Radio Flyer, Inc. E-mail correspondence, 10/07/02.
Pasin, Paul, president, Radio Flyer, Inc. E-mail correspondence, 10/09/02.

Rubik's Cube
Dohrmann, Bill, former employee Parker Brothers. Telephone interview, 5/6/02.

Slinky
James, Betty, developer of Slinky. Telephone interviews, 5/21/02, 7/2/02.
James, Tom, former president, James Industries. Telephone interview, 5/21/02.

Super Soaker
Johnson, Dr. Lonnie, inventor of Super Soaker. Telephone interview, 7/18/03.

Tonka
Wenkstern, Mary, daughter of former Tonka CEO, Russ Wenkstern. Telephone interview, 6/4/03; Personal interview, 6/5/03.
Laumann, Lloyd L., former vice president of manufacturing, Tonka. Telephone interviews on 6/18/03, 7/23/03.
Reed, Roger, former attorney for Russ Wenkstern. Telephone interview, 6/18/03.
Groschen, Charlie, former designer for Streater Industries, Mound Metalcraft and Tonka Toys. Telephone interview, 7/1/03.

Trivial Pursuit
Wurstlin, Michael, designer of game graphics and shareholder, Horn Abbot. Telephone interview, 3/5/03; E-mail correspondence, 6/5/03.

Gill, Richard, former executive vice president, Horn Abbot International Ltd. Telephone interview, 3/13/03.
Cornacchia, Joe, owner, Cornacchia Press. Telephone interview, 3/14/03.

Trolls
Dam, Niels, son of Dam Troll inventor Thomas Dam. Telephone interviews, 11/5/01, 11/15/01.

Twister
Dale, Don, former designer, Reynolds Guyer Agency. Telephone interview, 9/2/03.
Foley, Chuck, co-inventor of Twister. Telephone interviews, 12/17/01, 11/04/02; Written correspondence 8/28/03.
Guyer, Reyn, co-inventor of Twister. Personal interview, 11/7/01; Telephone interview, 4/23/02, 9/2/03, 9/3/03.
Palony, Pete, former art director, Reynolds Guyer Agency. Telephone interview, 9/1/03.
Rabens, Neil, co-inventor of Twister. Telephone interviews, 12/12/01, 8/28/03.
Taft, Mel, former senior vice president of research & development, Milton Bradley. Telephone interviews, 1/21/02, 1/24/02.

Uno
Robbins, John, son of Uno co-inventor Merle Robbins, brother of Uno co-inventor Ray Robbins. Telephone interview, 12/17/01.
Tezak, Bob, co-developer of Uno. Written correspondences, 12/27/01, 3/15/02, 6/4/02.
Akeman, Ed, co-developer of Uno. Telephone interviews, 4/18/02, 7/11/03.

WHAM-O
Malafronte, Victor, author. Telephone interview, 8/22/01.
Stingley, Norm, inventor of Super Ball. Telephone interviews, 9/06/02, 9/30/02, 11/18/02.
Carrier, Mike, co-developer of Slip 'n Slide. Telephone interviews, 9/19/02, 9/30/02.
Tolmer, David, son of Hula Hoop developer Alex Tolmer. Telephone interviews, 9/24/02, 11/25/02.

Wiffle Ball
Mullany, Stephen, president, Wiffle Ball, Inc. Telephone interview, 7/31/02.
Mullany, David J., CEO, Wiffle Ball, Inc. Telephone interview, 8/7/02.
Paine, Hank, owner, The Connecticut Store. Telephone interview, 8/13/02.

Index

Page numbers in *italics* refer to illustrations.

Index

Index

LANDLORD'S GAME

2 to 7 Players

No. 83. The **LANDLORD'S GAME** was designed by Mrs. Phillips to show the principles of the single tax. Players progress around the board buying and selling real estate, paying fines, and taking their chances from two packs of cards according to the space upon which their piece lands. The object of the game is to accumulate as much wealth as possible, and eventually to become the richest player in the game. It is played on an interesting board and should prove popular with all trading game enthusiasts.   Price, $2.00

Index

Index

Did you have fun?

If so, then give the gift of *The Playmakers* to your friends and colleagues

• Limited edition, 312-page hardbound book   • Over 420 color photographs
• 130+ additional images of vintage ads, illustrations and historical photographs
• 75 classic toys are profiled, offering the compelling origin of each
• Timelines, insider profiles and rare interviews provide an in-depth look at the toy business

Check your local bookstore or order online at: www.theplaymakers.com

( ) Yes, I want _____ copies of *The Playmakers: Amazing Origins of Timeless Toys* for $50.00 each.
( ) Yes, I am interested in having Tim Walsh speak to my company, school or organization. Please send me information.

Include $8.00 for shipping one book within the continental U.S. and $2.00 for each additional book. Please include 7% sales
     tax if you're a Florida resident. Canadian orders must include payment in U.S. funds, with 7% GST included.

My check or money order for $_____ is enclosed.

Please charge my ( ) Visa   ( ) MasterCard   ( ) Discover   ( ) American Express

(Please print clearly)

Name: _____

Organization: _____

Address: _____

City/State/Zip: _____

Phone: _____   E-mail: _____

Card #: _____

Expiration Date: _____   Signature: _____

Make your check payable to:
Keys Publishing
PMB 180
5370 Clark Road Suite A
Sarasota, FL 34233-3227

FAX orders to: (941) 926-8054
Payment must accompany all orders. Please allow 3 weeks for delivery.

Return a photocopy of this form by mail if paying by credit card/check/money order, or, by fax if paying by credit card. *Please do not cut or tear out this form.*

MONOPOLY

G.3

INVENTOR
W.B.GRUBER

WILLIAM H.

INVENTORS
MARVIN I. GLASS
BURTON C. MEYER

Fig. 4

Inventor
John Lloyd Wright

Fig. 1.
Fig. 2.
Fig. 3.
Fig. 4.
Fig. 5.

Inventor:
Charles B. Darrow.

LOUNGE GUN ROOM DINING ROOM KITCHEN
HALL CELLAR BALL ROOM
STUDY LIBRARY BILLIARD ROOM CONSERVATORY

Fig. 1.

FIG. 1.

FIG. 2.

Godt

United States Patent Office

Des. 183,626
Patented Sept. 30, 1958

March 5, 1963   A. K. MELIN   3,079,728
HOOP TOY
Filed May 13, 1959

Fig. 1.
INVENTOR
John B. Gruelle